Story of the Hutchinsons (tribe of Jesse) Volume 1

Hutchinson, John Wallace, 1821-1908

Nabu Public Domain Reprints:

You are holding a reproduction of an original work published before 1923 that is in the public domain in the United States of America, and possibly other countries. You may freely copy and distribute this work as no entity (individual or corporate) has a copyright on the body of the work. This book may contain prior copyright references, and library stamps (as most of these works were scanned from library copies). These have been scanned and retained as part of the historical artifact.

This book may have occasional imperfections such as missing or blurred pages, poor pictures, errant marks, etc. that were either part of the original artifact, or were introduced by the scanning process. We believe this work is culturally important, and despite the imperfections, have elected to bring it back into print as part of our continuing commitment to the preservation of printed works worldwide. We appreciate your understanding of the imperfections in the preservation process, and hope you enjoy this valuable book.

JOHN WALLACE HUTCHINSON

OF

THE HUTCHINSONS

(TRIBE OF JESSE)

BY

JOHN WALLACE HUTCHINSON

Compiled and Edited by
CHARLES E. MANN

With an Introduction by
FREDERICK DOUGLASS

VOLUME I

BOSTON
LEE AND SHEPARD, PUBLISHERS
No. 10 Milk Street
1896

Copyright, 1896, by Lee and Shepard

All rights reserved

―――

Story of the Hutchinsons

TYPOGRAPHY AND PRESSWORK
BY S J PARKHILL & CO
BOSTON

PREFACE.

At the request of the famous singer whose autobiography is contained within the leaves of this volume, the far from difficult task of writing the preface devolves upon me. The book is the result of our joint labors for many pleasant months. No apology is needed for its appearance. For nearly two decades the friends of reform and lovers of music of two continents — in the great centres of the British Isles, the leading cities and towns of the North and West, in the villages of New England, the hamlets of the West and Northwest, the cabins of emancipated blacks in the South — from the Atlantic to the Pacific — have been begging for the memorial narrative of the Hutchinsons.

For obvious reasons it has been deemed best that Brother John should tell his own story, and usually in his own way. To him it was given, more than any other member of the famous family, to be a participant in, or an eye-witness of, the scenes which have become indissolubly connected with the family name. The other tribes, after the "swarming," did good service in the concert-field, and never faltered in the work of upholding reform, but it was the "Tribe of John" that sang in the camps; that preached woman suffrage in the wonderful campaigns in Kansas and elsewhere; that talked and sung temperance in conventions in the North, South and West; and John, as the last of the "Tribe of Jesse," has stood by the biers of nearly all the eminent reformers with whom the family has been associated, and sung his requiem over the graves of all the members of his gifted family. On taking up the work with him I found the manuscript of the first two chapters and of the two foreign chapters written, and only needing editorial revision. We immediately began the work of reading diaries and correspondence and putting in narrative form the stories as told there. Our plan has been to read the diary as the record appears from day to day. A single sentence has often been all necessary to produce a flow of eloquent reminiscence from the historian, which, taken down from his lips, has resulted in pages of manuscript in the exact language, emphasized by the sensitiveness to odd situations, the irrepressible Yankee wit, or the pathetic sorrow of the last survivor of the Hutchinsons. Page after page has poured from his lips, while his eyes danced with that characteristic brightness and his mobile face glowed with that expression which has made him irresistibly attractive to his audiences for nearly six decades. Other pages have been dictated while tears of mingled grief and joy and hope coursed down the furrows of that grand old face. In telling the story of later years, the diaries of the lamented Henry have been of great assistance in furnishing additional details. The files of the *Liberator* have been freely consulted. As a general practice, wherever outside authorities have been used, credit is given.

Brother John's life-story is told; the desire of years is fulfilled in this book. May the reader find it not wholly uninteresting, nor without historic value.

CHARLES E. MANN

CONTENTS OF VOL. I.

	Page
INTRODUCTION	xv

CHAPTER I.— THE TRIBE OF JESSE. . . 1
Bernard Hutchinson — Genealogy of the Hutchinson Family in America — Mary Leavitt, mother of the Hutchinsons — "Old Grandfather," the Revolutionary patriot — The sixteen brothers and sisters — A musical mother — Milford, the home of the Hutchinsons — Early days in the old town — A susceptible schoolboy and his adored teacher — Match-making and hop-picking — A family of farmers — Coming up from the fields — The Milford brass band — Playing in the "Tippecanoe and Tyler too" campaign — Daniel Webster as a campaign orator — The drink habit in Milford — The first families.

CHAPTER II — BEGINNINGS OF SONG, 1839-1842 35
A boy's prophetic dreams — The Hutchinson Family's first concert, in 1839 — John and Asa start for Lynn — First concert in Massachusetts — Dr Lowell Mason advises — Professor Webb's opinion — John as a bar-tender — Bids good-by to the rum-traffic — Selling stoves and groceries — An embryo express line — Singing in the Washingtonian campaign — On the muster field — John afflicted with divers diseases — A week's concerts; profits, one dime — Better luck — Back to the farm — A community — Song and sentimentality — A long tour — The old "John" horse and carryall — A dangerous equine banquet — N P Rogers's tribute — In Vermont — New York turns a deaf ear — Saratoga unsympathetic — A friend in need in Albany — Success at last — A move upon Boston — Anxious days — Abby cannot leave mother — Another start — Judson has a love-fit — A dissolution

CHAPTER III.— SINGING FOR FREEDOM, 1842-1845 . 70
Frederick Douglass, the fugitive slave — George Latimer — Slave-hunting in Massachusetts — The Hutchinsons espouse

Abolition — Marriage of John — The great disunion convention — Faneuil Hall rings with cheers for the brothers — Playing ball with James Russell Lowell — The Brook Farm experiment — Colonel Higginson and George P. Bradford on the Hutchinsons — Visit to Brook Farm — In New York, singing for temperance — Introduced by Lyman Beecher — Dr. Beach and "Calomel" — Garrison and Jackson visit the Milford community — The "Tyler Grip" — Asa loses his heart — Longfellow and "Excelsior" — Morris and Willis and the Hutchinsons — Isaac T. Hopper — Rev. Dr. Cox and Abolition — Henry Ward Beecher, the Hutchinsons' true friend — At Philadelphia — "Home, Sweet Home," on a sliding scale — Charles C. Burleigh — Mrs. Burleigh's "Gobble" — At Baltimore — Hope Slatter Prison — Disgust with "The peculiar institution" — No boarding-house for Abolitionists — At Washington — John P. Hale and the vocalists — Levi Woodbury pays his respects — Meeting with Webster — Joshua R. Giddings — Taking tea with President Tyler — Webster argues the Girard case — Back to Philadelphia — The Second Advent excitement — Father Miller bids his hearers good-by — People with axes to grind — A big New York concert nets a half-bushel of money — Henry C. Bowen as a manager — Rev. John Pierpont, a family friend — Pro-slavery papers attack the Hutchinsons — At the Florence Community — "Get off the Track" — A great anti-slavery picnic — Among the White Hills — Hannah F. Gould — Pleasant times with Gough — Mob at the Portland convention — Judson's premonitions — Henry born — Death of Benjamin, and Isaac, Rhoda's husband — Community idea abandoned — A mob at a New York concert — Lydia Maria Child — The Garrison-Rogers controversy — Jesse buys High Rock

CHAPTER IV — IN ENGLAND, 1845–1846 142

The start with Douglass and Buffum — Life on the *Cambria* — Slaveholders seek to mob Douglass — Captain Judkins calls for the irons — Land at last — Début in Liverpool — Singing in Dublin with Douglass — Daniel O'Connell — Father Matthew speaks on temperance — Henry Russell makes an overture — Rebecca Moore, the friend of reform — At Richard Webb's, in Dublin; first singing of the "Bridge of Sighs" — George Thompson — His introduction of the quartet — Triumphs in Manchester — George Dawson — London — An evening with Charlotte Cushman and Eliza Cook — An evening at Charles Dickens's with Macready, Douglas Jerrold and Hon. Mrs. Norton — A concert — Adverse criticism from the papers — With William and Mary Howitt — Wellington's speech in the House of Lords — Wheeling gold in the Bank of England — Mary Howitt writes the family history — "Band of Young Apostles" — Tea with the Duchess of Sutherland — At Birmingham — Guest of John Bright — Richard Cobden — Visits to Windsor and Kenilworth — Singing the "Bridge of Sighs" to Mrs Thomas Hood

CHAPTER V. — IN SCOTLAND, 1846 199
Through the highlands of England — Visit to Harriet Martineau at Ambleside — A Scottish picnic — A concert on a lawn — Miss Martineau's story of the visit — At the grave of Burns — "Scotch Grab" — A snuffy Scotch kirk — "He that is filthy let him be filthy still" — Concert at Glasgow — In the land of Rob Roy — Sailing over Loch Lomond — At Edinburgh — In the Tower — Return to Liverpool — Farewell to English friends — The voyage home — Grandfather Leavitt dies — His love for the quartet — Kisses their picture and prays for their return from over the sea — Jesse's song, "Old Grandfather" — The Leavitt family

CHAPTER VI — A GOOD TIME COMING, 1846–1848 . . . 221
Dining at a hotel with Douglass — Other guests will not "eat with a nigger" — The landlord as a dentist — Brother Jesse's celebrated crow — At New York — Pro-slavery Philadelphia — Robert Purvis — A dough-face mayor — Colored persons must not hear music — Concerts given up — " We can earn our bread by farming" — Lucretia Mott's tribute — Hard work at rehearsals — Providence halls should be twice as big — Introducing rubber foot-balls at Yale — Gough again — "Zephy's" dyspepsia — Viola born — Seranaded by James Fisk, Jr — Singing to Henry Clay — Clay would be a teetotaller — John Quincy Adams' funeral — Judson " sadly taken in ! " — Visiting President Polk — 77 slaves escape — A tempest in a teapot — The "Hutchinsons' repentance" — Wendell Phillips and the Family — At High Rock — Going West — John Van Buren — Chats with Fillmore — An Indian funeral — At Niagara Falls — Free Soil singing — In Cincinnati — Abby married — A California venture — John sings "on his own hook" — Rejoined by the brothers and Abby — A picturesque serenade — Singing for Beecher — "The Good Old Days of Yore" — Judson's "Standing Collar" — The Rynders mob — " Psalm-singing" bad for riots —

Pleasant days with Greeley — The "North American Phalanx" — The Hutchinsons as sewing-machine agents — Bluefishing — Judson as a seer — Pierpont at Milford — Singing to Jenny Lind — "Wax Work" — Mishaps to Asa's viol

CHAPTER VII — LIGHTS AND SHADOWS, 1848-1854 . 271

Among the spirits — The Hutchinsons and Spiritualism — Jesse and Dungeon Rock — John's faith in the future life — At Rochester — Good and bad spirits — Judson's excitement — Days of watching over him — Sorrow in Syracuse — Concerts impossible — Back to Milford — Recovery of Judson — George Thompson mobbed at Faneuil Hall — John in Concord — "Squire" Whipple objects to Abolition songs — "The Bigot Fire" — Judson's whimsicality — Hannah F. Gould as an almoner — Death of the father of the Hutchinsons — Tributes to "Uncle Jesse" — A humble Christian — Singing again — Judson thinks the tickets too high — Dividends reduced from two hundred dollars to one dollar each — At seances with Mr and Mrs Greeley — "Blows" from the papers — Prof O S. Fowler — At St Louis — Hall refused — Mayor declines to give a license, with threats — No concerts there — Zephaniah's Illinois farm — Says Lincoln is the coming man — Cholera scare at Alton — Fanny adopts the bloomer costume — Brothers sing at Salmon P Chase's Democratic anti-slavery convention — Judson's money stolen — Brothers sing to the thief in jail — T C Severence — A Fourth of July riot at Painesville — The music quells the mob — Guests of Joshua R Giddings — "Sammy" — Happy hours with John G Saxe — Jenny Lind again — Jesse joins the Alleghanians — Joshua's successful concerts — Singing at Baltimore — Fifty policemen guard the hall — Meeting Mann and Sumner — Singing in a dissecting-room — Singing with Neal Dow and E H Chapin — Mrs. Stowe and the Hutchinsons — At Whittier's home — With Lucy Stone — Death of Zephaniah — Jesse's death — At Martha's Vineyard — John and Asa buy High Rock — Frank B Carpenter, a close friend — His picture of Abby — Death of Caleb — The "Ship on Fire" — How the song "sold" audiences everywhere — S F B Morse — The rendition of Burns — Judge Loring hung in effigy on High Rock — "Getting to be Know Nothings" — Lloyd Glover

CHAPTER VIII. — IN THE GREAT WEST, 1855-1858 . . 336

The Kansas excitement — History of the Free Soil agitation — The free colonization scheme — Judson, John and Asa determine to go West and settle — A discussion, the majority rules and a new decision — At St Paul — Through the big woods of Minnesota — At Fort Snelling — at Glencoe — On the banks of the Hassan River — Town of Hutchinson founded — John cuts the first timber and builds the first log cabin — Judge Flandreau "enters" the town — Music's power to lessen fees — Mississippi freezes over — Down the river-banks — Rev Charles G Ames — A ministerial door-tender — Rebuking a doughface — Faithful Blucher — Leaving Lynn "forever" — Preempting a claim — Singing again — Back to High Rock — A winter's concerts — Farming in Minnesota — Sunday in Hutchinson — John as both precenter and preacher — Running a saw-mill — The Sioux massacre of 1862 — Little Crow — John warns the settlers of impending trouble — Hutchinson attacked and burned — The Indians repulsed — The death of Little Crow

CHAPTER IX — THE SWARMING, 1858–1860 . . . 354

Three troupes growing up — John returns to High Rock — Daisy Cottage built — "Tribe of Asa" begins to sing — Judson and John together — "Mrs Lotty and I" — Abby singing again — "The Tribe of John" — The war imminent — "The Tribe of Judson" — Judson's poetic programme — Judson discouraged — The brothers' last concert — Judson's melancholy death — Joshua and John sing together — John Brown's raid on Harper's Ferry — The bells of Barre — John G Crawford — Wilson on the John Brown tragedy — Singing at Wilson's election — Singing in the Lincoln campaign — "Tribe of John" and Sister Abby together — The Hutchinson Family Young Folks — Joshua's many concerts — Early notices of the "Tribe of John"

CHAPTER X — IN WAR TIME, 1861–1865 . 370

The pusillanimous Buchanan — John B Floyd and the Springfield armory — Working for "Honest Abe" — Singing to Lincoln at Jersey City — At Lincoln's inauguration — The origin of "Secesh" — Douglas holds Lincoln's hat — The "Plug Uglies" — 'Dixie" — Star-spangled banner for a poster — Sumter attacked — Carl Formes — Singing for recruits — Helping the soldiers' aid societies — Henry Wilson as a drill-master — Singing at Theodore Parker's memorial — A call to Washington — Salmon P Chase — Chaplain Yard — At the White House — The lost piano-key — No music in the Buchanan administration — President Lincoln calls for the "Ship on Fire" — Simon Cameron furnishes a pass into the army lines — General Butler — In the Army of the Potomac — At Fairfax seminary — Two regiments attend — "Hark to the answer Slavery!" — A fuss — Major Hatfield — Surgeon Oakley the culprit — Confusion quelled by "No Tear in Heaven" — General Birney — A summons from General Kearney — "A rebel as good as an Abolitionist" — General Franklin takes a hand — General McClellan orders the singers removed from the camps — A respite — Sunday in the camp — Spilled from a buggy — At Alexandria — Back to Washington — The song submitted to the Cabinet — Lincoln says Hutchinsons can go anywhere — McClellan requested to report at Trenton — More concerts in the camps — General Farnsworth — A pro-slavery church trustee — Mayor of Alexandria could not stop the concert — Horace Greeley on the expulsion — What the correspondents thought — Colonel Welling describes the scene — Whittier compliments the Hutchinsons — Singing to McClellan's staff — Churches fear the Hutchinsons — A cautious Y. M. C. A. president — Willis and the Family — A good talk with Fremont — Pleasant hours at the home of Secretary Chase — "No concert here to-night" — A notable reception to the Tribe of John — George Burleigh's poem "Free song on the Potomac" — The fine art of "blowing" — Experiences with pro-slavery authorities — The year of jubilee — Back to Lynn — Mass concerts on High Rock — First singing of "Tenting To-night" — Walter Kittredge — Bernard Covert — Posing for Carpenter's emancipation picture — John B. Alley — "Cousin Maud" — Moll Pitcher's portrait — Hotel pie — A welcome in St. Louis — Gough again — Lincoln assassinated — High Rock observatory destroyed

CHAPTER XI — MORAL REFORM WORK, 1865-1869 . 430

At Washington — Schuyler Colfax — Closing of the United States Christian Commission — Bancroft's eulogy on Lincoln — A dream of finance — Among Lake Superior mines — Stuck in a slough — John gains a residence in Hutchinson — Peril on floating ice — Mrs. Bloomer — The Kansas woman-suffrage campaign — Shall there be a Hutchinson in Kansas? — A kicking horse — Viola engaged — A duet with a despondent bull — Story of the "Sweet By-and-By" — J. P. Webster — Lum B. Porter — "Vote it Right Along" composed — "The Fatherhood of God, and the Brotherhood of Man" and its history —

Address to Kansas people — A bee-line across Iowa — Miss Olympia Brown — "Susan" — Elizabeth Cady Stanton — Chief Justice Chase bids the Hutchinsons God-speed — Wendell Phillips does not enthuse — Handy Mr Whetstone — Singing at the polls — Hutchinson, Kansas, settled — Temperance work in the State — "Beware of Vidders" — Five dollars worth of life insurance — "Louisa" — Charles Dickens — Viola married — Graziella Ridgway — Richard D Webb — Ex-Governor Robinson and John's horses — John's hat confiscated by a hungry sow — A sad scene viewed by the sympathetic moon — The Grant campaign — Zephaniah's grave visited — "Dick" Yates — Mother of the Hutchinsons dies — General Logan — "Grant, our Great Commander" — Colonel Ingersoll — Joshua's letter from Minnesota — A strange Christmas package — Mary A. Livermore and woman suffrage — The Library Hall meetings — Singing for Dwight L. Moody — "Mary at the Cross" — With Camilla Urso — The Peace Jubilee — At the Vineyard — A choir of distinguished men — S. B Spinning — Colonel Higginson's tilt with Tilton — Rev H W. Conant — The literary bureau

LIST OF ILLUSTRATIONS.

VOL I

	Page
John Wallace Hutchinson	Frontispiece
Frederick Douglass	xv
Richard Hutchinson's Plow	2
The Birthplace of the Hutchinsons	8
Coming up from the Fields	20
The Hop-pickers	22
The East Wilton Concert	44
The Old Homestead	47
On the Road	50
John A. Collins	73
Nathaniel Peabody Rogers	76
Heralds of Freedom	88
Get off the Track	117
Parker Pillsbury	119
Ten of the Hutchinsons, 1844	137
Hutchinson Family Quartet, 1846	142
An English Souvenir	156
The Hutchinsons at Grasmere	202
Wendell Phillips	239
Tribe of Jesse at High Rock	242
Judson's "Standing Collar" Song	261
The Six Brothers	288
Freedom's Champions	298
The Trio of Brothers	300
Abby Hutchinson	324

ILLUSTRATIONS — VOL. I.

	Page
John in the Saw-Mill	346
Abraham Lincoln	370
High Rock in 1861	378
Singing to Lincoln	380
On High Rock in War Time	416
Closing Exercises, Christian Commission	431
Representative Women	437

FREDERICK DOUGLASS

INTRODUCTION.

It is no light task to write an introduction to this book of the Hutchinsons. They were a unique and striking family. In personal appearance and in moral and intellectual qualities, they were in the strictest sense, of the best New England mould. More than fifty years ago they were introduced to the country from the granite hills of New Hampshire, through the columns of *The Herald of Freedom*, by Nathaniel P. Rogers, one of the most brilliant and gifted writers of that day. He was an Abolitionist of the Abolitionists, and in thrilling words and at the very top of his sublime enthusiasm in that cause, he hailed with welcome the Hutchinsons, as did all Abolitionists, regarding them as a splendid acquisition to that then unpopular and persecuted cause.

To write worthily an introduction to this book, the record of their career, one should have, in some measure, the genius of the editor of *The Herald of Freedom*, for the Hutchinsons should be handed down to future generations in a light no less glorious at the sunset, than that which gilded their sky in the morning of their advent. The Hutchinsons were indeed an acquisition to the anti-slavery cause and to all other good causes. They were, when in England, fittingly called by Mary Howitt, " a band of young apostles." They sang for freedom, for temperance, for peace, for moral and social reform.

In their earlier days they were well described as a "nest of brothers with a sister in it." Judson, John, Asa and Abby were their names. They brought to the various causes which they served, the divinest gift that heaven has bestowed upon man, the gift of music — the superb talent to touch the hearts and stir the souls of men to noble ends, even when such hearts were encased with the hardest pride and selfishness.

No matter how high, no matter how low, this gift of music has, like the all-pervading love of God, power to reach, melt and fuse the souls of men into a sense of common kinship, common brotherhood and a common destiny. While it is of no language, it is of all languages, and speaks to the souls of men of all nations, kindreds, tongues and peoples, and like the overhanging firmament ever speaks forth the glory of God. To no singers whom I have ever heard was there given a larger measure of this celestial quality. Men and women who, at that early day, heard the Hutchinsons and who had heard other great singers, were compelled to confess that, in all their experience, they had never heard human voices blended into a concord of sounds purer or sweeter than those of this family.

There was something almost miraculous in the singing of these three brothers and one sister. I have heard them, in a time of great excitement on the slavery question, calm to silence and order a turbulent and determined mob when it was in full blast and fiercely bent upon breaking up an anti-slavery meeting. We had, in the old Tabernacle in Broadway, New York, an instance of this power. One of the most furious mobs that I ever saw, confronted the American Anti-Slavery Society and determined that its speakers should not be heard. It stamped, shouted, whistled, howled, hooted and pushed and swayed the multitude to and fro in confusion and dismay. It silenced the platform and threatened the speakers with violence; and when neither the prophet-like solemnity of Garrison nor the sublime eloquence of Phillips could silence that tempest of rowdyism and wrath, the voices of this family came down from the gallery of the old Tabernacle, like a message from the sky, and in an instant all was hushed and silent. Every eye was raised and every ear attent. The stillness was like that which comes immediately after the vivid flash of forked lightning and the crash of its thunder.

But the Hutchinsons were not merely a family of singers and sentimental reformers; they were actuated and guided by high moral principle. The world had much for them and courted them. It had wealth and popularity, but neither could seduce them from their steadfast convictions, nor could persecution drive them from the side of unpopular truth. Their fine talent for music could have secured for them wealth and fame; but, like Moses, they preferred to suffer affliction in the cause of justice and liberty than to enjoy the fruits of a concession to slavery. Jesse, the eldest brother, had the gift of verse as well as that of music; and well did he use it. He wrote on the spur of the moment and with surprising facility. He could frame words fitted to the immediate occasion; and these were sung with telling effect by the rest of the family. In answer to pro-slavery threats they sang

> "Party threats are not alarming,
> For, when music ceases charming,
> We can earn our bread by farming
> In the old Granite State."

While Jesse made no literary pretensions, some of his verses were as apt as any found in the songs of Robert Nichol or of Robert Burns.

Those who heard Judson, John and Asa and their angelic sister Abby sing, heard much, but heard nothing in comparison to what I heard in their home. I was permitted to hear the whole "Tribe of Jesse" sing in their old family mansion, where thirteen of the family poured out their souls together in pious song, till it appeared as if the very roof were rising skyward. The scene of that hour has been present to me during all these fifty years, and I still recall it as one of the most sublime and glorious hours I ever experienced.

I saw this family in all the vicissitudes of its career, covering a period of more than half a century. I saw it in times that tried men's souls. I saw it in peace and I saw it in war; but I never saw one of its members falter or flinch before any duty, whether social or patriotic, and it is a source of more satisfaction than I can express, to have lived, as I have now done, to bear this high testimony to the character of the Hutchinsons, especially now that only one of them has survived to write this book in perpetuation of their precious memory.

FREDERICK DOUGLASS

HISTORY OF THE HUTCHINSON FAMILY

CHAPTER I.

THE TRIBE OF JESSE.

"Ever hopeful, never doubting, always working for the right,
Loving, waiting, watching, longing, for the millennial day of light"

"The fatherhood of God, and the brotherhood of man,
The cause of true religion is spreading through the land
Oh, the fatherhood of God, and the brotherhood of man,
We'll talk and sing while on the wing, and ring it through the land"

In these modern times, when thinking minds are not satisfied to take people as they are, but seek for the elements that have contributed to success in state-craft, literature, the pulpit, music and the kindred arts by a study of heredity, a man or a woman is fortunate indeed if he or she can point to a line of ancestry which represents, as in the case of the Hutchinsons, sturdy worth, industry, public spirit and patriotism.

As the reader studies the biographical references that follow this paragraph, and notes how the musical faculty was shown in the various members of our family on the side of both my father and mother, he will, I am sure, find no reason for surprise that we, their children, should have had such success in singing the songs of freedom and progress on two continents. But before speaking of our immediate ancestry, it will be necessary to go back a few centuries, to the beginning of history, so far as our family is concerned.

Bernard Hutchinson, the progenitor of the English branch of the family, was born in Cowlan, county of York, in 1282, during the reign of Edward I. The English records show the line of descent in that country to have been: Bernard, James, James, William, Anthony, Thomas, Lawrence, Thomas, Thomas, Richard.

The family is entitled to bear arms described in heraldic language thus: "Per pale, gules and azure, semée of cross-crosslets or, a lion rampant, argent. Crest, out of a ducal coronet or, a cockatrice with wings indorsed azure; beaked, combed and mottled gules."

The motto is "Gerit Crucem Fortiter." The signification of this is "He bears the cross bravely."

Richard Hutchinson with his wife Alice and four children, emigrated to this country in 1634, and settled in Salem Village, now Danvers, Mass.

The first official notice made of him is in the town records, when it is stated that in recognition of his public spirit, as being the possessor and introducer of the first plow brought into this country, he was granted one hundred and forty acres of land by the town authorities.

He was a thorough agriculturist, and by assiduous devotion to his occupation and economy in living, he acquired a large landed estate, which on his death was divided according to the terms of his will.

He and his wife are recorded as members of the first church in Salem. He married three times, the last when he was seventy-nine years of age. He was born in 1602 and died in the year 1682.

His son Joseph, and three succeeding Josephs, continue the line to Elisha, who was born at Middleton, December 6, 1751. He was of the sixth generation. On November 10, 1772, he married Sarah Buxton, and

RICHARD HUTCHINSON'S PLOW—(p. 2)

in the year 1779 left Middleton (or Salem) with his wife and children, and removed to, and settled in the beautiful valley of the Souhegan River, near the present site of Milford, N. H., fifty miles from Boston, the town then being called Amherst. Here he took up land and began to follow on his own account, the occupation so long engaged in and made honorable by his ancestors, farming. In 1782 he was living in the southwest parish and was one of the prime movers in building the first meeting-house. He was one of the nineteen original members of the Congregational Church, which was organized November 17, 1788, and was the first clerk of the church, an office he held for several years. He was one of the first to answer his country's call, as a private, in Captain Jeremiah Page's company of militia, at Danvers, which engaged the British at Lexington, on the memorable 19th of April, 1775.

Grandfather came to Milford with his wife and two sons: subsequently a daughter was born. He was one of the first settlers, the place being then a howling wilderness, and the cry of wolves was frequently heard as they passed in close proximity to the rude settlement. Once a moose made his appearance; and on grandfather giving the alarm to his neighbors, they grasped their guns, and with a merry shout gave chase to the huge animal as he bounded away through the woods at lightning speed. It was a long and tiresome chase; but, buoyed up by their elated hopes and the novelty of the affair, the animal was at last driven to narrow quarters on Long Hill, and then he was quickly dispatched, carried home, and equally divided among his pursuers.

In addition to his own estate, he received from his father, by will, seventy-four acres joining westerly on his own bounds. From a rude structure which was demolished, he built the large house, still in existence, in which fourteen of the "Tribe of Jesse, sons of Mary," were born. He died in Milford, October 12, 1800, at the age of forty-nine years.

The two sons of Elisha, Andrew and Jesse, early evinced a taste and love for music. At about the age of fourteen or sixteen they purchased a violin on joint account, and often furnished the music at the farming and husking bees of the surrounding country; but, after some years, becoming dissatisfied with these performances, thinking them demoralizing, they resolved to dissolve partnership in the musical line and earn an honest living on the farm. Not being able to sell the violin so as to divide the proceeds, they decided to divide the instrument, and each made for himself a tobacco-box from his half. No comment is necessary on the moral aspect of this reform. "Consistency, thou art a jewel!"

The boys grew up to manhood on the farm; and Andrew, who was the older by about three years, married a Miss Raymond, of Mont Vernon, and had six children, three sons and three daughters. — Nathaniel, Elisha, Stillman, Phœbe, Mary and Martha.

Jesse, who was born February 3, 1778, on August 7, 1800, married Mary Leavitt, who was then only fifteen years old. On the death of the father, which occurred October 12, 1800, the farm was divided between the two boys, Andrew and Jesse, the latter securing the house.

Jesse had a mechanical cast of mind, and was by turns a farmer, cooper, shoemaker and carpenter, as circumstances seemed to favor. He did much of the shoemaking during the earlier years of his family. His expert coopering created considerable commerce from his shop to Boston. On the morning of the famous "shooting stars" he was packing off a four-ox load, for fifty miles to the city of Boston.

Mary, commonly called Polly, Leavitt, born June 25, 1785, was the daughter of Andrew Leavitt, a master-carpenter or builder. In his days the trade of master-carpenter embraced all the parts of the structure. He must go to the forest, cut the trees, haul the timber wanted for the structure, take it to the lot, frame and raise each piece to its position, select his timbers for shingles and clapboards, split and shave them by hand; with these and boards he must cover the building, make all the finish-work on doors and windows, do all the joiner-work, oversee the mason, hang the doors and sash, paint inside and out, fix the doors, locks, etc., lock the building and hand the key to the owner.

He was one of the heroes of the Revolution, serving as a faithful soldier during the seven years' struggle. At the battle of Bunker Hill he was one of the three hundred that kept the British at bay; and after the burning of Charlestown, he was detailed as master-mechanic to aid in rebuilding the burned district.

At the close of the war he received an honorable discharge and a pension, awarded by a grateful country in attestation of the high regard in which the thirteen original States held the defenders of the nation. He died at the age of ninety-four.

Deacon John Leavitt, the American progenitor of the family, was born in England in 1620, and died near Exeter, N. H., in 1650. Grandfather was born in Stratham.

The issue of the marriage of Jesse Hutchinson and Polly Leavitt was sixteen children, of whom thirteen grew up to manhood and womanhood. Their names were —

Jesse	Born February 25, 1802
David	" October 11, 1803
Noah	" January 26, 1805
Polly, or Mary	" June 7, 1806
Andrew B.	" August 19, 1808
Zephaniah K.	" January 6, 1810
Caleb, } twins Joshua, }	" November 25, 1811
Jesse, Jr	" September 29, 1813.
Benjamin Pierce	" October 3, 1815
Adoniram Judson Joseph,	" March 14, 1817
Sarah Rhoda Jane	" March 14, 1819
John Wallace	" January 4, 1821.
Asa Burnham	" March 14, 1823
Elizabeth	" November 14, 1824
Abigail Jemima (Abby)	" August 29, 1829

My mother, who, in early maidenhood, became the wife of my father and the future mother of four quartets with a sister in each, was possessed of a voice of peculiar sweetness, and instilled into her children the soul of melody, so that from infancy they imbibed this boon, a love of music, that was more fully developed in after years

At the time of the death of Sister Abby, in 1892, our dear friend, Frank B. Carpenter, writing in the *New York Home Journal*, spoke thus of the musical talent of my mother's family:

"She (Abby) came from a long line of musical ancestors Her maternal great-grandparents, William Hastings and his wife, were noted singers of their time One of the Hastings daughters married into the Leavitt family, also famous for musical genius Thus, of the union of the musical talents of the Hastings and Leavitts came the musical mother of the Hutchinson family"

In 1862, Prof. R. D Muzzey, of Dartmouth College, wrote to Rev. Dr. Davis, of Amherst, N. H., a letter containing reminiscences of his boyhood, when his father was a worshipper in Rev. Mr. Bruce's congregation at Mont Vernon, then the North Parish of Amherst. He speaks thus of my mother and her sister Sarah:

"There was one charm which was peculiar connected with the worship on that hill — it was the singing. There was a good choir, but the fascination came from a single voice, that of Miss Leavitt, an elder sister of Miss Leavitt who afterwards became the mother of the Hutchinson family, so renowned in song. The choir of Mont Vernon church met for practice on Sabbath morning before the hour of worship. Miss Leavitt always sang the alto. How many times, as we striplings ascended the hill, did we stop to drink in those rich and unearthly tones (oh, I can hear them now!) which filled the whole atmosphere, and seemed to come from an elevation far above that of the open windows.

"My dear sir, pardon my enthusiasm. I have since heard Madame Malibran, Madame Sontag, Jenny Lind, and an oratorio in St. Xavier's chapel from the choir of Pope Pius IX on the evening of his coronation, and I have not yet heard a voice so rich and inspiring as that of Miss Leavitt. Does such a voice come as often as once in a century?"

Sarah Leavitt married Chandler Averill, who was a fifer in the War of 1812.

Milford was an offshoot of Amherst. The village is situated about two miles in a southwest course from the old town, at the east end of a fertile valley, encircled around with sloping hills on the north and south, with Peterboro and Lyndeboro and the Greenfield Mountains on the west, where the Indian-named Souhegan River takes its rise — a fine, rapid stream, flowing majestically through the rich valleys, reaching the falls, where a dam is constructed forming a pond sufficiently large to supply the several mills. Here was built one of the first cotton factories in this country, which has been in operation for more than two-thirds of a century. Sawmills and other manufactories were dotted along its margin, all deriving supply and running-power from this source, and a small tributary stream which also supplies power for several mills, empties into the river near the town, and flows on toward the Merrimac and the ocean.

The family grew to such proportions at the old homestead that it was thought advisable to purchase another place. A farm was for sale some three-quarters of a mile distant from the homestead, coming down upon the meadow adjacent to the Souhegan River. Father made a purchase of this place. The farm contained about one hundred and sixty acres, with a very large house and convenient outbuildings. The house was built originally for a hotel by Colonel Joshua Burnham, and was constructed from lumber selected from the old growth in the pine forests upon the farm. The house was fifty-three by forty-eight, about thirteen feet stud, hip roof. Thence the younger portion of the family repaired, leaving the older members at the original homestead.

Brother Joshua, in relating the incident of moving, says he was detailed to carry his two younger brothers, John and Asa, in his arms across lots: they were very heavy, one being three years and the other one year old. Joshua was twelve. He conveyed them singly at the proper distance, and laying a child down went back and brought the other, and so alternately he reached the new home in safety.

The house contained eight large rooms, sixteen by eighteen feet in length and width, and a very large cellar under the whole.

Right in the vicinity of these premises was Colonel Burnham, living in the little red house on the hill, which had been selected by his children as a home for his de-

THE BIRTHPLACE OF THE HUTCHINSONS — (p. 8)

clining years, and situated where he could overlook the surrounding landscape, including a good view of the farm that was once the home of his family and which he had lost by unpaid debts. He was a frequent visitor to the place; and when the fruits were ripe, he would have free access offered by my father and the privilege of obtaining what fruit he desired. There was one very favorite apple, the flavor of which was delicious; and when the apples were ripe, this honorable old gentleman would be seen going and coming with his pockets full, and they were pockets! They were like bags, and he could carry almost half a peck in each one. He would come over, fill his pockets, and then trudge along towards home. He was occasionally visited by officers of the armies of the Revolution; and it was said that one of the staff of Washington was among them. My parents honored him by naming Joshua after him. He would frequently show his regard for his namesake by some token, and before passing into his dotage he called him to his house and presented him with a sash worn by him on parade while he was under George Washington's command. This article was carefully preserved, and is still, after the decease of both giver and receiver, an heirloom in the family.

In those early days among the pioneers, education was sometimes neglected. The colonel, though passing through seven years of renown as a discreet officer, could not write his own name, and while in business kept his accounts by characters. For instance, having sold cheese to a person, he would make a mark of that portion of cheese that that man received. His funeral was the first that I had ever witnessed, and the impression was depressingly suggestive. He died at the age of ninety-three; and engraved as an epitaph upon his tombstone, were these words composed by Brother Joshua:

> "Colonel Joshua Burnham,
>   Soldier of the revolution,
> Zealous in his country's cause,
>   Faithful to the constitution
> And obedient to its laws."

Our farm-house was sparsely furnished, and embarrassment in debt prevented any immediate change. One day a neighbor came into the house and looked about: no carpet on the floor, dining-table and a few wooden chairs; no pictures for the walls. She remarked, "Where is your furniture?" Mother pointed to the growing family about her and said, "These represent my furniture." There were ten children; and there was also room for expansion of the lungs, and music from father and mother and the older brothers went ringing up and down the hall-ways, with the broad open stairways extending up and down from the entrance. These quarters proved very advantageous to the harmonious development of our voices.

A spring of soft water was near, to supply the barn and a public water-trough, while a well of soft water supplied the house.

> "How dear to my heart are the scenes of my childhood,
>   When fond recollection presents them to view!
> The orchard, the meadow, the deep tangled wildwood,
>   And every loved spot which my infancy knew;
> The wide spreading pond and the mill which stood by it,
>   The bridge and the rock where the cataract fell,
> The cot of my father, the dairy-house nigh it,
>   And e'en the rude bucket that hung in the well."

The village of Milford grew to such proportions that it soon out-rivalled and challenged the competition and excited the envy of the town from which it sprang, though Amherst Plain held for many years the advantage, being the county-seat of Hillsboro County. We were a well-regulated town and a thrifty community, with all necessary requirements for a healthy growth.

The first Congregational Church was presided over for many years by a worthy pastor, Humphrey Moore, who was supported by the levying of a tax on all the people. He was a very industrious, economical man, displaying genius in the cultivation of his farm — for he was a practical agriculturalist — and prepared many of his sermons while in the field, he believing in the efficacy of out-door exercise and study from nature. There could be but one " Priest Moore." His wit manifested itself while at the divinity school, and it sometimes took a mischievous turn. One day he was caught tying a small tree or bush to the tail of a colt. When questioned by a member of the faculty, who said, " Mr. Moore, I thought you had sowed all your wild oats," he replied, in his peculiar lisping way, " Yeth, thir, I have, and now I'm going to brush them in." The professor said no more, but passed on. It is told of him, and the story is vouched for, that on one occasion he was asked to officiate at a Masonic celebration where a prayer was considered germane to the proceedings. All his denomination were opposed to the mystic order, and at first he hesitated, but finally complied, and at the appointed time and place made his appearance, and offered the following prayer, " O Lord, we pray for we know not what; if it is good, bless it; if it is bad, *cuss* it. World without end. Amen."

On one occasion he was addressing the Legislature of New Hampshire; extolling the thrift and productiveness of his people and town: he said there was one worthy gentleman in his town, Uncle Jesse Hutchinson, who was making money in raising a family of boys.

"Well, Brother Moore, how is your health?" said Joshua to him on one occasion. "I am perfectly thound above my knees," he replied.

Rev. Mr. Elliott came to Mason when father and mother were young people, and preached the Baptist doctrine. Father had no carriage, but being interested in the faith, he would put his saddle on his horse, and putting mother with a babe in her arms on a pillion behind, would trot over the Mont Vernon hills to Mason. As they passed Priest Moore's church from which they had withdrawn, the boys would hoot at them. Later Mr. Elliott was invited by father to come over and preach in the North School-house near the farm — from which father was afterwards buried. Soon father and Uncle Andrew built a Baptist Church, in which a Rev. Mr Evans first preached. Rev. Adoniram Judson, the great missionary, was a friend of Mr. Evans, and would sometimes come and preach for him. My brother Judson was named for him. A Mr. Bowles, and later Rev. Samuel Everett, preached there.

As time passed on and the children grew to the age of discretion, one after the other was advised to select a congenial employment. Most of the boys remained on their farms adjoining the homestead.

Jesse, at the early age of sixteen, repaired to the village of Amherst, and took a position as a "printer's devil" in the office of the *Farmers' Cabinet*, a paper edited by Richard Boylston, and there continued until he was proficient in the art and an expert at typesetting. Boys that serve as printers' apprentices often tire of the menial service, when in fact it is the best school that could be established as far as a thorough knowledge of grammar, orthography, etymology, syntax and prosody are concerned.

He was allowed once a week, and that on Saturday, to go home, a distance of two-and-a-half miles. His reception was an occasion of joyous enthusiasm as his shrill voice pealed forth in a shout or a song to announce his coming. The very family dog would scamper over the fields to meet him, his quick, instinctive ear catching the sound of his voice before any one in the house; and, this signal would first announce Jesse's coming. Then all the youngsters would rush out to greet him as he came bounding across the fields. Some pleasing reports he would bring us from our relatives who resided in Amherst. He would have a word about the Leavitts and how old grandfather was getting along. After he returned to the house would come the usual congratulations and a variety of sports, plays and recreations. On the day following, Sunday, he repaired to church with our parents, and on Monday morning early we would bid him farewell as he took his departure back to his trade

Andrew, at the age of sixteen, went to Boston and embarked in a mercantile business, becoming very successful.

Zephaniah went West, taking up lands for his farm in Illinois.

Joshua was a clothier, carding, dyeing, and weaving wool into cloth fabrics.

I, never supposing I was committing an unpardonable sin by letting my affections go out to lovable objects, early formed an attachment for a young lady schoolmate of my own age; and, learning what it was to have the intensity of a boy's love and devotion, I was perfectly contented whenever in her presence; and, whenever an opportunity offered, presented her with little tokens such as I might acquire, of affection and regard.

The pleasures of the district school were greatly enhanced by the attention and coöperation of this young lady in my studies. She was the best scholar in the school, and could spell them all down. At one time, noticing my timidity at reading my own composition, she generously volunteered to read it herself; and by her pleasant intonations and inflections added double interest to it, so that it was pronounced a worthy production, which made me very proud and grateful.

For years, as soon as I had entered the church and choir, I would first look down to her pew, would be cheered to know that she was present, and could thereafter sing with more spirit, for we were in fellowship and full sympathy, belonging to the same church.

Buoyed up under all discouraging circumstances, I built castles in the air and dreamed of a future and closer alliance. How often it is that we, by brush or pen, place before our gaze the name of our spouse! Caroline Bartlett was written one hundred times on the wooden walls that surrounded the old wash-room, where, being detailed by my parents to help do the washing for a family of ten, as we had many boys and few girls, I would immortalize her name in chalk. But, alas! at the mature age of fourteen my dream faded, for my presents were returned, and the incident closed.

The Baptist preacher, Samuel Everett, was quite dogmatic and very severe in all his utterances; and we were led to believe it very wrong to decide contrary to his mature judgment, as we felt we were the subjects of his watchful supervision. The school-committee engaged him to teach in the North District, and his sternness was very depressing to the pupils. He had a genius for corporal punishment. One of the boys was caught one day playing with a spring of an old tin candlestick. As quick as he discovered the device he snapped it on the nose of the boy, standing him up near his desk as a laughing-stock, and those who could not restrain their laughter were called up and awaited their turn to wear the badge. Of course he read the Bible and prayed, and so did all the adults in the school, but the discipline did not conduce to much spiritual growth. Compared with those masters who follow, he was kindly remembered. Fifty years subsequent I met him in Iowa City, where he had come to visit me and attend my concert from his home in the country, we found our experiences in varied paths led us in sympathy to broader views, and we spent one long and joyous day with each other.

We had some good teachers and some very bad ones. One in particular was quite offensive to the scholars; he generally would punish the older ones over the backs of the younger. This gave rise to revolt, which culminated in dissolution and dismissal. The facts were these: it came my turn to build the fire in the school-house, and I was on hand bright and early in the morning with my kindlings and started a blaze, putting on some large sticks as usual. Soon the smoke stopped ascending the chimney and began coming into the room. The teacher arrived and tried to stem the tide of smoke, but the place was soon filled, so that we were all obliged to seek the open air for breath. The teacher was then convinced that the chimney must be stopped up; a ladder was brought, and the "master so cruel and grim," ascending, discovered a board had been closely fitted on the top, with the intention of smoking him out. There was no more school that day. The news went abroad, and in the evening the whole neighborhood was brought to judgment. The scholars (all the male portion) were arrayed in single file, and the committee gave all a chance to tell what they knew about the affair. No one knew anything about it.[1]

It was thought best for the teacher to beat a retreat, and not stop to beat the little ones any more; and away he went, promising never to return. Everybody said, "Let him off too easy." About that time we played the "Rogue's March," in remembrance of the tyrant's departure. The work of repairing the school-house was soon finished, and a new teacher was engaged.

I well remember one gentle schoolmarm, who taught by love, and thus induced us all to respect her. She was only seventeen years of age. I was between seven and eight, and my affections were very tender; she attracted my whole soul and attention. I loved to obey her rules, and needed no chastisement. Oh, how precious those few weeks of summer tuition! Her example served to convince the people in later times; corporal punishment was abolished, and the principle of love was substituted. Then true progress was made, the best promptings of our nature were cultivated, and we stored up, with sweet affection and sympathy, the knowledge of our books, for we were guided by some magic spell, and our attachment grew stronger as the days passed by.

How sad were we all when we were told by the teacher to close up and pack our books, for the term was over! How we wept as we kissed her and said good-by,

---

[1] March 13, 1895. Attending a funeral in the neighborhood, I met an old school comrade, Captain Tim Curtis, who reminded me of this and similar incidents, as we conversed of our boyhood days — almost seventy years ago.

and watched her steps as she ascended the hill leading to her boarding-place! Oh, that I could go with her and live and love forever! Sobbing myself to sleep that night, I awoke very early, dressed, and stole out from the company of my three brothers, who still slept in the great square chamber, into the sweet, clear summer air. The song of the birds greeted me as I sped on, and my heart beat fast, and my spirits were buoyant, for I was soon to meet once more the dear love I longed for. How quickly I ran, and how short the distance between us! Soon I was standing outside the door waiting. Farmer Wallace coming out, surmised my errand, and said, "You want to see the schoolmarm, I guess." "Yes, sir, I do," I replied, with a tear in my eye. She was called, and we met once more, and then she kissed me a long farewell. She was leaving for a land far away. When the frosts of autumn came, her delicate constitution yielded to pulmonary disease, and her spirit took its flight. But the joy of sweet remembrance will cluster around that angelic form while all else of earth shall vanish; and in the "sweet bye-and-bye," I trust I shall be again blessed.

> "I heard a voice long years ago,
> A voice so wondrous sweet and low
> Oh, my love, I loved her so!—
> My love that loved me long ago"

Father was an early-riser: not much sleep after four o'clock for him. No astronomer loved more to bask in the glory of the heavenly bodies on a summer's night. He also delighted in witnessing the sun's first rays, for his well-laid plans for the farm work formed a stimulus to healthy action. The older boys were detailed for specialties, and the younger ones had to obey their commands — for "father said so"; and we all cheerfully fell into line and vied with each other to do our duty — to work well and fast. The short term of school in winter over, we hied to the woods to do some logging, cutting and hauling the season's supply of fuel; the best clean butts of hemlock, chestnut and pine were taken to the old saw-mill — still in existence near the Hardscrabble station built by grandfather — and converted into lumber, boards, shingles, clapboards, fence-posts, etc. This work was done while the sledding was good, and large piles of sled-length wood were heaped up near the house. Then followed the labor of cutting it into shorter lengths for the open fire-place and stove, splitting and piling it up in a loose manner till it towered to the height of eight or ten feet. Here it was allowed to remain for the sun and wind to dry it before it was piled up in the shed for future use.

Most of the people in our region not having funds to purchase whale oil for illuminating purposes, resorted to the dipping of candles. At the close of the butchering in autumn, the tallow was tried out and placed in an iron pot or kettle, and was kept warm by pouring boiling water into it, the tallow rising to the top: a dozen or more cotton strings, which were to serve as the wicks, were placed on a stick in order, about one-and-a-half inches apart, and all were let down into the liquid and held for a moment, then hung out to cool. This process was repeated about twenty times until the lot were considered of sufficient size for real tallow candles, and it was then ready for burning.

Notices were read in church, of prayer and conference meetings which would be held at the North School-house and commence at "early candle lighting."

But at times even this luxury of candle-light was

denied us, and we youngsters therefore sought and obtained from the ground, the roots of some pitch-pine stumps, whose trunks had been utilized long since for lumber. These treasures were put to good use during the long winter evenings while reading over our school lessons. At one time Brother Ben and I had brought from pasture to our door-yard a wheelbarrow-load of the roots — the result of an afternoon's struggle Brother Asa claiming some interest, said as he placed his finger upon the log under the uplifted axe, "Cut right there." It was done, and away went a portion of the index finger. Oh. then there was music that could not find room in the gamut! This was a mark for life, which in after years much inconvenienced him in playing his 'cello.

Brother David returning from a visit to Boston at one time, on the road learned the trick or secret of manufacturing "Loco-foco" matches. Space was soon cleared in the old shop; proper tools for cutting the maple timber into strips were made; and when ready Brother Ben was given a chance in this "trust." I felt glad to help, so dipped into the brimstone as first process. Then came the dip into the composition, a black substance covering the end of the stick; after that, the trial of igniting on a piece of doubled-over sand-paper, which proved a match for the match, and fire flew. I thought, "No more trouble with covering up the coals at night; no more running to the neighbors because our fire is out; no more snapping the flint over lint." A mighty revolution was at hand. There was a hidden million in it, and why the brothers did not continue in the new calling I never knew. They might not have been monopolists or bloated bondholders. but they certainly were the leading match-makers in New Hampshire.

I think all our brothers were good mechanics and quite ingenious inventors. They could do all repairing on the farming implements, could build a house, walled-in the farms; and as farmers they were experts in fruit-raising, and always kept the lands in as high a state of cultivation as was possible on the sterile soil of New Hampshire.

Almost all boys have a mark of some sharp tool on their hands or limbs, some scratch, as a result of imprudences. I have the scar of a hatchet and a shave near together, on my left forefinger. So we are taught by experience to avoid trouble. If in the moral world we are as fortunate, we may escape some flagrant blunder; but the healing may be a part of God's economy, and we escape as by the skin of our teeth, so that if we become angels in the ages to come we may be allowed to look with gratitude on our condition.

Spring, summer, autumn and winter, in season and out, we continued the work on the farm — ploughing, sowing, mowing, hoeing, reaping and harvesting the crops as they ripened. keeping up our rehearsals all the time

Jacob of old could not have been more proud of his numerous household, than our dear father, known throughout the town as "Uncle Jesse." All the boys were obedient and interested in the enterprises of the farm The members who were not away from home were gathered after the meal in the morning to listen to the reading of the Bible and prayers. He was a devout man, and the whole world came in for a share of his petition, all classes being recommended to the Merciful Then we hied to our allotted task. With some pressing job on hand we would work in gangs of six or eight or ten, and vie with each other to do a smart

COMING UP FROM THE FIELDS.—(p. 29)

job, so that we could secure father's approval. To him six faithful days' work was enough to merit a day of rest; and, therefore, though Sunday dawned on tired bodies, all gladly repaired to the worship in the Baptist Church.

We had three large pews besides one hundred free seats on the sides of the gallery, which father and Uncle Andrew retained when they sold the remaining pews: but we boys found places in the choir seats and with one of the brothers, Joshua, as chorister, sang to the acceptance of the visible if not the invisible spirits. Brother Asa was too young, or rather his voice was so low that he could not sing the common boy's voice, the alto, so being in the pew with father and mother, he found a vent for his desire for music by rubbing his forehead on the back of the pew, causing it to vibrate, which, mingled in with the other instruments, as the double bass, caused a quite noticeable effect, producing cheerful remarks from the hearers.

At the age of seven I had learned many hymns of my mother, and at the church I took my place in the choir, and carried my part, the alto, ere I could read a note of music. At the rehearsals my voice was quite conspicuous for clearness, and older singers would add a word of praise, as I would sound out above the loudest person, the hymns of Watts and other poets.

As I have said, years before father and Uncle Andrew had built a Baptist Church, so all of the family were early indoctrinated with the tenets of that persuasion, and when but ten years old I was labored with by the proselyters of that faith and was induced to connect myself with the church. I was enrolled as a member in good standing. This was in 1831. I had then been a singer in the choir for three years.

My mother, feeling an impulse, acknowledged that there was the same good class in all denominations, and cheerfully remarked to her son at one time that she felt that she was an Orthodox, Presbyterian, Congregationalist, Methodist, Universalist, Quaker, Baptist

For many years hop-raising was followed on the farm. Each spring poles were to be selected throughout the forest, of a suitable size for that purpose. Shaving these long, small sticks occupied our spare days during the spring while the sun was getting higher in the heavens. As soon as the frost was out of the ground, in with the plow, prepare the earth, open up the last year's hills, prune the superfluous vines or roots, apply the fertilizers, then re-cover with earth to wait the time when the poles should be set, two to a hill. When this was done, the whole field presented the appearance of an army with fixed bayonets awaiting a charge. This proved a lucrative business, but throughout the long summer until the last of August, when the crop was gathered, required much hard work. Some love and poetry clustered around the picking and drying, the girls, in a merry, social mood, stood around with us; clutching the vines and stripping the hops into large heaps in the well-filled boxes. Then would come the merry song and march to the house, as the bell or horn would sound the signal for dinner. The *menu* was very simple — corned-beef, cabbage, brown-bread, vegetables, sometimes pudding, and plenty of baked sweet-apples and milk for supper, with now and then a piece of white-oak cheese.

My oldest brother, David, succeeded in getting the contract of working the large three-acre hop-field for one season; and the time for gathering the crop having come, I, though quite young, inquired of David what he

THE HOP-PICKERS (p. 22)

would pay for the services of a big boy like me, being anxious to take part in the good-cheer of the occasion. He replied, "I will board you for what you can do, or I will give you one cent for the term and you board yourself." I was on hand when the morning came, and told him I would take him up on his first offer, reasoning that it would save father that much if I could earn my board. For more than two weeks I labored on, realizing that boys must have their promotion very slow, and then only when they grow or strike for it; but I made sure of a good time. In the evenings we sang our hymns and psalms together. Among the pickers was one quite talented girl, Lorena Smith, who amused the rest by playing her violin, one of her favorite pieces being, "The Old Hen Calling her Chickens over the Wall"; and the illustration she gave was a good imitation. These exercises made our joy complete.

The time passed merrily away, and we were sorry when the pickers left for their several homes. The hops were finally dried, baled and sold, and as David brought the proceeds of the sale and exposed them to view in a quart tin basin — fully a hundred dollars in silver halves and quarters — I suppose I manifested a rather covetous spirit as he withdrew the tempting sight, following him with my eyes. He soon stepped forward, and, holding an old-fashioned copper cent between his thumb and finger, requested me to accept this as a gratuity in consideration of my faithful two weeks' labor. What was accepted as a perquisite then with gratitude, would later have been spurned; but in our youth we learned not to despise the day of small things.

"Oh, the merry days, the merry days when we were young
Where the boy's will is the wind's will, and the thoughts of youth are long, long thoughts."

A respected citizen, the fisherman or angler of the neighborhood, with his rod and line, would pass our house, and, by instinct or sympathy with the finny tribe, was sure to have success in the brook, lake or river. He seemed to know the holes where to drop a line, and at evening would delight to show his luck to those who were compelled to stay behind. When he laughed the welkin rang, and through the neighborhood around the people were refreshed. At first the dread that some wild beast had broken loose from a menagerie and was roaring for its mate would possess the minds of the hearers; but as the tone died away after a prolonged "Ha-a-a-a," out-rivalling anything of the four-footed kind, then we all took a breath, and would shake his hand as we would ask him where he was going to fish next time, and if he would take us for luck.

Sometimes we coveted the leisure of our poorer neighbors. Generally they had patient, hard-working wives, who did more than their part in the support of the families. We, however, could get off sometimes for the sport of fishing after our stints were done. What enjoyment it was for me, alone or in company! One day I watched one of the neighbor's boys on the bank of the river at the mouth of the brook, sitting in a catching mood with his fish-pole and line, and I said to myself, "O dear, he will catch all the suckers and chubs, and I must wait till my rows are hoed!" The labor finished, how fast I leaped over the intervening meadow, stopping long enough by the low ground to get fresh worms, and, in a bound up the river bank, I was by the side of the fisher. I saw nothing had been caught; and lo, in the deep hole were daintily swimming around the hook of this boy ("Rid," as we called him) a school of fish. In went my freshly-baited hook, cautiously moving toward the largest one; the mouth opened, and I had him, first dangling at the end of my line and then upon the ground, safe. How proud I felt! In again, and out came another. Not a word was spoken between us; my luck was a mystery to him. In the space of twenty minutes I had secured eight of the hungry ones, when up got the boy and walked sullenly away home; and I could only say in condolence, "Fisherman's luck!" Moral, stick to your promised task and bide your time, but use fresh bait when you fish. Later, we Hutchinsons were made fishers of men, and made successes in proselyting.

Judson, four years my senior, purchased for three dollars a violin of a neighbor, Dimond Pearsons, and paid for the same by raising vegetables. This was when he was about sixteen years old. Encouraged by him, I followed suit, bought one, and paid for it in beans of my own raising; and we began playing duets. Some time subsequently, Asa, our younger brother, had the gift of a violincello from Andrew, which was once played in the Old South Church in Boston.

We were discouraged from practising our instruments in the house, and so sought the field; and many a good rehearsal we had by the side of the large granite boulder about one hundred rods from the house. Those rock concerts can never be forgotten. Phœnix-like the once despised viol of our ancestors came up from the ashes as it were, and was restored to favor, so winning the respect of our stern parent that we were permitted to come back to the house.

Later, Brother Judson and I joined the brass band: he chose the tenor and I the bass trombone, and our playing was much approved. I never was more elated in singing before the most popular audiences than heading with this band of twelve chosen musicians a company of infantry on the march. How everybody sprang to the doors and windows! the small boys rushing into the streets, following the trail. How the music "enthused" all in the towns where we played! "Tippicanoe and Tyler too," "Hard Cider," "Log Cabin," etc., all made up the campaign of 1840; and the Whigs elected William Henry Harrison in opposition to Van Buren. How the speakers worked! "Long Tall" Wilson, for instance, with coat and scarf off, sounding his stentorian voice as he faced the wind and his hearers for three long hours.

Daniel Webster, also, was active in this campaign. I well recall my first sight of him, at a gathering in Francestown. He was then in his prime, tall, with magnificent presence and noble face, his form clad in a blue coat and brass buttons, and a resplendent vest of buff material. The speakers in this campaign were fully as eloquent as those in the campaign for Harrison's grandson, a half-century later. The processions, especially those of the Whigs, were great affairs, with the log-cabins on wheels, and barrels of hard cider for free distribution to all who came, and veterans of the Revolution seated on the team.

In our band we had, of course, to play for both political parties, first for the Whigs and then for the Democrats. As the music was purely national, we considered that good taste was not violated in so doing. At one time we serenaded General James Wilson in his tent at Concord. He acknowledged the compliment by offering us brandy in tin dippers. To me it seemed rank and disagreeable stuff, and I simply smelled and tasted of it, and then threw it away. Some of the boys, I grieve to say, seemed used to it. To my unsophisticated political mind, there seemed a good deal of unnecessary fuss in all this speaking and parade.

At a convention at Wilton, Colonel Stephen Peabody, a prominent man of our town, and for a long time inspector of hops for our neighborhood, presided. Colonel Peabody was prominent in all the intellectual activities of our region. At this particular meeting in Wilton, he rose to introduce a Revolutionary veteran, and in most glowing terms referred to the services rendered the young nation by the men of seventy-six, one of whom he was glad to present to them — " What's your name, sir?" he added, abruptly turning to the old soldier. His memory had failed him in such a manner as to make his peroration appear laughable enough.

Drunkenness, or the drink habit, constantly infested every town, village, hamlet, neighborhood with which we were conversant. No station or condition was exempt from its blighting influence. Summing up the injury that has befallen the human race, and after long personal experience and observation, I am persuaded that the better portion of the body politic who have had their patience tried to the highest tension, may now demand of law-abiding communities what has been refused for centuries — an improved state of affairs, making peace triumph, and order to replace disquiet, drunkenness, confusion and anarchy. I believe it the duty of the present generation to diligently labor to so improve conditions that coming generations shall not inherit this incumbrance; and I abjure all the clergy of the land to fail not to declare the whole counsel with precept and example, to help establish man again in his primitive condition — not that they shall advise men to love and heed their spiritual well-being the less, but to work in the present vineyard the more, and emphasize the sentiment, "Thy kingdom come, Thy will be done on earth as it is in heaven."

I recall one man, who gave instructions on the violin, or professed to. My brother and myself were induced to become his pupils; but after a lesson or two his love of the art and occupation were well-nigh sacrificed and bartered away for the pleasure of the dram-shop. He so neglected his duty that we tired of the effort to excel under his tuition of bow and brandy. The bar of Buxton's Tavern was too interesting to this person of loose habits, whose will had become an easy prey to appetite and waywardness. His relatives were thrifty and industrious people. One was a banker, and was trusted and honored by all to the end. "Some for honor and some for dishonor." Both men were exposed to the same temptation, but one resisted. So I claim this habit becomes criminal and the indulger should be dealt with accordingly, and should not cumber the ground upright citizens should occupy.

The drink habit was almost universal in our neighborhood and town. Old New England rum was the white-faced devil that tickled the palate of more or less of the careless individuals comprising the population. It was considered a deplorable scourge by the better part of the community.

"Deep curse of mankind,
How remorseless the blast"

Scenes of squalor characterized the drunkard's home, as they have from time immemorial — a lack of thrift, and total neglect; rags and old hats taking the place of the panes of glass that had been rudely dashed out; together with the sad countenances of wife, mother and half-clad children.

"How often, oh, how often in the days that have gone by," was I sent on an errand of mercy, taking alms to one poor afflicted family whose father had ceased to provide and was a notorious sot. Sometimes I would meet him on the road, staggering to or from his old board house. At other times I would find him in a corner upon the floor.

The family, one by one, were put out to be brought up by strangers, and, strange to relate, only one of this family followed in the footsteps of his father, while the others grew to manhood, and proved to be men of energy, capability, thrift and reliability.

When sober this head of the family was considered a most capable mechanic and expert blacksmith and pleasant companion. Oftentimes did we refuse to give answer to his pleadings for a drink of cider.

He chanced to come into the mowing-field one day; and it was suggested that he was in a right condition to take up a bumble-bee's nest that was located in a little patch of grass which was still standing in the field that had been mowed. With reckless courage he volunteered at once to encounter the sting. Dropping on his knees in the presence of the nest, and thrusting his hands down, he began rubbing the bees between his fingers, to the amusement of the lookers-on. One moment up would go one hand to the side of his face or to the top of his head, wherever there was exposure, for the bees were flying in every direction. The rum that was in him ceased to be of sufficient potency to answer as an antidote to the sting of the bee; he rose and rushed away in a very excited state, grasping hold of some hay which he swung about him until they were dispersed. In spite of the misery he was in, he seemed to enjoy the feat, and regretted that there was not another nest to break up.

"No drunkard can inherit the kingdom of heaven."
"Look not thou upon the wine when it is red, when it giveth its color in the cup."

"O Rum, what hast thou done?
Ruined mother, daughter, father, son."

Who is there that, taking a retrospective view of the calamities that have befallen the race of human beings for more than half a century, could, with any degree of propriety and excuse, say that the cause of prohibition of this terrible traffic and the closing of the dram-shops of the country should not prevail? And to be consistent with our common love and estimation of the race of good citizens and true philanthropists, we should put forth strenuous efforts to relieve humanity from this deep curse of mankind.

"I've met with a beggar in rags,
　Who asked for a trifling sum;
I will tell you the cause why he begs,
　He once was a lover of rum

"Ask prisons and gallows and all
　Whence most of their customers come,
From whom they have most of their call,
　They will tell you from lovers of rum"

．　　　．

"But, O Rum, the time will come,
When the nation shall shout, 'Thy day is done!'"

An interesting character was Phenias Stimpson; a man whose principle was, "Live and let live"; disposed to treat everybody with civility, he served a useful part in his occupation and trade as a shoemaker and cobbler. He was at one time the town clerk. With a degree of culture in music, a lover of harmony and psalmody, he taught many singing-schools in our little hamlet. How well I remember the instructions that he gave, and taught with few of the rudiments, "Fa, sol, la, fa, sol, la, me, fa." He was noted for his good cheer and kind spirit, and was ever ready to second any occasion of fun and amusement.

I have sat with a degree of satisfaction in the little shop by the bridge waiting for some small job of cobbling that he was doing for me, and listening to his hum and whistle as he used the awl and drew the waxed-end through the sole of the shoe. The tune was always a merry and cheerful one.

A little misfit in the pair of calfskin boots which he had taken great pains to make and deliver to me the day before my marriage caused me great inconvenience. The right foot was quite cramped, but having no other foot-gear, I was obliged to wear them on my wedding tour, and from that cause I have worn a swollen joint on my right foot for fifty years. Few men who on their honeymoon have got in as tight a place can boast of as little inconvenience during half a century of married life.

Milford had one citizen who, though a "real live Yankee" in his ancestry and habits, was a thorough Hibernian in some of his remarks. "I have been sick," said he one day, "and had the brain fever in my head — the *worst* place I could have had it." He bought a barrel of crackers, so he could have some when he got out. He also said he liked to have bells on his sleigh, so he could see in a dark night. Said he, "I mean to be buried in the new burying-ground, if I live." "I saw a lot of muskrats," said he one day, "swimming *right* in the water."

Master Knight taught a country school not far distant from our locality. He was a very amiable, appreciative and capable teacher. He once related a circumstance that took place during the reading of the Scripture one morning. It was the rule of the school that it should be read by what is termed the "first class," which comprised usually the older boys and girls, and those who could read readily the language of the Bible. An ambitious youth, who considered himself competent because of his large size, kept in the first class, and having little knowledge of letters, secured a bright little lad that belonged in another class to assist and prompt him while the Scripture was being read. The class was requested to turn to the Book of Job, chapter two. The scholars who preceded this ignoramus read correctly and properly until it came his turn. The young prompter was crouched right at hand where he could plainly see the words, and in a whisper he said, "And the Lord"; and the brave avoirdupois student repeated the words in a loud voice, "And the Lord"; then in a soft voice again, "smote Job with sore boils"; then came the confident voice attempting to repeat the words, "And the Lord shot Job with four great balls." The lad, profanely witty, replied to himself in a soft tone, "H—l of a charge, wan't it!" And again the voice sounded out through the school-room, "Hell of a charge wanted." This was enough; the whole school was in a roar of laughter; the teacher, closing the book, said, "The further reading of the Scripture this morning will be deferred," while in a short conclusive prayer he said, "Oh Lord, we thank thee for everything. Amen."

Black as the ace of spades, a tall, well-proportioned, athletic, uneducated but witty African, came early into the neighborhood, at the abandonment of the slave system in Massachusetts, and was a convenient neighbor and servant, working among the different agricultural districts of Amherst and Milford. He was quite conspicuous on public occasions, like trainings, musters and holidays, with the "b-hoys" who were fond of scuffling and wrestling. He was always brought into the ring under the influence of a glass or two, which was freely furnished him, was sufficiently bold and sprightly, and could bring down to the amusement of all, almost any of those selected to scuffle or wrestle.

Some wag had learned of a resolution made by some woman in a family not far away, who had been discarded by her lover. She vowed in her madness at being jilted, "I'll marry the first man that proposes." This individual hastened down to inform the black man of the matter, saying "Miss So and So is very fond of you, and if you hasten before any one else and make a proposition for marriage — you will find her a white woman — she will accept." Consequently, this colored man dressed himself in his best overalls, repaired to the house, and boldly made his proposition; and to his great delight the lady agreed that he should be her suitor. Subsequently they married, and the result was that instead of one black man in our neighborhood, there soon grew up five boys and two girls of a lighter hue. They lived in comparative isolation; and although the inhabitants treated them with proper consideration and courtesy, still they considered the match a questionable one.

Some of the boys learned trades, others were put to work, and in the district schools were allowed to come in with the other scholars, yet there was observable a notable reservation and withdrawing from the common plays and sports of the children. One day, one of the sons, who was a very agreeable, pleasant man, speaking familiarly of his relation and his condition, said he would suffer to be skinned alive if he could rid himself of his color.

Each one of the boys was athletic and dexterous, whenever they were put in competition with an antagonist. They were fond of music. One played a 'cello or bass viol, and was accepted as a musician throughout the surrounding villages.

The father would trap for fur. Some individual up to tricks, desiring to surprise him with good luck, learned where he had set his "figure-four" along the banks of the brook, and placed a dead cat in his trap, leaving most of the body in plain view. Early in the morning he observed the trapper heading for the bank. He spied the animal at a distance, and making a standstill, uttered these sentiments in the hearing of the detective, supposing that he had a valuable fur in his trap. He halted, threw up his hands in expression of awe and delight, and he said, "Now Cæsar'll have some spending money; now Cæsar'll go to muster; now Cæsar'll get drunk if he's a mind to, and if he ain't a mind to he'll get drunk." He passed on, and to his consternation found only the body of a house cat.

"Fond memory brings the light of other days around me"

Friends and neighbors I loved, who dwelt on either side of the Souhegan, made the margin dear with friendships and loving associations. On the north and south of this stream once lived the Haywards, Hutchinsons, Pearsons, Burns, Bartletts, Wallaces, Averills, Peabodys, Crosbys, the Lovejoys, Ramsdells, Fullers, Simpsons, Buxtons, Knowltons, Gosses, Holts, Kings, Turners, Captain Kain, Dunklins, Fosters, Putnams, Millses and Knights.

CHAPTER II.

BEGINNINGS OF SONG

"We have come from the mountains,
We've come down from the mountains,
Ho, we've come from the mountains
Of the old Granite State !
We're a band of brothers,
We're a band of brothers,
We're a band of brothers !
And we live among the hills "

ALL through my boyhood, while engaged in labors on the farm, I had prophetic dreams or visions of scenes representing experiences, which in after years proved real. I saw our company standing and singing to numerous audiences, heard the plaudits and compliments as they dispersed, and witnessed the gathering-in of piles of money — gold, silver and quantities of paper.

We early manifested dramatic talent, and readily acquired a knowledge of elocution. The old North school-house entertainments became so popular that we soon had requests to exhibit in the village academy. We could sing our songs, play our several instruments, act as prompters, stage managers, costumers.

On Thanksgiving Day, 1839, the Hutchinson Family appeared together in public for the first time. Jesse had come up from Lynn, and Andrew from Boston, to celebrate the day. The plan of a free concert in the Baptist Church originated with Joshua and Jesse, each a choir-leader and music-teacher. Andrew demurred, on the ground that he could not spare the time from his business, but was told by Joshua that he *must* stay, and rehearsing immediately commenced. The advertising consisted of two slips of paper, one posted on the old Town House, and the other at the bridge:

> *The eleven sons and two daughters of the "Tribe of Jesse" will sing at the Baptist Meeting-House on Thanksgiving evening at seven o'clock.*

It was an anxious time for us all, but the older brothers secured "Squire" S. K. Livermore to speak on "Music," and the minister, Rev. J. G. Richardson, so that the concert might be interspersed with speakers and not fall through. Grandfather Leavitt, with father and mother were present, and sang with us on the old chorals. The church was packed with sympathetic listeners, and our hymns, anthems and glees were enthusiastically received. The next day Brother Joshua went to Ezekiel Mills, the sexton, to pay for the use of the church. He pushed him away, saying, 'The people of Milford owe *you*." The minister wrote the concert up for the *Farmer's Cabinet*, and after father's decease, the notice was found carefully preserved among his choice papers.

After our band was organized we began to discuss with earnestness the plan of giving public concerts, and by the time the school term of that year, 1841, closed, our plans were all made. Previous to this we had heard words from father that never were spoken to us before. Asa and I were the two youngest boys, and not being able to do our usual chores about the farm, owing to our attention to studies, he said, "After the school term closes, I want you boys to provide for yourselves"; which acted as a spur toward independent action. We notified father of our intention to leave the work on the farm and seek our fortunes in some other vocation. Getting his consent, he giving us our time, we packed the sparsely-filled trunks and bags of clothing in the one-horse sleigh, and he drove Asa and me to Lynn, where we arrived after a fifteen-hours' drive of fifty miles.

Arriving in Lynn, we met three of our brothers who had preceded us. Jesse, who had left home several years before, was established there, manufacturing and selling stoves, and doing a successful business in tin and hardware. He was also the inventor of improvements in the manufacture of air-tight stoves. Joshua had come from Milford, and Judson from Boston.

On consultation with our brothers, we decided to give a public concert, and the old Sagamore Hall was secured. (This was one of the old landmarks of the city, and remained standing until burned in the great fire which desolated Lynn, November 26, 1889.)

With a degree of timidity and embarrassment we started in on our first number, before a respectable audience, which had assembled to see what Jesse's brothers could do as singers. Jesse was very solicitous for our success. We were comparative strangers, while he had mingled with them all and was well acquainted. The concert was a great success, as evinced by the frequent applause throughout the programme to the final strains.

I said to my brothers, "We need more discipline and more culture." We therefore went to Boston, feeling that if we were to follow the business of giving concerts, we must have more practice, and that if we could get into some good business to earn our living, and still practice at the same time, we should be better able to please the public and ourselves.

We made a call on Dr. Lowell Mason, the great musical composer and teacher, then in the height of his fame. He hurriedly gave us, in reply to our request for advice in regard to vocal culture, a recommendation to use his recent publication, a new singing-book called the "Academy of Music," and expressing no further interest in our welfare, resumed his labors writing music. Saying no more, we departed with no material satisfaction. The urgent necessity he was under to fulfil the great obligation to the public resting upon him we deemed sufficient excuse for his action. Since then we have had our own experience with intruders. As time passed on, Dr. Mason spoke before his class in high terms of the Hutchinson Family's manner of singing, the great harmony they made, and the best manner of proceeding with public concerting, style of music. etc., as illustrated by our career.

We then waited upon Prof. George James Webb, who received us most courteously; and when the suggestion was made of our joining the Handel and Haydn Society, he desired to hear us sing. He selected a new piece of music and sat at the piano to accompany us while we sang, each taking his different part according to the rule. At the conclusion he arose and approvingly said, "I should be pleased to propose you to the society." He gave us a notice of a meeting they were to have the next week. My brother Judson and I accepted the invitation and were present at one evening's rehearsal. We retired from the meeting with a feeling that it would not be to our advantage to join them. Subsequently, after an absence from our boarding-house on Purchase Street, we learned that Mr. Webb had called and inquired for us, with the expressed purpose of soliciting our patronage as members of the society. We debated some time before giving an answer, but finally considered that by becoming members we should lose our identity (as we had somewhat light voices, which would be drowned by their style of chorus singing), and declined the offer.

We hired a capacious room on Purchase Street, Boston, where we did our own cooking and kept a bachelor's hall.

Jesse was engaged as a compositor in the *Advertiser* office on Court Street; and thinking I might like the business, I went with him to look for a job. Jesse still kept his store in Lynn, but came to Boston to keep us company. The *Advertiser* office was up in the top of a five-story building, and to reach it we had to climb the long stairs (the luxury of elevators was not then known), through dark hall-ways. Before we reached the top, I said I guessed I would not go any farther, turned around, and so retired and left him in his glory. I then tried sawing wood and peddling, but felt all the time that I was out of my element. One young coxcomb offered to loan me twenty dollars to buy a handcart.

I finally engaged myself to a grocer for eight dollars a month and board. Part of my duty was to tend bar and sell liquor by the glass, which was very repugnant to me. This was immediately before the Temperance Reformation, and it was customary to keep a bar in all grocery stores.

All this time we kept up our practising and rehearsing, meeting each week in a hall at the corner of Pearl and Purchase Streets, over the store of Brother Andrew, who had been in Boston ten years or more. Here the Universalist Society held their services, and Judson was leader of the choir. Rev. Mr. Spier supplied the pulpit.

Across on the opposite corner, the Rev. George Ripley preached Unitarianism, advocated the doctrine of Fourierism, and taught the brotherhood of man. He later established the Brook Farm experiment, and was afterwards for many years literary editor of the *New York Tribune*.

Finding, as we thought, that we could not make any further progress in Boston, we decided to retreat to Lynn. How glad I was to escape that fiendish liquor business, as it looked to me! Availing myself of an honorable discharge from my employer, I felt light-hearted and encouraged, believing that I could once more enjoy freedom of conscience, dancing and shouting for joy that I was out of rum-selling.

Asa joined Jesse in his stove business, tin and plumbing, and Judson and I started a small grocery store of our own. The stores of the four brothers were side by side, where the Sagamore Hotel now stands on Union Street, in Lynn, and we went on with success, for the business was not then overdone. The little grocery store that we occupied is still in existence, having been moved to Pearl Street; and as I recently purchased some goods at this store of the grocer, I reminded him that fifty years had elapsed since my brother and myself kept that store, occupying the room above as our sleeping and singing apartment. We still continued our economical habits, cooking our own food and retiring aloft to partake of the *menu*.

To facilitate our business, I purchased a horse for seven dollars, a superannuated harness and wagon for seven dollars, and with my fourteen-dollar team started an express route in conjunction with the grocery store. Several times a week we brought goods from Boston from the store of Brother Andrew, who kept a wholesale concern.

Though we labored diligently at our business, we still kept up our musical practice, and chartered a hall at the corner of Union and Silsbee Streets, where we went into systematic training.

We provided ourselves with the best music published in Boston — "The Kingsley Social Choir," "The Æolian Lyre"; and I sent by express the last dollar I had to Oliver Ditson's publishing house in Boston, for the cantata, "The Maniac," paying twelve and a half cents express.

On Sunday we joined our voices with the choir of the First Universalist church, where Jesse was chorister; and with instrumental music, two violins and a 'cello, we made the welkin ring, and enjoyed it as much as the listeners. Some slight momentary altercation occurred between the brothers, and to Jesse's criticism we took exception; and as *some singers* have been known to do before, we absented ourselves one Sunday from the orchestra.

Sitting in the body of the church, I was deeply impressed with the singing of the choir. Towering above the noise of the instruments, their voices pealed forth clarion notes that thrilled me, as it did the congregation, with delightful surprise. I was especially charmed with the sweet trumpet voice of my brother Jesse. It was most captivating to hear, and I felt proud of him. I said in my heart, "No feud shall more disturb us." Union and harmony was restored, and the brothers Judson, Asa and I, were again invited to take our positions in the choir on the following Sunday.

During this period, Hawkins, the reformed drunkard, came to Boston and inaugurated the great Washingtonian movement. We at once allied ourselves with the temperance cause, took the pledge, and on all public occasions we sang, "We are all Washingtonians."

During the early stages of the reform, the Old Deacon Giles distillery, of Salem, Mass., was converted into a temperance hall, and here, at a grand temperance rally, we first sang the trio composed by Brother Jesse, called —

KING ALCOHOL

King Alcohol has many forms
  By which he catches men,
He is a beast of many horns,
  And ever thus has been
There is rum and gin, and beer and wine,
  And brandy of logwood hue,
And these, with other fiends combined,
  Will make any man look blue

CHORUS.

He says, "Be merry, for here's your cherry,
And Tom-and-Jerry and port and sherry,
And spirits of every hue"
Oh, are not these a fiendish crew,
As ever a mortal knew?

Then came into the arena the immortal John B. Gough, with whom we fully sympathized. Such advocates as Hawkins and Gough in the field of battle against rum should have gained a great victory. Half a century has elapsed, and the great doctrines of temperance have been promulgated and advocated by thousands of reformers. Still the drink habit continues the deep curse of mankind.

In the autumn of 1841 I hired a suitable carriage, packed it full of such wares as I thought would be salable — confectionery, gingerbread and other eatables — and invited two of the members of the Lynn Band, Mr. Fisher, cornet, and Frank Lydston, portrait painter and trombone player, to go with me. We left Lynn for New Hampshire, fearless of the consequences. We drove all night, reaching the homestead in New Hampshire the next noon, where I had the congratulations of parents and neighbors. My sister Rhoda, who was noted for her palatable apple pies, supplied us with a dozen or two of this delicious food and packed us off. We started for the muster-field at Goffstown, N. H. Here my comrades sought for an engagement to play with the military band, and were successful in obtaining a small one, enough to pay their way.

I made a display of my wares, and hung a sign over my carriage which read thus: "Walk up, gentlemen! Here is your fine gingerbread and apple pies, mead and other palatable drinks." I secured a sufficient amount to pay my expenses. In addition to my confectionery, etc., I had a portfolio of prints, which I endeavored to peddle around the grounds. One was a picture of the steamer *Elections*, the first on the Sound. Some fellows came up pretending to purchase, and one took hold of the side of the portfolio and suddenly let go, and my pictures were at the mercy of the wind while they hurried away, and I had the mortification of picking the prints out of the dust.

Fully disgusted with such experiences, I was convinced that my forte was something other than catering to a promiscuous crowd, and after one unsuccessful attempt at Woburn, a week later, I returned to Lynn.

Owing to our irregularities of living, lack of proper diet and exposures over the marshes, driving a slow team from Boston to Lynn, I took a severe cold and was obliged to go to bed, having been pronounced by the doctor, sick with a bilious fever. I was fortunate in securing an interesting and sympathizing nurse, who with magnetic tact and wisdom, diligently watched over me for three weeks, until I was fully restored. This gentleman, now threescore years and ten, or more, still survives, and is no less a man than the Lynn caterer, Mr. Warwick Palfray.

Settling his bill, which was two dollars a day — and that for twenty-four hours daily — and paying the doctor, who was a proficient and expert practitioner, I had left out of my earnings and savings but seventy-five cents with which to commence business anew.

This was a season of misfortunes, and having passed through the whooping-cough, measles and bilious fever, I began to think that I was a sinner above all others.

During my most dangerous condition father, being solicitous on account of my sickness, came down from New Hampshire to see me and pray with me; but whether it was the prayer, or the laying on of hands, or the nurse that cured me, the spirits of the air may decide.

Autumn came, and we returned to Milford and gave our first concert in East Wilton. Deacon Bales, an old friend of the early years of the Hutchinson Family, made arrangements for our convenience and was present at the concert. The arrangements for a stage were the bare floor on a level with the audience, with a wide, rough pine board laid across on the heads of three barrels. On this board were six half-candles supposed to last till the end of the concert, and they stood in their own grease.

The deacon was considered an old-fashioned-mannered man, enjoying psalmody, playing his 'cello or bass-viol in a systematic manner. In directing and pitching the tune for the choir, he would place his fingers upon

THE EAST WELSON CONCERT — (p. 44)

his nose, press the tone up into the nasal organ to first take the pitch of the tune which he was to sing " la fawd la ' " This man spoke approving words of our concert, as we were bidding him good-by. In this and subsequent concerts for some time, we adopted the name of the " Æolian Vocalists." This concert netted six and a quarter cents after paying expenses.

In these first concerts, we sang from note and not by rote, having all our pieces arranged according to the programme in sheet music. In after years we found this was distracting to us; so we committed to memory all the songs we were to sing, and sang them with perfect freedom.

Being somewhat affected with hoarseness for several days, learning that pickles were good, at the next concert we procured some, about six or eight inches long; and between the songs we would stoop down and take a bite and pass it to the next. On one occasion we came pretty near strangling with the vinegar.

We gave concerts at East Wilton, West Wilton, Wilton, Wilton Centre, New Ipswich, Hancock and Peterborough. Returning, we found that the expenses had taken all except a dime, not leaving us enough to pay for the sleigh that we had hired at twenty cents a week of Brother Ben. This made Judson blue, and he said, "If we don't do better than this next week, I'll relinquish it, and give up the whole thing as a failure." " Better luck next week," said I, " in a better neighborhood "

Then came a week's concert tour through several of the towns in Hillsborough County. Small profits, but lots of praise. We divided some twelve or fifteen dollars.

Returning to Lynn, we took with us our youngest

sister, Abby, then eleven years of age, and hired Lyceum Hall, on Market Street, for a concert. Friends gathered around and arrayed her in a peculiar style, with a Swiss bodice or Tyrolean costume, giving her rather a foreign air, and she took her parts with the rest of us and sang songs at some of our country exhibitions. Thus far we had done very little singing as a quartet, but we soon found that adding her as making up the quartet, served to help in winning our way, and perfected the picture as we stood before the public. In the *New York Home Journal* in after years, N. P. Willis spoke of us as " a nest of brothers with a sister in it." The Lynn concert proved a grand success.

Then we went East, stopping at the towns of Beverly, Salem, Ipswich, Newburyport, Portsmouth, Kennebunk and Saco.

We headed our programmes with these lines, by Judson:

"When foreigners approach your shores
You welcome them with open doors
Now we have come, to seek our lot,
Shall native talent be forgot?"

In all of these places a lively interest was awakened in our favor. In Portsmouth we held three concerts, audiences increasing on each occasion. We sang in the hall attached to the American Hotel, kept by Barnabee, the home of Henry C. Barnabee, the singer, son of the landlord, whose musical laurels were won in after years.

Arriving in Saco we made the acquaintance of a musical person, Mr. Priest, who was considered then a leader among the singers of the town. He attended our concerts and spoke in complimentary words of them. We stopped at the Temperance Hotel, kept by Mr. Tufts. A grand temperance rally was held during our stay at

THE OLD HOMESTEAD — (p. 47)

this hotel, and we joined with the people. It awoke considerable interest among them. Fifty-three years later, at a banquet of the board of trade in Portland where I sang, the mayor remarked that he was a son-in-law of Mr. Priest, whose daughter, his wife, well remembered our singing at the time of which I speak.

Many friendships were made during this down-east campaign, which were lasting and renewed often in after visits with great pleasure. In each town was a cluster of sympathizing hearts, almost all young in years, who served to awake sweet memories in later days.

We repeated our concerts in the several towns on our return back to Lynn, starting late in December. Returning to Lynn in February, singing about in the region for awhile, we received a beseeching letter from our father, expressing an earnest solicitude for our welfare, and desiring that we relinquish our interests in public life. He expressed a longing for us to return home and help him on the farm, promising to give a deed of the home farm to the six youngest children. The deed was written, the conditions, that we were to give up our itinerant life, take care and provide for the wants of our mother as long as she lived, and continue a peaceful mode of living. He advised us to abandon aspirations for a matrimonial life, which advice we accepted with mental reservations, and entered into our vineyard of labor.

For some time we lived together, sharing all things in common, and father looked on with a degree of satisfaction. Many improvements were inaugurated. Buildings were moved, and some were torn down. The old hop-house, where we used to dry our hundreds of weight of hops annually, had become obsolete, and was also moved away; that business had been abandoned on account of our temperance principles years before. The old homestead and farm was put in thorough repair; new fertilizers were brought into requisition; and our labors were delightful, as all our interests were merged into one harmonious relation. The goods from the grocery store in Lynn we had freighted to a store on the farm.

It was a pleasure indeed to have our father so relieved from the burden of his great cares. That year he celebrated his golden wedding, simply by giving mother an outing. But the musical charm was by no means broken. Happy as was that spring with us young bachelors, and strong as our domestic feelings naturally were, we determined to try once again music as a means of living. Perhaps our musical impulses were a little excited by a circumstance which occurred about this time. Three young ladies of great personal loveliness came to our village from Lyndeboro and Bedford, for the purpose of attending the Female Academy. Being invited, they willingly became members of the choir, and very probably inspired the sensitive vocalists, for the music of the sanctuary so vastly improved that crowds flocked to hear it, and the minister, Rev. Abner B. Warner, exclaimed, "How much better I can preach now!"

How well I remember the singing of these girls! Our hearts and souls were kindled with a flame of sacred love; we worshipped at these shrines, and the associations ripened into harmony. At last we unitedly resolved to make propositions for engagement; and on Saturday night each repaired to the home of his sweetheart, and asked the question, "Will you be mine?" The answers were to be announced at our meeting the following day; but as the course of true love never does run smooth, the order was put in abeyance, and we were obliged to abide on probation:

"Better, some adviser said,
    To always court and never wed."

So affairs went on, — now giving a concert, now getting in a crop. While thus unsettled, a gentleman visited us, and observed, after hearing us sing, "Why, if you managed rightly, you might make as much in some places in one night as you do here in a year." This stimulated us anew, and, as soon as the summer came, once more we commenced preparations for a new tour.

Judson went to Boston, where he purchased a second-hand family carryall. From Brother Ben we secured a white mare which he had taken in part-payment of a debt. This, with the seven-dollar bay horse which I bought in Lynn, put us in a good condition for our venture. Judson took my horse — which we always called our "Old John" horse — to Boston to bring the carryall. In the excess of his enthusiasm, anxiety and humanity, he almost entailed upon himself and brothers a considerable loss. Of a warm and generous disposition and possessed of much feeling for animals, he determined to treat the old horse in magnificent style. Arriving at a hotel some miles out of Boston on the road to New Hampshire, and imagining a hearty feed would put him in good condition and enable him to get home all the faster, Judson gave the steed a half-bushel of oats, a peck of Indian meal and a large cribful of hay, all in one repast. The horse, unaccustomed to such plenty, devoured it all, and, of course, suffered from the banquet. The result was that Judson had to leave the animal behind to digest the monstrous meal, and procure another horse to take the carryall from Boston to Milford. Prior to the grand start, we — Judson, Asa, Abby and myself — gave a Fourth-of-July concert at Nashua, which was very successful, in connection with Mr. Lyman Heath, from whom we received some admirable songs of his own composition. The friendly advice of this gentleman was of much service. After this we set out on our northern tour, "sublime of hope and confident of fame."

As we passed on our way, David happened to be working in his fields, and hearing us, he paused, leaned over his fence and shouted, "Remember, boys, noise is not music!"

Having no travelling agent, we sent our bills by mail or by friends.

Our personal property was thus disposed of : a bag with our clothing was placed in the carryall; the violins, without cases, were hung inside; and the bass-viol was strapped on the top; the little hair trunk, containing Abby's simple wardrobe, was on the rack.

Many a night did we travel to meet engagements — often sleepy and cold, and longing for the luxury of a bed. Nor were we exempt from perils during some of these midnight excursions. The roads were strange, and whenever a guide-post was found, Judson, the tallest of the party, was deputed to examine and report thereon. Once we had a narrow escape. During a very dark night the horses stopped all of a sudden. Judson, who was ever on the watch, instantly jumped from the carriage; we were on the verge of a precipice; and had not the animals instinctively stopped, our progress might have ended in a "Dead March."

Arriving at Concord, we gave concerts and were very favorably received. Here we became acquainted with

ON THE ROAD.—(p. 56)

N. P. Rogers, editor of the *Herald of Freedom*, who in his journal devoted a column to a criticism of our performances. Mr. Rogers was always a warm and judicious friend of the Hutchinsons. He wrote admirable critiques on our performances, and repeatedly urged us to sing the thrilling songs of liberty and humanity; some of Burns' patriotic songs he also recommended. It was his ardent desire that we should not be mere birds of passage, but that we should ever cultivate home affections. At the time when this good friend was lying on his death-bed the Hutchinsons, then popular, happened to be in Concord. Mr. Rogers sent for us to sing him to sleep. One of us immediately repaired to the house, but while waiting for admittance to his room the last sleep had commenced. This was October 16, 1846. One of the daughters, by his request, sang the "Angel's Invitation." All of Mr. Rogers' family evinced great musical talent, and were excellent teachers of the art.

I insert one of his notices as copied from the *Herald of Freedom*, December 9, 1842.

THE HUTCHINSON SINGERS.

These Canary birds have been here again, charming the ear of our Northern winter with their wood-note melody. Four of them are here out of a nest of fourteen. All of them, I understand, are to flock together to warble at Nashua at our coming Thanksgiving, though one has to come from Illinois. The concert will be worth the long flight, and well worth a journey from here there to listen to. I had rather keep Thanksgiving (if at all) on the melody of these birds than on a whole poultry-yard full of dead turkeys and goslins, which make up the usual Thanksgiving feast, as well as the usual gratitude.

These "New Hampshire Raineis" sung here two evenings to rather small audiences. One night they were at an out-of-the-way hall, and the other night there was a sharp snow-storm. It would not have kept the people from the Baptist meeting to hear the brimstone melody of Jacob Knapp, but it kept them from hearing the simple, heart-touching strains of the "Æohan Vocalists."

Perhaps I am partial to the Hutchinsons, for they are abolitionists. It need not affright them to have it announced. It won't — if it would scare away their listeners it would not scare away themselves. But it won't. Human nature will go and hearken and be charmed at their lays, and the time is coming, if it has not come already, when the public conscience will feel quieted at the thought of having heard music from the friends of the slave and having patronized it. How natural for music as well as poetry to be on the side of humanity and the captive. And how gloriously employed it would be in humanity's special service. I wish the Hutchinsons had a series of anti-slavery melodies to sing at their concerts. "A Marseilles Anti-Slavery Hymn," for instance, with a Swiss "Rans de Vasche", an English "Rule Britannia", a Scotch "Scots wha ha'e", an Irish "Battle of the Boyne"; or a poor American anti-slavery "Yankee Doodle."

"Give me a ballad-making for a revolution," said some one of the sages, "and you may have all the law-making." What an agitation might the fourteen Hutchinsons sing up in the land with all their voices and instruments strung to the deliverance of the bondman! Would the South send on for our General Court to have them beheaded? The General Court would not touch a feather in their crests if they could only hear one of their strains.

A word of the music here the other night. Among the songs sung was "The Maniac." I have heard it recited with great talent, but I was not prepared to hear it sung. The younger of the brothers, John, performed it with appalling power. It was made to be sung, I think, rather than be recited or acted. Music alone seems capable of giving it its wild and maniac expression. A poor maniac is imprisoned, and starts the song at the glance of the jailer's light entering his cell. The despairing lament and the hopeless implorations for release, accompanied with the protestations that he is not mad, are enough to break the heart. It ought to have been heard by every asylum superintendent, though they have grown less of the jailer than formerly.

The airs were modern, most or all of them; and though very sweet, were less interesting to me than if they had been songs I knew. If they had had some of the old songs intermingled, I think it would better please everybody — some of Burns' "Bonny Doon" or "Highland Mary," for instance. Few professed vocalists, however, could touch either of these without profanation. I think the Hutchinsons might, for they are simple and natural in their music. I should love to hear them warble

"Ye banks and braes and streams
Around the Castle of Montgomery."

Their woodland tone, their clear enunciation and their fine appreciation of the poetry, together with their perfect freedom from all affectation and stage grimace, would enable them to do justice to the great Scottish songster, and it would do the people good to hear them sing him

Will they take the suggestion, and when they sing next, at least as far north as here, will they sprinkle their catalogue (in the singing, if not in the handbill) with a strain or two from the glens of the Scotch Highlands? And "Rans de Vasche," too, I would venture to mention to them the "Battle Chorus"; "The Lowing of the Cows upon the Alps," that makes the Swiss exile mad when he hears it in a foreign land Their spirited imitation would tell in that in grand effect

Oh, this music is one of God's dearest gifts! I do wish men would make more of it. How humanizing it is; and how purifying, elevating and ennobling to the spirit. And how it has been prostituted and perverted That accursed drum and fife, how they have maddened mankind! And the deep bass boom of the cannon, chiming in, in the chorus of the battle, that trumpet and wild, charging bugle, how they set the military devil into a man and make him into a soldier! Think of the human family falling upon one another at the inspiration of music! How must God feel at it, to see those harp-strings he meant should be waked to a love bordering on divine, strung and swept to mortal hate and butchery! And the perversion is scarcely less when music is profaned to the superstitious service of sect — its bloody-minded worship, its mercenary and bigot offerings How horribly it echoes from the heartless and priest-led meeting-house! But it will all come right by-and-by. The world is out of tune now; but it will be tuned again, and all discord become harmony. When slavery and war are abolished, and hanging and imprisoning, and all hatred and distrust; when the strife of humanity shall be who will love most and help the readiest, when the tyrant steeple shall no longer tower in sky, inspiring contempt of humanities, covering dwellings about its base, when pulpits and hangmen and generals, gibbets and jails, shall have vanished from the surface of the delivered earth, — then shall be heard music here where they used to stand The hills shall then break forth into singing, and all the trees of the field clap their hands.

Other papers now noticed us in most flattering terms, and the sun of prosperity seemed about to gladden us, for we did well and had some little money in hand; but funds are apt to fluctuate and clouds obscure the sun. A change came, and we were compelled for economy's sake to make more meals of codfish and crackers than was altogether agreeable. Like the babes in the wood, we sometimes picked berries from the hedge-rows, and fancied we had eaten a plentiful dinner. Imagination thus supplied the place of fact.

Little daunted, however, we went to Hanover, where we were well patronized by the Faculty and senior students of Dartmouth College. The ladies of Hanover, it would seem, were a little cautious, for at the first concert there was, wonderful to say, not a single bonnet in the building, somewhat to the embarrassment of the lady vocalist. But at the second they flocked in large numbers, for all voices had joined in the praise of the Hutchinsons.

Leaving Hanover, we now ventured into Vermont, in order to give the Green-Mountain State a taste of our quality; but fortune did not greatly befriend us. The tolls of the roads were very heavy and numerous, and in consequence of this and other causes, the exchequer began to assume an alarmingly small appearance. This caused us not a little uneasiness.

We were always glad when enough money was received at the door of our concert to meet the daily expenditures; and if a dollar or two were made over, we declared it a success. With the kind wishes of friendship won, more was in store for us, for we believed with Solomon, "A good name is rather to be chosen than silver or gold."

We succeeded in establishing a record which rose up to comfort in subsequent visits. Kind, encouraging words, printed in the papers at Rutland, helped us and partially established confidence among the curious, doubting ones on our way.

Whitehall, N. Y., was the next town where we attempted to hold forth. As we were not heralded, the audience was a motley crowd, made up of town boys and men who catch a handbill and take a man as they find him. A few musicians and one quite intelligent colored man were there. The barber of the village, Brown by name, seemed to be the oracle of the music circle. He boldly proffered his influence to assist us, and advised another concert; but the inhabitants heeded not the call, and did not come in to swell our receipts. Expenses at the hotels were just as exorbitant, regarding not the least the diminishing condition of our purse. This was a blue season for us, six weeks from home, and faith growing weaker. We walked to the top of the hill and thought of the martyrs and those who had suffered, hoping to gain consolation; but the present trouble was our own, to be realized and not to leave us. To return home without accomplishing our object was a disgrace; to send to friends for relief was mortifying; so we resolved to " go forward."

Just then we came across an old friend, a fellow-townsman, who some years before had left Milford, and was on a vacation from his Academy in Bethlehem, N. Y., over which he had presided for some five terms. This kind man, Mr. Josiah Fuller, gave us a word of cheer and invited us to his town, and the hospitalities of his Dutch settlement.

Bidding Whitehall and the kind musical ones goodby, we put out for the harbors of Sandy Hill and Glens Falls. Here many friends were made, but there were small additions to our sinking funds. Leaving Judson and Abby and the heavy carriage, Asa and I, with a light vehicle and the old white mare, rode twenty miles to investigate our chances in the land of the medicinal waters, Saratoga Springs. It was over a difficult, sandy road. After several unsuccessful attempts we arranged to hold entertainments at a pavilion near the recently discovered springs. The conditions were one-half net receipts.

We hastened back to Glens Falls through the sand, the most tedious road we encountered in all the summer route, fulfilled our engagements, hitched up the team and came to the famous resort of fashion, frivolity and frizzles, to say nothing of frailties. Twenty-five years after I published this song, presented to me by John G. Saxe:

WHAT DO THEY DO AT THE SPRINGS?

"Pray, what do they do at the Springs?"
   The question is easy to ask,
But to answer it fully, my dear,
   Will be rather a difficult task
     . . . . . .

Inspiring, my darling, the drink,
   The water so sparkling and clear,
Though the flavor is none of the best,
   And the odor exceedingly queer
But the fluid is mighty, you know,
   With wholesome medicinal things,
So they drink, and they drink, and they drink,
   And that's what they do at the Springs

In short, as it goes in this world,
   They eat and they drink and they sleep;
They talk and they walk and they woo;
   They sigh, they laugh and they weep,
They read, they ride and they dance
   (With other unspeakable things);
They pray, they play and they pay,
   And that's what they do at the Springs

Expecting to prolong our stay, we unloaded, and turned the horses out to grass. Though sanguine of success in the enterprise, we soon discovered we were a side-show, as the pavilion and springs were then little known and the management unpopular. Small audiences assembled, and only a sprinkling of the moneyed class from whom we had by the novelty of our manners and song, hoped to replenish our waning spirits and wasted purse. First three nights, no dividend; third, fourth and last, some three dollars and seventy-five cents were handed us by the doorkeeper as compensation. We drank of the bitter salina bubbling from the sparkling fountain, as the servant politely raised the cups in the reservoir when we stood by Congress Springs (as also at the several others in the vicinity), and saw from early morn till late at eve the throng of invalids come and go, leaving a little perquisite for the attendant, as they listened to Frank Johnson's Philadelphia Band, discoursing sweet music with hearty good cheer, while anon a good laugh from that inspiring son of Africa, came swelling up like a refreshing gust of pure air on a hot, sultry day. As the music from his bugle and band had suspended for a respite and the light gabbering compliments were spontaneously bestowed upon this merry master of music, Orpheus must have shook his sides to see so musical a soul flourishing amidst so shallow and heartless surroundings.

'Twas now we first observed our slave-holding neighbors, clothed in their wealth, displaying the elegance of their equipages, as they rolled in extravagance and splendor on the avenues, while we remembered this show was the product of the blood and sweat of the slave, who being forced could do no less than obey his master and submit to his fate. It seemed as though such inconsistency could not long survive in the republic.

Well, we looked and listened, and we also enjoyed, when we could forget our own deplorable misfortunes. But we had to drink the bitter cup almost to the dregs:

for when fate declared we must move away to other climes, when our bills were adjusted at the boarding-house, the old red and white horses once more in the carriage by the door, Sister Abby's little hair trunk lashed on the back, the bass-viol on the top, the bag with the entire wardrobe of Judson, Asa and myself in its place in the carriage, and we were seated in it, up came an officer with a charge that our horses had broken into his field, and had committed sundry and divers damages. This was a demand that must be met at once; so groaning in spirit, we drew forth the only money we had and gave it to him, and he went off satisfied.

I was no Methodist, but I felt like taking off my hat and asking for a collection. Still a little plucky, yet dreadfully disappointed, off we went, rather glad that our case was no worse, for we had joy in our hearts in the fact that we were together in misfortune, and sweet sympathy strengthened us. These trials could but knit us closer together

Schenectady was our next halting-place, and securing the co-operation of a New England man, Mr. Stevens, we were persuaded to announce a concert in the public hall, to be given free. Quite a large number of men and boys assembled. We sang with considerable spirit and freedom. The hat was passed around, and the sum of three dollars was collected, but on examination we found one of the bills was counterfeit. Availing ourselves of a chance to earn a little more, we went serenading with a party of young men; so with the collection given us we settled our hotel bill next morning, and leaving valued friends behind we travelled toward Albany. Arriving there, we took quarters at the old Delavan House, then, and for many years, a famous resort of travellers.

BEGINNINGS OF SONG.

Earnest for another trial, we contracted with the polite Albany caterer, Mr. B. F. Brier, to hold a series of concerts in his beautiful hall.

During the period in which the series of concerts were being advertised, we went to Bethlehem to spend a few days with our friend, Professor Fuller. While *en route* at night, we came on a strange road and were forced to inquire our way. Judson, then the pilot, testing the surroundings, nearly committed an unintentional assault and battery on an innocent villager. With whip in hand he was about to knock at the half-open door of a house; he raised the stick, but discovering a man standing in the doorway modestly withdrew it, and learning the way passed on to the home of the Yankee school-teacher.

While in Bethlehem we joined in a temperance gathering and witnessed the destruction of the remnant of a bar-room. A procession was formed at the tavern, and we marched to a hill, where the liquor was poured out of a demijohn, and fire set to it. We sang some temperance songs, and had a jubilee over the downfall of this potent instrument of Satan; for we still adhered to our temperance principles. A melancholy mishap occurred here; an insane woman climbed into our carriage in the barn, and busied herself by tearing our blank posters and programmes into little bits, leaving them as rats or mice would do, pulverized for their nests. We could but pity and not blame.

These Dutch settlers fed on what they called "Albany beef," *alias* sturgeon, a kind of coarse fish caught in the Hudson River. We were very lonesome, for in front of the house in the adjoining field, was the family burying-ground, where were interred the members of three generations — a solemn reminder.

"The marble doors are always shut;
You cannot enter in hall or hut
Never in dreams to moan or sigh,
Silent and idle, alone they lie."

And the people seemed to glory in rolling o'er our hearts a stone, by this burial-ground always in sight.

Bidding adieu to our Dutch and Yankee friends, we returned to fill our engagements in Albany. As before, the effort as far as finances were concerned, proved unsuccessful; a small surplus at the end of the week was handed us for our labor. We found a relative in the city who extended us some courtesy. Settling the hotel bill we had one shilling remaining, when up came the ever-importunate porter who pleaded for his usual perquisite. One of the brothers handed him our last shilling.

For a night or two we took cheaper quarters, twelve-and-a-half-cent lodgings on Broad Street, getting trusted for it, of course, and obtaining our food as best we might. Poverty stared us in the face. We seriously contemplated disbandment. A plan was devised to sell the team and take money enough to go home with Abby, for we had already kept her away from mother beyond the promised time. The lot fell upon me to go with her to New Hampshire, and leave Judson and Asa, who were to put off into the country and work their board until my return.

In the midst of these unsettled plans, there was a rap at the door and in stepped a tall gentleman, who introducing himself stated his errand. "Can you remain in the city till next Monday evening," said he, "I will give you a hundred dollars if you will sing for me that evening." A simultaneous smile passed around, and was equally shared by the brothers and sister. "A hundred dollars all to be ours!" "Who can this gentleman be?" "What good spirit has been laboring with his own and led him to this place?" We had witnessed a kindly-looking person at our little concerts, who seemed very delighted, and the hearty cheers that came from his vicinity were noticeable. "I may be a stranger to you, but you are not strangers to me; I have heard you sing, and am very anxious our Albany people should have the same privilege." We consented to stay "very muchly," and our hearts — though our thanks were modestly expressed — were jubilant. The dark cloud was swept away; for this noble Scotchman, Luke F. Newland, by his kind interposition at the nick of time had lifted our hopes into a realm of joy.

He arranged that we should sing on the Sunday following in three of the principal churches in the city. The *Evening Journal*, edited then by Thurlow Weed, announced the fact, while twelve prominent business men allowed their names to appear as high complimentary indorsers of the plan, which meant business. We took the hint thus furnished, and ever after sang in churches wherever opportunity was offered.

In acknowledgment of these kind offices, we were invited by an acquaintance to call around on some of his friends. He therefore took us on a serenading expedition, and among other calls we visited the house of Thurlow Weed. Surprising him with our songs in the open air, he invited us into his parlor and treated us with the greatest courtesy. After a collation, we bade him good-night and departed with his blessing, fully satisfied that we had been introduced into the presence of a great and good man, whose principles and patriotism were universally acknowledged, and sure that we had made the acquaintance of one who at all our subsequent visits to Albany, as the sequel proved, would be foremost in extending to us the freedom of the city, by giving us the influence and patronage of his valuable paper. Through the long vista of years that elapsed, we watched with intense interest his great political career — though politic, yet always advocating the best interests of his native land and people. From time to time we met and held pleasant converse with him, and on one occasion during his riper years, in company with my little family and my sister Abby, we visited him in his home in New York City. We sang him the old song "Good Old Days of Yore." Though very aged his memory was good and he referred to this visit to Albany long ago.

Sunday morning, accompanied by our new sponsor, we were escorted to the church of Rev. Dr. Sprague. The house was packed, and we sang our new sacred songs with spirit and understanding, the congregation, in respectful acknowledgment, rising at the conclusion. The pastor gave a notice of the concert, advising his people to go and hear the singers again. In the afternoon we were taken to the Dutch Reformed Church, where a similar effect was produced, the plan being indorsed and highly recommended. At our evening appearance the songs were most enthusiastically received, and Rev. Mr. Stillman, a Methodist Episcopal clergyman, complimented the singing and the singers, and like the rest advised patronage. How gratified were we to be thus received by the cultured and Christian citizens of the "West" as we deemed it then. The large congregation gazed with seeming admiration as they lingeringly passed by the orchestra into the street. The duty of the day was done, and all were satisfied.

The neat, acceptable hall of the Albany Female Academy was the scene of much interest the night of the concert, August 29, 1842. The wealth and the fashion of that town were there, it being advertised as a complimentary concert. We were introduced to as large an audience as could be convened, while hundreds were crowded out. We were cheered, and every selection sang elicited an encore. The evening passed swiftly away, and at the conclusion we received inspiring congratulations for our brilliant success. "God bless and prosper you, my young friends," came from many of the leading citizens, as they warmly shook our hands.

The programme consisted of selected and original songs and ballads, with humorous ditties, quartets, trios, duets, etc. "The Cot where we were Born," "The Grave of Bonaparte," "Snow-Storm," "The Irish Emigrant's Lament," "Crows in a Cornfield," "Indian Hunter," "Matrimonial Sweets," "The Land of Canaan," "The Angel's Invitation to the Pilgrim," "Alpine Hunter's Song," from the Swiss, "The Maniac," etc.

We did not attempt any performance that we could not master. At the suggestion of our amiable friend, Mr. Newland, we doffed the assumed name which we had sailed under, and resumed our own family name. "The Æolian Vocalists" were no more, and the "Hutchinson Family" thereafter took all responsibility of praise and blame. He also suggested our giving up instrumental performances as a prominent feature in the programme, and only using the stringed instruments as an accompaniment to the songs, thus making the instrumental music subordinate to the voices.

The leading characteristic in the "Hutchinson Family's" singing was then, as it always has been since, the exact balance of parts in their harmonies, each one striving to merge himself in the interest of the whole, forming a perfect quartet, which was rare in those early days. How often have we been questioned, "Which of you boys sings bass, tenor or the air?" So united were we in our movements there could be no strife and neither's voice could be distinguished until he arose and sang a solo; then the characteristic features of each voice could be identified. Judson took the melody, John the tenor, Abby sang a rich contralto, while Asa gave deep bass; each being adapted by nature to the part necessary for perfect harmony.

Judson accompanied his own ballads with his violin, while Asa with 'cello and I with violin, played accompaniments for him also. Abby played no instrument, and sang as did I, with Judson's and Asa's playing. The latter up to this time had not ventured any bass solos. Here we left our first original song to be published; and, not long after, we saw the "Vulture of the Alps," a descriptive song, issued in sheet form, displayed at the music-store of our ever-to-be-remembered friend, who, it should be added, extended us as the result of the concert one hundred and ten dollars, more being sent us after we reached our home in New Hampshire. So we bade adieu to the precious friendship so pleasantly formed, to seek other climes and new relations. "Come home," said father in his letters, and all the household repeated the same beseeching words. So we started for New England once more.

We stopped at Pittsfield, Mass., where we gave a concert that had been arranged in advance by an uncle, Colonel Nathaniel Leavitt, who had come to our assistance, and was our agent until we reached Boston, where in due time we arrived, singing in Springfield and Worcester on our way.

We boldly entered Boston, and advertised a grand concert in the Melodeon, at fifty cents a ticket. In this concert we made little money.

"How dare you come to Boston and take that great room to sing in, and at such a price too?" asked that hearty, prepossessing old basso profoundo, Mr. Richardson, of the Handel and Haydn Society, as he accosted us in rather a John Bull style in the anteroom, at the close of the concert. He was literally the "heaviest" bass singer in the country, his weight being upwards of three hundred pounds. I love to see size and sound correspond. (I sang tenor but admired bass.) The Handel and Haydn Society could boast of their "Lablache," as well as London; and the play was well cast when he sang in his chosen part "Goliath of Gath" in the oratorio of "David," "The youth as a feeble antagonist," "Come unto me and I will give thy flesh to the fowls of the air and the beasts of the field." Mr. Richardson never appeared to a better advantage; still the current of sympathy centred the more on the verdant country stripling with his sling.

So when we had declared ourselves and broken the ice by the first public concert in the Athens of America, and, by the novelty of our performance and variegated programme won the commendation of the lovers of music, our future coast seemed clear and success certain. The receipts at this effort reached very little above the expenses, but many valuable friends were secured, among whom was the notable Jacob Chickering, the eminent pianoforte-maker, and Prof. Benjamin F. Baker, who always expressed themselves friends of the "Hutchinsons" and of their efforts for musical improvement.

Meeting Professor Webb, a man of great culture, we

solicited criticism; and to the query, "What is your advice to us?" he answered, "Please yourselves, my boys, and you will please the public."

By this favorable *début* in the most cultured city of America, we felt our efforts were well repaid and we were ready for new conquests. The press was in our favor, and we felt true aspirations to devote our lives to the greatest usefulness in the divine art.

We resolved on a visit to the southern country, but first we must fulfil our duty to our parents and go home to New Hampshire. After singing in several of the largest places east of Boston, where we had a fair attendance, we came to Portsmouth and found the people ready to greet their old friends of a year's standing. We were pleasantly entertained for a time at the house of ex-Governor Levi Woodbury, he riding ahead of us on horseback as we entered his grounds. He was then a member of Congress with a strong Granite State Democratic constituency. He worshipped at the shrine of "Old Hickory"; and while in the mansion, we were shown a lock of gray hair that some Southern friend had sent to the ex-governor as a memento, it having been cut from the head of the hero, recently deceased. This, no doubt, is still cherished as an heirloom in the Woodbury family.

The Woodbury household patronized our concert and with most encouraging words advised us to come to the capital, Washington, which invitation we subsequently accepted. We were very well received by popular audiences at the Camenium, an amphitheatre-shaped building which made a very pleasant concert-room.

To the ancient town of Portsmouth we bade farewell, and taking the city of Lowell in on our route, gave two concerts to sympathizing listeners; and this place ever afterwards gave us a warm welcome

At Nashua we halted for the last effort previous to reaching our mountain home, for it was now November, 1842. Then we sang once more the precious "Sweet Home" to and among our own, while the old mansion rang with shouts of "welcome home again," all being gratified at the reunion. Mother seized hold of her darling child Abby, with a grasp that meant "Henceforth you are to stay with me forever." She had been apprised of our intention to go again into the field of concerting labor, to the far-off South. Dread seemed at the thought to paralyze her usual sympathies, and congratulations and her wonted courtesies were dispensed with toward the sons and her brother Nathaniel, who had been long absent in the West, but had returned with us.

I was more anxious than I have ever been since. We had struggled to reach this point of success and would not consider being disappointed in our aspirations. Our agent, Uncle Nat, was dispatched in advance, for the long autumn evenings, favorable to concerts, were upon us. Father tried to be reconciled, for he saw the union of our harmonies had resulted in success. Mother was fearful, and could not consent willingly that Abby should again go away from home — she, the youngest of sixteen, the baby, only thirteen years of age! We were very sorry to entreat her in this way, but could not return to the cities where we had just given such successful entertainments without Abby, so with a "God bless you," though grief was in the heart, we again launched our bark with hopes of luck.

At Nashua, early on the morning after we had given

our first concert in the Town Hall, I observed a team coming down the street. I soon recognized the old white horse, and my father sat in the carriage. "What's the matter? something is up or father would not have driven fourteen miles this early in our direction." My apprehension was soon verified. Father alighted, tied the horse to a post, and requested a private interview. The family were all summoned to our room, and the errand stated. "I have come," said father, "to take Abby home with me. Your mother has not slept all night, and is almost crazy." This was a trying hour; we felt it would be wrong to disappoint the public, and equally so to lacerate the heart so filled with grief. So a compromise was effected; we promised with a solemn attest to see Abby home in three weeks; so father believing us, bade us good-by, and we passed on towards our destination. I confess my name was not given on the document without some misgivings. However, we trusted in Providence, knowing "He doeth all things well." We were frustrated in arrangements, and our Southern tour was very doubtful. We next visited Lowell, where a concert was given. Here I met the young lady whom I subsequently married. With some reluctance we passed next day to Boston, and gave a popular concert in the Melodeon.

While many dear friends gathered to bid us a long farewell, as they supposed we were bound far away, Judson, who seemed before anxious to return with Sister Abby, acted at times unusually pleased, and a smile would play over his face when he was unconsciously oblivious to the subject and the audience before him. Judson was noticed by the clerk in the old Marlboro' House to go out quite early. He was missed from his room and from the breakfast table, but nothing more could be told of his whereabouts. Finally, some one discovered on the table of the public reading-room a note to the "Hutchinson Family." Being opened, in it was found hurriedly written these words:

"John, Asa, Abby, you go home — I go to Texas JUDSON"

Remembering Judson's sometimes desponding mood, the greatest alarm was excited among us. Suicide occurred to our thoughts. Search was vainly instituted and every probable place visited. Depots and other points of the city, including the wharves, were scanned by the friendly ones. We examined many places where we hoped not to find him. Abby and I put off for Lynn hoping Judson might be there with Jesse. Asa made a forced march to Milford, which place he reached by express from Nashua, at ten o'clock at night. With a nervous hand he rapped at the door, which after a tedious wait was opened by Brother Benjamin. Asa's first anxious question was, "Have you seen Judson?" Benjamin, smiling, said, "Where are John and Abby?" Then he said, "Come in; he is safe. He has gone to Bedford to see his Sally." The fact was Judson had been seized with a love-fit and had gone a-wooing. Meanwhile Abby and I were in Lynn in suspense, till the news of the safety of our brother was sent us the next morning.

CHAPTER III.

SINGING FOR FREEDOM.

"We're the friends of emancipation,
And we'll sing the proclamation
Till it echoes through the nation
From the old Granite State —
That the tribe of Jesse
Are the friends of equal rights"

WHILE we brothers were keeping our grocery and stove stores on Union Street in Lynn, a few rods farther down the street, in a modest building, dwelt Frederick Douglass. A short time before he had come panting up from the South with bloodhounds baying upon his track. My brother Jesse was identified with the very beginnings of the anti-slavery agitation, was in the fullest sympathy with the leaders and cognizant of all the thrilling details of the work going on through public meetings, in the *Liberator*, the *Herald of Freedom* and similar publications, to make sentiment in favor of the liberation of the bondmen. Through him we became familiar with the great agitation, which had our fullest approbation. We heard Douglass's story, and the result was an earnest desire to aid him in his work. It was not long before we joined him in many meetings, he telling his story, while we emphasized it with song.

In the preceding chapter the fact is stated that in the autumn of 1842, Sister Abby and I went to Lynn from

Boston, while Asa proceeded to Milford to seek for tidings of Judson.

The next morning the news was spread about the streets of that town that a flying fugitive from the South was pursued by a slave-holder and had been arrested in Boston. A company of about forty or fifty men resolved to make an effort towards rescuing this person. Brother Jesse and I joined them and were soon at the head of the delegation, marching through Washington Street, Boston, to Marlboro' Chapel, singing as we entered the large church, "Oh, liberate the bondman." I still recall my impression of the contrast between singing before a popular audience two nights before and the somewhat unpopular mission in which I was now engaged. A crowd was in readiness to greet us. While cogitating over plans of action, a man came through the aisle of the chapel, and mounting the platform, shouted out to the crowd, "He's free! he's free!" I can never forget the expression of joy on the face of every citizen present. The slave-holder was induced to manumit his slave, setting the price for his ransom at the low figure of four hundred dollars, which amount was paid over to him by the Rev. Samuel Caldwell, who acted in behalf of some members of the Tremont Temple Baptist Society; and George Latimer, for the first time in his life, was a free man.

If the nation could have followed up this scheme of purchase, like our English cousins, it would have saved a million lives and billions of treasure.

After that Latimer went with us to many anti-slavery meetings in Essex County. George has been a worthy, industrious citizen of Lynn for over fifty years.

After the Latimer incident Sister Abby and I returned to Milford. We found Judson obdurate. No more concerting for him at present; and so our Southern trip was given up.

Rejoiced at finding our family in circumstances of comparative health and prosperity, again surrounded by the familiar scenes of home and the general beauty of our mountain situation, yet saddened by the great disappointment of having to relinquish the mighty work that we had laid out, suited as it was to our ambitions and aspirations, it seemed to me doleful and wearisome in the quietude of our isolated home, for I disregarded the comforts and allurements of love and the warnings of experience. My soul pressed forward and longed to tread that path that was sure to lead to success, and still clung to the idea "Excelsior." But through the long, cold winter, being snow-bound in our New England home, I seemed to feel as Longfellow later expressed it in his great song, and could imagine that like the character represented in his immortal verse, even in death I would cling to this device and proclaim the progress of such aspirations of the soul in a higher sphere.

We held frequent meetings with our whole family gathered at the old homestead. A plan was suggested of giving some mass concerts in the region, and for a double purpose I went to Lowell, having in mind the young lady spoken of previously, and also arranging for some concerts.

Effecting engagements in Lowell, Nashua and Manchester, we went down at the appointed time with our double-sleigh team, thirteen of the family, including the quartet which had been giving concerts, and met with grand success in all of the three places, taking in with us the lady, Miss Fannie B. Patch, who, in the course of four weeks I married, intending to continue in the

JOHN A. COLLINS.—(p. 73)

pursuit of agriculture. She had been the leading contralto singer in the Freewill Baptist Church of Lowell for many years. Rev. Mr. Davis was the pastor.

We were importuned by an agent of the anti-slavery society, Mr. John A. Collins, to be present at the annual meeting of the organization to be held in Faneuil Hall, Boston.

Consenting to this proposition, the quartet, with Jesse, accordingly were present at the opening of the meeting which continued three days, January 25, 26 and 27, 1843. The first song we sung was "Blow ye the Trumpet, Blow!"

We were inspired with the greatness of the issue, finding our hearts in sympathy with those struggling and earnest people. We fully resolved to buckle on the armor, feeling proud to be engaged in such a great work for humanity. We were ready at any time to take up the cross and serve the Master, sympathizing with those in bonds as bound with them, and we sang for the emancipation of the millions of slaves in bondage. "The Negro's Lament," was one of the selections:

> " Forced from home and all its pleasures,
>   Africa's coast I left forlorn,
> To increase a stranger's treasures,
>   O'er the raging billows borne
> Men from England bought and sold me,
>   Paid my price in paltry gold ,
> But though slave they have enrolled me,
>   Minds are never to be sold "

As an illustration of the use made of the Hutchinson Family in the anti-slavery conventions of nearly two decades it may be well to quote extracts from the *Liberator's* report of this famous Faneuil Hall convention of

1843, where the Abolitionists first committed themselves to the doctrine of "peaceful disunion." It is from the issue of February 3, 1843. Without quoting unimportant details, the report says:

"The eleventh annual meeting of the Massachusetts Anti-Slavery Society opened at Faneuil Hall on Wednesday January 25th, Francis Jackson presiding. A song was sung by the Hutchinson Family, the celebrated vocalists from New Hampshire. Discussion immediately commenced on a resolution offered by Wendell Phillips: 'Resolved, That no Abolitionist can consistently demand less than a dissolution of the union between Northern union and Southern slavery as essential to the preservation of the one and the abolition of the other.' This was advocated by Phillips in a stirring speech. At the evening session the Hutchinsons sang again, and then the discussion on the resolution relative to the dissolution was continued by Messrs Jewett of Providence, Douglass of Lynn, and C. L. Remond of Salem. Another song by the Hutchinsons closed the meeting.

"On Thursday, after a most inspiring song by the Hutchinsons, the discussion of the resolution was continued by William Lloyd Garrison, Henry C. Wright of England, J. A. Collins and others. At the afternoon session a letter was read by John M. Spear of Weymouth, from Hon. John Quincy Adams. The discussion was continued, interspersed by two appropriate songs by the Hutchinsons. The resolution was amended, on motion of John A. Collins, so as to insert the words, 'between Free States and Slave States,' after 'Southern slavery,' and passed. On Thursday evening there was a meeting in the chamber of the House of Representatives at the State House, with President Jackson in the chair. It was opened by a heart-stirring song by the Hutchinsons, after which Edmund Quincy moved the following resolution: 'So long as Massachusetts pledges the physical force of her sons to protect her sister slave-holding States against domestic violence, she is practically a slave State; so long as she throws open her soil as free hunting-ground for the master in pursuit of his fugitive, she is practically a slave State — also when she sends back fugitives and requires her executive and legislative officers to swear to support a constitution which in some parts protects the slave system.' This was supported by Mr. Quincy, who was followed by Mr. Treadwell against it, and by Frederick Douglass — 'a chattel personal' — in its favor. Then came another song by the 'New Hampshire Raineis,' to the great gratification of the audience. C. L. Remond, William Lloyd Garrison and N. P. Rogers then spoke, and the discussion was closed by Wendell Phillips in a strain of thrilling eloquence. The resolution was adopted, and after another song by the Hutchinsons, the meeting adjourned

"Friday's meeting at Faneuil Hall was opened with a most inspiring song by the Hutchinsons. Rev Samuel May moved a reconsideration of the resolution on disunion adopted the day before, and the discussion was continued by Seth Sprague, J A Collins and the Messrs. Hutchinson (in an appropriate song on the subject) Mr Garrison then moved a substitute [which afterward became famous], and it was adopted · '*Resolved*, That the compact which exists between the North and the South is a covenant with death and an agreement with hell — involving both parties in atrocious criminality, and should be immediately annulled'

"The evening meeting opened with a song from the gifted sons of New Hampshire, which was received with thunders of applause, calling for its repetition, and another song was sung to the great gratification of the immense number assembled. William Lloyd Garrison presented and ably advocated this resolution, which was adopted by acclamation: '*Resolved*, That anti-slavery has rejoiced, from the beginning, in the aid of *Poetry*, which is naturally and instinctively on the side of liberty, it being impossible, in the providence of God, that Poetry should ever stoop her wing to the accursed service of slavery; and Humanity exults and rejoices in her other natural ally, *Music*, so gloriously represented here, in the old Liberty Cradle, by the "New Hampshire Rainers," whom Massachusetts abolitionism welcomes here from their White Mountains and thanks them for their free strains, in the name of down-trodden humanity.' During the evening's exercises the Hutchinsons sang three other songs"

On February 24th of the same year the *Liberator* said:

"The powerful description of the singing of the wonderfully gifted Hutchinsons at the late anniversary of the Massachusetts Anti-Slavery Society in Faneuil Hall, which we have copied from the *Herald of Freedom*, does not surpass the reality of their charming melodies. The effect on the thousands who listened to them was, in fact, indescribable. They added immensely to the interest of the occasion, and the manner in which they adapted their spirited songs (nearly all of which were original and impromptu) to the subjects that were under discussion displayed equal talent and genius"

The *Herald of Freedom*'s account was, of course, written by N. P. Rogers, who prided himself not a little on his success in enlisting our services for this and similar gatherings. He wrote as follows:

"The distinguishing incident of the anniversary was the co-operation of the New Hampshire Hutchinsons, aided by their brother from Lynn These singers I have several times spoken of, and, as has been thought by those who had not heard them, with exaggeration None, however, of those who heard their matchless strains at Faneuil Hall would have thought any degree of panegyric exaggeration, that language could bestow upon them All those who have heard their modest concerts, in suitable sized rooms, and in tolerably clear atmosphere, would have said the people could get no idea of their enchanting powers amid the tumult and depraved air of that great, overgrown hall But even there, it was a triumph for these 'New Hampshire Rainers,' as I have styled these unassuming young brothers, though the celebrated Swiss minstrels, who wear that family name and have made it so famous in this country and in Europe, have more occasion to covet for themselves the name of these singers from New Hampshire's Alps They are not mere vocalists They have hearts and minds as well as tuneful voices They are not wandering, mercenary troubadors, who go about selling their strains for bread or for brandy They are young farmers They work, *indoors* as well as out, in the noble kitchen as well as on the farm, and get a sound and substantial living by their useful industry. The more entitled are they to the most generous encouragement of their countrymen when they go forth occasionally to charm the community by their music That they are Abolitionists may engender prejudice against them in the pro-slavery breast, but their lays will banish the demon from the meanest heart, as David's harp played the devil out of King Saul

"The Hutchinsons were present throughout the meetings, and it is probable contributed considerably to keeping up the unparalleled attendance that thronged the hall They were not there as mercenaries in an orchestra They were not hired performers They were there as Garrison and Boyle were, as Douglass and Phillips, and the rest of us all, 'To help the cause along'; and they helped it They were always in order, too, when they spoke; and it was what they said, as well as how they said it, that sent anti-slavery like electricity to every heart. I never saw such effect on human assemblies as these appeals produced They made the vast multitudes toss and heave and *clamor* like the roaring ocean. Orpheus is said to have made the trees dance at his playing The Hutchinsons made the thousands at Faneuil Hall spring to their feet simultaneously, 'as it in a dance,' and echo the anti-slavery appeal with a cheering that almost moved the old Revolu-

NATHANIEL PEABODY ROGERS (p 76)

tionists from their stations on the wall. On one occasion it was absolutely amazing and sublime. Phillips had been speaking in his happiest vein. It was towards night. The old hall was sombre in the *gloaming*. It was thronged to its vast extremities. Phillips closed his speech at the highest pitch of his fine genius, and retired from the platform, when the four brothers rushed to his place, and took up the argument where he had left it, on the very heights of poetic declamation, and carried it off heavenwards on one of their boldest flights. Jesse had framed a series of stanzas on the spot, while Phillips was speaking, embodying the leading arguments, and enforcing them, as mere oratory cannot, as music and poetry only can, and they poured them forth with amazing spirit, in one of the maddening Second Advent tunes. The vast multitude sprang to their feet, as one man, and at the close of the first strain, gave vent to their enthusiasm in a thunder of unrestrained cheering. Three cheers, and three times three, and ever so many more — for they could not count — they sent out, full-hearted and full-toned, till the old roof rang again. And throughout the whole succeeding strains they repeated it, not allowing the singers to complete half the stanza before breaking out upon them in uncontrollable emotion. Oh, it was glorious!

"And it was not the rude mobocratic shouting of the blind partisan, or the unearthly glee of the religious maniac, it was Humanity's jubilee cry. And there was *music* in it. The multitude had caught the spirit and tone of the orator and the minstrel bards, and they exemplified it in their humanized shoutings. There is grand music in this natural, generous uproar of the mighty multitude, when it goes out spontaneously, as God made it to do. 'The sound of many waters' is not more harmonious, nor a millionth part so expressive — for there is not a soul in the unconscious waters. But I am exceeding my limits. I wish the whole city, and the entire country could have been there — even all the people. Slavery would have died of that music and the response of the multitude. If politics had been discountenanced altogether at the meetings — or suffered only to have their proportional attention — the whole tide of the proceedings would have been as overwhelming as the bugle cries of the Hutchinsons."

The verses of which the writer speaks were improvised by Jesse, as Rogers says, to enforce the oratory of Phillips. They were sung to the tune of "The Old Granite State." I cannot now reproduce the words.

A word regarding the noble, earnest agitators. Among those present were William Lloyd Garrison,

John A. Collins, Rev. John Pierpont, Wendell Phillips, Frederick Douglass, Mrs. Chapman, Charles Lenox Remond, N. P. Rogers, Parker Pillsbury, Stephen Foster, Theodore Parker, Francis Jackson, chairman of the meeting, and his lovely daughter Harriet. A noble gathering of pioneers!

Such a fold and such a unity was an inspiration to lofty resolutions; and when approached in regard to going with the selected advocate to hold a series of anti-slavery meetings, we most cheerfully acceded. The appointments were made, and our first meeting was announced to take place at Haverhill.

We left Lynn in two single sleighs, took in our family, consisting then of five members, with George Latimer, and joyfully did we make our journey over the well-trodden roads until we reached the Merrimac River.

In safety we crossed the ice to the opposite bank. In my sleigh was Latimer, the recently manumitted slave, whom we had taken in charge under the auspices of the anti-slavery committee. We had reached the top of the bank; looking in the rear we observed that as the second team was coming up the hill, the horse became fractious, and refusing to go forward had upset the sleigh and the company was thrown out, the sleigh capsizing in such a manner as to completely cover my sister Abby. George and I jumped over the back part of the sleigh in haste to help the party, when Jesse, who drove that horse, threw the reins, struck the horse with his whip, which rushed down the bank and upon the ice until he had thrown himself, and at last was captured with no injury to him or to us, excepting the great fright that we all received. We gathered up our belongings and rode to the church, where our meeting was just organized and upon entering we were met with the cheers of the audience, and in a few moments we were in their presence upon the platform. We were thankful to Providence that we had escaped injury and were able once more to sing our songs.

"Thus far the Lord hath led us on"

The meeting proved a grand success, and many proselytes were gained to the cause of anti-slavery. Lasting friendships were formed, and invitations were extended to us to visit them again; and, in fact, we were always welcome to that good old town in after years. The Essex County campaign was in every way successful, and many souls were won, who ever after adhered to their first love and were helpers in the cause of emancipation.

We accepted many requests to meet notable anti-slavery people west of Boston, in Cambridge and other towns; made the acquaintance of William A. White, a very interesting individual, and also came *en rapport* with James Russell Lowell, the famous poet.

We joined in their sports with them one day while playing ball. The balls in those days were flexible and not considered dangerous — very unlike the modern ball used by expert players which, when thrown with sufficient force and with the catching unsuccessful, would prove a fatal shot. They were quite bulky and soft, wound with woollen yarn, covered with leather; and if they struck a person, it would do them very little harm. Lowell and myself were playing together. He threw the ball, and I returned it with such rapidity that it went past his hands and struck fair upon his forehead. For a moment he winced under the stunning blow, but after passing his hand several times across his forehead, made no further complaint. My surprise, mingled with momentary regret, shocked me when I was aware that I had struck him with such force, as I fain would have received the blow myself. Little did I contemplate then that I had wounded a future minister plenipotentiary, for he later became such under the administrations of Presidents Hayes, Garfield and Arthur. He was called to fill one of the most responsible places that any man had occupied since Franklin, and he did the country great honor during the years he occupied that position at the court of St. James. For a long time his "Zekle and Huldy" was one of our most successful songs.

At this time we became interested in the "Brook Farm Experiment." This famous farm was located in West Roxbury, near the Dedham line, and is now occupied as the site of an almshouse. In the years of which I am speaking, however, it was the theatre where famous men and women were seeking to demonstrate not only the feasibility but the superiority of the apostolic mode of living, as a community. Horace Greeley's "North American Phalanx" became famous and the Florence Community was successful after that at Brook Farm was given up. But none of these experiments attracted so many of the class of people who were doing, or preparing to do, a great portion of the brain-work of the country for some decades, as Brook Farm.

The fact is, the Hutchinsons came upon the platform at a transition period, when various new ideas and "isms" were being preached. As this history proceeds, it will be easily seen that it was practically impossible for us to have embraced the anti-slavery reform without being under the influence of and affected by, several other related reforms and movements. Perhaps I cannot better illustrate conditions that obtained at the time than by quoting from the Brook Farm chapter of Colonel Thomas Wentworth Higginson's "Life of Margaret Fuller":

"It [Brook Farm] was one of the best — probably the best — incarnation of the ardent and wide-reaching reformatory spirit of that day. It was a day when it certainly was very pleasant to live, although it is doubtful whether living would have remained as pleasant, had one-half the projects of the period become fulfilled. The eighty-two pestilent heresies that were already reckoned up in Massachusetts before 1638, or the 'generation of odd names and natures' which the Earl of Stratford found among the English Roundheads, could hardly surpass those of which Boston was the centre during the interval between the year 1835 and the absorbing political upheaval of 1848. The best single picture of the period is in Emerson's lecture on 'New England Reformers,' delivered in March, 1844; but it tells only a part of the story, for one very marked trait of the period was that the agitation reached all circles. German theology, as interpreted by Bronson Alcott and Ripley, influenced the more educated class, and the Second Advent excitement equally prepared the way among the more ignorant. The anti-slavery movement was the profoundest moral element, on the whole, but a multitude of special enterprises played their parts. People habitually spoke, in those days, of 'the sisterhood of reforms', and it was in as bad taste for a poor man to have but one hobby in his head as for a rich man to keep but one horse in his stable. Mesmerism was studied; gifted persons gave private sittings for the reading of character through handwriting; phrenology and physiology were ranked together; Alcott preached what Carlyle called a 'potato gospel'; Graham denounced bolted flour; Edward Palmer wrote tracts against money. In a paper published in the *Dial* for July, 1842, on the 'convention of the friends of universal reform' in Boston, Emerson says of the gathering 'If the assembly was disorderly, it was picturesque. Mad men, mad women, men with beards, Dunkers, Muggletonians, Come-outers, Groaners, Agrarians, Seventh-Day Baptists, Quakers, Abolitionists, Calvinists, Unitarians and Philosophers, all came successively to the top.'

"Having myself attended similar meetings soon after, I can certify that this is not an exaggeration, but a plain, unvarnished tale. It is to be remembered, too, that all this stir came upon a society whose previous habit of life was decidedly soberer and better ordered than that of to-day, stricter in observance, more conventional in costume. There could hardly be a better illustration of this fact than when Emerson includes in his enumeration of eccentricities 'men with beards', for I well remember when Charles Burleigh was charged with blasphemy because his flowing locks and handsome untrimmed beard were thought to resemble — as very likely he intended — the pictures of Jesus Christ, and when Lowell was thought to have formally announced a daring impulse of radicalism, after he, too, had eschewed the razor. The only memorial we retain unchanged from that picturesque period, is in some stray member of the 'Hutchinson Family,' who still comes before the public with now whitening locks and vast collar that needs no whitening, and continues to sing with unchanged sweetness the plaintive melodies that hushed the stormiest meeting, when he and his four or five long-haired brothers stood grouped round their one rose-bud of a sister, like a band of Puritan Bohemians."

Brook Farm contained a gathering of people who represented the best element of all these conditions. It had the sanction of Emerson, Alcott, Theodore Parker and Margaret Fuller. None of these were members of the community, but all were frequent visitors to it and remained so long as to become fully identified with it. Colonel Higginson, then a youth, was another notable visitor. George Ripley was its projector and leading spirit. In the company, either as members or students, were John S. Dwight, for many years after Boston's leading musical writer; Christopher P. Cranch, artist, musician and poet; Charles A. Dana, then just out of college, now editor of the *New York Sun* and the Nestor of American journalism; Nathaniel Hawthorne, shy, retiring, yet observing, and fully illustrating the Scottish bard's warning, "A chiel's amang ye takin' notes," which were afterwards published in the "Blithedale Romance"; George William Curtis, destined so soon after to take his place as one of the best representatives of American thought in essay, editorial and romantic writing. These, with O. A. Brownson, George P. Bradford and many others, formed a community that should have fully demonstrated the blessings of the socialistic idea. It was proclaimed at first to be "a glimpse at Christ's idea of society." It was not until after it had been established some time that the attempt to apply Fourier's ideas was made. In time it was discovered that Nathaniel Hawthorne was designed for something better than milking cows, that Dana had a wider mission than washing dishes Though pleasant musicales, picnics, "conversations," and like interesting exercises varied the monotony of life, yet the disposition to do the farming and domestic duties by proxy made an expense as well as a perversion of the vital part of scheme, that, with the destruction of one of the community houses by fire, eventually led to the abandonment of the experiment. Then Greeley, who was in full sympathy with the ideas of Ripley, found a place on the *Tribune* for the man who had hitherto occupied a Unitarian pulpit, and as literary editor of that journal, Ripley was able to utilize the services of Margaret Fuller in a way that edified the public and greatly increased her reputation. Work for Dana and Curtis was also found on the *Tribune*, and so the abandonment of the experiment was the means of wonderfully enriching journalism. The literature of Brook Farm has in the last decade grown extensive, and perhaps the reader will not expect me to more than outline its story, which is to me, I confess, a most fascinating one. Dana has, as yet, never furnished the public his story of an enterprise in which he was a very important figure. I should like to see him give his version of it before his work is done.

At the time of which I am writing, we visited Brook Farm. We had looked forward to the event with happy anticipations. The distinguished communists gave us a most hearty reception. We understood the company to be formed with the purpose of inaugurating a thorough reform in our civil and social society, building up humanity and establishing such a code of character as to make them true lights and leading stars in the world. Every heart seemed bounding with hope, delightful to the soul; cheerfulness seemed to pervade every individual, man or woman; and they stood around, some fifty or sixty selected intelligent people, all evidently converts to the great idea of human brotherhood: "The Fatherhood of God and the Brotherhood of Man."

That occasion was one which lingered long in our memories; for with the delights that inspired us at that time, we seemed to catch a foretaste of a realm in which our spirits could bask and grow. All of the principles advocated we fully indorsed. It seemed to be truly the looking backward to the days of those loved ones who gathered around the Nazarene, whose mission when fully adhered to was love sufficient to redeem the race.

Embracing the influences pervading, we could sing the song of the "Right Over Wrong," or "The Good Time Coming":

> "Behold, the day of promise comes,
>   Full of inspiration,
> The blessed day by prophets sung
>   For the healing of the nation!
> Old midnight errors flee away,
>   And soon will all be gone,
> And the heavenly angels seem to say
>   The good time's coming on."

Finding the pervading sentiments in full accord with our loftiest aspirations, emphasized by our interview with such a nucleus of blessed spirits, we went forth filled with hope and a determination to do everything in our power to prove in our family and neighborhood the practicability of this high ideal in human life. We felt that we had struck the chord re-echoing down the centuries from the day of Pentecost and sung by the angels; and we gathered at our home in one group of affection, and more earnestly did we labor, rejoicing in the light of the true gospel

In the *Century* for November, 1892, George P. Bradford, now deceased, a survivor of the Brook Farm experiment, wrote as follows of the Hutchinsons' visit to the community. After speaking of the visits of Margaret Fuller, O. A. Brownson, Robert Owen, of Scotland, and others, he says:

"Then there were the Hutchinsons, a family well known at the time, and a marvel for their sweet singing, and this especially in the interest of anti-slavery and temperance. The accord of their voices was very pleasing A great charm of the singing was a sort of wild freshness as it taught in their native woods and mountains, and their earnest interest in the objects that formed so much of the theme of their songs"

For some time the old home in Milford was a family Brook Farm. Cheerfully did we take up the labor necessary, according to the season of the year and the different departments of the farm work, with one common aim and interest. We met all impediments with a determination to prove to all our surrounding neighbors that we were honest believers in the faith that we had embraced — the true community. In the cause of labor and progress we were united, each preferring one another. Our labors were joyous, and we were temporarily prosperous, for we were truly a band of brothers and sisters of one common interest. There were no differences or competitions in trafficking with one another, for we were genuinely interested in the welfare of all.

Music was the theme that filled our hearts and souls as we went singing forth to the different departments of labor on the home farm, for we earnestly believed in this manner of life.

While we were in Boston we were invited by the anti-slavery people to join with them in their May meetings in New York. We made ready, and were ticketed through by the Norwich route, railroad and steamboat. We were up on deck at early morning excited with curiosity to see Gotham, which we watched with intense interest.

Accompanied by our other friends we went to Apollo Hall, where the meeting was held, and when in full session we were introduced. We met with encouraging words from the anti-slavery people.

A mass temperance meeting was announced to take place at the Broadway Tabernacle. Making the acquaintance of the Rev. William Patton, D.D., later father-in-law of Abby, and other leaders in the convention who were aware of the interest we had taken in the cause of temperance years before, they invited us upon the platform, and Rev. Lyman Beecher, then a leading spirit in the great reform, at an opportune moment, favorably introduced us to an audience of 3,600 people. We little thought then how precious was to be our acquaintance with the great preacher's greater son. We were cheered, and somewhat elated and inspired as we sang our first selection, which took them by storm, and the applause was seemingly universal from men and women comprising that assembly. It was followed up with a like enthusiasm until we had answered the encore, when similar demonstrations were made. Then followed our family song, the "Old Granite State," after which we retreated to the anteroom, and though importuned, declined to go again upon the stage.

Then came an urgent request from numerous friends to give a public concert, which we did, and followed it up with several popular concerts in the different parts of Brooklyn and New York. With a promise that we would return again in early autumn, we bade farewell to the city and returned to our vocation as farmers at our home in New Hampshire.

Among other distinguished and notable men who showed us courtesies during our stay in New York was Dr. William Beach, an amiable gentleman of English antecedents. He had been present at both the anti-slavery and temperance meetings and had also attended some of our concerts. He had recently introduced a reform system of medicine on botanic principles. Calling upon us at our rooms he expressed his pleasure in listening to a song, "Calomel," which we had recently set to music:

> "Physicians of the highest rank —
> To pay their fees we need a bank —
> Combine all wisdom, art and skill,
> Science and sense, in calomel"

To express his appreciation of our introducing and singing the song he presented to us a large volume of eight hundred pages, called "The Reform Practice of Medicine."

During this season we had the pleasure as guests at our house of that blessed, firm, honest, gifted spirit, William Lloyd Garrison, with his coadjutor, Francis Jackson, from Boston. Later in the season came also that man from the mountains, N. P. Rogers, whose lofty expressions of his true inspirations were poetry in every syllable. He also was in full accord with our attempt to carry out our effort for "Peace on earth, good-will to men." He was a singer and a lover of the highest order of art and poetry, cultured in the letter of the law, yet more deeply inspired by honest hearts and a purpose to bring liberty to the captive. We believe that these pilgrims, though they sojourned but a very short period, enjoyed our house as much as we did their presence.

Following these notable lights, as leaders in the cause, came also many other dear friends whose hearts were in great sympathy with the anti-slavery work: Parker Pillsbury of Concord, Frederick Douglass, Henry Clapp, Jr., and others. It proved a time of joyous meetings and numerous activities. Important letters came from P. T. Barnum and others from all sections of the country, also from the great temperance leaders, soliciting engagements for legitimate concert tours. The cares of the farm in its different departments and numerous calls of church and public interest also demanded much of our time.

A special invitation came from an old organization, the New Hampshire Anti-Slavery Society, to join with them in a grand convention to be held at the capital, Concord. We made haste to answer the call, and were entertained at the house of N. P. Rogers. We heartily joined with them, and sang our songs of freedom, interspersing the selections appropriately between the speakers. Great unanimity of feeling then existed among the Abolitionists. Though differing as to their modes of conducting the great work, there were discussions and questions of policy raised and criticism expressed against the scheme of a third party; but the doctrine of no union with slave-holders, seemed to prevail without question.

HERALDS OF FREEDOM.

In addition to the five members of our family, a convenient carriage conveyed pleasantly across the country, a number of invited guests, thirty miles to Concord.

At the conclusion of this anti-slavery meeting, many friends expressed a desire that we might remain over one night and give a concert; but by persuasion and advice of Brother Jesse, as we had a very important concert coming off in Boston on June 17th, at which we had the promise of the presence of the President of the United States and suite, we decided not to remain.

The next day we took in with us as friends and fellow-passengers, Frederick Douglass and Charles Lenox Remond. Singing on our way as we came back through that part of Hillsboro County, we had the pleasure of these gentlemen for a day or two, at our home.

Soon followed the great complimentary concert. The fatigue attending the public receptions of President John Tyler induced his personal absence from the concert, but his representatives and suite honored the occasion by their presence, and in the reserved seats were Mr. and Mrs. Benson, whose friendship we were proud to acknowledge, Robert Tyler and wife, and Mrs. President Tyler and daughter. The concert was given in the old "Millerite" tabernacle, now known as the Howard Atheneum.

A card was issued printed on fine tissue or bank-note paper, representing the bank notes of that day with the exception of the extra border. This was one of our most notable concerts. The warm weather militated somewhat against us in a numerical way. At the conclusion we were introduced to the members of the Tyler family. Subsequently, when we had reached Washington, came an invitation for us to dine with the President at the White House.

We then set out for Nantucket. On our way we gave a concert in New Bedford, by invitation of a noted Quaker, John Bailey; we had an interesting audience, and were invited into the houses of many of the residents, among whom were several colored people, who presented us with testimonials and many little presents, a numerous variety of shells that had been brought from foreign coasts, for the New Bedford people then, as for many years before, followed the sea in whaling voyages for which they were noted, pursuing the profitable industry of securing great quantities of oil, for there was then "millions in it."

Reaching Nantucket after one session at the anti-slavery meeting, we were seized with an epidemic of influenza or what the inhabitants termed "Tyler grip," and although making strenuous efforts to produce our usual effect in singing, we were obliged to give up with a suitable apology and return to our hotel. After spending a few days with our friends, we again hied to our New Hampshire home. This disease, by the way, was not so fatal in its consequences as the modern *la grippe*, yet it proved a great annoyance, and in some cases terminated fatally.

With the temporary loss of his voice Asa came nigh losing his heart also, for he commenced wooing a daughter of Captain Chase, who followed the whaling business for a livelihood; and in 1847, the year after we returned from England, Elizabeth C. Chase became his wife, and went with him to his home in New Hampshire. "No great loss but there is some small gain."

During the remainder of the summer we were engaged in making preparations for our promised visit to New York, and early in September we put out once more for the Empire State, giving concerts on the way at Nashua, Lowell, Boston, Worcester, Springfield and Pittsfield.

On board the cars, at the conclusion of a song we had been singing on the way, a gentleman came forward and inquired if we had seen the new song just published, written by Longfellow, called "Excelsior." We answered in the negative, and he said, "I shall be very glad to send it to you." When we had reached New York we received this song from him through the mail. We at once set it to music of our own and sang it in our concerts.

At New York we first secured a good home in a boarding-house and then made a round of visits to the friends we had made the previous season. We found the field was broad and open and quite ready to harvest.

Our friend, Mr. C. M. Saxton, of the firm of Saxton & Miles, who kept a successful bookstore on Broadway, had officiated in our behalf, securing a hall, attending to advertising, etc. Friendly influence was secured through the medium of the *Tribune*, Horace Greeley, editor, and the *Home Journal*, edited by Morris and Willis. General good feeling was manifested among our personal friends, which bespoke us a large degree of success.

Noticing by the paper that Henry W. Longfellow was at the Astor House, one of us waited upon him with the request, that, if it was agreeable for him he would write an introduction for the notable song, "Excelsior." ["More lofty; still higher; ever upward' — Webster.] He gladly complied with our request, and before the day ended we received the note, which read thus:

"Excelsior" is a word in an unknown tongue; it represents the aspirations of genius. Disregarding the every-day comforts of life, the allurements of love, the warning of experience, it presses forward on its solitary path; even in death holds fast to the device, and the voice from the sky still proclaims the progress of the soul in a higher sphere."

Owing to our adherence to radical principles, the newspapers were cautious in their criticisms of our concerts, but through the interposition of many individual friends who seemed to be enamored with our songs, many editorials were favorably written of our work. Our patronage was particularly or generally derived from the masses of New England settlers from Connecticut and other States who in their enthusiasm induced the more staid and conservative Gothamites to at least indorse and come out and swell the interest of our entertainments, and we soon reached an elevated point of popular favor, for our halls and places of entertainment were being constantly thronged, as our temperance and anti-slavery sentiments were presented to their understanding, through the medium of sweet sounds, until at last we were wholly indorsed by the general public and were made to feel perfectly at home. One individual was heard, in conversation with another, to say, "They sing the sweetest harmony I have heard, but — their politics!"

Several very popular poetic contributions were furnished by our dear friend, General George P. Morris, among which were "My Mother's Bible," "Westward, Ho," "The Sword and Staff," "Washington and Franklin," "The History (or Origin) of Yankee Doodle." Jesse first enlisted Morris's sympathy, and through

Morris we became acquainted with Henry Russell, the author of "The Maniac," who then lived in Rochester.

We had frequent visits from a notable man, a Quaker friend, Isaac T. Hopper, though he could not make his appearance in our popular audiences, for it was against the rules of the Friends, but our best sentimental and freedom songs he was very much pleased to hear, and we accommodated him at our private apartments, in our hotel or boarding-house. Thrilling were the instances that he related to us of the slaveocracy, and his great display of wit in emergencies connected with underground railroading in which he baffled the slave-hunter by display of his sagacity, for he was wiser than a serpent and feigned to be harmless as a dove. He was one of the most congenial and loving souls the society of whom we were permitted to enjoy. We made frequent calls at his house and there met his intelligent and sympathizing wife, and also became acquainted with Lydia Maria Child, who was then acting editress of the *Anti-Slavery Standard*. "Owe no man anything," and "lay not up for yourselves treasures upon earth," were passages of Scripture which found a lodgment in Hopper's great heart. He was a friend of the slave and an enemy to all oppression. In after years at our frequent visits to that city and until he passed to glory he was very true and kind with his advice. We learned that his financial affairs were so arranged that there were no great investments made in bank stock or other securities, to be left to greedy heirs, but his mighty powers of mind, heart and will were so displayed that when he yielded up the ghost, all his obligations to every one were fully met.

Our reception in Brooklyn from the first was an ovation. The amphitheatre of the Brooklyn Institute was nightly crowded with interested and sympathetic listeners, and the hall rang out with enthusiastic applause for our best efforts.

We were favored by a call from the Rev. Dr. Cox of the Presbyterian Church in Brooklyn, and he stated to us the position that he had assumed in regard to the great question of emancipation before his congregation, the opposition he had received and his determination to abide by his resolution to devote himself to the cause of the oppressed. We were made glad by his announcement and trusted that, having put his hand to the plow, he would never look back or retreat a single inch. What weight of personal entreaty from domestic or church influence or pro-slavery threatenings, served to weaken his resolution, I never learned, but we know that it was more than his human soul could withstand, for when the whirlpool of anathemas and threatenings of loss of friendship, position and salary came, he was induced to retreat from his laudable position. The opportunity was passed, and another who could wield the sword, sceptre and pen, his chosen implements, in the face of the Goliath of slaveocracy, effectually slung his potent words with an honorable determination that challenged the highest respect and regard of even the vanquished foe. So Brooklyn saw another sight, and the earnest believers in an honest purpose sustained the great preacher of Plymouth Church, who proved a light and guide to honest patriotism and free religion. How often did I notice that brother beloved, fresh from his parish engagements with hymn-book and manuscript — Henry Ward Beecher — among the hearers at these Institute concerts.

We were most earnestly besought to join and take charge of the music, and become the choir at Beecher's Church, but declined.

After three months of continued successes in our concert enterprises throughout the city of New York and some of the larger towns environing it, we bade it adieu for a visit to our Southern friends and public, in Trenton, Philadelphia, Baltimore and Washington.

On reaching Philadelphia, we were greeted by some old friends who were cognizant of our efforts and by a few faithful spirits who were foremost in the anti-slavery enterprise in that city. The Hicksite Quakers were far more advanced in liberal sentiments than the Orthodox, and were ready to hear and receive truth from any source. Their kindly offered assistance in our enterprise was most opportune, and constantly awoke in our hearts gratitude and thankfulness, which forbade anything like grief or disappointment. We were previously heralded through the medium of favorable critics or notices in the papers, as also by correspondence from friends in New York and Boston. Here they came with their proffers to aid by work and deed. The names of Neil, the McKims, Motts, Davis, Palmers, Wrights and others, are all of those who let no opportunity go by to extend to us the right hand of fellowship, socially and otherwise, and we realized that we were in the midst of brothers and sisters. The friendships that were established in those early days were manifested increasingly, as the time passed, and never lessened in after years.

Our first entertainments were given to a very respectable audience, comprising some of the leading and influential people of the city, and Musical Fund Hall rang out to our delight the approval of this popular audience. At once we were favorably impressed by the acoustic properties of this hall, which were of a nature to give the best effect to our simple harmony.

This was inspiring. Our first number was heartily cheered and encored, and we were made aware as we proceeded with our programme that we had produced the best impression possible. We knew it was best to exercise wisdom in the introduction of our sentiments, for there was an intense, bitter spirit existing in the city; many of our audience had been called together out of curiosity, and some were ready to catch at anything that might be said or sung that should appear tinctured with the unpopular movement towards emancipation. Therefore, we confined ourselves to the introduction of a general programme of glees, sentimental and harmonious pieces that attracted the attention of the music-loving people, not forgetting the duty of fully declaring our position in the final song of the evening:

> "We're the friends of freedom,
> And the equal rights of man"

We also declared our opposition to the traffic in liquor and the custom of rum-drinking.

Concluding the concert, many of the audience gathered around us to congratulate us on our first effort and the request came from the president of the Philharmonic Musical Society, to join with it in its forthcoming concert. Fifty dollars was tendered and the use of the beautiful hall for another concert. This we agreed to and the engagement proved a great success. A few selections were announced on their programme, but answering to the encores, we were not able to leave the platform till we had sung four of our characteristic songs; and the delighted musicians, who had listened with the deepest solicitude, came down at the conclusion with vociferous cheering, and the exercise fully settled our status in the good opinion of the cultured scientific musicians of the City of Brotherly Love. Then followed a series of increasing audiences; and 1,700 people, for that was the capacity of the hall, nightly filled the spacious, magnificent concert-room.

One night the whole mass, as well as the singers, were destined to hum a tune as they were going out of the hall, towards "Home, Sweet Home," on the sliding scale.

The sky was clear, the stars shone out, while the audience gathered on this occasion. During the two hours' concert there came up a very thick fog which congealed upon the cold stony pavements and brick sidewalks, freezing as it fell, producing a glaze of ice of some thickness. The great throng, six or eight abreast, in making their exit from the hall in solid phalanx, pressed forward and as their feet came in contact with the ice, down they went. The unfortunates had only time to gather themselves up out of the way of the next falling crowd. Then came a great uproar and shouts of laughter, some with explosive and staccato notes of sudden or violent emotion, while others made points of exclamation, "Oh!" while there were some unpleasant tones on the minor key; and when the last row had fallen, at least 1,500 people had passed through the ordeal.

As we went out upon the street, we could hear in every direction, the merry shouts of those astonished and delighted people as they wended their way through the streets and avenues on that freezing night, "Homeward Bound." They were all in the ice business, chanting till they had come to rest at "Home, Sweet Home."

During this, our first visit, we had frequent invitations from our personal friends to visit the curious and remarkable places, buildings, etc., throughout the city. We were shown the great United States Bank, that was flourishing a few years before, with a capital of $14,000,-000, under the presidency of Nicholas Biddle. With the crash of this institution many people who had confidence in it lost their all. Many poor widows were ruined by this great crisis. The gentleman who escorted us said that he had had all his ready money in this institution, $13,000, sacrificed.

Our next visit was to the United States Mint, where we were very much pleased to witness the manner of coining silver, and a very interesting sight it was to see the quarters and halves dropping out of the hopper, with the national inscription and date — the eagles, the fives, the two-and-a-half and the twenties, all the varied denominations of the United States coin, gold and silver.

Then we visited the great Guard College, founded under the written declaration and bequest of Stephen Girard, who devoted his great energy to the acquiring of immense property. In his will regarding the structure he emphatically declared that this institution should be entirely non-sectarian; and, as far as I am aware, the city of Philadelphia has observed his declaration.

As is often the case, with America's great men idiosyncrasies appear that will not commend them to the good opinions of the generations that come after them. It was said of this gentleman, that he was unkind and neglectful of the interests of his wife and helpmeet, for she was left to spend her latter years in the almshouse, where she died and was buried in the Potter's field.

The grand structure at this time (1844) was yet to

be completed. Since that date thousands upon thousands have imbibed through the institution liberal sentiments; become lovers of humanity and true patriotism and great workers in the field of ethics.

Among numerous acquaintances we came across one old townsman, brought up in Milford, Luther Wallace. He was quite an expert player on the clarinet, and frequently played in an orchestra in choirs. He entertained us at his house, kept by his two maiden sisters. They together sustained a very good reputation for their kindness and uprightness of character. By trade he labored in a type-foundry. As we sat at the bountiful repast, the conversation was led to the scenes of our childhood, most vividly related as we recounted the early settlement of the varied families of Wallaces in Milford.

Rev Mr. Perry, pastor of one of the Baptist churches, extended the right hand of fellowship. He was also a native of New Hampshire and acquainted with our ancestry. He invited us to attend a lecture on "The True Matrimonial Relations of Man and Woman," and his criticism on the manners and shortcomings of the present civilization elicited encomiums and commendation. He ever proved a warm friend. He became a settled minister in the city of Cleveland, O., where we often met him in our frequent visits going and coming through the West.

Extract from my diary of January 9, 1844:

"Why are we highly privileged so much above our fellowmen? Is it because we are better than they? No We must give an account for all the blessings that we have in this world I fear sometimes we don't realize the responsibility that is resting upon us God help us to conquer our passions and prejudices, worldly honors and fame, for they will perish when God taketh away the soul, then we shall want a friend that sticketh closer than a brother."

We had calls from many interesting people, among them Mr. Swain, the notable manufacturer of a panacea so famous for its medicinal qualities that every family thought they must have a bottle. He had set up in his house one of the largest musical instruments in the country, of European manufacture.

Here in Philadelphia was the adopted home of our beloved friend, Charles C. Burleigh, with his worthy partner, Gertrude Burleigh. They were sojourning in a pleasant tenement, not far from our boarding-place, and we had frequent visits from them.

Mrs. Burleigh was a welcome guest at any hour in the day. She would go to the door and exercise her faculty of imitating one of our American domestic fowls, and it carried us back to the farm-yard, when we used to have turkeys fattening for Thanksgiving. It was certainly interesting to hear her "gobble."

While we were sojourning in Philadelphia, our brother Jesse sent us a request asking us to come to Boston to attend the American Anti-Slavery Society meeting, at which Jesse, Joshua, Caleb, and Fanny, my wife, having formed a quartet, were to sing. Brother Zephaniah was at this time acting as our agent.

We also had a very pleasant letter from our friend N. P. Rogers, of Concord, inviting us to come; but, however strong our inclinations to join with them in their grand crusade, we felt our duty call us to utter sentiments before people in Baltimore who had refused, years before, to listen to the voice of the prophets — where Torrey was imprisoned, so enfeebling his constitution that he went into a decline, and where Garrison, also, suffered imprisonment. Here the worst features of the slave system were practised. We visited Hope Slatter prison, where were confined slaves of every texture of skin, old and young, male and female, gathered up from all the surrounding country like cattle, forced into this den to fatten in preparation for the great Southern mart and the plantations of the South. Here to our great surprise we saw men, women and children — some so bleached out that you could scarcely trace the African blood. They gazed with the greatest solicitude upon us three peculiarly-dressed individuals, whom they apparently suspected were from the far South and were long-haired slave-traders.

While standing looking on these unfortunates a gate was swung ajar, and in came a company of stalwarts who went through the routine of some athletic exhibitions, cutting up some of their antics, by which they were taught to show their power, their health, their ambition and their spirit, so they would be purchased in all confidence as contented, happy servants. The keeper tried their muscles. They rolled up their sleeves to show what strength they had. Some would make good field hands, others were for domestic use.

This was a national institution, approved by the Constitution and laws of the land. Our hearts sickened at the sight. As we turned to retreat from the prison we inwardly cursed such an institution, and resolved and re-resolved to do everything in our power to ameliorate the slaves' condition, and wash from our escutcheon the bloody stain, and we emphasized with greater force that night at our concert,

"We're the friends of freedom and the equal rights of man"

Years before, Garrison, Whittier and Torrey, who had come on an errand of mercy and emancipation, were obliged to retreat from the city without a hearing, barely escaping with their lives. We had a less dia-matic experience, but still suffered inconveniences. We were conducted to our boarding-place, went into the parlor, and at once commenced to talk and laugh cheerfully, rejoicing that we had arrived at our destination and desiring to feel at home. When we had spent five or ten minutes talking matters over since we had come to the city, in came the landlady and said: "I am sorry to announce that the rooms that I had for you, were previously taken by a New York party; we therefore shall be obliged to dispense with you, and shall not be able to accommodate you." And out we put into the darkness. It was then about nine o'clock; but our friend, Jonas Hayward, said he knew of another place. We started off and met our baggage on the road bound for the first place, and told the man who pushed the hand-cart to follow us. We approached the house and asked the landlady if she could accommodate the Hutchinson Family — a musical company — for a few days, and she was very glad indeed that we had come to her. We went into the parlor, began to acknowledge ourselves living, and commenced to talk and laugh. Pretty soon Asa spoke out and said: "I went down to see the hall, and — what do you think? — it belongs to a Catholic." Pretty soon in came the landlady and said: "We have ascertained that the rooms we were to let you have are not vacated yet and we have no place for you in the house." And out we went again; and finding nowhere else to go, we concluded to go to the American House, went there and put up. It was a novel experience, then.

On the evening of January 23d we gave our first concert in Baltimore, achieving a pronounced musical success, although the audience was small. I remember that I sang the "Maniac." In the audience we noticed the faces of several familiar friends from our native town, Nehemiah and Jonas Hayward and Elizabeth and Mary Fuller. Mrs. Nehemiah Hayward, who was also there, wrote later in my album after listening to our song, "My Mother's Bible":

> "'My mother's gift,' that pleasing strain
> Still falls upon my ear,
> Revives the past, the mournful vein
> That memory loves to cheer"

We stayed several days in Baltimore, our brother Zephaniah, who acted for two years as advance agent for us, meanwhile going on to Washington and arranging for our appearance there. Our closing concert was given January 29th to a full house. On Tuesday, January 30th, we for the first time entered the capital of the nation. It was at an important era in the great debates that for three decades or more were focusing the eyes of the world upon the Congress of the United States. John P. Hale had just entered the arena where he was to win fame and an undying name as the champion of the oppressed. While we were there the great discussion went on regarding the "twenty-first rule," relating to the right of petition. Daniel Webster, the "expounder of the Constitution," was in the height of his then undimmed fame; John Quincy Adams, "the old man eloquent," was still wearing the harness, which he never laid off until Death's summons found him at the post of duty. In my book of autographs, collected at the time, is his name, written in trembling characters. Webster shows his pride in the Commonwealth which he so powerfully eulogized in his reply to Hayne, by the inscription, "Dan'l Webster of Massachusetts." Among other names in this little volume, which, by the way, no money would buy, are those of John P. Hale,

Jeremiah Russell, New York; Howell Cobb, Georgia; Hannibal Hamlin, Maine; Julius Rockwell, Massachusetts; Henry A. Wise, Virginia — the man who afterward hung John Brown; Alexander H. Stephens, later Vice-President of the Confederacy; James Buchanan, Pennsylvania, afterward president; Robert C. Winthrop, Massachusetts, and many others of the giants of those days.

After a short stay at our boarding-place, kept by a Mrs. Chisholm, we went immediately to the capitol. After a brief view of its architectural features and its beautiful frescos, we went into the Representatives' Chamber. The debate on the twenty-first rule, to which I have referred, was going on. A Georgia member made a few remarks and then John Quincy Adams spoke. Then the matter was laid on the table until the next day. We shook hands with the president in the evening, and made arrangements to pay a visit to the White House the day following. Early the next day Hon. John P. Hale called upon us. He was a man of determination, a great lover of liberty, his sympathies entirely with the North, a patriot indeed. We had previously met him at anti-slavery meetings in New Hampshire, although then he had not fully espoused that cause. He referred at this interview to criticisms which had been made upon a recent vote of his on a sectional question. I told him that we had added to our family song this verse, which we intended to sing at our first concert in Washington:

> "Liberty is our motto
> And we'll sing as freemen ought to
> Till it rings through glen and grotto
> From the old Granite State —
> That the tribe of Jesse
> Are the friends of equal rights"

He then made no objection, but offered complimentary comments. The *denouement* will come later.

After Mr. Hale's call, we went again to the capitol. When we came away Asa said he pitied this country. So did I. The subject of anti-slavery advanced slowly enough. A man from Tennessee, Mr. Johnson, spoke for an hour to no effect whatever. We believed the politicians, especially those in Congress, to be a curse to the country.

In the evening, in company with Ex-Governor Levi Woodbury, of New Hampshire, then in Congress, we went to the White House and were formally introduced to President Tyler, afterward dining with him. My impression of him, as recorded in my diary, was that he was not as bad a man as he had been represented to be. He wanted us to sing and we gave him "The Land of Washington," "A Little Farm well Tilled," "My Mother's Bible," "The Old Granite State" and "Good-Morning."

On the evening of February 1st we gave our first concert in the city in Assembly Hall. In the audience, together with many more of the greatest men of the time, were John Quincy Adams, Hon. Levi Woodbury with his family, Postmaster-General Wyckliffe and family, Hon. Charles Atherton, famous as "Gag" Atherton, of New Hampshire, Mr. Hale and others. There were many Southern men of note included. Mr. Hale, very solicitous for our success among such diverse elements, came into the anteroom during the intermission, and inquired, "Are you going to sing that verse you read to me?" I told him that we were "Don't," said he. "I beg you not to sing it to-night; I had rather give you my head for a foot-ball than have you do it." In deference to his desire that there should be no exhibition of sectional feeling to mar our first appearance, we omitted the objectionable verse, though not forgetting to embody its sentiment, in a less pronounced form, in other verses. Those were trying times and the effort to make an artistic success without doing violence to our consciences was no very easy matter.

After the concert we went to a social gathering opposite the hall, where for the first time we shook the hand of Daniel Webster. When Webster came in, before being introduced to the company, he stepped to the table, poured out a glass of champagne and swallowed it. Then he poured out another and gulped it down. This started his conversational powers; and as he lifted another glass, he paused, and inquired of his host, "Doctor, what makes this wine sparkle so?" It was a poser for the man of pills, scientist though he was, but my boyhood friend, Osgood Muzzey, whom I here met for the first time in many years, at once joined the group, and explained to Webster, for whom he acted as private secretary, the entire phenomenon. The "godlike Daniel," quite satisfied, then turned to his social duties. Webster was then some fifty-five years old. His appearance was impressive. His whole harmonious figure, face, form, carriage, was superbly grand. Men in public station rarely appreciate how much influence a little act will exert, or what will be the impression of their acts. It wounded us deeply, teetotallers as we were, to see this much admired and almost worshipped man partaking so freely of wine; but we could not forget that it was Webster, and listened and looked with respect and awe. We sang several selections, to his evident satisfaction.

To return for a moment to Muzzey. We had several

pleasant interviews with him during our stay in Washington. He had led a life full of adventure and incident in the fourteen years since we picked hops together for Brother David. I well recall how he used to sit in the hop-house and tell stories. He was a splendid specimen of a man, but, alas! died a few years later a victim to the drink habit.

The next day we made another call at the capitol, and heard Joshua R. Giddings, of Ohio, speak for the abolition of the twenty-first rule. His speech was able, heartfelt, and consequently effective. After an hour's session the House adjourned, and we departed, confirmed in our conviction that public men were nuisances. We were anxious for the triumph of freedom, and could not calmly wait for the slow processes of legislation.

While in Washington, news came that the harbors of Boston, New York and Philadelphia were frozen over, and that Long Island Sound was impassable. This was the coldest winter on record, and we were rather glad to be in a warmer climate. All travel was of necessity by land. As the fare from New York to Boston by rail was then fifteen dollars, we were rather interested to have the Sound become passable before our return.

Five hundred attended our second concert, in a popular hall known as Carusi's Saloon, and the most fashionable people from all parts of the country were represented. Mr. Giddings, that brave and noble Abolitionist, was there, to hear the Yankees sing. At the close of the concert the people rushed, almost *en masse*, behind the curtain to offer congratulations.

During the next week we spent an evening with the family of Postmaster-General Wyckliffe. We entertained them with songs, and they offered as entertainment champagne, oranges and chicken salad. We did not drink of the champagne, for we were teetotallers — a very good excuse, they said. Mrs. Wyckliffe we found to be a very motherly woman. The same week Mr. Hale took us into the Supreme Court, and we were privileged to hear Webster argue the celebrated Guard case. On February 8th we gave our closing concert in Assembly Hall, to a great concourse of people. The room was jammed. On the following day we returned to Baltimore, parting tearfully with many dear friends whom we had learned to love during our stay.

On the same evening we gave a concert in Assembly Hall to an audience which represented in money as much as we had taken during our entire previous stay. We notified them that we would repeat the concert on the following Monday night, and they received the announcement with cheers.

On Monday evening, February 12th, we gave what we intended should be our last concert in Baltimore, but the attendance was so large and enthusiastic that we consented to give another on the following Wednesday evening.

While this last concert was in progress, an incident occurred which illustrated the fact that our family quartet was made up of very human beings, and that, as Whittier says,

> "Before the joy of peace must come
> The pangs of purifying."

Amid the excitement of the concert, while we were in an anteroom, some word of criticism was spoken, and in an instant Judson and Asa had pitched into one another. I at once assumed the *rôle* of peacemaker, stepping in between, and as a result suffered the most damage. I began to rub my hurts, making fully as much ado as my injuries would warrant. This was enough. The anger of my brothers was forgotten in mutual sympathy and sorrow over my sufferings. A moment more and all three of us were on the stage, singing as sweetly as though nothing had happened:

> "This book is all is left me now,
>   Tears will unbidden start;
> With faltering lip and throbbing brow
>   I press it to my heart
>
> "For many generations past
>   Here is our family tree
> My mother's hands this Bible clasped;
>   She, dying, gave it me."

February 16th we reached Philadelphia. During our stay there I visited the grave of Franklin. On Sunday, the 18th, we went to hear Father Miller, the great Millennialist, preach in the saloon of the Chinese Museum. I never witnessed such a gathering in my life. He proved quite plainly, according to the record in my diary, made at the time, that the end of the world was near at hand. There was some disturbance, and an officer was sent for. When he came, the disturbers began to scatter, and the congregation thought there was to be a mob; but quiet was soon restored. Father Miller preached two hours, and then bade his hearers farewell forever.

On February 24th we left Philadelphia for New York, where we remained several days, giving concerts, and enjoying the society of old friends. While we were there word came of the terrible explosion on the ship *Princeton* sailing on the Potomac, of the big gun called the "Peacemaker." The President and his cabinet were on board, and Secretary Upshur and other prominent men were instantly killed. The tragedy was one of thrilling interest to us, for several of those with whom we had become intimately acquainted were on the vessel. The ladies, of whom there were at least two hundred, were in the cabin, having a social time; and just as the catastrophe took place our friend Miss Wyckliffe was being cheered for the toast, "The American Flag: the only thing American which will bear stripes!" None of the ladies were hurt. President Tyler had just been invited on deck, and had reached the cabin stairs on his way to the place of death when the explosion occurred.

While in New York each of us suffered more or less from sickness, occasioned, doubtless, by the life of excitement we were leading, and our inexperience in the business of making such long concert-tours. Our callers consisted of such cherished friends as General Morris, who was always more than welcome, and another class of people whom I find denominated in my diary as those with "axes to grind." Many of those who invited us to their homes were anxious to hear us sing, but the invitation was always very carefully worded. Just before we made our advent, an Englishman of note with his company had been giving concerts in the city, with great success. One of the class of individuals mentioned, with axes to grind, invited them to come to his house to a social gathering. The invitation was accepted, and soon after supper the host asked if he would not give the guests a little music. He hesitated and remarked that he did not know they were expected to sing. "Why," said the host, "that was what we invited you for." "Oh," said the artist, "then we will." He at once stepped to the door, ordered his coachman to go to his hotel and get his instruments, and when they came, stood his musicians in the corner of the parlor and went through his entire programme. The party was of course highly delighted. Then he said "good-night" and returned to his hotel. The next day the man who had invited him received a bill for eight hundred dollars. As a result of this incident, we found that when we went into similar gatherings, the form of request to sing was, "If you feel like singing, we should be very much pleased to hear you."

We made a short trip into Connecticut, singing at Stamford. On the day we started we arose, dressed and calmly waited until within a half-hour of the time of the boat's start for our carriage, and then learned that none had been called. Zephaniah hastened into the street and secured a hack, which landed us on the wharf just as the last bell rang. When we started back from Stamford, we were landed on the wharf only to learn that the boat did not stop. It soon steamed by, signalling that it would wait for us at a landing six miles away. We secured a carriage, and met it after it had waited a half-hour.

Our closing concert was given in the Broadway Tabernacle March 21st. For several days the indications had been unmistakable that we were to have an ovation. Our friend George Endicott offered us nine hundred dollars for our receipts, agreeing to pay all expenses. The old Tabernacle was full. All told, there was a little over fifteen hundred dollars, a half-bushel of bills.

While at New York on this trip we made the acquaintance of Henry C. Bowen, who has so long been the publisher of the *Independent*. He was then a merchant on Williams Street. He was so much impressed with the success of this last concert that he begged us to stay and give others. He said he would give us four thousand dollars for four nights if we would only stay.

Much as I longed again to greet my dear wife and the loved ones at home, I felt this too good an opportunity to forego, but it was of no use. Judson had been reading a book on hens, and had the fever badly. He must go home to his chickens; we had given our last concert and that was all there was to be said. Asa, too, had his plans, although he would have stayed had Judson been more tractable. Finding that plan was useless, Mr. Bowen then insisted that we must stop at Woodstock, Conn., the place which he has since made famous by his Fourth of July patriotic gatherings, and give a concert. To this we consented and he went with us. Our concert at Woodstock was given by daylight, between 11 A. M. and 2 P. M. We took ninety-four dollars and gave fifty dollars to the academy of the place. The people were so pleased that they asked us to sing on the following day, Sunday. So on Sunday evening we gave a free sacred concert in one of the churches.

We reached Boston March 25th, and in our boarding-place at Father Francis Jackson's on Hollis Street, counted up our gains for the three months and found we had $4,750 left in the treasury. Two or three days later we made a flying trip to Milford and greeted again the dear ones from whom we had been so long absent. We stayed about Boston several weeks, giving well-attended concerts in the Melodeon, in Charlestown, Cambridge, Salem, Lynn and other contiguous towns. We also heard frequent lectures from Wendell Phillips, Rev. John Pierpont, Garrison and others. Garrison came to us in trouble at one time, and seemed to sincerely appreciate the financial aid we were glad to give him.

On April 14th we left Boston on a three weeks' tour to Hartford, New Haven and other towns along the valley of the Connecticut. It was a trip full of pleasant, though not very exciting experiences. By a happy chance our good friends, Rev. John Pierpont and wife were on the train when we embarked, and we not only had their company on the journey, but met them frequently while in Hartford. We went to Springfield by rail, thence down the river by boat. It was the first time we had seen a propeller, and the other passengers seemed rather amused at our wonder over it. Brothers Zephaniah and Andrew were at the wharf waiting for us when we reached Hartford. Our first concert was given on Tuesday evening, all of the best people in the city being represented in the audience. We stopped at the Eagle Hotel, opposite the State capitol. My diary gives some interesting hints of the way we amused ourselves between our concerts. Up to the time our concerting commenced we had been more or less apart, but when our travels were begun our hearts became closer and closer knit together, and particularly when we were in new places we depended entirely upon each other for society. In the privacy of our hotel apartments we were like innocent children and played together like kittens. Mingled with our pleasures, however, was a vein of anxiety and foreboding, for Brother Andrew's spirits were far from light, Brother Zephaniah's health was poor, Brother Judson had a habit of viewing things from their tragic side, and all of us took rather a solemn view of life, joyous as we naturally were. At that time all the country was stirred up by the Second Advent excitement, and though we were not "Millerites," we naturally talked more or less on the subject. Thus, I find in my journal such entries as these:

"Andrew, Judson and I have been talking about that grim messenger, 'Death.' I believe we may live so that death will not be the king of terrors, but so that we can say with one of old, 'O death, where is thy sting, O grave, where is thy victory!' Then let us, brothers, try and get into the path of wisdom. God have mercy on us all, and save us in Thy kingdom at last to praise Thee without cessation, Amen."

Another entry, at New Haven:

"Asa wanted to go and hear the Virginia Minstrels to-night, but I persuaded him not to. So we had a family meeting, sang 'Old Hundred' and talked about heaven. How happy we shall all be when we get home!"

Later:

"I got scared yesterday at the noise of a lamp. Thought it was the last trumpet. Oh, that I might be ready when God calls!"

Again, at Northampton:

"Judson says 'Get ready, John, the time is at hand.' God have mercy on everybody. Amen."

But it was not all solemn, for I find such entries as these:

"All went to the hall this afternoon except Abby, and had a good play pinching one another. Andrew scratched me some accidentally."

Pinching was a favorite pastime with us, and our arms were black and blue most of the time from the exercise.

At another time:

"We have been playing at rubbing noses until the tears ran down Judson's cheeks."

All of us played ball a good deal for exercise. On our walks and other excursions, Asa and Abby, the two youngest, usually went together, while I paired off with my loved Judson.

While we were on this trip Brother Jesse published a new anti-slavery song, "Get off the Track":

SINGING FOR FREEDOM.

"Ho, the car Emancipation
Rides majestic through our nation,
Bearing on its train the story,
Liberty, our nation's glory

"Roll it along, roll it along
Through the nation,
Freedom's car, Emancipation"

This immediately aroused the antagonism of the proslavery press, and the *Boston Atlas* was especially bitter in its attack upon the song and upon us as its singers. At this time we distinguished our newspaper notices as "puffs," that is, compliments upon our singing, and "blows," criticisms on our anti-slavery songs and appearances at emancipation meetings. Much as we desired success, in an artistic sense, we desired to see the triumph of the cause of freedom more, and the result of the "blows" was only to make us utter a prayer for help to stand for the right.

At Hartford we made a call upon Mrs. Sigourney, the noted Connecticut poetess, leaving with her admissions to our concert, which she seemed to appreciate very much. We went to New Haven, where we enjoyed looking over Yale College. We attended an exhibition at the college chapel, where Johnson's Philadelphia Band was among the attractions. Then we went on to Springfield, where we gave a concert, and thence up to Northampton, a town that pleased us so much that it was with difficulty we tore ourselves away.

We spent two days, one of them a Sunday, with the Florence Community, and were loth to leave it. We looked over the farm, viewed the silk establishments and enjoyed the society of the communists, some one hundred and twenty-five in all. On Sunday, in the dining-room, Frederick Douglass spoke, as did one or two others, and we sang. The next day I made a trip to the summit of Mount Holyoke, which I greatly enjoyed.

While at Northampton we sang at an anti-slavery meeting in the town hall, at which Douglass spoke for three hours. This singing, of course, aroused more criticism, but we endeavored to take it patiently.

On Friday, May 3d, we were once more in Boston, our trip having netted us a tidy sum. Here I found my wife at Father Jackson's, and in a day or two a discussion commenced on the question of our future. Brother Benjamin was not satisfied with our plan of living together on the farm. Asa was opposed to it and it was not entirely agreeable to my wife. Judson and Abby agreed with me that it should be continued. I was a strong believer in the idea of a community, and so with me it was a question of principle. However, the decision was held in abeyance for the time.

The next week we all went home to Milford, where several weeks were spent in work on the farm. During this summer we erected what is known as the "Community Block," on the square in the village. It was four stories in height, with a hall in the upper part, which was at once devoted to the free meetings of the "Come-outers." On May 27th we went to Boston to attend the May meetings of the Anti-Slavery Society. The family was well represented at these meetings: Zephaniah, Joshua, Caleb, Jesse, Benjamin, Judson, John, Asa and Abby. We were all on the platform of Tremont Temple together. All the anti-slavery leaders were there. During our stay here we sang at a big temperance meeting on Boston Common, attended by at least twenty thousand people. The speakers included John B. Gough, Mr. Hawkins, the great Washingtonian

GET OFF THE TRACK.—(p. 115)

reformer from Baltimore, Gov. George N. Briggs and others. The temperance agitation in favor of moral suasion was then at its height. On the next evening there was another temperance meeting in the Representatives' chamber of the State-house, on Beacon Hill, at which the governor and others spoke. Our quartet sat in what is now the ladies' gallery of the old chamber, and sang at appropriate intervals.

At the last anti-slavery meeting of the week C. C. Burleigh presented a beautiful banner to Garrison, and eloquent speeches were made by each. There was a good deal of disorder, the disturbers sitting in different parts of Tremont Temple and hissing the speakers. The meeting ended in quite a flurry. Then we went back to our toil in Milford for a season.

I ought to quote N. P. Rogers's description of our singing at the convention, from the *Herald of Freedom*, June, 1844:

". . One word more — the Hutchinsons. No one will any longer tax me with hyperbole or exaggeration when I exult at these matchless anti-slavery songsters. They surpassed themselves at the convention. They came out with some new strains, and sung some that were not entirely new with prodigious and indescribable effect. Ames says it takes an orator to describe an orator, or to write his life. I say it would take musicians and music to describe these singers. Their outburst at the convention, in Jesse's celebrated 'Get off the track,' is absolutely indescribable in any words that can be penned. It represented the moral railroad in characters of living light and song, with all its terrible enginery and speed and danger. And when they came to the chorus-cry that gives name to the song — when they cried to the heedless pro-slavery multitude that were stupidly lingering on the track, and the engine 'Liberator' coming hard upon them, under full steam and all speed, the Liberty Bell loud ringing, and they standing like deaf men right in its whirlwind path, — the way they cried 'Get off the track,' in defiance of all time and rule, was magnificent and sublime. They forgot their harmony, and shouted one after another, or all in confused outcry, like an alarmed multitude of spectators, about to witness a terrible railroad catastrophe. But I am trying to *describe* it. I should only say that it was indescribable. It was life — it was nature, transcending the musical staff, and the gamut, the minim and the semi-breve, and leger lines. It was the cry of the people, into which their over-wrought and illimitable music had *degenerated,* and it was glorious to witness them alighting down again from their wild flight into the current of song, like so many swans upon the river from which they had soared, a moment, wildly into the air. The multitude who had heard them will bear me witness that they transcended the very province of mere music — which is, after all, like eloquence or like poetry, but one of the subordinate departments of humanity. It was exaggerated, sublimated, transcendent song. God be thanked that the Hutchinsons are in the anti-slavery movement — for their sakes as well as for ours! Their music would ruin them, but for the chastening influences of our glorious enterprise. It will now inspire all their genius and give it full play, and will guard them from the seductions of the flattering world, which, but for its protection, would make them a prey. I note them not to praise them. I am above that — as they are. I do it in exultation for the Cause, and for their *admonition,* though while they are Abolitionists they do not need it. Anti-slavery is a safe regulator of the strongest genius. I here take occasion to say, in defiance of all rule, that Jesse Hutchinson, Jr., is the most gifted song-writer of the times — so far as I know. None of our most approved poetry comes up to his, written in the hurley-burley of anti-slavery debate. It is, perhaps, owing to this and to the fact that he writes to sing rather than to read — writes under the influence of song — that the music precedes the poetry in his mind; that the words come at the call of the music, and are drafted into its service, or rather volunteer at its summons; that his poetry *sings* so much better than Pierpont's or Burleigh's or Lowell's or Whittier's or any of the bards. Burns wrote his immortal songs to match the tunes sent him by George Thompson. He couldn't sing like Jesse Hutchinson. I don't know as he could at all. His soul could, if his voice couldn't; and under its inspiration he poured forth his lays in songster verse. What songs he would have left us, if he could have written under such a spell of music as possesses the Hutchinsons! Jesse's songs remind me of him. 'The Slave Mother' is hardly surpassed by anything of Burns'. I only mention it to call the attention of the people to what is going on in the anti-slavery field. They'll all *miss it* if they don't come there."

As I look back upon the years of professional life no fact gives me greater satisfaction than this, that no matter how great were the artistic triumphs of the Hutchinsons, they were always more than ready to leave their

PARKER PILLSBURY — (p. 119)

public careers for the sweeter joys of domesticity One day we would be receiving the plaudits of the multitude, the next wending our way back to our fields. On our long trips, I find my diary contains constant expressions of longing for home and the dear ones left there. We placed the strongest emphasis on the joy and beauty of home, and to-day it seems to me that no institution exists which so distinctly bears the marks of the divine purpose and has a more sure promise of the blessing of the All-Father than the family. In this age of over-organization it is well to remember that the first, if not the only organization God ordained, was the family.

In June we went to a great anti-slavery meeting in Concord, where those present had the privilege of songs from Jesse, Judson, John, Asa, Abby, David, Noah, Caleb, Joshua, Benjamin, Rhoda and Fanny.

Then came haying-time. A regiment of Hutchinsons went into the fields for a family haying-bee — David with his tribe of boys and hired man; Noah with his crutch and cane, doing what he could; Caleb with his man; and Cousin William Marvel, Zephaniah, Jesse, Benny, Judson, Isaac, George, John and Asa.

On July 14th Parker Pillsbury preached to us at a "free meeting" in the old meeting-house. Judson tried to get Rev. Mr. Richardson to announce the event at the regular church service in the morning, but his request was refused. On the following Saturday William Lloyd Garrison and Francis Jackson came to our house for a stay of a day or two. On the following day the "Come-outers" enjoyed a free meeting with them in the old meeting-house. According to my diary, Mr. Garrison spoke at five o'clock, on "the Sabbath," and proved to my mind that it was as good as any other day. On the following day they departed, Asa driving them as far as Nashua.

During the latter part of the month I made a trip to Boston and Lynn. One day I spent fishing at Bass Point, Nahant, with such congenial spirits as Garrison and Pierpont. We took a sail-boat from Lynn, and enjoyed a fish mess, with Jesse as chief cook. Phillips came over from his cottage and dined with us. On another day twelve hundred of the finest spirits of the age went to Hingham for a great open-air convention. Garrison, Phillips, Douglass, Clapp, Charles C. Burleigh, Charles Lenox Remond, George Bradburn, Parker Pillsbury, Robert Purvis of Philadelphia, Stephen Foster, Abby Kelley, Francis Jackson, Edmund Quincy and others spoke. The quartet, Judson, John, Asa and Abby, with Jesse, did the singing for them. It was a picnic, and each one was supposed to bring enough food for himself and his neighbor. As many came for the loaves and fishes, the *menu* turned out to be rather slim. It was easily perceived that there was not going to be nearly enough for such a company; so the committee in charge of the tables set about finding any supplies that had been held back. It happened that I had brought my trunk, in which was my violin in its box, with me, and as the most safe place, had left it on the steamboat which had been chartered for the occasion. As soon as it was seen, it was surmised that it was full of eatables, and it was at once transported to the tables, to be opened if it was found that the bill-of-fare was falling short. I knew nothing of what had happened, until standing at the tables, looking vainly for something to assuage my hunger, I observed a man at it with a cold chisel. Before I could reach him, he had opened it and drawn forth the violin. I remarked that he would find nothing more appetizing than catgut and hair there. The managers of the affair, at Mr. Jackson's suggestion, made good the damage.

At sundown we were packed, several hundred of us, on the boat, and it started for Boston. Alas! the captain had missed his reckoning; the tide, instead of coming in, was going out, and soon we were stuck fast on the flats. There was nothing to be done but wait for the tide to come in again, although this was rather hard for people who were not only weary but who had been fed on little more than mental pabulum all day. But there we stayed, until nearly dawn. To make matters worse, the boat was so crowded that it was impossible to find sufficient seats, or other means of repose. I managed to find a loose cabin door, which seemed to be serving no very useful purpose, tore it off, and after placing blocks of wood under it, made it serve as a seat for six other weary ones beside myself. Finally, in utter exhaustion, I lay down under a table and tried to sleep, but the moving feet of the people sitting at the table soon demonstrated this to be anything but a bed of roses. Passing out towards the engine-room, I sighted my good friend Francis Jackson sweetly sleeping high on a pile of fire-wood. Meanwhile, Brother Jesse, with Frederick Douglass and Henry Clapp, were the life of the sleepy company. Deciding that there was no possibility of rest and small prospect of either supper or breakfast, they resolved to make the best of it, and so skylarked all over the boat. Robert Purvis was by the stairs in a sleeping position, when suddenly some one grabbed him by the nose. He woke and mildly protested against the undue familiarity. "Oh, beg pardon," said the intruder. "I thought you were a chair!" Jesse organized meetings here and there at which resolutions of the nature of solace for the inconvenience experienced were passed: "Resolved, that we had our usual quiet night's rest." "Resolved, that we have had our breakfast,' etc. Mr. Garrison viewed these performances with some disapproval, and quietly warned these young men against injuring their personal influence by too much levity; he could not forget that the party came to Hingham on serious business. But hard times and good times have an end, and at last we reached Boston, ate our breakfasts, secured some sleep, and soon the impression of everything but the good time we had had passed off.

This excursion was soon followed by one even more pleasurable, when I got my first impressions of the beauty of the White Hills.

In August I secured a big stage-coach, hired a man to drive the four horses which drew it (I saw this man, Granville Turner, hale and hearty in 1894), and made up a big family party for a trip through the White Mountains. There were twelve of us in the coach, besides several others in single carriages. We took the large tent belonging to the band, in which I had an interest, and on the first day proceeded as far as Concord. We pitched our tent, and gave a concert in the old North Church in the evening to a great concourse of people. Mr. Rogers' three daughters, Frances, Caroline and Ellen, joined our party at this point, as did John K. French, William M. White and Mary Lincoln.

After an enjoyable ride, we reached Sanbornton. We pitched our tent by a farm-house, and the men of the party used it for a dormitory, while the ladies slept in the house. We appointed a foraging committee to secure butter, milk, eggs and other supplies of the farmers, as they proceeded by different routes.

The scenery was sublime, the weather good and our spirits fine. The next morning, with cheers for the "Old Granite State," the farmers, and others, we started for Plymouth, where we arrived at noon, finding our family friend, N. P. Rogers, waiting for us. We stopped at the house of his brother John, a physician, and in the evening gave a concert in the village to a good house. Writing to the *Herald of Freedom*, Mr. Rogers spoke thus of this concert:

"The concert was in the Court House — a fine room for music, but too small for the audience — on a dogday night. It was crowded. Many people came in from the surrounding towns. The Hutchinsons have never sung to a more intelligent and tasteful audience, of any size, in any place. And they never sang more freely, or in freer spirit and strain. The air was somewhat oppressive and non-elastic, but they were in capital spirits. Some of their songs were absolutely wonderful. I wish I had time to particularize. I want to say a good many things about that little concert — to me the most interesting they can ever give. But I have no time. I was glad to see my old and venerated friend Judge Livermore present, at the age of near fourscore — though it was several miles from his residence, and a dark evening. And when they sang Longfellow's 'Excelsior,' and Judson sent down that chorus word, from the height of the high Alps young genius was scaling, 'It is your motto word, young men,' remarked the judge, enthusiastically, and in his own peculiar, 'excelsior' style, as rare as the music he was lauding. But I am interrupted, and must close."

Saturday we spent in the woods at Lincoln, trouting, with good success. On Sunday, at noon, we reached Littleton, our journey taking us through the Franconia Notch, a trip we greatly appreciated. We had a fine view of the "Old Man of the Mountain." A row upon Pemigewassett Lake was also taken. In the afternoon there was an anti-slavery meeting at Littleton. S. S. Foster, William A. White and Abby Kelley were the speakers, we contributing two songs. In the evening Foster spoke again, and we sang once more.

Monday we fished for trout in the Ammanoosuc River. On that evening we gave a concert, and the following day went to Fabyan's. The hotel was hardly as large as at the present time, and there were no accommodations for us, so the tent was brought into requisition once more. The eight women of the party were provided with one room in the hotel. The next day thirteen of us ascended Mount Washington, on horses trained by Mr. Fabyan for the purpose. We had a good time but a hard one. It was the roughest route I had ever travelled in my life. It was nine miles from the hotel to the top, and the ascent took about four hours. It was a romantic sight to see some twenty-four men and women on horseback, following one another single file over the rocks and crags, logs, ruts and ditches until they reached an altitude so high that trees or shrubs refused to grow. Then we left earth behind and went into the clouds, and at last reached the summit. I was the first of the Hutchinson party to reach the goal, excepting Mr. White, who walked the whole distance, up and back, eighteen miles. The guide refused to let the horses go beyond a certain point, but I had the reins in my own hands and urged my steed to the tip-top. It seemed poetic enough to be among the clouds, but it *felt* chilly, and after eating our lunch and singing a song, we came down. The clouds were so troublesome that we only caught one glimpse of the Saco River winding its way through the valley towards North Conway and Fryeburg. A severe headache spoiled my enjoyment of the view. When we reached the foot of the mountain, which was descended without accident, we had some sport racing our horses on the plains, and when we came to the travelled road we formed ourselves into a band, and so rode singing to the hotel. We were stiff enough when we dismounted from our horses and, of course, were a laughing-stock for those who had remained behind. I was very sick that night.

The next day we started on our return trip. Our bill for one and two-thirds days' board at the hotel was $73. We took dinner at the old Crawford House, near the Willey House in the Notch, and that night pitched our tent thirty-five miles from Fayban's, in North Conway, and in the evening gave a free concert to a delighted company which gathered outside. Then next day we went to Centre Harbor, stopping on the way in the woods of Tamworth for a picnic dinner. Mr. White made an temperance and anti-slavery address to the honest farmers who gathered about. The following day we spent rowing upon and swimming in Lake Winnepisogee. We returned through Plymouth, gave a concert at Sanbornton Bridge on our way to Concord, spent the last night of our journey at Goffstown and reached Milford August 14th. I was ailing most of the time on the return trip, and so could not enjoy it as much as I otherwise might. In those days I believed in hydropathy and had caught a serious cold from a superfluity of shower baths.

In the Milford column of the *New Hampshire Republican*, a few years since, appeared a reminiscence of this White Mountain trip, from a writer signing his name "E. M. S."

"In 1844 the celebrated Hutchinson family of singers decided on a pleasure trip through the White Mountains. In that year Granville Turner was driving the stage between Milford and Nashua, and as he possessed the confidence of Jesse Hutchinson, the father of the noted family, he was delegated to draw the ribbons over a double span of horses and guide the Hutchinsons on their journey. Mr Turner relates, that as he sat, reins and whip in hand, before the door of the Hutchinson home, with the brothers and sister about him, the father, Jesse Hutchinson, appeared upon the threshold and with raised hand gave into Mr Turner's keeping his sons and daughter, and bade him to return them to the parental roof in safety. Mr Turner solemnly replied that he would, and he did. On the journey many amusing incidents occurred All told, the party comprised eighteen persons. Not far from one mountain hotel they halted, and fished and sang and put up their canvas tent Later, a stage-driver coming into this hotel was asked if he had seen the Hutchinson singers, whom they heard were on the way His reply was, 'No, but I passed a band of tented Arabs who were fishing and singing not far away' None of the listeners imagined the people referred to, to be the Hutchinsons Later the 'Arabs' came driving to the hotel, singing, 'We're a band of brothers from the old Granite State,' and announced their identity, but the populace did not believe them They entered the hotel in their rough and ready rigs, procured rooms, and when evening came, they appeared in costume to the wonderment of all; and when they sang, they captivated and charmed and took that mountain house by storm."

The reference to father's solicitude for us is a reminder of Parker Pillsbury's description of a visit made to the old homestead at about this period. Milford was during these years one of the most pronounced anti-slavery communities in New Hampshire, and frequent conventions were held in the old church and other assembly rooms, as noted elsewhere in this history. On these occasions the members of the family quartet and Brother Jesse would come home, if possible, and share in the exercises, while the home would be opened to visiting speakers Pillsbury says on one occasion, he, with N. P. Rogers, stayed at the homestead. In the morning, after breakfast, "Uncle Jesse" rose to start for his daily toil in the fields; but just at this moment Brother Jesse said, "Father, shall we not sing you a farewell before we leave for our distant homes?" The father paused, and the dozen sons and daughters, led by Jesse, sang:

"Our father, we wish you well
  When our Lord calls, we hope you will be mentioned
    in the promised land"

To this prayer the father in sonorous, but grave and earnest tones, responded:

"My children, I wish you well
When our Lord calls, I trust you will be mentioned
in the promised land"

Both Pillsbury and Rogers were deeply affected by this ceremony, which, in the Hutchinson homestead was but the outflow of the sentiment of respect felt by every son and daughter for our sire, and something rarely overlooked in our coming and going.

September 11, 1844, the quartet, with Zephaniah as advance agent, started on another season of concert work. Our first stop was at Manchester, where we sang to twelve hundred people. The next night we sang in Nashua, taking nearly twice as much money as at Manchester. Then Brother Zephaniah went to Newburyport to arrange a concert, while we went on to Lynn, where a few days were pleasantly spent with old friends. On the 16th we reached Newburyport and gave a concert in the evening, six hundred being in the hall. While there we had as callers Rev. Samuel J. May, who desired us to stay over a day and sing at his anti-slavery meeting the following night, and Hannah F. Gould, the poetess, who consented to write us some songs. Mr. May found the native town of Garrison rather indifferent to anti-slavery. It had not then got to the point of raising a monument to its distinguished son. We were unable to stop and sing for Mr. May and the next day were in Portsmouth, where we had the pleasure of witnessing the launching of a man-of-war at the navy yard. Our Portsmouth concert was an artistic and a numerical success. Our next stop was at Saco; our house was poor, and we determined to leave the town out in our future trips.

On the 21st we reached Portland. We stopped at the home of our friend Oliver Dennett and had a most delightful stay. We gave two concerts, with good audiences, and at the close of the second were driven to the boat and steamed away for Augusta. By this time we thought ourselves pretty well "down East," but were told by the inhabitants that we must go on to Bangor before reaching that region.

Our concert at Augusta was successful. We were importuned to repeat it, but concluded to give one in Gardiner, near by, instead. The concert here was not numerically a success, however. Our next concert was given in Hallowell. There was a strong anti-slavery sentiment in this place. During this trip we brothers concluded to exercise as often as possible at bowling, and had many curious experiences finding alleys and making bargains for their use. In one place we had rolled the balls but a few minutes when the profanity and drunkenness in the place so disgusted us that we fled. At Bath we closed our concert as usual with "The Old Granite State," but immediately there were calls for "Get Off the Track." We sung it, and it was received with cheers such as we seldom heard from pro-slavery people. We were convinced that people would take in song what they would not in any other way.

October 1st we reached Brunswick. While at dinner in our hotel we noticed a man at another table who looked like John B. Gough. It proved to be the great lecturer, who was to speak in Bath that evening. He told us his stage was to start at once and bade us good-by. In a few minutes the stage came rattling back and Gough and his wife stepped out, as if they had forgotten something. He told us he thought the opportunity of spending an afternoon with us too good to lose, and so had come back. We had a jolly time until five o'clock, when he took the coach for Bath.

That evening we sang in a church, and the next day took a twenty-six-mile journey in a stage-coach to Portland.

We stayed several days in Portland, singing at a great anti-slavery meeting. This began in the City-hall, but after a day the meetings were stopped by the mayor, who refused to allow the hall to be used longer for such a purpose. This caused the loss of an evening, which the leading Abolitionists improved by a social gathering at the home of the Dennetts, where we were again stopping. Then Concert Hall was secured, and the convention proceeded. A Southern slave-holder made trouble at nearly every session by engaging in discussion with Mr. Garrison. On the last night of the convention, Sunday, October 6th, he, with a prominent Portland poet named John Neal, attempted to introduce resolutions declaring the poor, despised Abolitionists traitors to God and religion, Christianity and their country. Mr. Garrison met them with his strongest arguments. Finally, the confusion was so great that Mr. Garrison, in despair at making himself heard, called upon us to sing. We rose to give "The Slave Mother's Lament," facing as disorderly a gathering as I ever saw. Soon all was as still as death. We never had better attention. The audience was melted by our song, and the meeting continued without further interruption until a very late hour. We were so excited by the event that it was long after midnight before we retired. Mr. Neal ever after showed himself a kind, helpful and sympathizing friend.

The next day we went again to Portsmouth and from there to Newburyport, thence to Dover, N. H., giving successful concerts in each place. From there we went to Exeter, and thence to Haverhill, giving well-attended entertainments. We stayed over a Sunday in Haverhill, making a trip to Bradford and Georgetown, taking dinner with friends at the latter place, and returning, spent the night with friends in the former town.

Our next objective point was Andover, a conservative, but friendly town, where we greatly enjoyed the society of an old friend, Mr. Clark. A fine audience attended our concert. The next day we went to Woburn, where a good assembly listened to our songs in the town hall. The day after was spent with the Jacksons in Boston, and on the day following we were in Lowell, where our concert was given to a large audience in the Universalist church. On the following day we were again in old Milford, and stayed over Sunday. An anti-slavery convention was in progress in the hall, with Abby Kelley, Stephen Foster, Parker Pillsbury and a Miss Hitchcock as speakers. The meetings on Sunday were so largely attended that it was necessary to adjourn from the hall to the old meeting-house. We sang at each session. Monday we spent in visiting our brothers, and on the following day were back in Boston. This week we gave a concert in the Melodeon to the largest Boston audience we had ever yet had. The *Atlas* came out that afternoon with another diatribe against " Get Off the Track," which we were announced to sing, calling it " vile stuff." On Friday we went to Providence, and found politics raging, the Polk and Dallas campaign being in progress. Our concert that evening was largely attended and the audience enthusiastically demanded a repetition; but, alas! we had advertised for " one night only," and kept our word. On Sunday we heard a sermon by Rev Francis Wayland, president of Brown University. The next day we started for Worcester, stopping at Mendon on our way to spend a very pleasant evening and night with an old acquaintance Mr. Crooker. We reached Worcester Tuesday, October 29th, after a dreary stage-coach trip through the mud and rain. An overflowing audience greeted us that evening. The next day we set out for Springfield, fortunately meeting our friends, the Goughs, at the depot for a brief interview. At Springfield we heard several debates between George Bradburn and David Lee Child (husband of Lydia Maria Child) on slavery. Mr. Child had rather the worst of the argument. He believed Abolitionists should vote for Henry Clay; Mr. Bradburn did not. Our concert in this place was a success. On Saturday we reached Albany, where we found politics even more exciting than at Providence, and renewed our acquaintance with our good genius Mr. Newland, who was our friend in need in this city two years before. He believed that the Bible sanctioned slavery, and gave me a book which sought to prove it. On Sunday we called on Mrs. Mott, where we were glad to peruse copies of the *Liberator* and *Herald of Freedom*.

Election day came during our stay in Albany. It was an exciting time. One day Oliver Johnson came up from New York, and we had a pleasant time in his society. We gave two concerts to crowded houses, one hundred being turned away from the last, and meanwhile sandwiched-in a concert at Troy. Tuesday, November 12th, we gave a concert at Schenectady, where, two years before we were compelled to give a free show or nothing. On the 13th we sung in Utica, and went to a fire (a drug-store being burned) after the concert was over; and at two o'clock the next morning took the train for Syracuse. Here we gave a big concert Before it commenced a man came to the door-tender and asked the price of tickets. He was told fifty cents. "By George!" said he, "I never pay over two shillings." We told him he could go in for that, and if he did not think the concert worth it, he need not pay any more. At the close of the programme, he went to the doorkeeper and gave him the other two shillings, saying he would not cheat us. Rev. Samuel J. May was at the concert and before we departed we had a call from John A. Collins of the Community.

Our next stop was at Auburn, where we visited the State Prison, seeing seven hundred convicts at dinner. Our concert was given in the museum, to a good house. Then we went to Geneva, and thence on to Rochester and Batavia, and reached Buffalo November 22d. The trip from Batavia was very picturesque, although I missed a good deal of it because of my absorption in the works of Prof. O. S. Fowler. We had to be rather particular in our selection of a seat in the cars. The rails along the route were made of thin plates of iron nailed to wood, and sometimes the wheels had a way of turning them at the ends up through the car, making "goose-necks," and creating a good deal of havoc. We gave two concerts in Buffalo, successful, as were practically all on this trip.

There had been a great storm, and its effects were everywhere visible. A big steamer was landed high and dry on the shores of Lake Erie. Judson and I went down to see her. On our way we observed a little old house the lower story of which had been destroyed, all except the corner-posts, by the winds and waves. I noticed smoke coming out of the chimney, although it seemed impossible such a structure could be inhabited. We went on, but not being satisfied, returned, and noticing a ladder, crawled up, and knocked on a door lying horizontally on the floor. A delicate woman, with a half-starved baby in her arms answered our summons. The woman was thinly clad and almost frozen, for the tempest had washed nearly all her clothing away, and she was without means to get more. The next day, with Abby, we took them some clothing, paid their rent, and gave them money to move to a more secure dwelling.

Buffalo was the extreme western limit of our tour, but, much as we desired to return to home and loved ones, we felt that we must see Niagara Falls first. For some days before we took the trip we were filled with pleasurable anticipations. On November 26th we started. The cars in which we made the journey were mean, cold and uncomfortable. We stopped at a temperance house at the falls and warmed ourselves, and then went to see the cataract. It didn't look as we expected, and we were so nearly frozen that we cared very little how it did look. We bought some souvenirs and then went back to our hotel, and thence returned to Buffalo. Taking a summer trip to them in later years gave me quite a different impression.

On our return tour home we revisited many of the cities we had so recently seen, and all our concerts were successful. But there was a shadow over us all the way. My brother Judson had many of the qualities of the seer. He was very gloomy during our stay in Buffalo and afterward. It was his regular assignment during our trips to write letters to the folks at home. One day in Rochester I happened to pass behind him as he was writing a letter to father and mother, and glanced over his shoulder at the sheet. He had drawn the outline of a coffin on the margin of the paper. I stopped in dismay, and as I stood there he drew another, the coffins being head to head. I do not know what he wrote in the letter. We were not in the habit of reading one another's missives, and none of us said anything to him about it. From that time, though we were constantly meeting dear friends, were having the highest success in our concerts, and were seeing sights to be remembered for a lifetime, we were full of forebodings. I had my own personal reasons for anxiety, and in addition was an indefinable fear of an unknown sorrow.

Our last concert was given in Worcester. We arrived a day early, and in the evening went to hear Ole Bull play. In the language of my diary, "He played me mad." But great as his success was, he had an audience only half as large as that which gathered to hear the Hutchinsons on the following night.

Friday, December 4th, we reached Milford once more. We were told in the village that Brother Benjamin and Isaac Bartlett (Sister Rhoda's husband), were sick. We found them so, but able to be about the house. On the following Wednesday Isaac was so very sick that Dr. Shaw was called. On Friday Brother Benjamin grew suddenly worse, and Dr. Shaw was also called to him. On Saturday, Jesse and Andrew, who had been summoned, came to Milford to bear their share in nursing the sick men. On Tuesday evening, December 17th, my wife gave birth to our first-born, Henry. As he heard the first cry of the little infant, Brother Benny awaking from his stupor, said, "One comes into the world, another goes out."

During the excitement following the birth, Sister Rhoda came hurriedly in, and said Isaac was dying. I went to him, and he was bidding father and mother and the brothers good-by. He lingered, however, for several days; and meanwhile Benjamin grew rapidly worse of the same disease, typhoid fever. Isaac died on Sunday, December 22d, and on Monday Benjamin bid farewell to earth.

As I was standing by his bedside, he raised his eyes, with a look of intensity, and said: "Victory, victory, this is a day of victory." These words I afterwards used as a closing strain of a song which we have sung many times at funerals and other occasions, entitled "A Brother is Dead."

Meanwhile Asa became very sick, and with the shadow resting over the bereaved household he, too, calmly prepared for death. He had the same disease, but ultimately recovered.

Three hours before his death Brother Benjamin sang a farewell song with Jesse, who was watching with him. The double funeral of the brothers-in-law was held from the old home on the following Tuesday. As I passed through the hall and saw the two caskets, head to head, instantly the recollection of Judson's letter, written in Rochester, flashed through my mind. It was a touching funeral service. We were all there, excepting our sick brother Asa. We realized all that human skill could do had been done to save the lives of these two loving, earnest, whole-souled brothers, but that God had called them and they had cheerfully obeyed the summons. Rev. John Richardson of the Baptist church conducted the service. Brother Jesse's words I can never forget. He said: "We have adjourned our family meeting to Heaven. Blessed be God!" The family, with broken, but hope-inspired voices, joined in songs of love and heaven. It was the first break in the family circle since most of us had come to maturity. Alas! how frequently came the broken ties afterward!

The demise of these our brothers led to the dissolution of the community. As has previously been stated, the home with its eight large rooms, eighteen by sixteen feet square, and the farm of one hundred and sixty acres were given to the six younger children — Benjamin, Judson, John, Asa, Rhoda and Abby, on condition that they should take care of mother. Father had a great idea of doing missionary work as a preacher. He had the farm where all the children but Abby and Elizabeth were born, and also a house in the village, and to his mind there could be no reason why he should not deed the house to us. As a matter of fact, it may be stated, he did not preach, and it was very rare indeed that he was away from home over a night. When we formed our community, it was with an idea of "settling down," and farming; but as time wore on, the attractions of our life of song were too strong, both artistically and financially, so we started out once more. All our earnings as a quartet, however, went into the common treasury; it was understood Benny and Rhoda had as much interest in it as either of the others. A great deal of our money was loaned out at interest. Two thousand dollars was expended in improvements on the farm. Five thousand dollars was invested in the Community Block. There was no bank in town, so the rest of our money was put in a shot-bag, which was in turn put in an earthern pot, and that was buried under the cellar arch. We kept father informed of its location, and made him understand that whenever he wanted money, all he had to do was to go and dig it up.

Meanwhile Brother Judson, Sister Rhoda and I married. This complicated matters, and made life as a community more difficult. Then the older brothers began to hint that it was not quite fair to deprive them of their interest in the farm. The death of Isaac made no

ASA   ANDREW   JESSE   JOSHUA   DAVID   CALEB   NOAH   JUDSON   ZEPHANIAH   JOHN
TEN OF THE HUTCHINSSONS, 1844 (p. 175)

difference in Rhoda's status, of course, and the death of Benjamin, as his father was his only legal heir, should have made none. But it brought matters to a head in such a way that after many conferences it was deemed best to make a division, and give the community plan up. So far as the house and farm were concerned, the deed had never been recorded, so that all that was necessary was to destroy it, but there had been such an increase in personal property that an auction was necessary before there could be a division of that

It was a great trial to me to give up the life in the old home. It not only meant a relinquishing of a form of life in which I fully believed, and the partial separation from the brothers and sisters whom I so dearly loved, but it meant a farewell to the home of my boyhood, to which I was tenderly attached. However, we did not separate at once. Judson went to housekeeping in the "milk room," Fanny and I in the sitting-room, while the rest of the children kept house with the old folks. Our lives were very quiet for a couple of months. Domestic cares occupied most of our time. On February 18th we gave a concert at Wilton. Prior to that the whole family of brothers with Abby made a trip to Boston and sung at the anti-slavery meetings in the Representatives chamber of the State-house. Our hearts were heavy as we thought of our brother, with us but a short year before. We also made a trip to Fitchburg, and sung at a meeting where Wendell Phillips was the speaker.

During the last of February we started on a concert tour, first singing in Manchester to a crowded house; and then, going back to Milford long enough to get my wife and little Henry, we went to Lowell, where a successful concert was given. Leaving Fanny there, we went to Boston, where a few days were pleasantly spent. March 10th we went on to Providence, and on the 12th gave a concert. While here we visited Governor Dorr, in prison for rebellion. He was painting fans. Another concert was given in Providence on the 14th to a crowded house, though it was stormy. After a concert in Pawtucket, we went to New York, arriving March 17th. Here we had a triumphant, though rather stormy experience. The *Express* warned us we should lose our popularity if we sang such songs as "Get Off the Track," and our friends advised us not to sing it. New York, as well as the rest of the country, was very tender on the subject of slavery at this time. The blows of the Abolitionists were beginning to tell. But a warning in those days came to us in the similitude of a command. As long as nothing was said, we could take our choice; but if we were told we must not sing a song that expressed our convictions, we then felt that, come victory or defeat, we must cry aloud and spare not, and the song was sung, with a serene sense that God would help us to do our duty. Well, our first concert came off in Niblo's, on the 19th. We gave a second on the 24th, and two days later sang in Palmer's Opera House. When we sang "Get Off the Track," the audience hissed; then some began to cheer, and there was a tug of war; finally the cheers prevailed. Our friend Henry Dennison was in the audience, and threw a request for a song, attached to a copper cent. It hit my violin, and as many thought it a stone, a good deal of unnecessary indignation was shown. We went into the ante-room, and waited during the uproar until we feared that it would be said that we were hissed off the stage. Then we went back. The hissing continued, and also the cheers; but finally the cheers triumphed, and we were able to sing our next song, "My Mother's Bible." Henry John Sharp, an English reformer, was present, and was very indignant at the treatment we received. This noble man, who wrote many songs for us, was a frequent attendant at our concerts, and always would bring a fine bouquet for Abby.

Several more concerts were given in New York and Brooklyn. Instead of references to applause, I find such entries as, "Not much hissing," in my diaries. April 4th we gave our last concert, at Niblo's, and five hundred were turned away for lack of room, which showed to what extent the prophecy of the *Express* that we should lose our popularity had proven true. During this stay in the metropolis, we saw a good deal of our valued friends George P. Morris and Mrs. Lydia Maria Child.

April 7th we sang in Philadelphia, and on the 9th sang again in Musical Fund Hall, to as many people as could get in. We stopped again in New York on our return, and during this stay visited Sing Sing, and sang to the convicts. When we sang "My Mother's Bible" to the female convicts, every one was in tears. After concerts in the city and Brooklyn, our *finale* was given in the Broadway Tabernacle. Returning, I went to Lowell, where my wife was waiting me, stayed over a Sunday, and then went to Boston, where two concerts were given.

May 5th we were all in Milford once more, and most of the time for a few months was devoted to the pleasant duties of a farmer's life. Asa and Abby put in a few months' schooling in the academy in Hancock. Judson and I worked on the land, made soap, butter, pickles; we fished and hunted, put in our quota of time on the highways, and altogether had a happy time

On June 4th we attended an anti-slavery convention in the old town-hall in Concord. It was a stormy time. Pillsbury, Foster, Phillips, Douglass and others debated, until words waxed so hot that Garrison, who took no part, left the hall. The main trouble was over the *Herald of Freedom*. The paper was edited by N. P. Rogers, and his son-in-law, John R. French, who, after the war, was sergeant-at-arms of the United States Senate, was its business manager. All the New England Abolitionists were interested in the paper, and it was our frequent habit to send contributions of money to aid it. Mr. Rogers, who had an expensive family, had left a lucrative law practice to take up the anti-slavery agitation. At this meeting an accounting was asked. The first causes of the trouble were Foster and Pillsbury, who expressed a feeling that they had beaten the bush for the paper in their meetings, but that Rogers had caught the bird. Another cause of trouble was Mr. Rogers' ideas as to meetings. He had invented a sort of free meeting, with no chairman, where each said what he had to say as he found opportunity. This did not meet the views of Mr. Garrison, who was disposed to insist that everything in the anti-slavery line should be carried on strictly in the Garrisonian way, decently and in order. They also disagreed on the subject of an independent party organization. The upshot of it all was that the convention displaced Rogers and put Pillsbury in his place. The people of New Hampshire were very much attached to Rogers, and rather indignant at this proceeding. Consequently, when he started another paper in Concord, it at once gained a large circulation, while the *Herald of Freedom* languished. But Mr. Rogers' spirit was broken and he never recovered from what he felt to be an injustice and desertion by his friends. His health gave way and he survived but a few years after. We held aloof from participation in all this trouble. Our friends were arrayed on either side, and we said nothing. When the debate waxed too warm for comfort, we would put in a song, which seemed to smooth things over somewhat

During this spring Jesse purchased High Rock in Lynn, and this in after years became the home of several of the Hutchinsons.

Meanwhile, we were thinking of Europe. It had been Jesse's idea to have the whole family go into concerting, but the death of Benjamin changed that plan Early in August we had a pleasant tour through New Hampshire towns and then went to Lynn, intending to have a few weeks of rest by the seashore. But our plans were suddenly altered, as the next chapter will show.

CHAPTER IV.

IN ENGLAND.

"Old John was frank, and every rank
  Gave us the welcome hand,
And her noble men did now and then
  Make us love our fatherland.
The women, too, were kind and true,
  And we scarcely found a foe
In the days we went to England, boys,
  Long time ago

"We saw the great in Church and State,
  In all their pomp and pride,
The little queen who reigns supreme,
  Her lords and dukes beside
But dazzling sights brought no delight
  When the poor were crushed so low,
In the days we passed through England, boys,
  Long time ago"

DURING the spring and summer of 1845, we had been singing through the towns of New Hampshire, and were in hopes of having a vacation, and to pass it in fishing and rustic enjoyments. We were, in the early part of August, giving some concerts in Massachusetts; and in Lynn on the 11th, we met Frederick Douglass and James N. Buffum, an anti-slavery sympathizer of that town, who, having purchased their tickets, and made arrangements for a trip to Europe, were expecting to sail on the 16th on the steamship *Cambria* of the Cunard line. They urged us to go with them, and as we had been contemplating a tour of England for some time, it did not take much persuasion to induce us to go: we straightway began to make preparations for our departure.

HUTCHINSON FAMILY QUARTET, 1846 (p. 142)

We returned to our home in New Hampshire to take leave of our dear ones, which we did not find a very easy matter. They all said "Don't go, don't go"; and when mother found we were bound to go and take Abby with us, she was almost heart-broken, for a journey to England in those days was looked upon as being attended with more danger than at present, and they were all afraid they would never see us again. But they being finally reconciled, we set to work in earnest, as time was short. We had to raise about two thousand dollars, which we finally succeeded in doing, and we were ready to start. As we had to give a concert in Gloucester on the evening of the 14th, we left home early on the morning of that day for Lynn, where we took a carriage to meet our engagement, accompanied by our sister Rhoda and Harriet Jackson, daughter of our anti-slavery friend, Francis Jackson. I had not slept any the night before, being kept awake by the entreaties of my wife to stay at home, and was up before daylight. Mother was up, and all our brothers came to say good-by. The time to depart had arrived; and I had given my watch and some tokens to my wife to keep in remembrance of me, as though I never expected to see her again. The dear old father, whom we all revered and honored, was solemn and very prayerful, saying but a word, "Be true to each other, my children." Then the blessed mother let us go, with tears in her eyes, watching us till the darkness of the early morn hid us from her sight; but her voice still sounded over the hill as the last echo died on our ears. I shall never forget the ring of that voice as the old horse drew us from the "cot where we were born."

That day, so mother related to us afterward, she climbed to the summit of the steep hill in sight of the house, seven miles away, and sat under an old chestnut-tree, a journey she had longed to accomplish, and wept when she thought of her children gone so far away. Meanwhile, we prayed for our precious ones gathered in the home by the old Souhegan, among the granite hills, and stole away in the morning twilight, our hearts sad and oppressed. The next day came the final preparations in Boston: buying the tickets, getting the baggage on board, and taking leave of the many friends who had gathered to see us off; the getting on board the small tug-boat, as the steamer could not get up to the wharf; the parting of the two sisters, Rhoda and Abby, the former a widow, left behind to go back to the Granite State and comfort the old folks at home till we might return. These things all touched our hearts. The attempt to sing under these circumstances seemed almost sacrilegious, but as Jesse had composed some verses for the occasion, we attempted to put them into music. The first verse was gone through quite respectably. As the bell rang and the friends were about getting on the tug to return to the shore, the second verse was begun, when catching sight of Sister Rhoda, whose earnestness bespoke the deep sympathy of a feeling heart, we broke down, and gave only a last farewell as the old ship carried us away over the bounding deep.

When we became accustomed to our confined quarters, the motion of the steamer and the surroundings, we began to feel quite at home. We early formed the acquaintance of Captain Judkins, whom we found to be a bluff old sterling Englishman, full of music and good cheer. We passed much of our time in his society on deck, and many a night we sat and sang together and told stories till midnight.

We of course suffered from sea-sickness a part of the

time, and were confined to our staterooms, but soon got regulated so that we could enjoy the bountiful table which was spread for us.

Life was quite monotonous; but between eating, sleeping, reading and singing, we managed to pass the time very pleasantly, often gathering on deck with some of our English and American friends, who seemed very glad to linger with us to enjoy our harmonies. We saw some big waves, some big icebergs, and some big fish, while on board we had some big slave-holders from Cuba, who somewhat marred the pleasure of the voyage. One of them, at the table one day, accidentally spilled some wine on the dress of my sister; his profuse and distressing apologies, coming from such besotted lips, were much worse than the wine stains on the silk skirt.

Frederick Douglass, for the crime of color, was forced to take passage in the steerage, where Mr. Buffum accompanied him. It was only by sufferance that Douglass was allowed to come on the promenade deck, and then had no freedom except when with a friend. We frequently invited him to walk with us, when he freely expressed to us his feelings and sentiments on the subject of slavery, and among other things said he would rather trust his liberties with the English government than with the American rabble.

The curious of both nationalities were interested in him, and after reading his little "Narrative," which we took pains to circulate among the passengers, the desire to hear him speak was expressed. We obtained permission from the captain to give him an audience on the forward deck. Most of the foreigners and some of the Americans were assembled; and our colored brother began at first standing under the awning, but I persuaded him to come into the open, by the main-mast, where he read from a pamphlet containing the statutes of South Carolina on the subject of slavery. We soon saw that the reading was not relished by some of the auditors, as the sequel proved. The cluster of slave-holders and slave-drivers were preparing to resent what they claimed was an insult to them. They soon so disturbed the speaker that he was forced to suspend, and with a sentence half-finished, he retreated under the awning and thence down the stairs to the steerage, his only hiding place, where he was sheltered from the wrath of those blood-thirsty Americans whose "chivalry" was so much shocked. Then followed threats of killing, and throwing the "nigger" overboard, and for a few minutes anarchy ruled and the war spirit was rampant.

The captain was sent for; he came suddenly from his quarters, where he had been enjoying a siesta after a luxurious banquet tendered him by his friends. He took in the situation at a glance, and when one of the fire-eaters approached him, threatening insult because he had allowed a "nigger" to speak, the old British lion awoke in him, and asserting his authority as captain, he shouted lustily for the bos'n to bring the irons. This at once quelled the disturbance, and quiet was restored.

The captain then turning to us, said, "I was once the owner of two hundred slaves, but the government of Great Britain liberated them, and I am glad of it." We struck up "God save the Queen," and followed by singing "Yankee Doodle," "America" and "A Life on the Ocean Wave."

We made some very pleasant acquaintances on the voyage, but were more strongly than ever prejudiced against the institution of slavery from this exhibition made on board ship by the scions of southern aristocracy, as also by the supercilious airs they put on.

Everything was done for our comfort while on board, and we were almost sorry when land was announced, though we were anxious to reach the shores of Old England and ascertain what fate had in store for us.

On August 26th, the captain informed us we could see land that evening, which caused a small commotion on board, each one being anxious to be the first to discern it. At about 10.30 P. M. we saw the first light, which we were told was at the southern extremity of Ireland; and the next morning before breakfast we hailed the land with delight. It was the Emerald Isle: the mountains loomed up in their grandeur; and dotted here and there with their fields of grain, white unto harvest, the land presented a very picturesque and interesting appearance. Our hearts bounded with rapture:

"The cold cheerless ocean in safety we've passed,
And the warm genial earth glads our vision at last"

One man hailing from Philadelphia exclaimed as he came on deck, "Oh, the dear spot where I was born!"

Soon we were in sight of Wales. We had just finished our dinner, toasts had been given to the Queen and the Army of England, and to the United States. Jesse gave the following toast, "Our country is the world, our countrymen all mankind," which was received with warm applause.

The next morning broke bright and clear, and we were up early making preparations to go ashore. Books were laid aside, and we were engaged packing trunks, putting off our sea-scented clothing and Scotch caps, and donning our long coats, broad collars and beaver hats, assuming the airs of strangers, we, who but a few hours before were intimate friends or hail-fellows well met with everybody on board. We ranged ourselves on the deck in position to give a lusty cheer to the people of Liverpool as the steamer drew alongside of the wharf. Here we were in a foreign land three thousand miles from our own native home — though in the land of our forefathers — in smoky old Liverpool.

We disembarked, and getting our baggage through the custom-house with some trouble, even being required to pay a duty on a daguerreotype of our family group, were conducted to a hotel, and in company with Edward N. Wright, one of our own countrymen, and Edmund Sharpe, a clever Englishman, were soon seated at the sumptuous table of a foreign hotel.

How odd and singular everything appeared! The meat looked delicious, tasted some like pork, cut like beef. We ventured to ask the name of it, when our English friend answered with a smile, "This is the famous Southdown mutton." We often called for that dish during our eleven months' stay in England, readily perceiving why the English bragged, and still brag, about it. Judson called for some molasses, being very fond of this sweet; the servant seemed disturbed, not understanding the order, took a few steps backward, then tried to comprehend what the gentleman wanted. The request was repeated, at which the girl was completely non-plussed. Our friend Sharpe, being familiar with the language on both sides, informed the girl that "treacle" was wanted, whereupon she jumped for the article and Judson's wants were at once supplied.

We were settled for the time in very comfortable quarters, Douglass and Buffum being with us, and spent the time in looking about and observing the manners and customs of the people, which seemed strange to us. When we left the steamer and walked up the street we were struck with the order and decorum of the working-classes as they passed along to their daily toil. As it was early in the morning they were just going to their work, lunch in hand — the tin-pail parade — dressed according to their different occupations, apparently cheerful and happy. But everywhere poverty, in the form of human beings, came under our notice to mar our pleasure.

"Begging, begging, England's squalid poor,
　For scores of hungry beggars met at almost every door"

Our hearts grew sick to see the suffering and distress there was in the city.

The next day after our arrival, being the 29th of August, and the birthday of our sister Abby, we all took a trip into the country to see the estate of a famous marquis, to reach which we had to go to Eaton Hall, a distance of nineteen miles from the city, and to cross the River Dee, the bridge or arch over which was the greatest in the world at that time. This estate was one of the largest in England, covering an area of sixty-three square miles, and the income from it was said to be two million dollars. Passing through the walled town of Chester on our way, we were shown some very ancient buildings, among them a chapel which was said to be six hundred years old, in a good state of preservation and still used regularly as a place of worship.

On this estate, we were informed, there were two hundred men kept constantly employed. We soon came in sight of the mansion, a most splendid structure of white marble. After waiting about half an hour, we were admitted and conducted through the principal rooms. The hall through the centre of the house was very wide and four hundred and seventy-two feet long, the floor laid in marble. The rooms, besides containing family portraits, were hung with the most gorgeous and expensive silk and worsted fabrics. Everything was on a magnificent scale, and displayed not only the wealth but the taste of the occupants. After we had inspected the interior of the house we went into the garden, where the same evidences of wealth and taste were shown: flowers, trees, shrubs and plants in profusion. On our return to town we passed fields of grain which were all loaded with a bountiful harvest; the land seemed to be good and under a high state of cultivation. It was just harvest time, and thousands of people, men, women and children, were out from the cities, some of them hundreds of miles, working in the fields.

At this time rumors of war with America were very common; but they gave us little uneasiness, as we told our English friends that Uncle Sam had whipped John Bull twice, and could do it again if necessary. But next to our own native land our hearts went out in love to this merry Old England.

We found the season was early for concerting, and in addition to this, began to fear we had brought our coals to Newcastle, for many of the singers in the street had fine voices, yet made only a precarious living. We began in earnest to seek an engagement to sing, realizing that we must soon begin to replenish our treasury. Board bills were coming in, expenses going on. New clothes, cut in the fashion of our English cousins, were thought indispensable; so we doffed our long tails for the "stubs" of John Bull. We had already spent a good deal of money, and knew that unless some resource was soon provided we should be "broke." We tried to find some one who knew us or had confidence enough to make an engagement with us for a concert. Nobody came to the rescue.

A few friends came to see us at the hotel; we sang for them to gain their approval; they all cheered us, shook hands and expressed a wish that we might succeed, but left us alone in our glory. We soon realized that popularity in our own country gave us little fame here, and that we must begin over again and sing our way into public favor and thus overcome the prejudice we found existing against Yankee talent. Some people seem to delight at times in doing what they know will make them miserable; that is the only reason I can now give for our often repairing to the pier, at that time, to witness the arrival and departure of the steamers from and to our own land, and we would turn away from the scene and sigh that our mission was still unaccomplished.

Edwin Forrest was in Liverpool at this time, called upon us several times with his wife, and encouraged us much by his words of cheer.

We finally succeeded in getting an engagement for the evening of Wednesday, September 10th, in Concert Hall, Mechanics Institute, for which we were to receive ten pounds. We had two days in which to look around and prepare for our first appearance before an English audience. The Disston family was giving concerts in Liverpool at this time, and being attracted by the novelty of their instruments (sax horns), we went to hear them and decided it was the sweetest music we had ever heard. The family consisted of the father and four sons: we advised their coming to this country, and I think they met success by taking the advice.

Dining at our hotel, the boarders, men and women,

all drank a sort of ale or beer or some kind of wine: glasses were put at our plates, some of the liquor poured into them; but we being teetotallars, the color of the liquid aroused our suspicions, and not being certain what it was, we declined to partake, fearing we should find the "old critter" in it and break our pledge. Not wishing to expose our ignorance, we decided to take some of it to our rooms and find out what it was; this we did, and all together, found the stuff tinctured with the "Fiendish Reaper." Then we realized that we had broken our pledge, and resolved to sign over again, and relinquish all drinks of this description during our stay in the kingdom.

Later, while in Dublin, under the hospitable roof of Richard Haughton, we all signed the pledge. The article of agreement, I am informed, hangs to-day in the parlor of that honorable gentleman; and his daughter, surviving him, thirty-one years later pointed with pride to this pledge. Abby, who saw this only a few years ago, wrote, "The precious signatures are in as good a state of preservation as when made, with the signers now, some in the spirit world, others surviving, all the living true to the pledge."

Messrs. Isaacson and Atkinson were the proprietors of the Zoölogical Gardens, and being asked by them to go out there and sing a few songs, we walked out, a distance of about two miles. Of all the sights I had seen up to that time, this was the grandest: beasts of all kinds, from the monkey to the elephant; birds from all parts of the world; and flowers of the most brilliant hue. The gardens, about ten acres, were laid out in a most artistic manner. We sang a few songs, hoping to get an engagement at no distant day.

As the time drew near for our *début* before an English

audience, we all felt nervous and excited. We found that our voices had not improved by crossing the Atlantic. We went to the hall to familiarize ourselves with the surroundings, and were on the anxious seat all day. The hour having finally arrived we went to the hall. With trembling step and throbbing brow we entered our dressing-room; met Jesse, who seemed very much excited, and asked him what kind of a house, "Oh, not very full." He had expected a full house.

Our hearts beat fast as we went in before the audience. Thunders of spontaneous applause burst forth from every part of the hall. Every eye was fixed on us as we took our seats and laid down our instruments. When we stood up with trembling limbs and voices we were received with another round of applause. When this subsided, we commenced the song, "The Pirate's Glee, or Blow on." When we had finished the cheering was renewed; our confidence was restored, and we went through our programme, being cheered on every number. We were relieved, feeling that our reputation was made; and though fifty dollars was a small sum for our effort, considering that we had sacrificed engagements in New York, Philadelphia and other cities in America which would pay us one thousand dollars a night, we were well satisfied, and encouraged to believe that we should soon have the people with us, and be able to reap the reward for which we came, appreciation, fame and cash, the latter of which we needed very much. There were quite a number of Americans present, among whom were the Forrests.

We felt that now we had broken the ice: our first concert had been given, and as we thought very acceptably, so we should have no trouble in getting further engagements. But the first thing to do was to have one of our number act as agent for the family. As Jesse had already acted in that capacity at home, and his voice could not be much addition to the quartette, the duty was put upon him, and he continued to serve as our business agent during our stay abroad. As a result we were engaged nearly every evening, either on our own responsibility or on special terms.

After giving one or two more concerts in Liverpool we began to receive letters from all directions soliciting engagements.

On the ship coming over was a Scotchman by the name of Mackintosh, who made us promise to come over to Dublin, and receiving letters from Douglass, who was there, we at last decided to go, and wrote that we would be over very soon.

About this time Jesse came near getting us into a scrape by bringing into question our musical abilities and judgment as critics. An aspiring individual applied to a committee for a professional engagement, referring to us as to his musical abilities. Jesse was approached, and having heard the man sing, he inadvertently said the man was a clever fellow, which was enough and he was engaged. His performance on the first occasion was so displeasing that the audience left the hall in disgust, so we heard, before the programme was completed, and he was left to sing to empty seats. We were taken to task for recommending such a fellow, but when it was understood that what we meant by "clever" was simply that he was a good-natured fellow, possessing an agreeable disposition, instead of possessing skill or talent, as they construed it to mean, they had a good laugh over it, and we were exonerated from blame.

We watched the manners of men and of the times with wonder and surprise, trying to realize the conditions we saw in society. Such extremes of wealth and poverty we could not reconcile.

One day as we gazed from the hotel window there came into the public square a woman, poorly clad, with a basket on her head. She was gathering with her hands the offal from the streets, and as she continued to fill the basket the rain, which was falling, saturated the contents and ran down upon her person. When she had filled the basket she trudged away with it, a sight to behold. We thought, what a contrast to the wealth we see all about us, and felt inclined to murmur against Providence for allowing such a wretched state of society. Good sweet-voiced singers came and sang their doleful, sympathetic strains under our windows, and we would remark, "What a pity such gifts could not be better appreciated and utilized!" To us it was soul music, and our enjoyment in listening was only marred at the thought of the condition of the singers, and we would sing a verse of our song,

> "New England, thou land of the brave and the free,
> Our country and home, we are looking toward thee,
> And we long for the day when again we shall stand
> On thy rude sandy soil, but our own native land."

The very next night we were listening to delightful music rendered by no less personages than Grisi, Mario, Miss Whitnall and Signor Lablashe, who were singing in concert, and their voices charmed all who listened. But, strange to say, they were singing in the magnificent opera house for the small price of one and two shillings, and sixpence for the poor, and a small house they had, too. Of course we could not expect to approach the character of music they sang. Novelty and harmony were all we could count on for success, but we thought we could give just as acceptable a concert as they.

After being in Liverpool about two weeks and giving concerts to crowded houses, we started for Dublin to keep our engagements there. In crossing the Channel, which we did on Sunday, September 21st, on the steamer *Madrid*, we were more than sick; it was ten times worse than the Atlantic. But we finally found ourselves on the sod of the Emerald Isle, and met a reception which only the sons of Erin could give. We found, awaiting us at the landing, Mr. Buffum and a Mr. Thomas Webb, who escorted us to Dublin, a distance of seven miles; we took rooms at the Hotel Northumberland, and were invited to spend our first evening at Mr. Webb's house, where we found Frederick Douglass and Mr. Haughton, with whom we became very well acquainted, and at whose house we spent very many pleasant hours during our stay in Dublin.

Just before leaving Liverpool we were called upon by a warm-hearted, burly Englishman named Scott, who, when he saw we were disposed to be down-hearted and home-sick, said in his broad accent, "Cheer up, my Yankee lads, in spite of British fashion you will succeed if you continue in the path you have struck out." We had already begun to have some misgivings as to our success; though we had been well received so far, we had not been able to obtain engagements at prices which we thought we ought to be getting, and were afraid the people were too far advanced for Yankees like us.

Our first concert in Dublin was given under engagement with Mr. Mackintosh for ten pounds, and on the evening of Monday, September 22d, we repaired to the hall. As we entered all was still, not a person but an officer and the doorkeeper were at the door; all looked gloomy. I looked into the hall, and there sat one solitary Irish woman in the pit. We went into our dress-

THE HUTCHINSON FAMILY.

AN ENGLISH SOUVENIR.—(p. 156.)

ing-room, a little narrow place with a small fire in it, a single gas-light, and that just on the point of going out, apparently. There we all sat down to wait till we should hear the signal for beginning the concert. I don't know what thoughts passed through the minds of the others, as not a word was spoken; but it was just as well that quiet was maintained if they all felt as I did. I had just been reading the life of Napoleon, and had a presentiment that we were near the city of Moscow — disappointed ambition. The avalanche of public opinion seemed about to fall upon and crush us. I wanted to go home to the granite hills of our native land, and hummed to myself the lines:

> "Ah! why from our own native land did we part,
> With its mountains and valleys so dear to each heart?
> Ah! why did we leave the enjoyments of home
> O'er the wide waste of waters as strangers to roam?"

When the band, for one had been provided consisting of about twenty pieces, struck up an air, every strain seemed to strike daggers to my heart; and as soon as it was ended we entered the hall and took our places on the platform. There were but few people there to receive us, and most of them were invited guests — among others Messrs. Haughton, Webb and Douglass. One old man sat away down in front near the platform, and in his expressions of enthusiasm he almost disconcerted us; he would pound on the floor and the edge of the platform with his cane, and shout "Encore!" "Bravo!" as loud as he could shout. We made up our minds to go home after this concert. The steamer *Hibernia* was to sail on the 4th of October, and we thought that none too soon for us to get out of the country.

Frederick Douglass was at this time endeavoring to

arouse an interest in the abolition cause, speaking every night, and selling the books which we had helped him circulate on the vessel coming over. We attended some of his lectures, and singing to the audience were cheered most vociferously. The Lord Mayor was present and presided at one of the meetings. We concluded to join forces with Douglass, and for two or three evenings we had grand good meetings and made hosts of friends, who advised us not to go home; so we decided to stay a little longer.

We called at the house of Daniel O'Connell, who was then in his prime; not finding him at home we felt honored in being allowed to sit for a few minutes in his big armchair.

We now decided to give another concert on our own responsibility, and had the assurance of the attendance of the Lord Mayor and O'Connell.

About this time we went into a field, where we saw some women digging potatoes, as this was a part of their duty, and noticed that about one-half of the crop was bad, good for nothing, which proved to be the case all over the country, and was the cause of the famine the following year.

We went to the summit of the Dockey Hill, a distance of about eight miles from the city, where we had a splendid view of the Sugarloaf Mountains and of the sea. We were followed all the way up by a troop of beggars whom it was almost impossible to rid ourselves of. The eminence reminded us very much of High Rock, on the beauties of which Jesse expatiated to the friends who were with us.

On the way back to town our attention was attracted by a crowd of children surrounding and following a man in the street, and on asking who he was were told he was Daniel O'Connell. We turned and followed, then passed him, and seeing him smile and say a word to the children, we felt that he was indeed a great man. The next day we had the pleasure of seeing and hearing him speak in Constitution Hall on "Repeal." He touched on American slavery; and one sentiment he uttered was, "He that commuteth crime gives strength to the enemy." I thought I had been in packed assemblies before, but I never saw anything to equal the crowd on that occasion. I had to get out before the close of his speech, or suffocate.

We gave our next concert, and had a better house than before; were cheered tremendously, and felt comparatively happy. Mackintosh, who had rather forsaken us since the failure of our first effort, was now ready to make amends and give us more engagements.

We went out to Kingston one day, where we had the pleasure of seeing, and shaking hands with that friend of humanity and advocate of temperance, Father Mathew; we heard him talk and administer the pledge to a number of people. He was then in his prime, a strong, well-built man.

Henry Russell was in Dublin at this time giving concerts; was having fine houses and giving great satisfaction. We saw a good deal of him, sang and consulted with him. He discouraged us very much by saying he did not think we should be able to make any money in that country, at the same time trying to engage us to sing for him. On one occasion we were at his concert and agreed to sing on the chorus of one of his songs. We were behind a screen, out of sight of the audience, and when we struck into the chorus of the "Boatmen of the Ohio," it seemed as if the house would come down. He rushed in to us, and telling us to sing louder, it was repeated.

Then we were invited upon the stage, and sang "The Old Granite State." This so captivated the audience that Russell thought it advisable not to make his appearance in the one or two numbers that remained on the programme, and the concert closed with the selections we sang in response to enthusiastic encores. Russell then offered us one thousand dollars to make the tour of England under his auspices! We declined to accept his offer.

In one of our walks about the city we came to the poor-house. We passed through all the different departments, and were surprised when told that there were fifteen hundred inmates. We afterwards visited the prison in which O'Connell was incarcerated for one hundred days.

We were still in Dublin, undecided what to do. Some said, "Go home." Jesse said we could go to New York for fifty dollars. This was the third time we partly decided to go. Judson related a vision he had when he was fourteen years old, that he was to die at the age of twenty-eight; and as this was the year, he was very despondent. I told of a dream that I had the night before, to the effect that I was going to be drowned on my way home from England; and when Abby told us that she had just dreamed that we were all drowned on our way home, we concluded there must be something in it, and that we had better "bide a wee."

On the evening of October 14th we left Dublin for Manchester, going *via* Liverpool. In crossing the Channel the boat was crowded with hogs, cattle and horses, with which the Irishmen were to "pay their rent"; between the noise of which and the roughness of the water we got very little rest. Arriving in Liverpool in the morning, Judson and Asa went directly on to Manchester to engage lodgings, the rest of us stopping in Liverpool to see our friends and get the mail. In the afternoon we followed, and joined in the hunt for lodgings, which they had not yet been able to find.

We were soon settled in comfortable quarters, and began to feel more at home than at any time since we had been in the country. There seemed to be a different atmosphere surrounding us. Though the town was very smoky and dirty, we were in good spirits. Judson had just heard from home that the letters he had sent had been published, and just having come from Ireland, said he was willing to stay in England till he went home

We soon began to find friends. A Mr. Peacock, to whom we had a letter of introduction, did everything in his power to interest us, introduced us to a great many free-traders and friends of freedom, among them Mr. Robert Moore, husband of Rebecca Moore, who became a life-long friend of the Hutchinsons.

We stopped in the Bazaar, where an exhibition was in progress, to see the sights and get a view of a live duke from India. He came in, accompanied by his grotesque and brilliant suite and interpreter, when every eye was fixed on the lion of the hour. He passed through the room and took a seat in the orchestra with the music. We were invited to sing a song, and coming to the platform, we sang "Come on"; being encored, we sang "Over the Mountain," when we were loudly cheered Thinking we had already been highly complimented we descended and were introduced to the duke, who expressed himself as much gratified with our singing.

Having concluded to change our boarding-place after being in it three days, we notified our landlady early on

Sunday morning that we wanted our bill, as we were going to leave. She handed the bill to us, and on finding it made out for five pounds, a full week's bill, told her we would not pay it. At the same time we had our trunks all packed ready to leave. She got mad and very much excited, said we ate so much more than Englishmen that our board was worth more, and she would make no reduction. We then told her we would stay the week out, and forthwith ordered breakfast. It was produced in due time, and we so astonished the good woman with our voraciousness that she was glad to let us go at half-price.

Mrs. Rebecca Moore, at whose house Abby had been staying for a day or two, we found to be a highly intellectual, refined, sensible, loving woman, and the more we saw of her the more she grew into our affections; the many happy hours we spent in her society, in her house and at our own boarding-house, can never be forgotten, but will always be cherished by me as the pleasantest of my life. She still lives, and I often now receive tokens of friendship from her.

We found our new boarding-house a very pleasant place, and that it was where Edwin Forrest, the Disston Family, and other public characters stopped when in the city.

Mr. Bennett, a corn dealer, to whom we had a letter of introduction, was very polite and kind to us. He invited us to dine at his house. We found him living in fine style just out of the city, and we were beautifully entertained, and treated with marked attention and hospitality. After an early dinner he and some other friends whom we met at his house accompanied us back to the city. As we returned in the early evening the factories, of which the town was full, were all lighted up. The lights shining out brightly made a very brilliant effect.

We remained in Manchester only about a week at this time, making no engagements to sing, meeting some old American friends and making many new ones; then returned to Dublin, where we had to give some concerts.

The passage over this time was not so disagreeable as our former ones had been, as we were in a first-class boat, and the water was comparatively smooth. Among the many new acquaintances we made was a family of Quakers named Wells; they were very fond of music, and what was remarkable with that sect, they were very demonstrative in their manifestations of approval.

After remaining in Dublin for two weeks, giving concerts in the city and some of the surrounding towns, we began to make arrangements to go back to England. Not expecting to return to Dublin, we began to take final leave of our friends, and we thought they were as sorry to have us go as we were to leave them. They had all treated us handsomely, and on leaving gave us many tokens of their regard.

We spent our last evening at the house of Richard Webb, a party being given in our honor. During the evening Mr. Webb brought in a periodical which he had just procured, containing the "Bridge of Sighs," by Tom Hood, published then for the first time.

> "Take her up tenderly,
> Lift her with care;
> Fashioned so slenderly,
> Young and so fair!"

After reading it over, we took it into his library, and putting our heads together, we put the poem up in plain sight of each of us, began to adjust our different parts to the lines, and in a short time came out and sang it to the company: after making some slight changes in the music, it became one of the selections on our programme, and we sang it on almost every occasion.

We crossed the Channel again, this time from Kingston, on the steamer *Iron Duke*, and had a very rough voyage. On the morning of November 7th we arrived in Liverpool, and on the following evening gave a concert to sixteen hundred people, who greeted us with long-continued applause.

Mr. Buffum rejoined us here, having come on from Birmingham, and gave us quite a shock when he said he had had a falling out with Douglass, and could not stay with him any longer. He proposed to stay with us for a few days and wait for Dr. Kittredge, who was on the way over from America, when they were going together to France. We were very glad to have him with us, as he was full of fun, always in good spirits and cheered us up while we were in his presence.

On the 18th, Dr. Kittredge, of Lynn, or "Noggs," the *nom de plume* under which he wrote, arrived, and the next morning left for France with Buffum. It was very hard to part with these true hearts. "Noggs" had a claim of the first class on my affections. My diary says:

"God bless every hair of his head, every inch of it is wit and good-humor; and were it to grow twice the length it now is, 'twould still be on the head of Noggs ' continually ' [The last was his great by-word]

"Farewell, you Yankee, true and witty,
We'll meet again and sing this ditty.

"I shall never forget the time when first we met in England, in this old smoky Liverpool"

We were engaged now nearly every evening, either in Liverpool or some of the suburbs, and were quite happy and contented.

We went one evening to hear that good, faithful friend of humanity and equal rights, George Thompson, M. P., speak on the India question. I knew him the moment he entered the door, from descriptions I had received of him, and was prepared for the treat he gave us. His lecture was a fine one, full of poetry and feeling; his address was pleasant and impressive, his eloquence grand and powerful, and he had a magnetism that carried his audience with him.

We were introduced to him after the lecture, when he received us very cordially, and invited us to breakfast the next morning, where the conversation turned on the controversy then going on between Garrison and Rogers, which we all deplored.

This was the beginning of an acquaintance which was kept up between us to the day of his death; and we always found him the same kind, genial friend and formidable defender of any cause he espoused He called upon us the same afternoon in company with Miss E. Pease, to bid us adieu, as we were about starting for Manchester, and said that he would meet us there the next day.

On the way to the station Asa and Abby went on ahead, walking at quite a rapid pace, and as it was quite dark they did not pay much attention to anything except to keep on the sidewalk. All of a sudden he went down, dragging her after him. When I came up I found they had fallen into a coal-hole which had just been opened. As they scrambled out they looked somewhat the worse for wear, not much hurt, but very much astonished We had only time to caution the careless coal-heaver never to do such a thing again as to leave the hole open without some protection.

The road was very rough, and the cars were so tossed

about that we found it almost impossible to get any rest; and to add to my discomfort there was a man sitting next to me who seemed quite fatigued and likewise desirous of getting some rest; just as I would get into a doze he would jog his lymphatic corporosity up against me, seeming to say at every lurch or nod, "Keep awake, or you'll take cold," which would have been good advice to follow, as some of the passengers had their windows open, and I did take quite a severe cold. We took a second-class coach, not that we despised the lowest, or abjured with homage the upper, but it was congenial to our ideas. "Give me neither poverty nor riches."

The next morning George Thompson called on us and suggested that we should sing a song or two at his lecture in the evening; and we consented. A short time after Jesse came in and said, "Boys, did you know you were announced to sing to-night?" To our surprise posters had been put out announcing us to appear in company with George Thompson. When evening came we entered the hall with him; and previous to commencing his lecture, he introduced us to the audience in a very neat, complimentary manner, and we sang a song. Being encored, we sang another. At the close of his lecture, which was on the ancient history of India, we sang "The Old Granite State," and such a round of applause as we received did us good, and made us think of home. He afterwards gave us, together with Mrs. Moore, a very graphic account of his visit to India, the character, habits and customs of the people. It was like reading a novel, only much more interesting.

We heard Willson, the great Scotch singer, and admired him much in his description of the character of Burns, and singing of his songs.

On the way out to Chester, where we gave a concert, we had a fine view of Easton Castle, a huge mass of rocks, perched up on a steep hill, looking like an iceberg, as viewed against the background of a clear sky.

From my diary:

"November 27th This is Thanksgiving Day in our far-away New England home. We think of the father and mother and all the brothers gathered around the hearth to celebrate the day in prayers and hymns of praise, and wish ourselves there with them As I look out and see the new moon just settling behind the hills, my memory reverts to the scenes of my youth I think of the many happy hours of my earlier life, when I knew not what care or remorse was; of my school days, when I was filled with buoyant hopes of the time when I should be a man in active life The bright side seems always to present itself in anticipating future events The present never satisfies me Little did I think, when trudging through the snow to the old district school-house, with my book in one hand and a piece of 'Johnny-cake' in the other, singing as I went, and hurrahing for Jackson, who was then President of the United States, that I should ever visit Old England But time and fate have brought it about, and here I am, a lonely, self-exiled, ignorant man, left to deal with the future What is past I know; what is before I cannot tell; the present I have learned to improve and enjoy. I might say I regret the neglect of my books; that would only be folly I will make the best of what I have, and improve all I can. I am happy of life, and hope for a future that will satisfy the mind Many of my old friends and associates have gone home, with the memory of whose spirits I now hold sweet communion. Ere long this spirit will be separated from its tenement, and eternity begin its work of clothing it with celestial robes of immortality Now, a transient home, but soon an everlasting one; now with anxious fears, soon peace and joy without alloy

" The stars are shining now o'erhead,
This clear and frosty night;
So will they shine when we are dead,
As countless and as bright
Other poor souls from dust shall rise
By our good Saviour's aid,
When the last trump shall sound,
Sun, moon and stars shall fade."

Returning from Preston, where we had been singing, to Manchester, we were enveloped in smoke and fog so thick we could hardly see across the street; which reminded us of a man who had told us a few days before, that he had been waiting forty years for a pleasant day to leave the city.

Asa, Judson and Jesse went one day with a friend to see one of the large cotton mills, and came home tired, but delighted with the sight, and covered with evidences of where they had been, in shape of fine particles of cotton all over their clothing.

Being engaged every evening in giving concerts of our own, attending others, or being entertained by our numerous friends, time passed very pleasantly and swiftly with us. We visited all the churches, at some of which we heard fine singing; the colleges and fairs, where we saw many interesting curiosities. So much dissipation was beginning to tell on us, and we were pretty well used up; but kept up our spirits, as we were just beginning to feel repaid, in a financial way, for coming.

In Manchester was located the largest and best equipped machine-shop in the kingdom, which we visited one day on the invitation of the proprietors, Sharp Brothers & Co. We were shown all through it, and were very much interested in watching the nine hundred employees at their work. There was a mammoth clock in the establishment, the pendulum of which weighed 312 lbs., and all the work in the place seemed to be going by that clock, at least it was as regular as the swing of the pendulum; but we were weary before we got through, watching the ponderous engines and the great variety of machines.

The largest and most enthusiastic meeting we attended was at about this time in Free Trade Hall. It was an anti-corn-law meeting. The hall was crowded, not less than eight thousand men being present, besides hundreds on the outside who could not gain admittance. It was a splendid sight to see such earnest, attentive, upturned faces. Yes, they were the working classes, who had come together mutually to seek redress for grievances; they were seeking the repeal of the corn-laws, that cursed system of keeping food from the starving poor of the country. Thank God, the laws were about to be repealed. Willson was the chairman of the meeting; Gibson, Cobden, Bright, Fox and Brotherton were the speakers; Fox was the orator of the occasion, his language being true eloquence. The audience was very enthusiastic; it must have been inspiring to have such an intelligent mass of human beings to address.

Bolton was another of the large manufacturing towns which we visited. We were met on our arrival by the committee of working-men which had engaged us. We were conducted to our lodgings, which, though humble, were very neat and comfortable. We gave a concert to one of the largest and most appreciative audiences we ever had. Next morning the sun shone out bright and clear, which was a great relief, as it rarely shines in this country unless obscured by the fog or smoke — here we found pumpkins a curiosity and a fair day a novelty. The town was dirty, everything begrimed with soot, but it was a manufacturing town, and we could expect nothing else. We were awakened in the morning by the ringing of bells and blowing of whistles, and kept awake in the early hours by the clatter of the wooden shoes on the pavements as the men, women and children stamped along on their way to the mills. There were some very large, high chimneys at some of these factories, one of them being thirty-six feet in diameter at its base, and three hundred and sixty-six feet high, octagon in shape, and built, as we were informed, without visible staging, the material all being carried up and the work done from the inside. There were not many fine houses or buildings in the town, but a fine free-hearted set of people.

As we came into Manchester on our return we saw that we were billed to sing the same evening at the Colonial Institute with Professor Greenbank. We sang four songs; by request I sang "The Maniac." Then we returned early to our rooms, Judson not being at all well, and for three or four evenings our concerts had to be given up or postponed on account of his sickness. On one occasion we engaged the services of Miss Whitnall, but she did not fill the vacancy in our quartet, though she was a fine singer. An apology was made for us by the mayor of the city.

We received letters from home; and among other matters of news, we learned that our brothers, Zephaniah, Caleb and Joshua with our sister Rhoda, were giving concerts in America, styling themselves "The Home Branch," and trying to sustain the reputation of the family.

From this time (about the middle of December) up to leaving Manchester, January 24th, we were engaged almost every evening in giving concerts. We sang in Bolton, where the house was full when we arrived. The crowd standing in the aisles was so dense that we had hard work to squeeze through; and after we were through, the gap closed up like water resuming its place after being disturbed by some body thrown into it.

We sang in Halifax, another manufacturing town of about seventy thousand inhabitants, nestled among the hills which were covered with snow; these reminded us very much of our own native hills. The scenery all the way coming out from Manchester was grand, through a beautiful valley about six miles long, and on either side hills or mountains: in another place through six or eight arches of solid masonry, one of them two and three-quarters miles long.

We sang in Ashton, which had the finest hall we had yet been in, though it not being sufficiently heated we suffered very much with the cold. We gave a concert in Darwin, a town about nine miles off the railroad, to reach which we had to take a coach. The hotel here was a great mass of stone on the side of a hill, it looked like a prison, but we were well treated both in the house and at our concert

As Christmas approached, we could see preparations being made for its celebration everywhere. The rich and poor alike were providing their gifts, and mistletoe boughs were seen on every hand.

On Christmas Day news was received of the ill-fated steamer *President*, which was lost three years before. It was now said that she had been taken by pirates, but none of the passengers were ever heard from. We spent the evening at our friend Peacock's, where he entertained us reading portions of the "Cricket on the Hearth," which had only just been published

We had received a barrel of New Hampshire apples, as well as some chestnuts and hickory-nuts, right from the old farm, in time for Christmas, and they tasted good to us, and to our friends whom we "treated."

We gave concerts in St. Helens, Rochdale, Macklesfield, and all towns around Manchester, and were receiving letters for engagements all the time. We received one anonymous letter, advising us not to meddle with English politics; to let free-trade alone!

George Dawson was delivering a course of lectures at

the Atheneum at this time, and we became quite well acquainted with him. He was a young man, only twenty-four, and a man of a good deal of ability. We attended some of his lectures, and at the conclusion of one of them he pointed up to one of our bills on the wall, and expressed himself as much gratified that we were singing such songs — in a word, gave us a good puff; and when he spoke of poor Tom Hood, the author of some of the songs we sang, the audience sympathetically responded to the eulogy he pronounced upon him. He afterwards invited us to come to Birmingham, saying that he would do all he could to make our stay pleasant and profitable.

As we had several calls from London, Jesse went on there to make arrangements for our appearance in the metropolis of the world.

Our last concert in Manchester was given January 23d, and we prepared to leave for London the next day. Our friends all came to say good-by and God speed; and, telling them we should see them again two or three months hence, we got aboard the cars, singing the refrain:

> "Now farewell, friends and brothers,
> Fathers, sons, sisters, mothers,
> Manchester people, and all others
> In old Lancastershire
> From our first appearing
> Have your smiles been cheering,
> And the thoughts endearing
> We shall cherish evermore
> May the choicest blessings
> Ever rest upon you all"

Riding all day in the cars through a beautiful country — hills, valleys, meadows and streams, mansions and castles — we reached London at about five o'clock, where we were met by Jesse, and conducted to the quarters he had selected for us, at 21 Hollis Street.

We awoke bright and early the next morning, which was Sunday, January 25, 1846, to find ourselves in the third story of a boarding-house near Hanover Square. We had sung in Dublin, Liverpool and Manchester most of the time since we arrived in the country, and had had an experience which we prized as highly as we did money. We found ourselves a few hundred dollars ahead of what we had when we left home, and were now in London, the great and mighty city, all well and in good spirits. The surrounding houses impressed us as being very handsome, most of them five and six stories high, no blinds on the windows, and everything orderly and refined. Toward evening, after the rain had subsided, we walked out to St. James Park, where we saw Buckingham Palace, the home of the queen. It was a magnificent building, surrounded by a high iron fence, around which soldiers were stationed. In front was an arch built by George III, of solid marble.

I cannot now describe the impression formed upon my mind on this, my first visit to London; it came up to our fullest anticipations, and reminded us of the pictures we had seen of Babylon.

The next day we spent in looking about the city in company with our old friend "Noggs," who had returned from France. We called on George Thompson at his office, and found him just as pleasant and glad to see us as he was in Manchester, and promising to do everything he could for us. We also saw Mrs. Charles Dickens and her sister, with three other ladies, sang them some songs, with which they seemed much pleased; she invited us to her house on the Wednesday following.

George Thompson having obtained an invitation for

us to attend a Buckingham Soirée, which was held in the hall of the British and Foreign Institute, we repaired to the hall at about half-past eight, and were ushered into a room full of aristocratic people, with white gloves, etc. We took an obscure seat behind the piano, and as soon as quiet was restored we began to sing — first "The Cot where we were Born," which we followed with "Excelsior" and "Over the Mountains"; all of which were received with applause. Then George Thompson gave a short history of our family, and of our intentions in coming to England (a most favorable introduction); after which Abby was asked to sing the "May Queen," which was received with pronounced marks of approbation. Having spent a very pleasant hour we returned to our rooms, light-hearted and full of hope for the future, for we had a promise of a command to visit the queen shortly. This was a courtesy expressed by royalty to visitors, a command instead of an invitation.

We were boarding ourselves, as we did in Dublin, and found it the most convenient and pleasant way of living. It was the custom followed by most foreigners at that time. We hired our rooms, furnished our own food, which was cooked for us in the house and put on a private table, for all of which so much a week was paid. George Thompson was a frequent guest at our cheerful board where he wittily related many of his American experiences.

We visited the gallery of fine arts, where we saw some very fine paintings. Then we called on the American minister, found his clerk in, and he gave us a Democratic discourse on politics.

We were invited to spend an evening with Charlotte Cushman, who was just starting in her professional career: arriving at the house we found quite a large party, and being asked to sing, we contributed several selections. During the evening she, together with Eliza Cook, the author of the song, and the author of the music, also present, sang the new song, a parting glee, "Come, let us part":

> "Come, let us part with lightsome heart,
>   Nor breathe one chiding sigh
> To think that wing of rainbow plume
>   So soon should learn to fly
>
> "We scarcely like the chimes to strike
>   That tell of pleasure's flight,
> But friendship's chain when severed thus
>   Is sure to reunite.
>
> "Then why not we as merry, merry be
>   Though the song be the last,
> Believing other days will come
>   As bright as those just passed"

It had just been written, and was still in manuscript. (This was the last song I sang with my sister Abby in Boston, in 1892, but a few weeks before her death) We often met Miss Cushman afterward, and esteemed her highly for her grand womanly qualities of heart and mind.

On the day appointed we called on Mrs. Dickens and spent a very pleasant, social hour. We did not see Dickens, he not being at home.

Having made arrangements to give our first concert in London on February 10th, we had some time to look about and see the sights, of which we took advantage by visiting a great many people and places of interest We saw Charlotte Cushman in "Romeo and Juliet," attended the Julian concerts, and went to Westminster Abbey. One day we took a steamer down the river to the Thames Tunnel, which we found a wonderful structure indeed. I walked through it with a Scotchman; it was lit up with gas, and all along the walk were fancy stations or booths, where men, women and children were offering little trinkets for sale. We saw three little boys, the youngest six years old, playing a harp and violins, and they made very sweet music. Asa tried to get his phiz cut out for a sixpence; when it was done it resembled Sir Walter Scott more than it did him, and because he found fault with it the sculptor was quite wrathy and threatened to black his eye and inflict all manner of corporal punishment upon him.

We passed up the river about two miles, lowering the smoke-stack of our little steamer as we ran under the many bridges with which the river is spanned. The "London" bridge was a splendid structure, but the "Suspension" was far superior. We returned to the city in the early afternoon, having passed a very pleasant day, and seen many places of historical interest, among which was Westminster College.

Abby and Jesse repaired to the house of Charles Dickens, where they had been invited to dine; and in the evening we all joined them, in company with "Noggs." After taking some coffee we were shown into the parlor upstairs, and ushered into the presence of some of the most notable characters of the day. There was Macready, the actor; Douglas Jerrold, the author of the famous "Mrs. Caudle's Curtain Lectures"; Samuel Rogers, the celebrated poet, the Hon. Mrs. Norton, author of "Bingen on the Rhine"; and a number of others no less noted. By request we sang "The Bridge of Sighs," "Good Time Coming," and other selections, which were well received. "Noggs" got into conversation with Macready, not understanding who he was, and said to him, "I know I've seen you somewhere." "Very likely you have," he replied, "I have been in America, all through the States, etc." After they had finished, Asa said to "Noggs," "Did you know you were talking to the celebrated actor, Macready?" When "Noggs" realized it, every muscle in his face contracted and relaxed alternately; he was much surprised and embarrassed. After spending a very pleasant evening we retired, often calling at the house afterwards, always being welcome, and receiving calls from Mrs. Dickens, who came to hear us sing.

While dining with Mr. and Mrs. Dickens, Charles Dickens sat at Abby's right, and Douglas Jerrold at her left. In accordance with her pledge, she declined the wine when offered. Dickens said, "Well, Jerrold, after dinner we also will give up wine — until to-morrow."

We found that we had every kind of talent to contend with in London, from the street musicians to the finest operas; as this seemed to be the Mecca of all who were after fame, popularity and money. We soon made up our minds it was no place for us to succeed, as it would take a longer time than we had at our disposal to create a sentiment in our favor. We found not the best of feeling existing toward the Yankees, and as we were more distinctively American than any other company ever introduced in the country, there was a good deal of prejudice against us, and it was only among a certain class, and that the industrial, that we could hope for much appreciation. We accordingly decided that our stay must be short in London: we could give a few concerts in the city, visit some of the suburban manufacturing towns, where we could always command good audiences, see all the points and places of interest in and about the town, and then return to Manchester or Liverpool.

We spent a delightful evening at the house of George Thompson, and found his wife, though an invalid, a most charming lady.

Our first concert in London, February 10, 1846, had been well advertised, and our friends all assured us it would be a success. The evening came; we went to the Hanover Square Rooms, called the "Queen's Concert Rooms," and sang, we thought, as well as usual, and were well received by an intelligent audience of about five hundred. Seated in different parts of the crowded hall might have been seen the notable William Howitt; Mary Howitt, the poetess; Eliza Cook, author of "The Irish Emigrant's Lament"; George Thompson, M. P.; Charlotte Cushman, the greatest actress of the nineteenth century; Douglas Jerrold, the great author; John Forester of the *Examiner;* Hogarth, the London musical critic; Hon. Mrs. Norton; John Ross Dix, author of "Pen and Ink Sketches"; Samuel Rogers, the celebrated poet; and many others.

Among those noted people, and seated in the most conspicuous place in the front part of the hall, was Charles Dickens with his wife and children. After forty years had elapsed I met his son, who was visiting the prominent places in America, at a lecture in Lynn and he spoke with enthusiasm of the delight that he experienced at that notable concert in the Queen's Concert Rooms. Referring to the occasion, he said, "Among the brightest recollections of my early years was attending that concert of the Hutchinson Family, in company with my father, mother, brothers and sisters."

At this concert appeared a man whose business was

something like that of the man who likes to clean gravestones in the cemeteries, for whatever sum friends of the buried might give. He had met Brother Jesse previously, and proffered courtesies to the family. On this evening he sat in a conspicuous place, and at an opportune time threw upon the stage offerings in the shape of a wreath and bouquet. These were given to Sister Abby. When we returned to our anteroom, who should appear but this man, asking where his wreath and flowers were, with the explanation that he desired to throw them to another artist the same evening. We pointed them out to him and he seized them and vanished into the night.

Congratulating ourselves that we had made a hit, there came a reaction in the way of cold criticism in the papers the next morning. A dramatic critic of one of the papers advised us to throw away our fiddles, and we found the notices in some of the other morning papers still worse. The *Morning Chronicle* was an exception. Not knowing what to do or where to go, we started out to walk off the "honors," each going in a different direction. We were later cheered by some of our friends telling us we would yet succeed in changing the opinions of the press. When the *Times* came out, we anxiously looked for its verdict; then all hope seemed to desert us, as we thought it the meanest notice we had ever had in any newspaper. They called us the "second batch" of American singers. The cause of this we attributed largely to a feeling of hostility against the Yankees, as there were rumors of war with the United States. Our friends rallied around us, and tried to console us by saying,

"A blow is as good as a puff,
 They're both windy"

Judson said he wouldn't sing again, he was going home, and began to pack up his fiddle at once. With my sister Abby I was rather more sanguine than the rest, having prepared myself for adverse criticism; but it was hard to stem the current of opinion that they must go home, which had set in in the minds of all the other members of the family. In a few days this feeling wore off in a measure, and getting more favorable notices from the press, we "braced up," determined to win our way to favor while we stayed in London.

On February 14th we attended service in Westminster Abbey, that grand edifice about which so much has been said and written. On our way we passed through St. James Park, and were attracted by the crowds that congregated there on Sunday. Two novelties we saw attracted our favorable attention; one the presence of a number of goats harnessed into little wagons for children to drive; and the other the keeping of numerous cows to be milked for the benefit of the many children. Our friend Stephens from America was with us, and told us of meeting an Englishman in the town, who was pointing out to him the cannon that had been captured from foreign countries. Stephens asked him where they kept those taken from the United States. "Oh, we haven't got any." "But you must have some you took at Bunker Hill." This made the Englishman bristle up; but he had nothing to say, and the Yankee only laughed and left him.

In Hyde Park we often saw some of the queen's troops parading, with a band of about sixty pieces. The troops in their bright uniforms, with the instruments of the band glistening in the sun, presented a very fine appearance, which was very much enhanced by the display of grand equipages, coaches and carriages of every kind and description.

Our second concert was given with a little better success than the first, inasmuch as it elicited quite favorable notices from the press, though in a financial way the receipts were not enough to pay the expenses.

We visited the Houses of Lords and Commons in company with George Thompson. They not being in session, we were admitted to the floor and had the honor of sitting in the seat of the speaker, and had the seats of all the prominent members pointed out to us by the attendant.

We spent an evening at the house of William and Mary Howitt, where we met a goodly company of the friends of freedom, among whom we always felt at home. On Washington's Birthday, which was Sunday, we took breakfast with Mr. Millville, Secretary of the Legation, and dined with our good friend George Atwood, who gave us a real Yankee dinner of beans and brown bread. There we met a number of American friends and passed the evening, for about two hours, in singing good old-fashioned hymns and patriotic airs.

We visited the Polytechnic Institute, the Zoological Gardens and the London Literary and Scientific Institute, where we sang some songs. We went to see the curiosities in the Chinese Museum, and on the way passed the house of Lord Wellington, in front of which was a monument erected in his honor, which was composed of the cannon he captured from Napoleon. We went to St. Paul's, where we saw the statues of Pakenham, Sir John Moore and many others; and on paying sixpence we went up into the whispering-gallery, which was one hundred and thirty feet in length and across which we could hear the least whisper. Ascending about one hundred steps higher we had a fine view of the city, but could have seen more, as the air was clear, but for the dense smoke arising from great chimneys in all parts of the town. From here we went to the Tower of London, through which we were conducted by a soldier who fought under Wellington at the battle of Waterloo. He told with pride of a French bullet he had in his head. After inspecting the ancient weapons of war used in the days of Cromwell, Queen Anne, the Georges and other tyrants, we ascended the steps, saw the block on which Anne Boleyn was beheaded; and the axe, too, was there. We then went into the room where the treasures of the realm were kept, and saw the several crowns belonging to the kings and queens of England, resplendent with precious stones, which alone were valued at one and a half million pounds sterling. The diamonds, pearls, rubies, gold and silver ornaments there displayed were said to be worth ten million pounds. We then went to see Madame Toussaud's collection of wax statuary. There was the royal family, Parkinson, Napoleon, and a hundred more of the great characters who had died, but seemed to be still living, so true to life were they.

After giving our fourth concert in London, Judson and Asa, as well as Jesse, were bound to come home, and all signed an obligation to start in April. I would not join with them, and Abby being opposed to going back so soon, they concluded to stay a little longer.

We went to the House of Lords again, and were more successful this time, as they were in session. We expected a treat in hearing some of the peers of the realm speak, but we were much disappointed. Wellington, the Iron Duke, got up in a pompous kind of a way, and complimented the English army, who fought so well, and killed so many of the Sheiks, during the war in India. Every word he spoke was followed with cheers. He began, "My Lords [cheers] — My Lords [cheers] — the army [cheers] — in India [cheers] — the Sheiks [bravo, bravo!]" That was about all he said; but the next morning the *Times* came out in a two-column article on the thrilling effect produced by the eloquent words of the noble lord. Two others of the members tried to say something, but they were very uninteresting; Lord Brougham was one of them. The whole affair seemed like a farce; they would leave their sentences half-finished for the want of words. Well might *Punch* say, "They ought to be turned out to grass."

We went to see the Bank of England; were shown through the vaults, a privilege rarely accorded to strangers; had in our hands millions of dollars worth of notes; and wheeled about in a wheelbarrow all the gold we could lift. We went from the bank to the Exchange House, where was a splendid statue of the queen. From the Exchange we went to the Temple, a church one thousand years old, where we saw some of the same old figures put there a "long time ago."

On the evening of March 6th we gave our fifth and last concert in London for the time being, having made an engagement to return and sing again on the 30th. At this last concert we sang our new song on Oregon, singing verses alternately in the tunes of "God Save the Queen" and "Yankee Doodle." This seemed to delight the audience very much. We had to stop at the end of each verse for the cheering to subside. This was composed by George Thompson, Judson and Jesse.

We now made up our minds to leave London, and

seek our fortunes in some of the smaller towns, in a good many of which we had already secured engagements. The first town we went to was Islington, the home of the late Tom Hood. Here we had a house full of enthusiastic listeners, who seemed to enjoy every moment, and it did us good to sing to such people. We were entertained here by Mrs. Thomas Hood, and sung to her her late husband's "Bridge of Sighs."

We then went to Birmingham, where we gave three concerts to crowded houses, visiting, during our stay there, the Silver-Plating and Galvanic Manufacturing Company, as well as many other places of interest in and about that busy town. After our three concerts in Birmingham we left for Manchester, where we were greeted by all our friends, who were glad to see us returned, and we began to feel at home again.

Jesse, here being anxious to leave us and go home, offered to sell out to us for a thousand dollars. After consultation with Asa, Judson and Abby, it was decided best to let him go; so we accepted his terms, and he left for Liverpool to start for America. He afterward regretted the step; and we being loath to have him leave, he concluded to rejoin and stay with us until he could induce us all to return home. The financial phase of the incident was amicably adjusted.

In Manchester we gave a concert to one of our old-time assemblies, and were very much cheered and encouraged by our reception. While here Judson received news of the sudden death of his father-in-law, Abel Hutchinson; at which he was very much depressed and again talked of going home. Going on to Liverpool we found the *Cambria* lying at the wharf, when Judson and Jesse went aboard and picked out their berths, determined to return home June 19th, or July 4th at the latest. After giving one or two concerts in Liverpool we returned again to Manchester, intending to make that our headquarters while giving concerts in the surrounding towns, until we should return to London to keep our engagement made there for the 30th. In Bolton we gave two concerts in a fine temperance hall to very large appreciative audiences. Miss Ashworth, an estimable lady, whose acquaintance we formed, took us in her carriage out about three miles to see a huge water-wheel; and on the way stopped to introduce us to a Quaker woman, for whom we sang some songs, to her great delight. This wheel was to us an enormous affair, made of solid iron, sixty feet in diameter, and costing £10,000.

On Sunday Abby and I attended a Quaker meeting. There we sat for two long hours without hearing a word spoken. Though it was very tedious and monotonous we bore it with all patience, as we had a number of good friends in the meeting; and they were such dear, good creatures, and so sociable and pleasant in their houses, that we could well put up with their silence in meeting. And on the whole I am not sure but the service impressed us more than some of the long faces, long prayers and long sermons we had been accustomed to see and hear at home.

Back to Liverpool we went, and gave a grand good concert to a very large, enthusiastic audience. Captain Judkins of the *Cambria* was present and wanted us to promise to return with him to America on July 4th, which we nearly made up our minds to do

After giving concerts in Rochdale, Berry and Crew, which were very satisfactory to us in every way, and very pleasing to the audiences, if their demonstrations of approbation were any criterion, we returned to London, where we arrived on Saturday, March 28th.

On the evening of the following Monday we went to the Covent Garden Theatre, where we found an audience of five thousand people awaiting us. It was nine o'clock before we went on the platform. This entertainment began at six o'clock and lasted all night, being an annual complimentary concert to the talent of the kingdom. Abby sang the "May Queen," which she had to repeat, in answer to the applause which greeted her; Judson sang "Down East"; then we all joined in the "Old Granite State." The other attractions before this vast audience were the elder Braham, Russell, Phillips, who all sang finely; some Italians, Jews and Germans, who all sang and played very creditably; but none of them seemed to secure the approbation that our simple ballads and melody elicited.

Our good friend George Thompson, with his wife, called for us on the following morning to escort us to Windsor Castle. We arrived at the station, where we ordered dinner to be ready for us at three o'clock, then took a coach with postillion for the castle. The surrounding country was beautiful; through the trees we could see the old towers of the castle looming up in their grandeur. We soon arrived at the base of the hill, where leaving our coach, we began the ascent to the castle. We were conducted by an attendant through the various apartments, saw the portraits of the ancient kings, queens and noblemen with which the walls were adorned. Then we ascended the tower, singing as we went. At last we reached the top, and had the whole country round about for fifteen or twenty miles spread out as a panorama before us, the most magnificent sight I had ever beheld. Our guide was very communicative and inquisitive in regard to us, and on questioning Mr. Thompson, was told that we were Yankees, that we came from the backwoods, and on our arrival we were wild, but having been in the country for about nine months we were pretty well tamed and perfectly harmless, and could speak a little English; also that we were black, but the climate had bleached us out; and a good deal more in the same strain, all of which the credulous Englishwoman swallowed with open-eyed wonder.

We had a fine view of the Thames, as it wound its picturesque way through the valley; it inspired us with song, and we sang all the way down and out. We took a cab and went on the Government land, a splendid hard, smooth road, straight and bordered on each side with old English elm-trees. The sight was grand as we ascended the hill opposite to look at the castle. We passed herds of goats quietly grazing and stopped by the side of a beautiful little lake, in which the queen and royal family were said to fish for gudgeons. We skipped stones on its glassy surface, got under the trees when it rained, had a general good time, enjoyed our dinner immensely when we returned to the hotel, and reached our rooms late in the afternoon, pretty well tired out but feeling that we had spent a very delightful day, and seen one of the greatest objects of interest in England.

We gave one or two more concerts in London, which we considered very successful in every way, and then we began to take leave of our many dear friends. Mrs Mary Howitt was one of them. We felt under great obligations to the Atwoods, the Goulds, Dickenses, Putnams, Lords, and our numerous friends in London for the many kindnesses and attentions shown us.

Among the brightest recollections connected with our visit to England was the many pleasant visits in a social way to the home of Mary and William Howitt, and their presence at the concerts given in the different parts of the city of London.

From the first introduction to them they seemed to me England's best production. Such culture of heart, spirit and intellect — full of enthusiasm, love and faith; always so cheerful and hopeful.

Our visits to their home were frequent; and whether the occasion was one of a strictly private nature or we were to meet other invited guests, we were made happy and our resolves were made stronger to labor on in the right.

We were surprised on one occasion, accepting an invitation, to find that we were to sit for our portraits. The artist was ready with brush and easel, and we were to sit for the painting. Mrs. Howitt, in the mean time, took her relative position and with paper and pen instituted a series of queries relative to the rise and progress of the Hutchinsons in America, of our personal relations and environments, of genealogy, of the parents of our numerous tribe, of our religious sentiments, of our labors in the cause of human elevation, emancipation and temperance. Both artist and historian were busy in their vocation; and as our interview closed after the sitting, we found a beautiful painting of the quartet in water-colors. Forty-seven years after, this painting was sent to New York to Sister Abby, she showing it to the artist Mr. F. B. Carpenter. It was pronounced a true likeness as he remembered the family in earlier years.

Mrs Howitt at this time published the following lines in our honor:

BAND OF YOUNG APOSTLES

Band of young apostles, teaching love and truth,
You have come before us in your glorious youth,
Like a choir of angels missioned from above,
To make our souls acknowledge how beautiful is love.
Taint of earth I see not in your clear eyes shine
You to me resemble natures all divine —
Pure seraphic creatures, from some higher sphere,
Who but for love and pity never had been here,
Who but for human fellowship had never shed a tear.

Band of young apostles, such to me ye seem,
As I list your singing in a rapturous dream —
Now with choral voices, like the birds of May,
Warbling in tumultous joy that winter is away;
Now like angels weeping o'er a sinner's bier,
With their white wings folded and low voices clear,
Mourning for the sorrow which sin has brought on earth,
Mourning for that pity that man has made such dearth,
Teaching to a callous world what a soul is worth.

Band of young apostles, teaching love and truth,
Onward go, high missioned in your joyous youth!
Onward go, God's blessing on your path alight!
Still lift your kindred voices as prophets of the right.
Onward go, undaunting herald of that day
When all mankind are brothers and war has ceased to sway
We have seen and loved you, we have pressed your hand,
We have blessed you, and we bless in you your native land
Farewell, and God's blessing guide you, ye young and noble band

On April 6th we bid farewell to London, not expecting to return, and on the same evening and the two succeeding ones gave three concerts in Liston, a beautiful little town about four hours' ride from the great city It seemed so quiet and retired that we could almost have been persuaded to settle down and stay there.

On leaving London our landlady said we were exceptions to the common itinerant singers, in that we paid our debts.

Our next concert we gave in Loughborough, where we found ourselves in a great company of teetotallers, who had come there to hold a meeting. The hotel was so filled with them that we had hard work to get anything to eat. We repaired to the hall where their meeting was being held, and being called upon to sing we gave them some of our best temperance songs, which pleased them very much; and in the evening our concert was a grand success, and it cheered us very much to find ourselves in such an atmosphere, feeling we were just where we belonged. Jesse made a speech, and on the whole we thought we had passed a very happy Good Friday.

We returned to Liston, where we spent two or three days very pleasantly among our newly-found friends. We were entertained very handsomely at the house of a Mr. Briggs, who had a very fine establishment about two miles out of town. In company with Mrs. Briggs, Mrs. Mott and Mr. and Mrs. Hawks, we visited the ruins of an ancient abbey, walked through the gardens surrounding it, and on the banks of a little lake we sat down and gave our friends a specimen of Yankee whittling; but we finally had to tear ourselves away from this place and these friends.

At Nottingham, where we gave our next two concerts, we were well received, stopped at a temperance hotel, and spent a large part of our time in seeing the sights, among others the ruins of the old castle, which had been destroyed for the second time, about fifteen years before our visit, by a mob. This was one of the oldest castles in England, was the nursery of several of the English monarchs, and was destroyed during Cromwell's time, when it was defended by Colonel Hutchinson. We saw the secret path, cut in the solid rock, by which the garrison escaped. It was on an eminence commanding a fine view of the town and surrounding country, though Jesse thought it could not be compared to High Rock. Another very attractive feature of this town was the extensive lace factories, which we visited.

Near the castle gate was hung in full view the sword of William Wallace, once waved as a dazzling inspiration to his followers, as he led them on to victory at the head of his clan. The blade appeared to be five feet long, and so weighty that any modern leader would find it wearisome to wield upon a charge.

Derby was our next objective point; we gave two concerts to well-filled houses and very appreciative people. Mr. Cook, the Unitarian preacher, and his good wife were very attentive to us here, took us in the country to see another old castle and a church which was twelve hundred years old. It was built of stone, and the walls were covered with moss, and little trees and shrubs growing all over it. Our friend Sharpe took us from here to Swadlincote, where we met with the warmest reception accorded us anywhere in England. This town we found not so attractive in appearance as some we had seen, but the people were very hospitable, and all seemed to vie with each other to see which could do the most for our comfort and enjoyment. This was the home of the Sharpes, and going to the house we were introduced to the father, an old man nearly ninety, who told us he had always been a temperate man and was still enjoying good health. Our friends were the proprietors of very extensive pottery works here, and they made the finest kind of crockery, some samples of which were given us by the employees, for whom we sang two or three songs. On leaving England for home we were presented by the Sharpe Brothers with three large crates, containing a full dinner- and tea-set of their manufacture, some of the pieces of which I still have in my possession. We remained here over Sunday and returned to Nottingham, where we gave another concert.

In Leicester we gave a concert to seventeen hundred people, who all cheered us till they were hoarse and we were tired. Then going to Sangton, we were met by a Mr. Bloor, at whose house we were invited to stop during our stay in the town. We found his a very pleasant family, consisting of a wife, who was an elderly lady, kind-hearted and good, and several daughters, who made our visit of two or three days very agreeable. We gave two concerts to very large and good audiences. Remaining here over Sunday, we went to church in the morning, and heard a sermon preached by the rector, which I thought the most bigoted of anything I had ever heard. In the afternoon we went to the church attended by the Duchess of Sutherland and her family. She drove up in her coach, drawn by four splendid white horses, and with about half-a-dozen liveried servants We received an invitation from her to visit her gardens and take tea, which we accepted, and saw the most beautifully laid out and kept gardens that we had seen anywhere. We took tea with the duchess, and after a short stay left for home. We gave another concert the following evening, then one in Macklefield, and then went back to Manchester.

We went from here again to Birmingham, where we gave two concerts in the town-hall, which was crowded on both occasions, not less than seventeen hundred people being present. A little party of about twenty-five was gotten up here to visit Warwick and Kenilworth Castles, which were a distance of about twenty miles from the city.

We first arrived at Warwick, which we were told was the only castle, with the exception of Windsor, spared by Cromwell in his desolation of the country. We walked around and about it, over it and through it, viewing it from every side, and were impressed with the massiveness of its walls, and could but think of the many cruelties and outrages that had been committed inside. We went out on the battlements, and from one of the turrets we had a fine view of the surrounding country. On the walls and stairways were carved the initials of tourists, who seemed very desirous of immortality, or at least that their names should not die. In the observatory was a bowl said to have been taken from the ruins at Pompeii; it would hold about three hundred gallons, and looked as if it had been filled with punch a good many times. Inside everything was grand, and showed signs of having been at one time magnificent; the paintings on the walls, the massive tables, gold-engraved and gold-plated, and the furniture hundreds of years old, all showed what it had been. We sang a song in the large dining-room, and our voices echoed through the whole house.

Kenilworth was the best specimen of a ruin we had seen; the foundations were there, but the walls were scattered in all directions, covered with moss and ivy. It was on high ground overlooking the country for miles around. But we were getting hungry, and making a table of a plank we found, we soon were doing justice to the excellent dinner we had brought with us, consisting of cold roast beef and mutton and pigeon-pie, to say nothing of the lemonade, and wine for those who drank it. It did not take us long after dinner to see all there was to these ruins, and we started for home, reaching there at about two o'clock, pretty tired, but feeling well repaid for our fatigue.

Staying in Birmingham another day we visited the extensive glass-works, and being urged to sing again, gave another concert to at least eighteen hundred people. After the concert we drove out a mile and a half to the house of a Mr. Carpenter, where we stayed until about one o'clock engaged in social intercourse. On our return to Manchester we took with us a splendid edition of Shakespeare, presented to us by our friends in Birmingham, and gave another concert to a thousand people, the hall, aisles and steps so crowded we hardly had room on the stage.

From Manchester we went to Oldham, one of the dirtiest places we got into, but we had a good audience. Then we started for Warrington, which we reached after much tribulation, missing trains, impressing broken-down teams, and at last having to depend upon generosity of strangers to drive us into town in a private conveyance.

We gave another concert in Bolton, and returned to Manchester; from whence a Mr. Ryland took us to his house, about two miles out of town, where he had very large cotton factories. He entertained us most royally, but could not understand why we would not join him in some of his wine, twenty-five years old. In the evening we sang to his operatives, after which he took us back to town.

At one time during our stay at Manchester we went with Mrs. Moore to hear George Dawson deliver his celebrated lecture on "Oliver Cromwell." He came before the audience with the greatest degree of *sang froid*. At once he commenced talking to the people. He had one of the largest heads I ever saw on a man, and it was filled with knowledge. His only gesture from beginning to end was simply a moving of one finger. He was just about my age.

Subsequently, we called on John Bright, M.P., and spent one of the pleasantest evenings we ever enjoyed. Mr. Dawson came while we were there. Bright treated us right royally. I can now see his smiling, joyful, hopeful countenance. He lived an earnest life, with high aspirations for a position which he could fully adorn. He was one of the noblest men whom we met, and with whom we conversed. Cobden and Bright were the Garrison and Phillips of England. With George Thompson and Robert Moore they constituted the quartet which went through the country and held great conventions in opposition to the corn laws.

On Saturday, May 16th, we were advertised to give our farewell concert in Free Trade Hall, Manchester, and felt a little anxious and nervous over the prospect; but when we found ourselves confronted with an audience of six thousand people, and learned that hundreds were turned away, we felt reassured and gave one of our best concerts. We felt very much elated.

We went to Leeds, where we gave two concerts to good audiences; then to Henly, where we gave two more with good success — at both places stopping with friends who treated us with greatest courtesy.

The weather was getting quite warm, so it was really uncomfortable singing in the crowded houses which greeted us everywhere, and we felt glad to think we had really decided to leave for home on the *Cambria*, July 4th. While we were consoling ourselves with this fact, the news came that the *Cambria* had gone ashore on Cape Cod, so our hopes were dashed again for a short time, till we learned it was a false alarm, or rather that the damage to her was very slight and would not interfere with her regular trips. Within eight years after, the *Cambria* went down with all on board, excepting the engineer. She had then been taken off the Cunard line.

We left Henly at ten o'clock one bright Saturday morning on the outside of a coach for a drive of forty miles to Swadlincote. The air was clear and bracing, the country beautiful, a part of the way in the valley of the Trent. The passengers were sociable and pleasant, and everything combined to make the ride delightful. At Burton we met our good friends Edmund and Frank Sharpe, with carriages, in which they took us the rest of the way. The people seemed very glad to see us, and the gratification was mutual. We passed Sunday quietly, going to church with some friends morning and evening; and on Monday, after visiting an old ruined castle at Ashby, we gave a very acceptable concert to a big assemblage of delighted people. We were engaged here by a blind man, who was a great lover of music; and after the concert we returned to Swadlincote, where we gave a concert the next evening. From the latter place we returned to Birmingham, where we met all our good friends again — Mr. Patton, Miss Bennett, the Porters and Miss Carpenter. Here we heard that Henry Russell was going to sue us for singing his song, " The Maniac," but he discreetly refrained from pushing the matter. We gave two concerts, after which we took leave of all our good friends. In Birmingham we went through the factories where steel pens and also hooks and eyes were made; and spent one of the days very pleasantly in the country with a party of about thirty friends. Here we first learned of the beginning of the Mexican War. On Sunday we went to hear George Dawson preach, and were very much pleased with his manner. He spoke without notes and was very eloquent and interesting. After the service in the evening, we went behind the pulpit and spoke to him, calling him "brother," as he really seemed to us. He promised to come to America some time, and later he did so.

All good friends must part, so we had to leave these people, as we were advertised to sing in Sheffield. A number of our friends accompanied us ten miles on the road; when we reached Derby we met some more who had driven the seven miles from Swadlincote to shake hands with us. About five miles farther on our road we were joined by Edmund Sharpe, who accompanied us into Sheffield, where we gave our first concert in the theatre, and were well received by a large audience.

Here we visited the world-renowned establishment of Rogers, where the finest cutlery was made. We saw many fine specimens of the art; one knife with two hundred blades, others with one hundred, seventy and sixty. We bought some razors, knives and forks.

The town was beautifully situated on the sides of two hills, most of it in the valley between. We met here a Mr. Stanburn, the editor of a paper, who was very attentive to us. On June 4th, after giving two more concerts to appreciative audiences, we left Sheffield for York, where we entered the Minster or York Cathedral, which we found to be very magnificent. As services were being held we stepped in to hear the singing and the playing of the organ; then, on payment of a small fee, we were allowed to ascend to the top of the tower, which was a very long, tedious climb of two hundred and eighty-five steps of about nine inches each.

From York we went to Leeds, in both of which places we gave concerts, then started back to Manchester. During our concert at Leeds a Mr. Buitt was selling the *People's Journal*, containing Mrs. Howitt's article on the Hutchinson Family, together with picture of the group. On our return to Manchester we attended a concert in Free Trade Hall, and were cheered by the audience as we entered, though we only helped make up the audience. We were greeted, between the numbers, by Richard Cobden and his friend Harland. We heard the celebrated violinist Vieuxtemps, who was creating a great *furore* at the time.

We went to Haslington, a small manufacturing town, seventeen miles distant; gave a concert, and enjoyed the hospitality and enthusiasm of the people. Here we experienced our first thunder-storm in England, and it was a grand sight indeed to see the light and shadow cast upon the intense green of the surrounding hills.

After driving out to Langton, a distance of about forty miles, on a coach, and giving a concert, we returned to Manchester, where we prepared to give our farewell, take leave of our friends and start for Scotland, where we had promised ourselves we would spend about two weeks before returning home. We were receiving letters from all parts of the country bidding us farewell, and were packing up preparatory to leaving for America.

CHAPTER V.

IN SCOTLAND.

"And we are friends of emancipation,
In its broadest acceptation,
This we sing through every nation
From the old Granite State
  We are friends of freedom,
  And we'll plead the right of all.
Men should love each other,
Nor let hatred smother,
Every man's a brother,
And our country is the world."

Our last concert was given on the evening of June 13th in Free Trade Hall, before an immense audience, and was a grand ovation. After the concert we were surrounded by our friends, who had all come to say good-by. The next day we spent a quiet Sabbath, the afternoon and evening at the house of the Peacocks, where we found Mrs. Moore and Mr. Ireland. We sang some songs with them that will never be forgotten as long as life lasts; we left them in the evening with hearty hand-shakes and tears in our eyes.

The next morning we left Manchester for Liverpool, intending to make our start from there to Scotland. We were received by good Rickerby, who was always glad to see us, and in the evening gave a concert to a large audience in Lord Nelson Street. Mr Smith, editor of the *Mercury*, came into our dressing-room, and we found him a fine specimen of a real old English gentleman.

We journeyed through a part of the highlands of England in our route to Scotland, which compelled us to travel by various conveyances, as the railroad, stage-coach, canal-boats, etc., and we rode the last fourteen miles in a barouche that we had chartered for that purpose.

Harriet Martineau had cordially invited us to visit her at her country home, some time previously, while we were in Liverpool. As we approached the town where we were to visit her (Ambleside), the sun was slowly declining in the west, as if separated by a cloud that capped the top of the surrounding hills; it formed one of the grandest spectacles that eye hath ever seen, silver-lining the landscape and presenting a most gorgeous aspect, on which we would gladly have feasted and never left if it had been possible to preserve such a picture:

"The sun's rich rays shine through the day,
But flashes deeper still
When darting forth its farewell beams,
Behind the western hill."

In the sweet valley surrounded by these hills was clustered the village of Ambleside. Near a beautiful lake of fine location, was the residence of Miss Martineau, a picturesque cottage of rough stone.

"Bright things can never die,
E'en though they fade,
Beauty and minstrelsy
Deathless were made."

It being June it was even more than ordinarily beautiful, and we soon came down into the valley and up toward the town and learned from the postmaster where the good lady resided whom we were to visit. Miss Martineau greeted us at the door, for she had been previously informed of our arrival and was ready to receive us. She was extremely glad to see us and gave us a hearty welcome. Sister Abby remained with her in her house, while Judson, Asa and I, took quarters at a hotel.

It had been planned by our good hostess that we should enjoy a visit or an outing to a lake, a distance of about three miles; so on the following morning we set out for it, where we joined a company of her choice friends. Reaching the lake we took a boat across to the opposite shore, where we would be sheltered from the heat of the day.

"A boat, a boat to cross the ferry,
We are going over to be merry."

We commenced in earnest to enjoy the occasion and having no regular programme, things took their own course, of singing, running, dancing, wading in the stream, climbing the surrounding hills, piling up stones for landmarks and monuments and behaving much like little children on a picnic, and so passed some of the first hours till at last Brother Jesse, who was to join us, having stepped off the previous day to get the mail, came to the opposite shore and we saw him, but beyond hearing distance. He crossed over in a boat, and as he approached we sent out a song. He answered us back, and we soon greeted him and received our mail. The time passed joyously. We sang songs, spoke pieces, told stories, and were as happy as mortals could be. Thus passed the never-to-be-forgotten day.

The next day we took a comprehensive view of the town, village and farm-home of our hostess. It was haying-time, and we were much pleased to have the opportunity of a little farm-work, as we were allowed by the gardener to take his scythe and mow. We soon found it was very heavy mowing, and that we could not do it. Miss Martineau came on the piazza, and asked us if we would not like to try a lady's scythe. We consented, and she brought her own implement: it was about twice as heavy as our Yankee scythes, the blade about three inches and a half wide. It was a fatiguing effort to handle even such a woman's-suffrage scythe.

Learning that the hall where we were announced to sing was small and low-studded, and taking into account the extremely warm weather, we concluded to find a place where we could sing in the open air, consequently I was introduced to Mr. Harrison, who had a very fine mansion with a beautiful lawn in front. He cordially offered us the use of it; arrangements were made and the stage erected.

The concert commenced about six o'clock in the evening, and some three hundred people had gathered on the lawn, while as many more of the populace were seated on the walls. Each part of our programme elicited the warmest approbation and the applause was hearty. We greeted the audience with "The Cot where We were Born"

> "We stood upon the mountain height,
>   And viewed the valleys o'er,
> The sun's last ray, with mellow light,
>   Illum'd the distant shore;
> We gazed with rapture on the scene,
>   Where first in youth's bright morn
> We play'd, where near us stood serene
>   The cot where we were born"

We would dash upon the stage, sing our piece, receive our encores, and then disappear among the bushes until our next number.

Our good lady sat at the right, about four seats back, and with her trumpet to her ear seemed to catch every

THE HUTCHINSONS AT GRASMERE. (p. 302)

sound, and was apparently enjoying the entertainment. About midway of the concert there came up a black cloud. the lightning flashed, the thunder roared and the rain fell, but not upon our audience. Still we could see it outside the apparently charmed circle. Soon the sullen rumble of the retreating storm could be heard in the distance. Our farewell refrain was:

> "Though we love with true devotion,
> Our dear home across the ocean,
> Yet we feel a warm emotion
> For our old fatherland
>   May the kind relations,
>   And the obligations,
>   Of the Saxon nations,
> Be good-will and brotherly love
>
> "Now, farewell, friends and brothers,
> Fathers, sons, sisters, mothers,
> Harriet Martineau, and all others
> In old Ambleside,
> May the choicest blessings rest upon you all,
> Farewell, farewell!"

The concert over, we said our parting words. Seated in our carriage that was to convey us to Patterville we sang again our last good-by; our dear lady standing upon her piazza waving her white scarf, her farewell fraught with the tenderest affection with a "God bless you all."

I append a description penned by Miss Martineau of the whole visit, which appeared in the *People's Journal.*

THE HUTCHINSON FAMILY IN GRASMERE

We all remember the singing group, and the Memoir which Mrs Howitt gave us It is pleasant to me now to connect them with our lake scenery, to think that our valleys have resounded with their harmonies Mrs Howitt wrote to me that the Hutchinsons were coming to Kendal, and I forthwith settled in my own mind that they must sing to us at Ambleside. Everybody about me wished to hear them, and they wished to come, so the whole affair arranged itself easily enough. The large room at the White Lion was engaged and filled with benches, so as to hold the greatest possible number, two hundred. As the time drew near, however, I met a shake of the head whichever way I turned. Everybody was sure that many more than two hundred people would want admission. People were coming from Bowness, Grasmere, Hawkshead, and even Kendal, and if they should be turned back from the door, how could they be expected to bear it patiently? And then the heat was excessive. Everybody was afraid of it. But what could be done? Here was the largest room that could be had, and the Hutchinsons could not stay to give a second concert. Such was the state of things — the tickets almost all sold, everybody wanting to go, and everybody dreading the heat — when the Hutchinsons were to arrive, on Tuesday evening, June 16th. I had advised their coming by Newby Bridge from Lancaster, so as to finish their day's journey from Liverpool by the Windermere steamer. A trip by steamer from end to end of Windermere is the prettiest finish of a summer day's journey that can be imagined.

It was as lovely an evening as any during this glorious June of 1846. As I stood on the shore at Waterhead waiting for the steamer, I endeavored to look upon the landscape with the eyes of a stranger, and thought that if I were then seeing it for the first time, it would appear to me the true paradise of this world. The soft ruddy evening light on Wansfell, the purple hollows of Loughrigg, the deep shadows of the western side of the lake, pierced by lines of silver light — the white gables of the houses at Clappergate, peeping from the woods which skirt Loughrigg, and the little gray church on its knoll in the centre of the Brathay valley, — these made up such a vision of delicious coloring that I imagined my friends on the deck of the steamer saying, that never, in any lustrous evening of a New England autumn, had they enjoyed a richer feast to eye and mind. Then came the steamer, rounding the point from Low-wood. There seemed to be but few passengers on deck — no signs of any band of brothers, with a sister in the midst. They were not there, and I had only to hasten home, lest they should arrive some other way. Before I had been at home many minutes, I saw from my terrace a barouche coming rapidly along the winding road, with one bonnet and several gray caps in it; it entered my gate, drove up to the porch, and I found myself among hearty Americans once more.

The first business to be done was to go down to the White Lion, and see the room. When there, we could only agree, like other people, that the room could only hold two hundred and that it would be dreadfully hot. Then the brothers and sister stepped on the platform, and tried the fitness of the place for music. What those few notes were to others I know not. I saw afterwards that a number of people had on the instant gathered in the street and a little friend of mine observed that he now heard music that he thought beautiful. As for me, long years of solitary sickness had passed since I had last heard harmony, or anything that I could call music, except one song in my sick room from Adelaide Kemble, and this was almost too much for me now, in full health. It thrilled through me, as if I were a harp played upon by the wind. It seemed to me that I never before heard such harmony, such perfect accord, as between those four voices. I believe the echo never sleeps in the ear of those who have once heard it.

The next day, Wednesday, was reserved for a glorious country holiday, and it turned out a day of pleasuring without alloy. Rare as is the event of a pleasure day without alloy, for once it was so. A party of seventeen persons, aged somewhere between seventy-six and twelve years, met on the shores of Grasmere — about three miles from my house. We had three boats, and in them — rowed by ladies, children, young men or servants, as the fit took us — we crossed to a shady, shingly spot, before the greatest heat of the day came on. There, on the shingle some lay down, and talked, or played "Duck and Drake," while others dabbled in the cool ripple, or dipped their heads, and let the water stream from their locks.

Abby Hutchinson, the youngest of her parents' sixteen children, and therefore called "the baby," dropped asleep for a few moments with her head upon a stone — her sweet face looking as calm and innocent as any baby's. Other young ladies pushed off in a boat to practice rowing, and came back relieved of the toil by a spirited little fellow of twelve who wielded their oars manfully. Then off went one or the other of the Hutchinsons, rowing away suddenly, as if for his life, and coming back no less vehemently. It was a gay little party, on the margin of a clear lake at the bottom of a basin of mountains all green to the summit — dappled with woods and slopes, gay sunshine and deep shade. In the midst of the lake was its one island, green and bare, except on the side where a pine grove casts its shadow on the waters. On the opposite margin was the village of Grasmere, with its old church — its low and square tower showing itself from among the trees. Immediately behind it rose Helm Crag, the most beautiful summit in all the neighborhood for form, light and shadow. To the left branched off the mountains, now gray and purple, which encompass Easedale. To the right ascended, winding round the skirts of Helvellyn, the road to Keswick. Scattered nearer at hand, among the nooks and on the slopes of the hills around the lake, were dwellings whose aspect might tempt wandering spirits of earth or air to stay and rest amidst Nature's peace. In this scene was our morning passed.

Then came the merry dining, the spreading of the tablecloths on the grass, the finding rocky seats to eat on conveniently, and the grouping (as if they could help it!) of the Hutchinsons to sing, their breath of song stirring up the quietest spirits of the party, like a breeze breaking the glassy calm of the lake, and then the lazy rest after dinner; broken by the arrival of a fourth brother of the Hutchinsons, bringing letters and newspapers from Liverpool by the last packet. When each on his separate stone had read his letters and dispensed his public news, all who were ready for enterprise, and not afraid of the heat, began to climb in the direction of High Close. What a scramble was the first part. Tempted by the shade of a wall, we went straight up the face of the hill, where the grass was as glassy and slippery with the dry weather as so much satin, and for almost every step forward, we slipped one back. After a few laughs, some sensations of despair, many slides and universal vows to return another way, we all reached the road, half-way up the ascent, and from thence all was easy. Cool air soon came to us over the ridge before us; we got some water at a farm-house, and then attained our object. We stood in a field whence we commanded the finest view of Westmoreland. Far to the left stretched away Windermere among lessening hills. Near to us lay Loughrigg-tarn, a round little lake on higher ground, though beneath us. There it lay blue and clear, under the dark slopes of Loughrigg. Immediately below us spread Elter Water — looking like a group of ponds amidst green meadows. To the right stretched Langdale, the winding narrow valley which is overhung at the further end by the glorious Langdale Pikes, our landmarks amidst the billowy hill region in which we live. Last of all, arose Bowfell, — the mountain mass which closes in the whole. Such is the mere outline of the scene which sprinkled over with dwellings of every kind from the great castle on a promontory of Windermere, to the gray hut on the mountain side — where farm-steads, hamlets, mills, cottages — a chapel here, a bridge there, a sheep-fold below — such is the scene which is rightly called the finest view in Westmoreland. The Hutchinsons will never forget it. They noted down the names in their tablets, and the features of the scene in their minds. In the midst of it all, however, sweet Abby, looking herself as fresh as a daisy, had in her hand a basin of clear cold water for the benefit of the thirsty.

After returning to the boats, the next thing was to row across to Grasmere, as we were to go a mile beyond the village to a friend's house in Easedale to tea. That was an evening to be remembered. Our venerable hostess sat in her beauty under a shady tree, happy among her happy guests. The tea tables in the shade looked cool and tempting. We were in a garden in front of a white cottage — an elegant, rambling cottage, all covered with roses, whose porch was almost one mass of blossom and spray. The sun let us alone under our trees, while it shone everywhere else, making the wild and sometimes dreary Easedale, one scene of light and greenness.

Soon, the Hutchinsons grouped themselves, as if by some irresistible attraction, and sang piece after piece, to the rapture of their hearers. Those who had heard them sing "The Cot where We were Born," "The Ohio Boatman," and "Excelsior," may conceive something of our delight. And, of all things to be doing, they were teaching us to play "Fox and Geese" on the green below. They themselves played with great humor; and in the midst of our fun, I saw that all the servants of the house were looking on from the corner of the terrace, and not a few laborers from outside the gate.

The appointed day for the concert had arrived. The evening before, a neighboring gentleman had kindly and beneficently offered that his lawn should be the scene. His servants should move the benches, put up the platform, attend at the gates, and save all trouble.

In the morning the hot weather melted away all doubts. It seemed clear that all parties, those who could not be consulted and those who could, would be pleased to be sent to a shady spot in the open air, where any number of people might hear without any crowding. The Hutchinsons themselves begged that all the townspeople who liked might hear them, those who could not pay as well as those who could. That concert will never be forgotten by any who were so happy as to be present. The Hutchinsons enjoyed it more than any they had given in the country. Abby left her bonnet in a rhododendron bush out of sight; and the family group came up a green slope from the thicket below. The little platform was erected under the deep shade of spreading sycamores. In front and on either hand were collected a larger audience than any house in Ambleside could have contained; and among them were some who could not have enjoyed the pleasure elsewhere — an invalid lady, who lay on the grass and an infirm old gentleman, whose chair was wheeled into the circle. There was row behind row of the tradespeople, servant and laborers of the neighborhood; and in the centre, behind all, the parish clerk — zealous in the psalmody and all the other good objects of the place, and most active in promoting our concert. He deserved the enjoyment which I am sure he had.

And now when I am most anxious to convey some impression of this festival, I am least able to do so. How is it possible to give an idea of the soul-breathing music of the Hutchinsons to those who have not heard it? One might as well attempt to convey in words the colors of the sky or the strain of the nightingale as such utterance of the heart as theirs.

One can only observe the effects. There was now hearty laughter, and now many tears. Nothing can be said of the interior emotions which found no expression. Everybody congratulating everybody else on having come. A young servant of mine, who went all in high spirits at the prospect of an evening's pleasure, cried the whole time, as did others. At the end, when every heart was beating in response to the brotherly greeting and farewell offered in the closing piece, "The Old Granite State," the parish clerk sprang up and called for three cheers for the Hutchinsons, which were given by as many as had unchoked voices. I think no one could have come away without a strong impression, consciously or unconsciously entertained, of the good and beauty of a free nurture and exercise of our human powers. There must be many among us with powers, of one sort or another, equal to those of the Hutchinsons. If we could be wise, and take courage to follow the lead of our natures, it cannot be but that many of us might be as free, as simple, as happy, as beneficent as they, as able as they to speak to hearts and to awaken souls.

As for me, I crossed the road to my own gate in a mood which the Hutchinsons described to me as theirs when I entered the room where we met for the last time — "We are happy and sad," said they. I was happy and sad; and, I dare say, so was everybody who was at that moment returning home from that green spot under the trees. The most moving thing, however, was yet to come. When they had dressed themselves for a night stage to Patterdale, and had supped, and said farewell, and seated themselves in the carriage, they stopped the horses on my terrace for yet another minute, and sent forth a sweet and most mournful chorus of farewell to me, in notes swelling and dying away in the still night air. I was "happy and sad," as I turned in to my solitary lamp. I could not let the glass door be closed, late as it was; but again and again I went out on the terrace to look for more stars to light my friends' way over the mountain pass, and to watch the summer lightning — not without some impression that their sweet strain of farewell was still floating over the valley. To me it can never die away into silence.

THE KNOLL, AMBLLSIDE, June 20, 1846.

POSTSCRIPT. — Mr. Hartley Coleridge was present at the concert, and the effect on him of Abby Hutchinson's singing of the "May Queen" may be judged of by the following sonnet, which he permits me to append to this paper.

TO ALFRED TENNYSON

I would, my friend, indeed thou hadst been here,
  Last night beneath the shadowy sycamore
  To hear the lines to me well known before;
Embalmed in music, so translucent, clear,
Each word of thine came singly to the ear;
  Yet all was blended in a flowing stream.
  It had the rich repose of summer dream,
The light distinct of frosty atmosphere.

> Still have I loved thy lines, yet never knew
>   How sweet they were, till woman's voice invested
> The pencill'd outline with the living hue,
>   And every note of feeling proved and tested.
> What might old Pindar be — if once again
> The harp and voice were trembling with his strain!

How joyously and delightfully passed each and every hour through that starlight, moonlight and twilight night, as we posted far away over the winding mountain paths leading toward our destination. As we thought of its being only a couple of weeks before we should be sailing for our home, it seemed as though the best wine had been reserved for the last. The scenes thrilled us with such delight and — accompanied as they were with the memory of the beautiful scenes and friendships we had just left behind — so enthused us that we bade farewell to sleep and joyously and mirthfully sang our songs and conversed with each other until sunshine dawned, enlivening our pathway till we alighted at Patterdale. In Scotland during June the twilight lasts all through the night.

It could not be possible for mortal creatures to enjoy more of the beauties of nature than this — one of our brightest experiences in all our tour, with a background as interesting as the picture itself, and it was all without alloy.

Leaving our chartered team, we entered the regular stage-coach at five o'clock on the morning of the next day, and were driven through a very interesting portion of Scotland leading to Glasgow, where we arrived at seven o'clock in the evening.

As we passed through Dumfries, the driver kindly drew up his horses and allowed me to jump into the field where Burns ploughed up the mouse. I picked a few daisies which I have pressed in my book as a memento. Learning that the great poet was entombed in the churchyard of that town, we resolved to visit it. While they were changing the horses, we hastened to the spot, and as we could not wait for the gate to be unlocked, scrambled over the wall, and as if by instinct took a direct course to the grave. We found his monument, the finest among four or five hundred, on which his figure was sculptured in marble holding a plough. We then went into the church and sat in the pew once occupied by the Scottish Bard. 'Twas solemn to be there. As we proceeded on our way we passed a marketwoman with some strawberries. I purchased a shilling's worth. When we arrived at the hotel, found Judson and Asa had also purchased a bag. We had a feast indeed, sweetened, and with cream.

As we advanced onward in Scotland, we perceived marked characteristics of their nationality in the inquisitive countenances of the people.

One of the curiosities which attracted our attention here was a tree which was pointed out to us, said to have been planted by the great Scotch warrior, William Wallace, when a boy

One of the great annoyances throughout Great Britain which we could not become reconciled to, was the exorbitant perquisites of the servants at the hotels, public places and resorts. Every one of the employees, from clerk to bootblack, came streaming in after we had paid our regular charges, with their demands for perquisites. From the clerk even to the chamber-maid, every one wanted their fee. It was both extortion and imposition upon us. In the present case we had paid our fare, some fifty dollars, for a ride in a coach — higher rates than we paid in our own country; but as we approached the city where we were to take the train, we learned from some persons that the "whip" intended to come the "Scotch grab" on us for the sum of five shillings each, and there were five of us. I ordered him to leave the baggage at the depot where we were to take the cars for Glasgow; instead of that, he deposited the baggage right opposite the tavern. We had barely time to get it to the depot, but we immediately chartered a hand-cart, and found a man ready and willing to take it as fast as he could for the sum of three or four shillings. As I secured my tickets I met this driver at the train. He was exceedingly insulting. I said to him, "You can't come the 'Scotch grab' on these Yankees." The police were very near, if there had been any outbreak.

Usually while we were travelling any great distance we took a regular first-class coach, with a door on each side, which held six or eight passengers, and we were fastened in by the train-man. The coaches had very fine seats, cushioned thoroughly for the whole length of the body and with arms upholstered.

It was frequently the case at the starting of a train from some of the depots, that a man was deputized with trumpet in hand to play some patriotic air familiar to the people travelling, and that was a signal for the starting of the train. This man would get partly through his tune when we would start off with the music ringing in our ears. The trumpeter at Manchester would recognize us as we approached the train, and would play some of our national music, "Yankee Doodle," "Star Spangled Banner," "Sweet Home," "Auld Lang Syne," which we considered a compliment to the Hutchinsons.

Every nation, as far as we have learned its history, has been inclined to dissipation in some particular, persuing courses that are both injurious to health and demoralizing. The great tobacco habit is an illustration. Tobacco was an Indian weed discovered in America only about three hundred years ago. It was first introduced into Europe for medicinal purposes, but afterwards resulted in an imitation of the native aborigines. The white man became addicted to the habit of using this narcotic on account of its so affecting and exhilarating the nervous system. Though there was a heavy embargo on this product, yet the people of Great Britain would not forego the privilege of the substance, but secured it at whatever cost, to their mouth's content.

It was evident that the Scotch people in Glasgow had embraced and practised the habit of using it in the form of snuff. Sunday morning I repaired to one of the kirks. The moment the door was opened, the pervasive atmosphere of the place came with such a stunning power upon my olfactories that at first shock I was inclined to withdraw, but staggered through the thick fog and was ushered to a seat with a large congregation around me, and soon observed that the male portion of the audience at very short intervals were taking their pinch of snuff from a box situated almost directly in front of each of them upon a desk. The preacher took his text from that passage of Scripture, "He that is filthy let him be filthy still," the only passage in the Scripture that appears to sanction the habit; and often in his gesticulations, pronouncing the curse upon original sin and sinners, he would reach his hand to a deposit shelved under his Bible, and pausing in his sentence, as he was about to pronounce his anathema upon the poor sinner of old, he would snuff his tobacco, and then finish out his gesture.

For exercise we perambulated about the city and

noticed the peculiarities of the buildings; some were very ancient in their architecture, some six and seven stories high on the great thoroughfare, the upper stories overhanging the sidewalks in a very ancient style.

We learned to our surprise of the strict observance of Sunday and the general acceptance of that day. In a private apartment of our hotel some one of us happened to sing a few bars. The landlord came to our room and requested us not to sing a note, as it was annoying to a divine who was boarding in the same house Of course, we refrained from further disturbing incidents and determined that while we were sojourning in Turkey we would do as the turkeys did

The following Monday we gave our first concert and were received with the greatest *éclat* and vociferous applause. Such a greeting was exceedingly gratifying to us, and the tender recollections of that scene and reception will ever abide with us as an honor from those peculiar and interesting people.

The United States Consul showed us great courtesy, and there came a request that we should repeat the concert, but our engagement at Edinburgh the following night prevented our remaining. The next day we started for the Highlands of Scotland. We visited Loch Lomond and the Mount Ben Lomond, 3,200 feet above the level of the sea. This is the land of Rob Roy. The atmosphere was most invigorating and electric, constantly ministering to our esthetic joy as we viewed from this height the beautiful lakes and the grand scenery of the country, the silver cascade and waterfall perfecting the scene. The tempest, too, to make the scene more beautiful, was upon us. A sudden gust of wind coming upon my umbrella nearly threw me over the precipice into the raging stream. Seeing my dangerous position, my brother Asa sprang and seized me and balanced me back into life.

Thence down the lake we sailed across Loch Lomond to the opposite shore. Here they supplied us with mountain ponies, and we crossed five miles over the mountains. Halting upon a crest, we gathered in a group and sang Sir Walter Scott's words to our adapted music, "McGregor's Gathering," in full view of the lake.

> "The moon's on the lake, the mist's on the brae
> And our clan has a name that is nameless by day;
> Our signal for fight, which from monarchs we drew
> Must be heard but by night in our vengeful hallu
> Then hallu! hallu! hallu!"

Several Scotchmen gathered around and listened, expressing great delight with the song, the words of which were, of course, familiar to them.

Descending to the landing, we took a steamboat, seven miles across the lake, and saw the cave of Rob Roy. We stopped at a hotel named Ardcheanachrochdam. We mounted the hill near this unspeakable hotel, and sang "God save the Queen," and "Yankee Doodle," then passed on to Sterling where we gave a popular concert and were very well received.

Leaving Sterling *en route* for Edinburgh, we took a seat on the top of the coach for the pleasure of viewing the country, and, arriving at the station, took cars to our destination. On our arrival we improved the opportunity of viewing the capital of Scotland, where we beheld many places of much interest. We saw Scott's monument, which was the finest specimen of architecture I have seen for many a day. We also visited Sterling Castle. We here met Mr. Comb, the phrenologist. We went to the Parliament House, and to George

Harriett's institution for poor children. This, I think, is the best method a man can take to use his money and do good. There were eighty children in this institution. Edinburgh University, or College, was one of the grandest buildings I had seen since leaving New York. The only monument we saw in this institution was that of Robert Burns. Bonaparte's table, which he used while a prisoner at St. Helena, we also saw. We then went on to Arthur's Seat, the view from which has been so magnificently described by Carlyle; and thence to Royal Chapel, where among the many curiosities, we saw the bones of the kings and queens of Scotland. We went to the Tower and saw the crown of Scotland that Sir Walter Scott found in a little room in the walls of the structure; also a very large cannon that was used in the time of the Scotch Rebellion, belted with wrought-iron hoops, one and one-half inches thick, and six inches wide, a rude-looking piece of ordnance.

Returning to Liverpool by way of Glasgow, we met many of our recently made friends, who congratulated us on our safe arrival. We then gave two more concerts before our departure, the time intervening being spent in social gatherings. We took the opportunity to invite all our English friends to Uncle Sam's domain, as he was "rich enough to give them all a farm."

On the morning of July 4th we went on board the *Cambria*. Many dear friends from the different parts of the country came to see us off. Among them were Douglas Jerrold, Frederick Douglass, Henry Clapp, Mr. Ireland, of the Manchester *Guardian*, Mrs. Bright, the Misses Brady, and many others.

On the trip we had frequent gatherings on board, at which we entertained the people, introducing many of our nautical songs, interesting to the captain and supernumeraries as well as the passengers.

A London cockney having shipped on board, bound for Canada, made himself a nuisance by lying in the thoroughfare or walk on board, where we would have to step over or on him in passing a given point towards the awning. Day after day we would find the man in that position, stupid with his homesickness and seasickness. Some friends had gathered to hear us sing a song. At the closing of the melodious song, "Happy and Free," and while the others were applauding, this man awoke from his stupor, turned up his face and ejaculated this sentence as a compliment to the performance, "That's infernal good." After hearing this song he never spoke more, and we passed on. Who would not sell a farm and go to sea?

Nearing the American coast, the warm, genial earth gladdened our visions at last, its beauty enhanced by a splendid sunset watched by passengers and crew, pronounced as the finest view that they had seen. One Englishman in his enthusiasm remarked, "Well, if that is a specimen of your sunsets, I shall want to stay in America."

About midnight the pilot was taken on board; and when morning came, with a fair wind, the sails were set and wafted us onward, and we had a safe conduct to Halifax. We saw the sun rise once more in America; we went ashore and saw the forts; took on some ice, provisions, etc., with twenty-five passengers, then went on to Boston. The day passed merrily by with high hopes: we speculated with one another on the prospect of again meeting our American friends. The ship was merry with song; and as a complimentary reminder of our nativity, as we passed around the rocks of Marblehead, the captain dined us upon pork and beans. The occasion was notable for friendships and congratulations. We sang our songs, and in the evening we gave a concert in the cabin, and all went "merry as a marriage bell."

Notwithstanding the seeming idiosyncrasies of that confiding and capable officer, Captain Judkins of the *Cambria*, we treasured him among the nobility, such a one as England is proverbial for placing at the head of her greatest and most responsible enterprises, Captain Judkins was a friend and brother.

The following day, July 17th, we arrived in Boston at two o'clock. Passing Cape Cod we saw twenty-five fishing schooners all in one company. We were all jubilant, especially Brother Jesse, who having caught a glimpse of Lynn and High Rock, seemed to be overcome with delight, and going to and fro, scattered smiles to high and low, all the time in great danger of losing his hat. We all joined in singing "Home again, from a foreign shore."

We were greeted at the landing, as millions have been before us, by our dear friends, with whom we were glad indeed to meet. Among the crowd at the landing stood Elizur Wright, editor of the *Chronotype*. We made many pleasant calls on our Boston friends, and were again greeted by our dear friend Francis Jackson and his daughter Hatty, on Hollis Street.

Having been absent eleven months, we treasured the experience of that period as among the brightest, loveliest and most profitable of our lives.

We then hastened to a happier meeting and greeting at the home farm, which we had left the year before — father, mother, brothers and sisters, wife and little one. We met with many queries and questions — and they became very monotonous, though coming from friends and neighbors as they met us in our perambulations about the town at every corner — like these: "How did you like sailing?" "Did you see any big fish in the ocean?" "Did you meet with any accidents on the way going and coming?" "Sure, by Jabers, did you see O'Connell?" "Did you visit Scotland?" "How do you like the English brogue?" "What was the highest price for tickets you got at your concerts? We heard you got eight dollars a ticket" "How much did you take at any one concert?" "Do you think they'll be inclined to go to war with us again? I guess we could whip them out every time" "Are they inclined to aid us in our great struggle for emancipation, and will they be sincere in it?" And, to cap the climax, "How did you like the queen?" By the way, Jesse was the only one of us who saw Victoria, after all.

Upon our arrival from England, we were informed by a relative that grandfather Leavitt was very ill and was extremely desirous of seeing his grandchildren. I gathered up some material for his comfort, my brothers and sisters contributing to this donation, carried them to the house and presented them to my Uncle William, who had charge of grandfather. I found him lying on his couch, but he still had his memory and senses. He was then ninety-four years old. He expressed great delight at our safe arrival, and said, "I shall never see you again." In a very few weeks after we heard of his demise, on the 29th of August, 1846.

Hanging upon the wall of his room was a lithograph picture of brothers and sisters, the quartet, that we presented the family some little time before we left for England. We were told by our Uncle William Leavitt that daily our grandfather requested him to take down that picture, bring it to where his feeble sight could distinguish the individual members, and as he kissed them he would murmur a prayer that we might safely return and that he might behold us once more.

The funeral was arranged at the Congregational church, of which he was a member in good standing. He had assisted in building it seventy-four years before. During the services we arose from among the mourners, stepped into the aisle and sang "The Angel's Invitation to the Pilgrim."

> "Come pilgrim, come away,
>   Why shouldst thou be lingering here,
>   I hear the voice of angels calling,
>   Come away, come away"

The occasion was very impressive and one of deep interest. He being well known by the citizens and the oldest man in the town, great sympathy was manifested.

A very excellent notice of him appeared from the pen of Richard Boyleston, the editor of the *Farmer's Cabinet*, his familiar acquaintance.

I here submit several verses, the lines of which were penned some years subsequent to this by Brother Jesse, in memory of his life and demise.

OLD GRANDFATHER

Old Grandfather lived till he was ninety years old,
  But he died long ago, long ago,
He had many friends, and it never was told
  That the good old man had a foe.

Chorus

Then lay down the mallet and the maul,
  Hang up the chisel and the saw,
There's no more labor for the good old man,
  He has gone to his home far away

His grandchildren all will remember him long,
    For a smile always sat on his brow,
As he told a good story or sang a good song;
    Methinks I can hear him sing now

He built many houses while he lived upon the earth;
    But never a house did he own,
Except the old cot where he lived so many years,
    And the house where now rests his bones

Oh, well I remember the day that he died,
    And they laid him out on his bier,
As we followed to the grave the little children cried,
    And the old men wept many a tear.

His body now sleeps in the old churchyard,
    And the stone marks the spot where 'twas laid,
And in heaven his soul has found its reward,
    And the good, all shall meet him again

Chorus
Then lay down the mallet and the maul,
    Hang up the chisel and the saw,
There's no more labor for the good old man,
    He has gone to his long home awa.

He married three times, and had nine children by his first wife and two by his second wife. His youngest daughter Nancy took for a partner a brother of the great preacher Theodore Parker, of Boston. The youngest son, Kendrick, following the calling of his father, pursued his trade as a carpenter in the city of Cincinnati, where, in the very early days of slaveocracy he assisted and was a member of the first anti-slavery society of that vicinity, in which Salmon P. Chase acted an important part. He also lived to the good old age of ninety-three.

CHAPTER VI.

A GOOD TIME COMING.

> "There's a good time coming, boys,
>   A good time coming,
> There's a good time coming, boys,
>   Wait a little longer
> We may not live to see the day,
> But earth shall glisten in the ray,
>   Of the good time coming
> Cannon-balls may aid the truth,
>   But thought's a weapon stronger,
> We'll win our battle by its aid
>   Wait a little longer."

Soon after our return from Europe an incident occurred which well illustrates the peculiar political and social conditions of the time, and indicates how necessary was our work of arousing the public conscience to a sense of its inhuman treatment of the despised and down-trodden black man, even though in so doing we encountered a form of social ostracism, and risked the loss of popularity and money.

I had invited Frederick Douglass to dine with me in Boston, at the old Pearl Street House. Arriving a little ahead of him, but fully persuaded that he would come, I tipped up a chair by my side at the table, and commenced my dinner. Perhaps I was two-thirds through, when I descried his familiar figure at the door. Immediately rising, I beckoned to him to come to me, and seated him at my elbow. At once a hundred chairs went back with a bang, and every guest excepting ourselves, rose and vacated the apartment, repairing to the corridors and hotel office, indignantly declaring, with much more profanity than could by any stretch of imagination be considered necessary, that they did not propose "to eat with a 'nigger.'" Meanwhile, though rather surprised at this demonstration, I calmly remarked to Douglass that we would go on with our dinner, and beckoned to the waiter to come and serve us. He, a white man, defiantly placed his towel behind his back, and refused to respond. Then I called another, and another, with the same discouraging lack of success. By this time I was desperate; going to the side-board, where the dinner was dealt out, I seized a whole roasted chicken, and placing it before my despised friend, told him we would serve ourselves. As we came out of the dining-room, having finished our dinner, the cook came up from the basement, wearing his white headgear, and boldly declared that he'd be —— if he would cook for a nigger. As we glanced from the windows we saw at least a half-dozen drays drawn up to the sidewalk, receiving the baggage of the "insulted" guests, which was being removed to more acceptable quarters. The proprietor of the hotel took a noble stand on this occurrence. He said to me, "I take the responsibility. This is your guest, and you have a right to have him here."

At a later date during my stay, I had a rather unpleasant experience with this same landlord. I was afflicted with a severe toothache. He sympathetically remarked that he thought he could help me, and I consented to let him pull the offending molar. So he produced an instrument closely resembling a logger's canthook, known to the profession as a "turnkey," and adjusted it for action. He used a neighboring tooth for a fulcrum When he began to bear down, I found that one of my front teeth was likely to be sacrificed, and cried out, "Hold on! you'll spoil my front tooth." As a matter of fact, I now, a half-century later, carry a loose front tooth, with a dent in it, as a result of that operation. Well, the tooth came out, and my Boniface dentist looked it over, said it showed very little decay, and after scraping it, put it back in my jaw. He showed me one in his own mouth which had been put back in the same way. For six weeks after that I suffered from neuralgia and every form of pain that ever proceeds from a diseased jaw. Finally I went to Lynn, convinced that another tooth was the sinner, and calling on a dentist, had it extracted. Then I told him of the tooth I had had pulled and reset, and he exclaimed, "You have run the risk of your life! It must come out at once." So the second one was taken out. I found it a great deal more painful than when it was pulled the first time.

On the 1st of October, 1846, we started on another tour, very successful financially, but which came to an abrupt ending, owing to our regard for another cultured black man, Robert Purvis, of Philadelphia, and our determination that whites and blacks should have equal facilities to hear the Hutchinsons sing, or we would refuse to sing to anybody. Three profitable engagements, at an average of eight hundred dollars each, were hanging in the balance of our decision; but we did not falter and rather than yield to the pro-slavery prejudice of Philadelphia, expressed through the high-handed officialism of its mayor, we returned to our farms and our freedom. We could earn our bread by the sweat of our brows, and preferred to, rather than submit to the tyranny of misguided and prejudiced magistrates, even though we knew an impatient public was waiting for our songs.

On January 8, 1847, Mr. Garrison made the following comment on the Philadelphia incident, in the *Liberator:*

"The Hutchinson Family, after giving three concerts in Philadelphia, were denied the use of Musical Fund Hall for a fourth by the trustees, on the ground that the mayor had given warning that the admission of persons of color could not be allowed, and would be positively prohibited, otherwise the city would be exposed to the danger of a mob! There is another exemplification of American liberty — another story to travel to England of opprobrium of our country. Shade of William Penn! has not thy miscalled 'City of Brotherly Love' long since become the abode of every foul spirit? Of course the Hutchinsons indignantly refused to exclude colored persons from their concerts, and consequently shook off the dust from their feet of this mobocratic city."

We gave Philadelphia a lesson that she did not forget, and she profited by it. But to my story.

Our route led us through Manchester, Concord and Nashua, to Boston and Lowell. At each place we gave good satisfaction, except when we sang what the Democrats called "politics." Then we usually received a volley of hisses. But hisses did not frighten us. We gave two concerts in Salem, and recalled how once we had to go begging for an audience in the City of Witches; but a name abroad had changed all that. We found it harder to sustain popularity than to earn it, for our audiences grew critical. At a concert in Lynn some one made a remark from the auditor's seats, and in response Brother Jesse gave one of his celebrated crows, with which he was wont to awake all the roosters in town at dead of night during his youth and young manhood. The effect upon the audience was to cause a commotion that may be better imagined than described. We went to Worcester, where two concerts were given, and on October 14th reached New York

City. My diary tells the story of our stay there as follows:

"On Wednesday the 18th, sang in the Tabernacle to about two thousand people. It did seem good to be with the Gothamites once more. We got through the concert without much trouble. With the exception of a little hissing all went off smoothly. We sang against war with Mexico, and against the 'honorable' system of enslaving the human race. The papers came out the next day roaring like lions against such sentiments being uttered in a concert-room by persons singing for the public favor and money. This had its effect, and now we feel more like singing against these public sins than ever. On Monday the 21st, we had our second, and another good house, but with some falling off from the first. One paper is on our side, the *New York Tribune*, edited by Horace Greeley, formerly of Amherst, N. H. He is a very moral man, and one who wishes well to all the human family. Peace to his posterity!

"On Tuesday, December 1st, we gave our third entertainment, at the Tabernacle. Had a good house. My wife was present. She came on in the steamboat *Atlantic*, arriving in New York on that morning, just two days before the boat was wrecked on the coast of Long Island Sound, forty persons losing their lives. Oh, what an escape!"

On the day of one of our concerts in New York Abby was suffering with a severe cold, caught on a trip to Sing Sing, where we spent Thanksgiving Day singing to the prisoners. The doctor said she could hardly talk, much less sing; but we had the programme to go through, and we went through it, Abby singing with the rest, to the satisfaction of ourselves and the public. To the last our concerts in New York were well attended, but much opposition was manifested, especially when we sung such lines as the following:

> "War and slavery perplex us
> And ere long will sorely vex us,
> Oh, we're paying dear for Texas
> In the war with Mexico.
> Such a demonstration
> Is beneath our station
> When by arbitration
> We can settle every war."

Our two opening concerts at Philadelphia were of the pleasantest kind. We took about fourteen hundred dollars. We stayed with Edward Hopper, son of the eminent philanthropist of the same surname. Mr. Hopper's wife was the daughter of Mrs. Mott, the noted Quakeress and Abolitionist. The week preceding Christmas was one to be long remembered. We occasionally found amusement skating with friends, Edward Davis, Miller McKim and others. On the eve of Christmas we had a fine time at the home of our friends the Palmers, with games and song

On Christmas night we gave our fourth concert at Musical Fund Hall, and encountered some opposition to our anti-slavery sentiments. But we felt it our duty to tell the sins of the nation, and preach humanity to the whole race. At this concert our friend Robert Purvis, an educated mulatto, to whom I have previously referred, a fine speaker and in every way an able man, attended, sitting with Lucretia Mott and one or two other "plain bonnets." Some few people, having constitutional objections to colored persons beside them in a public entertainment, made complaint to the mayor, and that dough-faced functionary at once notified the head of his police force to place officers at the door to stop any one black enough to belong to the proscribed race from coming in to hear us sing Also informing the trustees of the hall that he would not be responsible for the damage to it, if this was not done. This order we considered an infringement of human rights, and we at once came out in a card in the papers, stating our convictions in the most emphatic manner, and announcing the cancelling of the dates of three concerts advertised, on the ground that we were virtually driven from the hall:

> "Party threats are not alarming,
> For when music ceases charming
> We can earn our bread by farming
> In the old Granite State."

On the evening of the 29th we were given a farewell reception at the home of Lucretia Mott. I shall never forget that scene. Many friends of freedom were gathered. It was a happy meeting, though the words of Mrs. Mott affected us to tears. In thrilling language, she eulogized us as martyrs for principle, saying we should be classed with the martyrs of old, and prophesying the greatest good to come from our act. And she was right. At the close of the meeting we felt more determined than ever, on our course, and consecrating ourselves anew to the good work we went forth, realizing that for the achievement of any great end, we must, in the language of the poet,

> "Strike like a hammer, steady, strong,
> That beating shapes the glowing steel;
> Strike for the right against the wrong,
> And be each blow a thunder peal."

The name of Lucretia Mott will long be revered, and her good works live in history, for the seeds of love and kindness sown by her in the hearts of many will bloom centuries hence. Many hearts echo the worthy tribute paid to her by Fanny D. Gage, from which this is an extract:

> "I never think of that woman,
> But my heart throbs high with love,
> And I ask, Can she be more beautiful
> In the blissful realms above?
> I can scarcely in my dreaming,
> See her face more fair and bright;
> She seems to me now with her radiant brow,
> A spirit of love and light

"The poet may sing his praises,
  Of the glow of sweet sixteen,
But there is a holier beauty
  Of eighty-three, I ween;
For the girlish face if moulded,
  By a true and loving heart,
Will brighten as the heart throbs on,
  Rechiselling every part."

Of course, the real trouble in Philadelphia was that we were singing anti-slavery songs, and were converting the people, and the pro-slavery sympathizers couldn't stand it. The papers took sides for and against us, and great good was done for the cause of equal rights. Meanwhile, we shook the dust of Philadelphia from our feet, as a testimony against it, and went to Wilmington, in the slave-holding State of Delaware, where we found a less proscriptive spirit than in the City of Brotherly Love, and were treated with perfect courtesy. Then we went home, with aching hearts, for it was hard to be reconciled to the Southern custom of suppressing free speech and free song. Two days later, we brothers had shouldered our axes and were merrily at work logging, as if there were no such unpleasant functionaries as pro-slavery mayors in existence. In the course of a week I had purchased the Wheeler farm in Amherst, near the Milford line, and soon began moving my household goods to it, and set up in real earnest as a farmer.

With the exception of two or three short trips, details of which will be given later, most of the year that followed was devoted to the multifarious cares of farm life. My journal shows that I worked fully as hard to earn a simple livelihood on that farm as does the average poor man who battles with the elements, and depredating specimens of the animal and feathered kingdom, in getting subsistence from the rocky soil of New England, in lieu of some better and easier mode of life. Meanwhile, I confess that I was unhappy. To be sure, singing was a severe tax on one's physical and nervous system. We boys were in the habit, in our rehearsals, of practising for perfect accord and harmony until in sheer exhaustion of brain and nerve we would resort to an extreme expedient for relief. Each of us would take a separate tune, in different keys, and sing them simultaneously for about an half-hour. By that time we would be sufficiently refreshed to go on with our practising. But, notwithstanding the cares and trials of professional life, it seemed to me, picking up stones in the east field, or toiling at haying in the hot July sun, was a far harder mode of making money, and vastly less remunerative.

In January, 1847, we all went to Boston to sing at the anti-slavery meetings. Before leaving Boston we gave concerts there and in Woburn, and then went to Providence, where at our first concert the rush was so great that a thousand people were unable to gain admittance to the hall. A Mr. Willard was very kind to us during our stay here. We sang in Pawtucket, and again in Providence, and the demand to hear us was so great that on the day of our departure we gave a morning concert to a large audience. The next night we sang to fifteen hundred people in Springfield. Here we met George Hills of West Cambridge, now Arlington, and a Mr. Coggin of New Hampshire, both of whom were very friendly to us. I made a short visit to my old friend Lydston, the painter, who was also very proficient on the trombone and a good fellow. Then we proceeded to Hartford, where our friend Rev. William W. Patton, afterwards president of Howard University, soon appeared, and made life look pleasant. He was Ludlow Patton's brother.

February 15th we reached New Haven, where we sang to a full house. The next day we had a fine time kicking football on the college green. By the way, I was the first to introduce the big rubber football at Yale College, for so many years the home of football champions, and also at Amherst and other colleges. I had seen them at the store of a relative in New York, and immediately bought one. During this trip we for the first time saw the workings of the magnetic telegraph. Our concert was given on the 17th. It went off well, but our anti-slavery songs were hissed by a coterie of Southern students sitting together in one part of the hall. Judson looked calmly at them during a pause in the singing, and remarked: "There are no snakes in Ireland, but there are lots of geese in America." That squelched them, and we had no further trouble. Meanwhile, we had become very much aroused, and sung with more spirit than ever. The next day we returned to Hartford, and in the evening gave a closing concert. We were hissed some, and the following day the *Times*, a Democratic paper, paid its respects to us, coming down on our freedom songs "like a thousand of brick," as my journal says.

Going back to Springfield, we gave concerts there and at Cabotville, and then went to Albany, where we stopped at the Delavan House, in company with John B. Gough. We went to his lecture, where he kept the people in a roar for three hours. After the lecture we had an hour of good fellowship with him. The Albanians turned out well to our concerts, and so did the Trojans, when we went to Troy on the 25th. At Troy we stayed with Rev John Pierpont. We heard him preach on the Sabbath during our stay. While at Troy, Brother Zeph came in one day feeling unwell, and whimsically remarked, "I haven't eaten anything since yesterday till to-day — and to-morrow will make three days."

On our way back we stopped at Albany and gave a farewell concert. A little negro girl in the audience disturbed some of our pro-slavery hearers very much. Judson had been quite averse to going to New York City, but we finally persuaded him to go and sing for the benefit of the starving poor in Ireland. March 3d we reached that city. Here we were met by Ludlow Patton, who soon became the husband of Abby, and had a most enjoyable time in his company. Soon after our arrival Joshua joined us, he having been himself on a concert tour. On the 5th we gave a concert in the Tabernacle, with comparatively little hissing. On the 8th we had one of our most successful concerts in Brooklyn. After a monster concert in the Tabernacle we returned to Boston, where we stopped a few days. On the Sabbath I heard Theodore Parker preach, and was highly edified. I made a practice of hearing him often after that. Took a day's run out to Lynn, to see Jesse in his new house on High Rock, and then home to Milford again.

On Sunday, April 18th, my daughter Viola was born. My diary says, "The Lord has blessed me, and I hope to be always thankful." To-day, cheered as I am in my declining years by the loving ministrations of this affectionate child, I gladly repeat the sentiment.

Home cares fully occupied my attention for many months. In August we made up a family party, and started for a trip through the White Hills. With us were Caleb and wife, Judson and Jerusha his wife, Rhoda and Abby, with Joshua driving; Asa with his new bride Elizabeth, Frank, and her sister and the baby in the team with me. Others joined us as we proceeded. Our route was through Manchester and Concord, singing at each place, and making a pilgrimage at the latter to the grave of our honored and lamented friend N. P. Rogers. Plymouth, Bristol, through Franconia Notch; Fabyans, where we found the hotel much enlarged, and did not have to camp outside as before; Littletown; Bath; Haverhill; Hanover, where we gave a concert; Woodstock; Windsor; Claremont; Bellows Falls; Brattleboro; Keene; Peterboro; giving concerts in nearly all the latter towns; and home. While in the White Mountains we were fortunate in meeting the Baker Family twice, and had a good sing with them. At Brattleboro we were serenaded in the dead of night by the Burdett Family, a fine organization of young men. It seemed to me if I could have such singing over my body at my funeral I should be satisfied. In the group was a boy, James Fisk, Jr., then fourteen years old, with a beautiful alto voice. He afterwards became the noted stock operator with Jay Gould, and died a tragic death in New York.

The year 1848 was an eventful one to us. In February we spent three weeks in concerting in the vicinity of Boston and then departed for New York. On our way we heard that Henry Clay was to be the guest of the city, and the fact started up the poetic muse of Brother Jesse, who was with us at the hotel in New Haven and he wrote his song, "Harry of the West." He showed the words to me, and instantly an appropriate melody came into my mind. This we sang over several times, and then started for the New York boat. On board, we sought a retired spot, and commenced to rehearse it again, Jesse taking the bass and I the air. Judson and Asa came sauntering along, attracted by the new tune, and uttering remarks in comment on our singing a song of which they knew nothing. "What have you got there?" said one. "Join in," said we. They took their parts, and we sang the song, until a large number of passengers, attracted by the harmony, gathered about, complimenting us upon it. We had no thought of singing it in public, but at our boarding-house in New York, we sang it over again. Captain Knight, of the new and famous ship *Henry Clay*, called upon us, and invited us to go on board the vessel. Complying, we went into the captain's cabin and standing in a group, struck up the song. We had hardly finished, when an alderman of the city, who was on board, said to us enthusiastically, "You must go and sing that song to Henry Clay this afternoon." We began to consider whether we ought to go or not. Jesse immediately added another verse to the song to make our convictions clear, for we well knew Clay to be a pro-slavery man:

"For the glorious day is coming now
When wrong shall be redressed,
And Freedom's star shine bright and clear
On 'Harry of the West'"

And we consented to go.

Going ashore, we took a hack and went after Abby, at our boarding-house. She was rather reluctant about going, as she had heard so much against the "great compromiser," but finally yielded. We soon arrived at the hotel where the reception was taking place. The mayor with his chief counsellors and their distinguished guest were just about taking their wine at the banquet when we were ushered in. The Hutchinsons were at that time very popular in New York. The leading people in all departments of life were frequenting our conceits, and we were pretty well known to everybody. The mayor at once arose and expressed his pleasure in announcing our presence, and said we would sing an appropriate selection. The four brothers sang —

> "Come, brothers, now let's hurry out
>   To see our honored guest,
> For lo, in every street they shout,
>   'Brave Harry of the West'
>
> "The women, too, and children sweet,
>   Are singing with the rest,
> And weaving garlands in the street,
>   For 'Harry of the West'
>
> "Old Broadway now is all alive,
>   And in her laurels dressed;
> As the word goes round, he'll soon arrive,
>   Brave 'Harry of the West.'
>
> "Behold the aged statesman comes!
>   In highest honors dressed,
> No conquering hero ever shone
>   Like 'Harry of the West'
>
> "Nor shall a party feeling dare
>   To raise one narrow test,
> But all shall in the tribute share
>   To 'Harry of the West'
>
> "For th' glorious day is coming near
>   When wrong shall be redressed,
> And Freedom's star shine bright and clear
>   On 'Harry of the West.'
>
> "Then, hail, all hail, thrice-honored sage,
>   Our most distinguished guest!
> We'll venerate thy good old age,
>   Brave 'Harry of the West'"

As we were singing this, Mr. Clay's eyes opened, and his chin dropped with astonishment and surprise at its appropriateness. At the close, he rose and came to us, saying, "What can I do to repay you for this great honor you have conferred upon me?" Instantly the response came into my mind, "Liberate your slaves, and we'll make you President of the United States." But it did not seem appropriate to say such a thing, under such circumstances, and we simply made some response of thanks for his expression of gratitude, and he returned to his place of honor. Subsequently, he sent his wine down to us, but we sent him back word that we were teetotallers, and could not drink with him. He left his seat, came up to us and responded, "If I were a young man like yourselves, I'd be a teetotaller, too." Later, with Abby, we sang a temperance song, "Cold Water," and "The Old Granite State," thus giving him both temperance and emancipation.

A reporter of the *New York Tribune*, Elias Smith, was present, and wrote out a very elaborate account of the incident, and included the song. Other papers also printed accounts of it. This made trouble for us, for the papers went to Boston, Garrison read them, and the next week the *Liberator* came out, and in a scathing article attacked us for going back on our principles in doing honor to Clay, the compromiser. We said nothing in response, but bided our time.

In referring to our meeting with Clay, my diary says: "It did seem good to hear the old man speak, but he is 'Clay' like all of us."

Another experience of our first week in New York was witnessing the funeral cortege of John Quincy Adams pass through the city.

On this trip Brother Joshua acted as our advance agent. March 14th my diary says:

"We gave our second concert last night Had a jam We are rather glad to make money of course, but not so fast as to distract our attention from the great subject of humanity. This evening Jesse joins us in song for the first time since we left the Old World"

We stayed several days in New York, giving many concerts in the city and vicinity, usually with crowded houses. Then, with concerts in Morristown and Trenton, we went to Philadelphia, the city we had left so abruptly the year before, for conscience sake. We were unable to obtain the Musical Fund Hall for our concerts, owing to our determination to admit any colored people who were likely to come; so our three concerts were given at the Assembly Rooms. All were largely attended, and to our surprise, not the slightest disapprobation was manifested. In Baltimore two concerts were given to rather unsympathetic audiences, and here we met the Haywards, Lovejoys, and other cherished friends. We had the pleasure of a Sunday with that faithful friend to the cause of humanity, Mr. Snodgrass, and then proceeded to Washington.

At Washington we stopped at Willard's Hotel. We visited the capitol, and paid our respects to our valued friend, Senator John P. Hale. Congress was discussing resolutions regarding the French Revolution.

At our first concert, where we sang well and were but little hissed, a rather laughable episode occurred. Judson was singing his solo, "The Humbugged Husband," and was just delivering the line, "I'm sadly taken in," when the platform gave way under his feet, and he was "taken in" before the eyes of the audience, which was, of course, convulsed with laughter at the remarkable coincidence. He fell up to his chin, with violin in one hand and bow in the other, outstretched in air.

On April 11th we took a trip to Mount Vernon, the home of Washington, eight miles by boat and the rest in a hack, ten miles. The house and tomb of Washington were in a sadly dilapidated condition. We went into the mansion, and sang "The Land of Our Fathers" to old Mrs. Washington, a family connection of the great man, cut some canes for souvenirs and came away after witnessing the squalor of the slaves of the Washington family, feeling that slavery was a curse to our country, indeed. The same evening we went to the White House to see President Polk. "Shook the old fellow by the hand, and found him to be nothing but a man, and rather small at that," says my diary. We met James Bowles and other old friends there.

The next day we went to the capitol again, and heard speeches from John C. Calhoun and others. In the afternoon Judson and I called upon Mr. Tuck, Representative from New Hampshire, and Joshua R. Giddings, who was still doing his glorious work for his fellow-men.

Sunday, the 16th, we had as company all day Dr. Bailey and another friend, Mr. Chaplin, a man who only the night before had succeeded in starting seventy-seven fugitive slaves toward a land of freedom. He had kept his secret well, and no one suspected him of complicity in a plot that had set the whole city, and later the country at large in an uproar. He was very anxious, and it was a relief to confide his story to us. The next morning I had business at the American Hotel. The man whose guest I was begged me to excuse the absence of a bootblack and other supernumeraries of the establishment. He said the servants were among the party of fugitives that had escaped. He did not seem to know the manner of their departure, and I was discreet enough not to inform him. All the slaves were recaptured near the mouth of the Potomac, and a few days later were auctioned off to planters farther South, against the protests of Northern papers, as a punishment for attempting to make their escape.

We returned from Washington *via* Baltimore, where two more concerts were given. Dr. Snodgrass got up a fishing-party, and we had a fine time. Rebecca Codman, a woman of culture and public spirit, was in the company. Then we went back to New York, a city where we were always successful. In fact, New York, with Boston, Hartford, New Haven, Springfield, Worcester and Providence, would have given us all the business we desired in those years. The other places we visited were usually at the solicitation of admiring friends, rather than by our own volition.

April 22d, I find this entry in my diary:

"Astor House, up five stories from the ground, sitting at a table by the light of two candles, Jesse on one hand and Asa on the other, one writing to Hale of the senate, and the other to that good man Giddings of Ohio, words of congratulation for their success in standing for the freedom of the whole human race, black and white. I wrote a word in each letter. I hope we may do something in this great and glorious work of freedom. These are great times. I know we must have a revolution in less than six months and our slaves must be set free. ''Tis coming,' sure. I am thinking the second coming of Christ is also near on the earth. Perhaps the millennium is about to dawn. I am full of hope and fear. O Lord, hasten that glorious time when we shall live in peace and harmony together; when the spirit of fraternal kindness may exist between all nations! The world is in commotion. We have all been very much excited for the past week, because of the news of the day. There seems to be a mighty shaking up amongst the tyrants and slaveholders, and I guess the 'good time' is really coming.'

Four days later I wrote:

"The Irish hold a meeting to-night to raise troops to send to Ireland. The feeling is very strong. I hope Ireland will get her freedom without much fighting, for the people there are determined to have a republic. Well, I can say, 'God be praised for doing these great and good things for his creatures.' This boarding at the Astor House at two dollars per day and waiting till three o'clock for one's dinner isn't exactly the thing. But there's a good time coming. I am glad I live in this great time."

WENDELL PHILLIPS — (p. 239)

The next day:

"We had our good friend Dr William Patton to dine with us Talked about the glorious revolution in the world, and had a good time of it"

After this we went home for a week, and then were off to New York again to attend the anti-slavery anniversaries. On our first day we heard John P. Hale speak for the Liberty party, sang at the American Anti-Slavery Society Anniversary, and in the evening listened to a lecture by Horace Greeley. The next day we went to the anti-slavery breakfast of the Liberty party, and later proceeded to the Minerva Rooms, where the anti-slavery meeting of the old society was going on. We usually took these meetings in on the wing, as we were likely to come in late or go out early to attend temperance meetings or fulfil concert engagements, and so had contracted a habit of sitting, not on the platform, but about two-thirds down the hall, in seats sufficiently near together so that we could strike up an appropriate song whenever opportunity presented itself. So this morning we followed our usual custom. Soon we sang "The Slave's Appeal." When we had finished, Wendell Phillips immediately took the platform, and remarked that if the song that had just been sung was to be understood as a confession of sorrow for the indiscretion of the vocalists in singing a fulsome song in honor of that apologizer for slavery, Henry Clay, it would be welcomed. This remark astonished everybody, for the audience was in ecstacies over the song. The usual method when criticisms were indulged in these meetings was for the criticized to reply, and Phillips was the last man to fear an answer of that sort. When he paused, Brother Jesse started to rise to respond. It did not seem to me that that was the best thing to do, and I pulled him down in his seat again, saying, "Let us sing; sing 'Liberate the Bondman.'" At once we sang the song that had for so many years melted hearts and converted thousands from pro-slavery to friendship for freedom. It was the inspiration song of many a campaign for the down-trodden, and was a far more silencing answer to allegations of lukewarmness toward the bondmen than any words of defence that might have been uttered. When we ceased singing the assembly was in tears. There was an exhibition of the deepest feeling I had ever seen in such a gathering. Our victory over our critics was complete. Phillips grasped his hat, and springing to the platform, swung it over his head as he shouted, "Three cheers for the Hutchinsons!" They were given with a will. This episode closed the meeting. Our friends gathered around, and we were showered with congratulations from every quarter. Among those who came to us was Phillips. He was immensely pleased at the way we had completely ignored his remarks, and won our vindication by means of song. This closed the incident as far as we were personally concerned. Henry C. Wright wrote an elaborate story of the affair to the *Liberator*, in which he pictured the "repentance" of the Hutchinsons in such colors as to arouse the mirth of Elizur Wright, and he replied to it in the *Chronotype* at considerable length. This provoked other articles in the *Liberator*, Douglass' *North Star*, the *Lynn Pioneer* and other papers.

We were making the New England House our headquarters on this trip. I gave Frederick Douglass a very cordial invitation to become my guest during my stay, informing him that there was extra room and a bed in our suite and that we would be glad to have him occupy it. He was rather reluctant at first, saying he did not care to have a repetition of such a scene as had occurred at the Pearl Street House in Boston. I told him that I would leave my door unlocked, so that he could come in at any hour in the night without molestation. He was reassured, accepted my invitation, and was with us during the convention.

While in New York we attended a meeting of tee-totallers at the Tabernacle. Among the speakers were John P. Hale, a Mr. King of Dublin, and a Frenchman from Lyons, who talked in his own language, and was interpreted by the celebrated Rev. Dr. E. N. Kirk of Boston.

On May 12th we returned to Boston, having Mr. Hale and Christopher Robinson of Lynn for company. The next day I went home. On May 31st, with my wife and daughter Viola, and in company with the rest of the family — father and mother, brothers and sisters, fourteen in all, and in our own teams — a start was made for Lynn, to visit Brother Jesse in his stone cottage on High Rock:

> "In the State of Massachusetts in the good old town of Lynn
> There's a famous range of ledges as ever eye hath seen,
> Two hundred feet the highest point, looms up its rugged block,
> And it's known throughout New England as 'Old High Rock.'"

Brother Jesse gave us a royal welcome. We made a happy party, although a rather good-sized one for the accommodations of the large stone cottage. The next day Brothers Andrew and Zephaniah joined us. We spent the day in song and plays like so many children. We were a hungry and happy band. On the following day we went to Swampscott, chartered a fishing boat, and went to the "Grounds," where we had rather poor luck as fishermen. Father caught the most of all.

I remember one day during this happy family reunion we all gathered in a big cleft about half-way up the face of High Rock, and sang "Land of Our Fathers." This was an appropriate song for this family of New Hampshire birth to sing, for in this region our ancestors for five generations had lived, and father was born only a few miles away, though removing to Milford, N. H., with his parents when only a year old.

The next day, father, mother, David, Noah, Andrew, Zephaniah, Caleb, Joshua and Rhoda went home, and the remaining brothers separated and arranged concerts in Ipswich, Beverly and Gloucester. The next week we gave our entertainments in each of those towns, with good success. On the following week we had arranged for concerts in Providence and Pawtucket, a part of which we gave, but suddenly I had word from Milford that little Viola was very sick. My wife and Henry were with me. We went to her as soon as possible, taking Dr. Kittredge from Boston — my old friend "Noggs" — with us. Skilful nursing for a few days brought my little daughter around well again, and I returned to Providence. A concert was advertised for the evening I arrived; but Asa and Judson, thinking I was not coming, had gone to Boston with their wives, and cards of postponement were out. I immediately had them taken down and availed myself of the benefits of the then rather new magnetic telegraph to reach my brothers and get them back. Our concert was given that night to a crowded house. Concerts in Fall River, Woonsocket and vicinity were given. We spent a Sunday in Woonsocket with our anti-slavery friends, the Adamses. Also had some pleasant interviews with our friend Blaisdell. Mr. Adams was a delegate with Garrison and Rogers to the World's Anti-Slavery Con-

TRIBE OF JESSE AT HIGH ROCK — (p. 242)

vention in London. When we went back to Providence I met Mr. Chaplin, who, as I have stated, made an unsuccessful attempt to free seventy-seven slaves in Washington. We gave him money to help three more to freedom.

One of the pleasantest friends I met in Providence was Andrew L. Willard, who later in the season visited me at my New Hampshire home. Concerts in New Bedford and Taunton followed. At the former city we renewed acquaintance with Joseph Congdon and the Coffins, with whom we went on a fishing trip. I suffered a good deal with a cough and other bodily ailments on this tour, but had many pleasant times notwithstanding.

During the following summer I sold my farm in Amherst, and moved to a new home in the village of Milford temporarily. In September we attended a Free Soil Convention in Boston, at Tremont Temple. One of the chief speakers was John Van Buren, son of the ex-president, who had also taken up the cause of freedom. Mr. Van Buren was our guest a part of the time during our stay. We went to Lawrence, then a very unfinished city, and gave a concert at this time. Following this came concerts in Manchester and Concord, the great Free Soil Convention in the latter city, at which we sang, and then a great concert in Boston. My journal says: "Had a full house. Friends, or at least acquaintances, came in at all hours to see us — and get tickets." This was a form of courtesy that we never refused, however numerous the calls.

This was the start for a trip farther west than we had ever been before. Perhaps a quotation from my diary may give a good idea of how we felt in making the trip.

"WORCESTER, September 16, 1848 — Came to Worcester to-day Gave a concert in the City Hall. Had a large number of the good people to hear us sing. This probably is the last time but once we shall sing in this goodly city. Oh, my soul is full of poetry! The recollections of the past rush through my memory, and I feel both sad and joyous at times. This season is full of suggestions to call forth the emotions of the soul. We have to leave home, separate ourselves from home friends and wander out into the world to meet and form new associations and friendships. There is something about it sad to my mind, especially the uncertainty of meeting those at home again in this world. Yes, it is sad to leave father and mother and all the home scenes, to die out West, or have them die before we return. We cannot insure our lives until we come back. Life is uncertain. But what makes this parting doubly sad is this. We have left our brothers, all of whom occupy a tender spot in our souls' affections, cherishing hard feelings toward us. God forgive me if I have ever injured any of my brothers. I have always wished them well, and now I would gladly share all I have equally with them all. Oh, what a happy band we might make, to be united to combat the world! I am a sinner, but a humble man, and a well-wisher to my race. I have longed to see a state of things brought about in which the society of which we form a part might grow healthier, richer in knowledge and brotherly love. But that day of hope and sunshine seems to be about passed over, and I have nearly concluded there is no use of my flattering myself any more. So God have mercy on me. Thy will be done.

"Sunday, September 17th.—Our concert last evening was a good one, and we sang a Free Soil song that brought down the house, in a tremendous cheering. The ball truly is in motion, and slavery trembles. God speed the right! Our visit out West is fraught with some dangers, and we must take care of ourselves, or fall victims to the unhealthy climate. To-day a Mr. Washburn gave us a Free Soil song. Such a man we seldom find. God bless him."

This Mr. Washburn was a brother of Israel, Elihu B. and William B. Washburn, and one of a family of governors, senators and diplomats. From Worcester we went on to Northampton, where we gave a concert in the First Congregational church, the Baptist church having been previously engaged, and then taken from us, the authorities fearing desecration. While here we saw and had a long talk with Garrison, and were more impressed than ever with the fact that he was a very earnest and conscientious man. We spent two days in

Pittsfield, giving a concert in a hall jammed to suffocation. Among our pleasant calls was one from Ex-Governor George N. Briggs and a Mr. Barr.

From here we proceeded to Albany, and stopped once more at our old hotel home, the Delavan House. Mr. Newland, our kind friend of early times, had failed, and it was a privilege to offer him our assistance. The next night we sang in the female academy. The lights went out during the concert, a much worse misfortune than a few hisses. Hon. Millard Fillmore, then a vice-presidential candidate with "Old Zach. Taylor," was present at the concert, as at others we gave later. John Van Buren was also there. After the concert, Fillmore, who was also at the Delavan House, asked us into his room and talked very freely to us, giving us his sentiments on anti-slavery. He reminded us that as a member of Congress he was recorded in some test votes as a friend of freedom. This conversation pleased us very much, but we recalled it with feelings of regret at his change of front, when he subsequently, as president, signed the "Fugitive Slave Bill."

The next day I called on Frederick Douglass, then visiting Albany. It will be noticed that we never neglected to pay our respects to the abolition leaders wherever we found them, and yet we were carrying on our work for the emancipation of the colored race in our own way, and in a perfectly independent manner, glad, however, whenever we could give a lift to those carrying the burden of the great agitation, or join them in felicitations over the progress of the cause we all had at heart.

On September 27th we attended two weddings, one that of our old friend Benjamin Brier, at Albany; and then, at Troy, that of Caroline Pierpont, daughter of the great reformer, John. I remember how our joy at the latter ceremony was tempered by the reflection that this daughter of an original Abolitionist had linked her fate with that of a slaveholder.

Our route next took us through Lansingburg, Schnectady, Utica, Rome, and on to Syracuse, a favorite stopping-place with us. We had big audiences at each of the places mentioned. While in the cars *en route* to Syracuse, Judson feigned insanity, and I officiated as his keeper, to the great consternation of our fellow-passengers. While in this city we attended an Indian funeral. It was a strange experience to see the ceremonies, and hear the moans of the women. We rode to Oswego in a two-horse carriage, and greatly admired the flour country through which we passed, with log huts on either side the road. The great flour mills we saw were equal in size to many of our eastern cotton mills. From here we went back to Syracuse, for a second concert, and then went to Auburn. We fell in with a conductor on the train who took us hunting, and we got some squirrels, after a five or six mile tramp. We went to a farmer's house, and I found him a Massachusetts man. He had a beautiful farm, and I talked with him about getting the brothers all to go West, a scheme I cherished many years, though those of us who finally aided in the development of this great region were much farther west than this Auburn farmer. We spent some time with our friends the Wrights, in this city — a daughter of this family, niece to Lucretia Mott, married Wm. Lloyd Garrison, Jr. — and were called upon by the Messrs. Clark, good fellows and first-rate singers. Over forty years after, at the World's Fair in Chicago, I met one of these brothers. He was still giving concerts.

Our trip from here to Geneva was by four-horse team between Lakes Seneca and Cayuga. It was a country as rich as a garden, and as we had the stage to ourselves, we could stop as often as we pleased to pluck the beautiful flowers beside our route. Canandaigua came next, and then Rochester. Douglass was at this time living here and editing his paper, the *North Star*, established with material given him by his English friends. He came to see us as soon as we arrived. We sang in Minerva Hall in this city. I recall that Judson sang "The Bachelor's Lament" to such good effect that a child in the audience cried, greatly amusing everybody. Buffalo was our next objective point. We sang there and at Lockport during our stay. We were pretty well known in Buffalo. We had a habit of grabbing a shovel as we passed the men at work on the highways, and showing them that we knew how to handle the implement. The boys in the streets as we passed would shout, "There go the Hutchinsons!" The anti-slavery friends were few, here, however, and as my diary expresses it, our songs took "like cold bread."

Next we sang at Niagara Falls. I had another opportunity to gaze on the cataract, and recorded my reflections in my diary as follows:

"Roaring, foaming cataract! Thou seems't to me nature's noblest curiosity. Thy hurried waters for ages have travelled but to roll and tumble over these rocky cliffs. The mist that rises from thy spray is caught up in the clouds and in the round of time comes again with other waters to fall over thy brows. Thou flood of living water, roll on! Eternity is the length of thy days, and of it thou art emblematical. The world is full of thy praise, thou proud, rolling waters. We leave you with regret as thousands do, but to give place to others who learning of thy beauties come hither to learn wisdom. Let not mortal man attempt to imitate thee. Not even music, 'the theme of every noble heart' can represent thee. Niagara, fare thee well!"

From this place we took a run into Canada. Once more we gazed upon Englishmen at home. At Toronto, Ludlow (Patton), who was acting as our advance agent on this our longest trip, left us, and went to Ohio to arrange for our coming. We sang in Toronto and Hamilton to small but fashionable audiences. Then we returned to Buffalo, intending to depart at once for Erie. But we were unable to get a boat, and so remained over night. It was the night before election and we went to a Free Soil meeting in a big stable and sung our last campaign songs for the time being. The next day the Alleghanians, a popular band of singers, spent a good deal of time singing with us. We enjoyed all this very much, though a slightly different face was put upon the matter a few weeks afterward, when we found they had fallen in love with our songs to the extent of preceding us over our Ohio route, singing them all the way.

Well, we finally reached Erie, and found the people disappointed at our delay in coming, so we advertised and gave a concert. Then we went on to Ashtabula and Zanesville, where we had crowded houses and seemed to do some good, and after a chilly ride all day in a closed carriage — we had seen a man shaking with the ague and were more than afraid of it — arrived in Cleveland. We gave our first concert November 15th. There was a big attendance. We found Cleveland a thriving and rich place, and met many friends. We had one day's pleasant riding with Rev. Mr. Aiken, I remember. Our second concert was even more successful than the first.

Elyria was our next stopping-place. Here we had such a jam that it was almost impossible to sing. People came from as far as Oberlin, seven miles away.

They filled the aisles of the church where we sang, and crowded upon the platform so that there was hardly room to stand. A son of Governor Slade of Vermont came many miles to hear us. Next we went to Sandusky.

On the 23d, we arrived in Cincinnati. On the evening of the same day we sang to a thousand people. Here we met Henry Marvel from Milford, N. H., my cousin, and my mother's youngest brother, Kendrick Leavitt, who would hear of nothing but that his distinguished relatives, whom he had not seen for twenty years — in fact, he had never seen Abby — should make their home with him. We found him a good, Christian man, and greatly enjoyed our visit. We made side-trips to Hamilton, Lawrenceburg and other places, and gave many concerts in Cincinnati. We also renewed our acquaintance with our life-long friends, the Muzzeys; Osgood Muzzey was then there with his father. We made a trip to Coventry, Ky., by a steamer we chartered to cross the river. The slave-holders cheered our anti-slavery songs, and we had a good time, though the concert was not financially remunerative. When we got back we were made happy by the arrival of Brother Jesse from the East. We met a Dr. Miles here, and arranged with him to look up some land upon which the family might settle. We went to Dayton. While at that place all hands took hold and made a song, " A Trip to Ohio," which afterward became very popular.

Leaving Cincinnati, we went to Springfield and Columbus, where we had a pleasant time with members of the State Legislature and others. We went back to Uncle Kendrick's for Christmas. On December 30th we bid our many friends a long farewell and took the boat for

Wheeling, stopping at Ripley on our way with Rev. Mr. Rankin, a noble Abolitionist. We had hardly got aboard when we were shocked by news of cholera. Judson was especially frightened, and at once announced his determination to go home. As time passed on, the excitement subsided; but Judson had made a vow to return home if spared, and we could not move him. We had a service on board the vessel on Sunday, and we all agreed to sing. But when Judson was asked, he solemnly refused, and said he never would sing with us again. When we reached Pittsburgh, we made another effort to get Judson to stay, but he would not and went off, and Jesse went after him. We still had a quartet left, for Ludlow was a good tenor singer; but the next misfortune was the illness of Asa, which made it necessary to give up concerts we had planned.

My birthday, January 4, 1849, was spent in crossing the Alleghanies toward Baltimore. After finding that Jesse and Judson had gone North, we left Baltimore, and went to Philadelphia. Here Asa left us for New York and home. From here the trio that was left went to Bristol, and were invited to give a concert. Two evenings later Abby, Ludlow and John appeared in concert and gave good satisfaction. Forty-three years later the same trio sang together at the funeral of John Greenleaf Whittier. It was our last public song together. A few weeks more, and our darling sister's human song was hushed forever.

From here we went to New York, where Jesse rejoined us, but that was the end of our singing for the time being. Three days later I was in Milford again, more than happy to be with my wife and children.

On Wednesday, February 28, 1849, Abby and Ludlow were married in New York City. In a few days they came home, and during the following week had their wedding-party. We were all there, and had a royal good time, singing songs and otherwise amusing ourselves. I was anxious to go on the road, singing again, and a good many hours were spent planning. Judson was obdurate for a time, but finally yielded. We had a big family conference, and endeavored to make a plan to have the entire family own property and practice and give some concerts together. The idea did not strike Jesse favorably, and Ludlow threw cold water on it; so nothing definite came of it. Meanwhile, David, Judson, Asa and I had entered into a compact to build a house on the Dr. Fuller place, which we had purchased. This was an important transaction, by the way. Dr Fuller was stopping in another place with a son, a minister, and it was known that he was very averse to selling his property, which was in the centre of Milford, especially to any Milford man. I was determined to have it, however, and recalling that my friend Cyrus Bradley, the painter, had been able to buy from the land the lot on which he purposed building, rightly decided that he would be the best agent to buy the property. So I engaged Bradley to go to the place, and put in a week at painting, or anything else, but to see and talk with the doctor at all hazards. He went, and in a few days returned with the good news that he had bought the place for me. On this land now stands the Milford town-hall, the public library, the bank building, the brick school-house, and numerous stores and dwellings. Before we began the erection of the house of which I have spoken, Judson sold out his interest to the other three brothers; and as the work went on, David became the agent of the others to look out for it.

On May 15th, we started on another tour of the

quartet, which for so many years had been before the public. Ludlow went with Abby, and each of the brothers took their wives. We sang in Lawrence, Concord (Mass.), Lexington, Woburn, Haverhill, Exeter, Dover, Great Falls, Rochester, and reached Portland June 1st. We spent much time with the Dennetts, and received many callers at the United States Hotel, which we made our home. While here, we found Prof. H. W. Longfellow was stopping at the same hotel, and we were invited into his apartments, where we sang three songs, the words of which were composed by him, one of them "Excelsior." About this time I invented a new form of water-wheel, and put it into the hands of my friend H. F. Casson, of Nashua, who happened to be in town. Then we went on through Lewiston, Augusta and Hallowell. At the latter place I went trouting and for my first fish landed a big fellow, weighing two pounds and two ounces. Asa fished for pickerel; he caught 23 pounds in all. Thence we went to Skowhegan, and to Bangor. Here we stayed several days, and made hosts of friends. Concerts were given here, at Orono, Oldtown, Bucksport, Belfast, East Thomaston, West Thomaston, Damariscotta, Wiscasset, Bath, thence we went back to Portland and home.

Soon after our return Sister Abby was taken seriously ill, and for two months her life was despaired of. Then she went to Connecticut with her husband, and we feared that was the end of her concert work with us.

But it was impossible for me to think of giving up a mode of life I enjoyed so well; and so, when I found that my brothers were averse to going with me, I determined to strike out for myself. So in a short time I went to Boston and had some hand-bills struck off. Then I went back to Milford and advertised a concert.

I had the Milford Brass Band to assist me, and had a fairly good house. I sang fifteen songs, and recited "The Gambler's Wife." I followed this up with concerts in Mason, Townsend, Hollis, Lyndeboro, Wilton, Hancock, Peterboro, Jaffrey and Mont Vernon.

At about this time I made a California venture. A man named Darrow in our town wanted to go to the promised land, but had no money. He came to me, and I lent him five hundred dollars, stipulating that he should give me half of his earnings. For security, I insured his life, making the policy payable to myself. He was gone many months, and I heard nothing from him. Then some one told me he was earning eight dollars a day, and I was quite willing to wait, if the investment was to bring me half of it. Finally his wife, then staying in Nantucket, came to see me, and began negotiations looking towards buying me off. She offered to pay the loan and one hundred dollars besides; and as I was glad to get even the principal back, regardless of interest, I quickly took her up, accepted the money and released him from his agreement. I saw Darrow in California in later years. At one time he was worth a hundred thousand dollars.

My success in concert-giving "on my own hook" in New Hampshire gave me courage to strike out into other fields; and on October 26th I left home and went to Boston. From there I went to Hartford, where Abby and Ludlow were stopping. I at once made an arrangement with Mr. Patton to act as my advance agent. While here I heard Father Mathew, the apostle of temperance, speak several times. He remembered seeing us in Ireland. It was a great comfort to me to be near Abby, but I felt the absence of my brothers Judson and Asa keenly.

November 2d, I commenced my Connecticut tour with a concert in Farmington. Then followed successively concerts in Plymouth (which were repeated), Bristol, Wolcottville, Waterbury, Meriden, Waterbury again, Wolcottville again, Meriden again, Middletown (three successive concerts, audience increasing each time), Farmington, New Haven (where I was very unhappy, recalling the many times I had sung there with my sister and brothers, but determined not to despair), Bridgeport, Springfield (Mass., where I sung for the benefit of Henry B. Brown, a runaway slave, and gave two concerts), New Haven again, Hartford (giving two concerts), Cabotville (Mass.), Chicopee Falls (Mass.), Winsted, Terryville, Wolcottville once more, Winsted again (I had trouble here with rowdies who jeered me as an aristocrat because my tickets were twenty-five cents instead of twelve and one-half cents), Litchfield (Brother Jesse met me here, and for a short time assisted me on the business end), New Hartford, Litchfield again, Meriden again, Hartford again, and after a quick trip to Milford, another in Hartford, Willimantic, Windsor Locks, Willimantic again, Cabotville again, North Brookfield (Mass.), Worcester (Mass.), Lynn (Mass.), Woburn (Mass.).

During most of my trip in Connecticut, which lasted over three months, I made my headquarters in Hartford, either at a hotel, at Rev. Wm. W. Patton's or at my friend John Comstock's. The principal reason for this was that Abby was usually in that city. Not all of these concerts were numerically successful, though they averaged well, and I was all the time gaining a reputation that was bringing me frequent offers from other singers to join with them. I was still hopeful of again singing with my brothers, however, and paid no attention to these offers. Ludlow and Abby, and Jesse when he came, were able to write the folks at home of my success. My health was fair, but loneliness and homesickness told on me, and I had days of physical weakness when the future looked dark. At such times I would write farewell words in my diary, for it seemed as though I was never to see the dear home faces again. But this was usually at night, and in the morning I would remember that my motto was " Excelsior "—still higher — and would go at it again with new courage.

At one time during my trip my wife came to see me, and she told me that my brothers Asa and Judson had been to our house and inquired very particularly as to my progress. She thought the tone of their inquiries indicated a desire to be with me. They had been hard at work chopping trees in my absence, and probably concerting looked a little more attractive to them than it did when on the road. I said nothing, but waited developments. After my concert at Woburn, I went home, a little nettled, I remember, at a rather unusual habit the Woburn selectmen had of taking in an entertainment through the windows of the hall. A stay of a few days and I was off again, and on February 16th gave a concert to an audience of six hundred people in Lyceum Hall, Lynn. Then back to Milford again, where I got my wife and son Henry, and proceeded to try my luck in Woburn once more. By an accident, the notices of this concert were not put out until my arrival, but I sung on the 19th to a small house. On this occasion Henry sang with me, his first appearance in a paid entertainment, though he had previously sung with me at the hall in Milford. He created quite a sensation.

During the latter trip to Lynn, I met both Judson

and Asa. It was a little hard getting at it, but in the course of our conversation they made me understand that they would not be averse to doing some concert work. I suggested that they should sing a little, and we began. They had had no practice during the winter, and I was grieved to perceive that their voices were a little rough, and that we did not blend as formerly. Finally I stopped playing, and looking at them said, " Boys, I'll sing with you again on one condition, that we get Abby." "Done," they responded, and at once we laid our plans to go to her, and see what persuasion would do. On the 20th of February we all met in Boston and took the train for New York. While *en route*, we formulated a plan of giving her a serenade to announce our arrival, and I at once went to work and composed the words of an appropriate song. When we reached New York we waited until evening, and then walked up to her boarding-place to sing our serenade to Abby. We made inquiries, however, and were disappointed to find that she was away. We went back to the New England House with heavy hearts. The next day we took a boat up the Hudson forty miles to Rockland Lake, where we had learned Abby was likely to be found. Landing three miles from the place we took supper at a hotel, and then started on foot, over the mountains and through the mud, for our objective point. We found the house in a sightly location, overlooking the beautiful lake. The moon was shedding her lustrous beams over lake and mountain, and it was just the night for nocturnal choristers to warble serenades.

But we had been frustrated once. We determined to find whether our bird was caged before we began. Asa boldly ventured to the door and rang the bell, while

Judson and I fell back into the shade of friendly shrubbery. An aged gentleman, Mr. Duncan McMartin, came to the door. "Can you direct me to the steamboat landing?" asked Asa. "Certainly," was the reply, and the obliging old gentleman closed the door, and walked down to the gate in order to better give the information desired. It was correct, for we had just come that way and were posted. "By the way," pursued Asa, "there is a man named Patton stopping at your house, is there not?" "Yes, do you know him? Won't you drop in and see him?" Asa had met him, but would not stop, thank you. He supposed Mrs. Patton was there also. The answer was in the affirmative, and the traveller went his way.

A few minutes later Mr. McMartin and his guests were engaged in family devotions, when from the moonlighted terrace under the window there floated up the voice of song:

"Strains of love our hearts are bounding,
   Sister dear, sister dear,
As on you these strains are sounding,
   Sister dear, Abby dear
Your brothers three before you singing
And to your heart we joy are bringing,
Oh, open the window and hear the ringing,
   Sister dear, O sister dear!

"Once more on earth we've come to greet you,
   Sister dear, Abby dear,
And happy are we now to meet you,
   Abby dear, sister dear
Blissful thoughts do now inspire us,
As now this scene of love comes o'er us,
Oh, will you join with us the chorus,
   Sister dear, O sister dear?"

The good man reached his "amen" with some haste, and in an instant Abby exclaimed, "Oh, my brothers!"

and rushed to the door and over the intervening terrace. When we paused she broke the echoes of the dying strain by singing:

"Welcome, brothers, welcome."

We could hardly suppress our emotion as we drew our beloved sister to our hearts. We were invited into the house, and royally entertained for several days. It seemed like a paradise in that beautiful home. We discussed our plans with Abby and Ludlow, but were unable to get a promise that she would sing with us. Meanwhile, I drew up an agreement that we brothers would stick together for three years, for I had had enough of uncertainty.

Monday, February 25th, we bid Abby farewell once more, with sad hearts, for we had been unable to get her to promise to sing for us. We went to Poughkeepsie, while she, with Ludlow, went to New-York. We gave a concert three days later to six hundred people. A few days after we gave another in a church. People seemed to enjoy us, but Abby was not with us and we were dissatisfied. On March 2d we sung in Newburg. The concert seemed to go harder than ever. The boys' instruments sounded harsh, and we missed Abby's voice in our harmony. I went back to my room, sadly disappointed. What should we do? I sat down, and soon Judson came in, looking and feeling morose and desperate. Then Asa came in, threw down the bag containing our evening's receipts on the table, remarking, "That money is hard earned." This showed that he felt as the others did. Then there was an awkward pause. None of us cared to express what was in our hearts. Suddenly we heard a voice:

"Sing, sing, what shall I sing?
The cat's run away with the pudding-bag string!"

"That's Abby!" Asa exclaimed, rushing to the door. And so it was, but where was she? We hunted through the corridors, looked under the windows, and finally under the bed, where we found the intruder, together with Ludlow. They had slyly visited the concert-room, heard us sing, come in ahead of us, had been let into the room by the clerk, and secreted themselves. There was no more moping that night after that sweet surprise. She could not join us right away, but gave us assurances that in a short time she would. We started out on a trip to fill in the time with light hearts after that good news. The next day was Sunday, and she sang with us at church and on the following evening appeared with us in concert in the same place. After that we three brothers filled engagements in Fishkill, Poughkeepsie again,— where by a breakdown of our carriage we smashed Asa's cello all to pieces, and were compelled to walk five miles into town — and Kingston.

During this rough ride Judson's violin bow became loose in its box, and kept thumping, thumping on the body of the instrument, until it nearly wore a hole through it. Not long after he swapped it off for another violin with a teacher, who twenty years later came to me with the identical instrument and offered to sell it. I bought it for my son Judson, its former owner's namesake. I soon recognized in it an old friend, by the marks; and within a week of this writing have played upon it in concerts.

From Kingston we went to Catskill and Hudson, two big concerts in each place; and then back to Milford for a short stay.

On Friday, March 22, 1850, we opened a series of concerts in New York City, at Niblo's, Abby being with us. On the following Sunday we sang in Plymouth Church, Brooklyn, for Henry Ward Beecher. The same week we gave a concert in that church, before a thousand people. Later we gave another. We stayed several weeks in New York giving concerts in Niblo's, the Rutger's Institute and the Broadway Tabernacle.

March 12th we went to Albany. On the following Sunday we sang in the Congregational church, Mr. Beecher, whom I had seen often during our stay in New York, and learned to love as a brother, being the preacher. We gave concerts in Albany, Troy, Newark, Elizabethtown, and then back to New York for another series of concerts.

During this season's work we brought out two songs, in particular, that gave great satisfaction. One of them was Jesse's song, "Good Old Days of Yore." He came from home, and met us at the beginning of our work in Newburg. On the following day, as before stated, we went to Poughkeepsie, and he went with us. From there he went ahead, and cared for our business interests through the season. At Poughkeepsie he produced and read to us the words of his beautiful song, written while in bereavement by the loss of a little child:

> "How my heart is in me burning,
> And my very soul is yearning,
> As my thoughts go backward, turning
> To the good old days of yore,
> When my father and my mother,
> And each sister dear, and brother,
> Sat and chatted with each other
> Round that good old cottage door
>
> .   .   .
>
> "Then were words of kindness spoken,
> And each heart renewed the token,
> Pledging vows not to be broken,
> Broken never, never more

JUDSON'S "STANDING COLLAR" SONG (p. 261)

> And though now asunder driven,
> With the ties of childhood riven,
> Still we cherish pledges given
> Round that good old cottage door."

There were four verses in all, and they affected us deeply. When he had finished, and while we were each sitting under the spell of the sentiment, I said, "Jesse, cannot you carry the thought a little farther and bring it to the meeting at our Heavenly Father's door?" He thought a minute, then seized a pencil, and went apart from us. In a short time he returned with a verse added:

> "Though our days on earth are fleeting,
> And all temporal joys retreating,
> Yet we hope for another meeting —
> Better far than days of yore —
> When through heavenly courts ascending,
> And with angel voices blending,
> We shall sing on, without ending,
> At our Heavenly Father's door —
> Sing the New Song forevermore."

The other piece referred to was Judson's "Collar Song." As all our friends know, we had many years before adopted the wide Byron collar, which became a distinctive feature of our dress. While we were in England, the standing "dicky" became so popular as to be universally worn, and our turn-down collars were sadly out of date. But they were comfortable, and we continued to wear them, although our neckwear became the subject of a good deal of comment. In composing the "Collar Song," Judson and I stood before a mirror and turned up our collars, thus nearly extinguishing our ears. Verses of this song were:

> "The standing collar is all the rage,
> And we want to keep up with the spirit of the age,
> And we know not how high the fashion will go,
> So we thought we'd make 'em eight inches or so —
> Ri tu, di nu, di nu, etc.

"While travelling in Europe with our collars turned down,
  Whether in a big city or in a small town,
  As we passed through the streets the boys would holler,
'Just look at those Yankees with the great wide collar'—
    Ri tu, di nu, etc."

The May meetings of the anti-slavery people were held in the Broadway Tabernacle during our second stay in New York. The aggressive pro-slavery forces, instigated by certain pro-slavery papers and headed by a bright tough named Isaiah Rynders, determined to break the meeting up. On the morning of the first day of the convention we entered the great ampitheatre and took our places in the centre of the upper tier of seats. Garrison was the first speaker. He was very radical in his utterances, I remember, speaking of the dead and living Christ. Suddenly Rynders and about a hundred of his satellites swooped down upon the platform and took possession of the meeting. There was a great uproar, and we were fearful that the Abolitionists would receive bodily harm. The police were in sympathy with the disturbers, and no help could be expected from them. I thought of the expedient to which we had resorted in so many previous meetings when the debates waxed hot, and suggested that we sing. So the quartet struck up a selection. I have often since heard Frederick Douglass describe the effect of the song. The uproar ceased immediately, and all eyes were turned to us. This did not suit Boss Rynders at all. He desired to monopolize attention. He left the platform, and strode up the aisle toward us, and when he got near enough to be heard, shook his fist and shouted, "Stop that —— psalm singing!" As our only idea was to create a diversion from the crisis on the platform, and that had been done, we subsided, when the end of the verse was reached. Then Rynders proceeded. Calmly ignoring Mr. Garrison, he called on an alleged scientist in the gang to lecture on the close connection between the "nigger" and the monkey. His argument was received with great delight by his sympathizers. He concluded. "Now," said Rynders, turning to Douglass, "you may speak." I shall never forget the fine sarcasm in Douglass's voice and manner as with a low bow he acknowledged the "royal permission" vouchsafed him to defend his race from the aspersions of science, falsely so-called. It was a glorious effort and the anti-slavery people were delighted. Not so, Rynders. He stopped the orator, remarking that he was not a "nigger" anyway, but more than half white. Douglass retorted: "Then by your *royal* permission — (bowing low) — I will introduce a man who is not *guilty* of having a drop of white blood in his veins." Ward, the great colored orator, who afterward shook the dust of this compromising country from his feet and went to Liberia, then took the platform, and talked until Rynders adjourned the meeting. The next day the contest was renewed, the mob taking possession, but I was not there. The excitement and anxiety of the first day upset me, and I took to my bed for the first time in nine years, where I suffered from prostration several days.

It was during this stay in New York, also, that we made a trip to the "North American Phalanx" in New Jersey, the community founded by Horace Greeley, and in which he took so much interest. We went on a Saturday, remaining until the following Monday. Mr. Greeley and Mr. Spring, one of the chief promoters of the enterprise, went with us. We found the community not as large as that at Florence, but with a much finer farm than that, and far more comfortably housed than the people engaged in the Brook Farm experiment. On Saturday evening there were dramatic representations in the big kitchen, and on Sunday we had services in the same apartment, Mr. Greeley giving an address, we contributing some songs. Sunday was a stormy day, but we greatly enjoyed it. On Saturday we had a chance for a good game of football. This year we had more fun with this game than any other. In many of the towns visited I organized clubs. The rubber footballs I took with me were novelties, and often a collection would be taken and I would be commissioned to buy them a ball in New York.

Another incident of this period was a call from a man named Martin, who had invented a sewing-machine. He bargained with us for the right to sell in the county of Hillsboro, N. H., and gave Jesse the right in Lynn. Jesse took a machine to Lynn with him, highly elated, but never did anything definite towards introducing it, and it finally went to decay. Hillsboro County never saw it.

May 23d we left New York for Bridgeport, Conn., where we called on P. T. Barnum at his beautiful home, "Iranistan," afterwards destroyed by fire. He talked to us of his project of bringing Jenny Lind to this country, and showed us the wine bottles he had taken from his cellar and smashed, he having become a temperance man. We sang some songs in his music-room. After a concert here, we went to New Haven, where I was shown great courtesy by my friend Governor Seymour, the hero of Chapultepec, who, when we reached Hartford, a little later, devoted much of his time to entertaining me. We had a game of football, I recall, with two legislators.

We sang for a few weeks in many Connecticut cities, and in Springfield and Worcester in Massachusetts. Then we went home for a time. In June the three brothers started on a tour without Abby. We sang in Salem, Danvers, Marblehead, Milford (Mass.), Holyoke, Northampton, Amherst, Deerfield, West Springfield, Westfield, Pittsfield, Great Barrington, New Britain, Norwich, Plainfield, and thence returned home.

During the summer we made a short trip, first to Stonington, where we not only gave some pleasing concerts, Abby being with us, but had some very happy days with Rev. Dr. William Patton, Sr., and his family. We had a bluefishing trip to Block Island, I was seasick, fearfully so, but when our small boat reached the fishing grounds, and I heard Asa scream out, "I've got a bite!" I revived at once. When Dr. Patton caught one and shouted to me to take his line, I responded with alacrity. Soon I was pulling a real bluefish towards the boat. Oh, how he did pull! He would take a tack and draw hard on the line, but all the time I was getting him nearer. Then he would hop out of the water to extricate himself; but he was hooked fast, and in about one minute I had him in the boat. We caught forty all told, my catch being nine, and then we had another siege of seasickness getting home But the fun was worth it. Dr. Patton had quite a number of ministerial friends with him on this trip. While we were going over to Block Island all the company were seated in the middle of the boat, when Judson suddenly jumped upon the forward deck, and waving his hat, shouted, "Come up out of the mighty deep!" Instantly a big fish, apparently ten feet long, leaped out of the water and seemed to stand on his tail for a moment and then disappeared. We were not partial to sharks, and fearing it might be one, armed ourselves for resistance if he should chance to leap up again and come aboard. The dominies, meanwhile, gazed on Judson with new respect, as on one gifted with prophetic powers, and it was evident ever after that Dr. Patton considered that he had an unusual gift in that direction. The next trip we made to Block Island was on an excursion steamer, there being some four hundred on board. We agreed to go for one-fourth of the receipts, and sang at intervals in different parts of the boat to admiring audiences.

Next we went to New London, my first visit. Here we sang to general acceptance, and had some very pleasant experiences. Then we proceeded to Norwich, gave a largely attended concert (where we had the vexatious experience of seeing the gas fail us and having to substitute candles, which smoked), and visited the grave of Uncas, the Indian chief, and the birthplaces of Benedict Arnold and Mrs. Sigourney. Leaving Norwich, we sang in Worcester, then in Providence, where our former triumphs were repeated, it being impossible to get all who came into the hall, and on to Newport, where we found it hard to reconcile our simple songs and ways to the spirit of aristocracy we found prevailing. So we went back and gave another concert in Providence and then went home.

In the interval between the last trips recorded I succeeded in arousing an interest in Milford to hear our old friend, Rev. John Pierpont. By invitation of many townfolk he came up and spent a few days, preaching in the town hall on "The Resurrection," Joshua, Caleb, Asa, Judson and I forming the choir for the occasion; he also gave a temperance lecture, touching particularly on the tobacco question When we returned from Providence I found great results from his work, a large number of young men having sworn off from the use of the weed.

On September 14th, Judson, Asa and I left home once more for a musical trip. Joshua went ahead as advance agent. We had an accident as we started. The stage-driver turned his horses with a flourish and threw Asa's 'cello from the roof of the stage; it was badly smashed, box and all. That old bass-viol had a good many smashings during our experiences, but it is said to improve such an instrument to glue it occasionally. We had much rather have our instruments broken than our bones. It is a matter for congratulation that in all the years of our journeyings to and fro, we never were in a railway or steamboat accident of any account, and none of us suffered any personal injury. We sang in Manchester, Concord, Groton, and Milford, Mass. Then, after a short rest at home, we went to New York. All New York was in a *furore* over Jenny Lind. In company with P. T. Barnum, who was the projector of her wonderful tour in this country, we visited her at her hotel and sang her Jesse's song of welcome, which became so popular in our concerts:

> "From the snow-clad hills of Sweden,
>   Like a bird of love from Eden,
>   Lo, she comes with songs of freedom —
>   Jenny comes from o'er the sea!
>   Though afar from home endearing,
>   Yet her heart no danger fearing,
>   For she hears a nation cheering —
>   'Jenny, welcome to the free!'
>
> "While the great and honored hear you,
>   Let the poor oppressed be near you,
>   Then will every heart revere you —
>   Jenny, sing for liberty

> Thou, indeed, art not a stranger
> To the palace or the manger;
> Welcome, friend, and fear no danger —
> 'Jenny, welcome to the tree.'"

She seemed to be very much pleased with the song, spoke of her home and how she longed to go back to it, and shook our hands warmly when we parted. The same evening we heard her sing to eight thousand people. I cannot express the joy I felt in hearing her sing, with such a rich voice and sympathetic manner. I sang the song quoted above, by the way, at the Swedish building during the World's Fair.

September 23d we sang in Newburg, Abby having joined us. From there we went to Poughkeepsie, where we sang to a crowded house. Next we sang in Catskill, Albany and Utica. At the latter place, I remember, we succeeded in getting a tune for our "Cold Water" song, which had been waiting for an appropriate setting for many months.

October 1st we sang in Syracuse. The mayor of the city with a party of officials, and General Wool, the Mexican hero, were in our audience. We sang in a church, and were rather cramped in our accommodations in the pulpit. Oswego came next. We sang at an anti-slavery meeting at which Gerrit Smith spoke, and gave a concert to a fine audience. Auburn was next visited. I sang the "wax-work" song, the words by George W. Putnam. This for many years was a favorite with our audiences. It told the story of two Yankees who were visiting the South on a speculative tour and got short of money. They concluded to perpetrate a sell on the populace, and so advertised an exhibition of wax-work. Previous to the show they provided themselves with a couple of pounds of shoemaker's wax.

The most gentlemanly of the two stood at the door and received the money of the people, which came in liberally. The other, who for the purposes of the show was temporarily without a palate, gave the lecture and exhibition. He talked "youn yin ees yote"— that is, down in his throat:

>"Of course the people thought to see
> A mighty show of figures —
> Of Napoleon, Byron, George the Third,
> And lots of foreign gentlemen,
> Of Mary, Queen of Scots, you know,
> And monks in black and white,
> And heroes, peasants, potentates,
> In wax-work brought to light."

But when the curtain was drawn aside, our friend without a palate was disclosed with his shoemaker's wax in his hands. This he pulled as one would pull candy, and as he began to "work" it, addressed his audience.

> "Said he, 'My friends, how some folks cheat,
> I never could conceive,
> But this is the *real* wax-work,
> For I stoop not to deceive,
> This is the *real* wax-work,
> For your quarters and your twelves;
> Ladies and gentlemen, please walk up,
> And examine for yourselves.'"

The wondering people soon saw the joke, and proceeded to make preparations to ride him on a rail, but he had an open window and a ladder, and as he went out of sight turned and held his wax up to view, saying with a saucy grin:

> "'My friends, there's no deception,
> For I scorn to take you in,
> This is the *real* wax-work,'" etc.

In this song it was necessary for me to mimic the palateless man, and also to seemingly work the wax, this pantomime having much to do with the success of the piece. I have had auditors ready to swear that I had wax in my hands, this being, I considered, quite a compliment to the realistic character of my performance.

CHAPTER VII.

LIGHTS AND SHADOWS.

ON Saturday, October 5, 1850, we reached Rochester, N. Y., and were, as my diary says, "among the spirits." Perhaps I can illustrate the peculiar condition of our minds at this time by a quotation from my diary, written while there

> "What is conscience? 'Tis no substance, but an article of merchandise that can be bought and sold Still, it comes with intelligence I think it altogether a matter of circumstance with every one It is good or bad according to education Still, I think it may be made up of departed spirits, who dictate to us, according to their characters. An erroneous idea of the commitment of deeds is the suggestion to us of evil, while the promptings to good are the suggestions of good spirits Truth is never ashamed It takes a bold front in the war with sin and falsehood The absence of truth causes fear The commitment of one evil act will cast a shadow of darkness over a multitude of honest impulses The honest man is brave in good works Intelligence is the key to human progress."

It was natural for us, brothers and sisters, to be radical We were "real, live Yankees," and were constantly in association with the progressive, radical element which had so much to do with shaping the thought of New England in the two decades that preceded the war If there was one man we worshipped more than Beecher, it was Theodore Parker. Horace Greeley, with his pronounced views on the anti-slavery question, on the community system and on Spiritualism, was one of our idols. We were quite accustomed to the extreme utterances of Garrison, of Rogers, and other men who had by their devotion to emancipation won our hearts. Earnest, Christian parents had brought us up to love God and hate sin; but the compromising and hesitating attitude of the churches on the crucial questions of the hour had naturally tried our faith and our patience. A gradual change in our views, the result of constant contact with the radical spirits who were so stirring New England and the North, had led some of us who were younger members of the family to withdraw from the church associations of our early days. I think I was the first "come-outer" in New Hampshire. We were waiting for great developments in the line of social and ethical progress. We believed that old systems of society — including slavery — of theology and practice, were to be done away. We were looking for the new light with eager, longing gaze, determined that no one should welcome it sooner or more heartily than ourselves. Some one has said the Hutchinsons were "highly subjective." This delicate suggestion perhaps covers the ground as well as pages of explanation. Nearly every one of my older brothers had embraced the new doctrine of Spiritualism. My brother Jesse was enthusiastically devoted to it. It also took a strong hold upon some of us who were younger.

The romantic story of Dungeon Rock, in Lynn, has often been told. Whether it is history or legend, few can read the traditions of the pirate band — which sailed up the narrow Saugus River in the early days of the settlement, hid for months in the almost impenetrable thicket of "Pirates' Glen," and finally found a refuge from the law in the cave in Dungeon Rock, now the outpost of the beautiful park, "Lynn Woods," where a famous and authenticated earthquake is supposed to have swallowed them up with their booty, the mouth of the cave being closed forever — without a tingling of interest. Soon after he began to believe in the spiritualistic philosophy, Jesse conceived the idea that there could be no more convincing proof of its truth than to find that supposed treasure through spiritual guidance. He therefore went at the work with drill and powder, seeking light from mediums in his effort. His active temperament was not adapted to such laborious processes, however, and he soon abandoned the task, it being later assumed by Hiram Marble, who devoted the rest of his life to it, in conjunction with his son Edwin, who continued to work at it after his father's death until his own demise, over a generation of time being given to the search for the hidden treasure, under mediumistic guidance. Hiram Marble told me he would either prove the truth of Spiritualism or dig its grave. So for decades those earnest, honest men, whom the world may call mistaken, drilled and dug and tunnelled, until they had made a gallery in the solid porphyry for one hundred and seventy-five feet, turning, twisting to the right or left or up and down, as the mediums directed. The work was done by lamp-light, and the stone was carried out in buckets. There, at the mouth of the tunnel — which is large enough for two men to walk abreast and erect for its entire length — it remains, an eloquent evidence of what men will do to prove their faith. The bones of Tom Veal and his pirate band still moulder undisturbed in the cave, if cave there is. Jesse is dead. Hiram and Edwin Marble, too, are gone, and the truth of Spiritualism, so far as Dungeon Rock goes, is still a matter of faith. The rock came into the hands of the city soon after Edwin Marble's death.

I am a firm believer in the future life. I believe too, in the ministry of angels, and that the spiritual world is a present reality. To quote Mrs. Stowe:

> "It lies around us like a cloud,
>   A world we do not see;
> Yet the sweet closing of an eye
>   May bring us there to be."

I have full sympathy with Longfellow's sentiment:

> "There is no death! What seems so is transition;
>   This life of mortal breath
> Is but the suburb of that life elysian,
>   Whose portal we call Death."

And with Bulwer Lytton's even more poetic thought,

> "There is no death, the stars go down,
>   To rise upon some fairer shore;
> Where, bright in Heaven's jewelled crown
>   They shine forevermore.
>
> "There is no death, the leaves may fall,
>   The flowers may fade and pass away,
> They only wait, through wintry gloom
>   The coming of the May.
>
> "There is no death, an angel form
>   Walks thro' the earth with silent tread,
> He bears our best loved friends away,
>   And then we call them dead.
>
> "Born into that undying life,
>   They leave us, but to come again,
> With joy we welcome them, the same,
>   Except in sin and pain."

Brother Asa, before his death, did not hesitate to bear testimony against Spiritualism, and attribute to it whatever of disappointment and loss the brothers experienced for many years. The belief was too dear to those who have gone, many of them dying in fullest sympathy with the doctrine, for me to desire to say a word in adverse criticism of it. That it has been misrepresented and injured by many who professed to be its exponents, every spiritualist believes. It is still a subject to be tested and like every other honest inquirer I am to-day as ever "looking for a test." As to myself, for many years I have made it my motto to live in one world at a time, and I simply refer to the question at this time because as a truthful historian, I could not tell the story of the months which followed and leave it out.

Judson was a man of the most ardent, loving and susceptible nature. His nerves were always tuned to concert pitch, and he could stand no more than the ordinary limit of excitement in our eventful experiences without breaking. He was deeply impressed with such spiritualistic phenomena as we were able to observe on this trip, but the effect on his mental and nervous temperament was to make him the prey of sensations he had never experienced before, and finally to unfit him for the task we had set ourselves in starting, and so to make the trip a failure. We all saw it with sorrow, except Jesse. The latter, sanguine, enthusiastic, and ardently devoted to the new idea, saw in Judson's experiences new proofs calculated to establish the truth of Spiritualism.

He urged him on to new tests. Judson, always thinking elevated and noble thoughts, was lifted by the clairvoyant or mesmeric — we to-day should say hypnotic — state in which he often found himself, to a height far above common humanity, seeing in his new sensations the beginning of a new dispensation.

Immediately on our arrival at Rochester we called on our old friend Frederick Douglass, then editing his paper in the place, and saw his wife and "little black children," as my diary puts it. Perhaps it will be well to quote portions of the diary for the days which followed:

October 6th. Spent the evening with some friends who are engaged in spiritual rapping. Not very interesting, owing to some disturbance by some spirits which were not congenial. We returned to our hotel feeling quite weary.

Monday, October 7th. We spent the forenoon at Mrs Fish's, hearing the rappings. Judson was very much wrought up. Cried. We were all much excited with the demonstrations. We thought we were conversing with spirits of departed friends, who professed to be our guardian spirits. A minister was present and was melted to tears, for he was conversing with departed souls.

October 8th. We had a second time at the rappings. Much excitement. After the added excitement of a concert Judson and I went to Mrs Fish's after Abby's parasol. She took his hand and he seemed to be falling into a magnetic state, when I made some objection and she ceased and withdrew her influence. She told some stories respecting her experience in mocking the spirits, etc. We retired feeling quite excited.

October 9th. Took the cars to Buffalo. On the way Judson came in from another car, stating the case of a poor fugitive slave on his way to Canada. Raised six dollars for him and bade him God-speed. Sang to a full house. This was the best concert we ever gave, for we were all united in spirit and happy. Judson was particularly interested.

October 10th. Took steamboat *Queen City* for Cleveland. Judson was quiet, but did not feel like laughing and playing with us. Several times he got Abby to magnetize him.

October 11th. On our arrival at Cleveland Jesse met us with spirits of enthusiasm. After dinner we went to the house of a friend of Jesse's. While we were in the parlor waiting, the gentleman came in, and his presence caused Judson to feel badly. He went to the door to get air. I went and exerted myself over him. Our host said, "Come in and I will remove all the bad effect of this meeting." Jesse manifested a desire to see something remarkable done. The clairvoyant was sent into the spirit land. She said she saw some spirits about Judson. They were magnetizing him. Judson seemed very much excited and was happy. He wanted to go home to heaven. He saw the blessed spirits, heard the music of heaven, the harps, etc. He was recalled, but was quite bewildered with excessive joy.

October 12th. Jesse took Judson to that place again, and he got into a bad state. In the evening we gave a concert, but it was a total failure. Judson was all out of spirits. The influence was upon him, and if I looked at him he would shiver and tremble. He refused to sing any comic songs, and I had to struggle through the best I could. Friends think strange of our depreciation. What is the matter? Oh, how I felt! Judson quit chewing tobacco . . Sad, sad! I visited Jesse, and charged him to leave town and get away from Judson. He said he should do nothing of the kind. Soon Judson was in great agony. We called a physician. No relief, until Mr. Clark was sent for, who ministered to his wants and quieted him. All night we were in sorrow for him.

October 13th. Got a carriage to take Judson to ride. He would not go. Jesse and he were together all day. Later I rubbed Judson's head, and he was much better. He went to dinner, hurried through and left the table with Jesse before the rest were done. We went to his friend's. He had Judson in a magnetic state. Hurried him through. We went to Mr. Severance's, and from there to one of his neighbor's where we sang. On our way to Mr Bradburn's, our next stopping place, Judson hurried ahead, and went without much ceremony into the house and to the room where a poor girl lay dying in consumption. Sympathy caused Judson to try to do her good. She was frightened. She left the room, Judson remaining and making passes across his chest to relieve her. He magnetized water and sent to her. We watched the movements with intense anxiety and sorrow of heart. We succeeded in getting him home after much trouble. All night he called for Jesus Christ, Mr Clark, and others. He had no rest. It was a terrible night.

October 14th. Postponed concerts. Disappointment seems to mark our progress out West. Judson worse. We are much used up.

October 15th. Took Judson to Mr Severance's. Jesse will keep him in his company. He thinks he can do him good no doubt. How kind of Mr S to have invited us! Asa and I went into the garden and wept bitterly. Many good friends came to comfort us.

October 17th. Judson no better. A magnetizer called to see him. We talked on the subject of spirits all the evening. Judson was quite easy. At ten o'clock he got out of bed, stood in the hall, and preached for an hour. At four o'clock (18th) Mr Severance and I went for the doctor. Judson was worse. At two o'clock that afternoon we took sail for home with our brother. We watched him all the time, fearful of his jumping off. He did work well to deceive me. Once I had to take him into the cabin by main force.

On our arrival at Buffalo we found we had missed the express train, and so a little later we took another train for Syracuse. As we passed through Rochester, where he was first magnetized, we had hard work to prevent Judson from jumping from the train. At Syracuse we stayed several days. We were going on, when friends suggested that we try a magnetizer, and see if we could not get Judson out of his unnatural state in the way he got into it. The effort was of no avail. Our old friends Dr. Weating, Rev. Samuel J. May and his son John, with others, were very kind to us. One day Mr. May invited us to bring Judson to visit him. Judson was so charmed with his visit that he refused to return to his hotel, and it finally took the united strength of four men to secure him, and take him back, he having gone part of the way and then refused to go further. He was conveyed in a wagon, Dr. Weating, Mr. May and his son drawing the conveyance, while Asa and Ludlow pushed it, and I sat in the vehicle and attended to the stricken man.

On October 21st we started for home. By using anodynes Judson was kept quiet, and we made the journey without difficulty. In a few days we were all at Milford again; and in the time Judson recovered, so that we were able to resume our singing.

On November 15th I made a trip to Boston, in company with my wife, and in the evening went to Faneuil Hall to hear our friend George Thompson, the great English Abolitionist, speak. He was not permitted to lecture. A mob, with pro-slavery proclivities, from the North End, completely filled the body of the hall, standing, as is the usual custom in that historic place. I sat in the gallery with my wife. Mr. Thompson would begin: "Gentlemen," and then the mob would sway back and forth and groan, so that his voice would be inaudible. Over and over he would repeat that rather misapplied word, "Gentlemen," but it was of no use. Mr. Garrison observed me in the balcony, and called on me to sing, hoping thereby to quell the tumult, but I was alone; without my brothers' voices with me I felt myself unequal to battling with such forces of disorder. It grieved me deeply that I was unable to extend a welcome in song to this noble man. This scene has often been described at length by historians.

Early in November I sang alone in Nashua to a full house. The next week I gave two concerts in Lowell. November 28th I gave another in Amherst. December 4th came another in Pembroke. Then I went to Concord and arranged with Messrs. Burr, who were lecturing, to have the use of their hall one night. I gave one concert in the Manchester city hall, my little son Henry, who had been brought over by his mother, assisting me, and then went back to Concord to fulfil my engagement. At this concert a rather interesting incident occurred. The hall was full and in a conspicuous place sat "Squire Whipple" a noted Democrat. At this time a delegation of prominent Southern politicians had come to New Hampshire to confer with Franklin Pierce in regard to his acceptance of a nomination to the presidency, and some of them, with their wives, were in Mr. Whipple's party. At one part of the programme, I had sung this song, Henry, with his shrill treble, joining in the chorus:

"Come freemen, listen to my song, a story I'll relate,
It happened in the valley of the old Carliny State,
They marched me to the cotton-fields at early break of day,
And worked me there from morn till night, without a bit of pay

CHORUS

"They worked me all the day,
Without one bit of pay,
So I took my flight in the middle of the night,
When the moon had gone away"

At the close of this selection, Mr. Whipple arose, and remarked that he did not come to hear an anti-slavery sermon, and protested against such songs being sung. The audience hissed this demonstration, and he sat down. But my indignation was wrought up to the highest pitch, and later in the evening I stepped to the front and recited "The Bigot Fire," a poem by my friend John Ramsdell, a native of Milford:

> "Oh, kindle not that bigot fire,
>   'Twill bring disunion, fear and shame,
> 'Twill rouse at last the Southron's ire
>   And burst our starry band in twain.
>
> "Theirs is the high, the noble worth —
>   The very soul of chivalry;
> Rend not our blood-bought land apart
>   For such a thing as slavery
>
> "This is the language of the North,
>   I blush to say it, but 'tis true;
> And anti-slavery calls it forth
>   From some proud priests and laymen too.

(To make my rebuke more effective, I substituted "politicians," for "proud priests" in the last line.)

> "What! bend forsooth to Southern rule?
>   What! cringe and crawl to Southern clay?
> To be the base, the supple tool
>   Of hell-begotten slavery!
>
> "No, never! while the free air plays,
>   O'er our rough hills and sunny fountains
> Shall proud New Hampshire's sons be slaves
>   And clank the fetters round their mountains
>
> "Go, if you will, and grind in dust
>   Dark Afric's poor, degraded child;
> Wring from his sinews gold accursed —
>   Then boast your gospel, warm and mild!"

How the audience did cheer at the conclusion! Whipple immediately arose and left the hall, leaving his wife and friends, remarking to the doorkeeper that he had got as much as he could stand. I never received more genuine compliments than for this act.

Leaving Concord, I sang at Franklin, Sanbornton Bridge, Meridith Bridge, and closed the week with another concert at Concord, where the audience asked for a repetition of the song that had so aroused Mr. Whipple's ire. It was cheered handsomely.

Next week's concerts opened at Fisherville, and then I went to Plymouth, where I renewed old friendships with John R. French and others of the Rogers Family. Another concert at Concord and one at Nashua closed this trip.

Next came a trip to Boston to attend the anti-slavery fair. I again recited "The Bigot Fire." December 28th, I gave a concert in Lyceum Hall, Lynn, where Judson and Asa, who were there at the time, sang two selections. This was followed by concerts of the three brothers in Marblehead, again in Lynn, in Salem, Beverly, Newburyport, Dover, Portsmouth, Exeter, and then we went home.

At all these latter concerts my brothers sang with me, always with success, but with some very peculiar occurrences sprinkled in, occasioned by the whimsical workings of Judson's mind. An example was at Newburyport, where he was impressed that it was his duty to do something for the poor of the town, and therefore proceeded to draw from his pockets handfuls of silver half-dollars, previously secured, which he threw into the broad aisle, requesting Hannah F. Gould, the poetess, who was present, to act as almoner and see that the money went to the worthy poor only. Sometimes he would speak as if inspired, to the astonishment and delight of the auditors. Sometimes his speech would be of a comically edifying nature. More often than otherwise, it would be an address on the sinfulness of eating flesh, or wearing any garment that necessitated the killing of animals for its construction. Because of these theories he had discarded boots and shoes, clothing his feet in socks. His food was fruits, cereals and honey. However, though his idiosyncrasies caused the rest of us a good deal of uneasiness, they were never of a nature to harm any one, or to seriously shock an audience.

In February, 1851, while singing in Chelsea, we received word of the serious illness of both my father and mother. After a few days, mother recovered, but it was my father's last illness. He had always been a very well man. We learned when we went home, which was as soon as the trains could take us, that a neighbor's barn had been set on fire by a disaffected son. He had purchased cattle, and his father had refused to let him keep them in the barn; hence the act. When the alarm was given, father hitched up the old mare and rushed over to render assistance. He reached there in time to help save the granary, and was of course in great excitement at the act of the undutiful son. He got into a perspiration and then, riding home in the severe weather, took cold. He tried hard to overcome the effects of the cold, but was unable to do so, though he still kept about the house attending to his "chores." One day he was bringing in a basket of green wood, when he was seized with paralysis, and fell over the wood. He was taken up, put to bed, and it was found that his frame was nearly all paralyzed, and his speech almost so. He lingered several days (about a week), roused occasionally, and one day asked to have his revered friend, Deacon Pearsons of the Baptist church, come in and pray with him On Sunday, February 16th, he fell asleep in Jesus:

> "How blest the righteous when he dies,
> When sinks the weary soul to rest;
> How calmly beam those closing eyes,
> How gently heaves the expiring breast."

"Uncle Jesse," as he was called affectionately by all the people of the town, of which he was a selectman for many years, was all his life long a faithful, humble, devout Christian man. He was gifted with a resonant, high-pitched voice, and loved music as passionately as any member of his family. He was all his life a farmer, and for many years whiled away the hours of toil singing many old ballads and hymns, in which his boys, mowing and raking at his side, joined him heartily. He was always proud of the success of his family, but also solicitous for its welfare in the truest sense. For this reason he sometimes questioned whether the life of travelling vocalists was as healthy and happy a one as we might live in other ways, and his voice was always in favor of a life of contentment on the farm. Notwithstanding this, he sometimes gave evidence by his own disposition to go out into the world and hit up his brothers, that he was in no small degree responsible for the zeal for reform shown by his children. He was a man who pondered much on his own spiritual condition. It grieved him to feel that his religious joy and fervor was not sometimes as great as at others, and he was more than willing to sacrifice himself to gain peace of soul. A while before his death he talked with Brother Judson about this subject, and his son's advice was to give up eating pork and chewing tobacco, as a means of grace. The good old man thought the advice was timely, and at once he quit both. A good many of our neighbors had a feeling that his giving up pork in the winter season, when he had been in the habit of eating it all his life, shortened his days, as it deprived him of a means of nutrition which was essential to his well-being. There was quite a discussion concerning this for some time after his death among the townspeople.

The funeral was in the school-house near our home, as it furnished better accommodations than the house for the large numbers of sorrowing friends who gathered. Mother was still in bed, and the sons tenderly carried the body to her room, and she gazed for the last time on the loved face. It was a sorrowful scene, but hope buoyed us up, and kept us from despair. At the school-house Rev. Mr. Pearsons, pastor of the Baptist church, led in prayer and read a hymn. Then Judson spoke of the causes of disease and death, Andrew on the course of sin and death, and Joshua tenderly referred to the love of the father for his children. Then we all, brothers and sisters, joined in singing " My days are gliding swiftly by." After that the ten sons bore the body to the grave. Abby was overcome with grief. Then each returned to his own home.

Soon we took up the work of concerting once more. We were gratified in two senses in this work. First, our ambition was gratified, because fame and fortune came to us, sweetened by the reflection that it was won in a good cause. Again, we knew we were battling for the right, and though we took some chances of loss, yet the militant spirit within us was often so aroused that we rejoiced to meet and overcome opposition:

> "For right is right, since God is God,
> And right the day must win;
> To doubt would be disloyalty,
> To falter would be sin."

We sang first in Pawtucket, then in Woonsocket, Attleboro, Taunton, Valley Falls, Foxborough, Stoughton and Providence, where we gave several concerts to audiences numbering fifteen hundred and eighteen hundred people. Until our arrival at Providence the concerts were given by Judson, Joshua and John. There Caleb, Asa and Jesse joined us.

Our next concerts were at Worcester, Springfield, New Haven, and so to New York, where we were joined by our older brothers, David and Noah. Our first concert was given at the Tabernacle and we found our old friend Rynders, the rowdy, there to hear us. He had some of his crew with him and there was a slight disturbance. David and Noah did not sing with us, but were active in assistance in other ways. While on this trip we attended a seance by the Fox sisters, with Mr. and Mrs. Greeley. It was an exciting time. About this time our dividends began to diminish in a manner we were unaccustomed to in New York. Brother Judson had decided that our tickets, at fifty cents each, were too high. He refused to sing unless we placed them at twelve and one-half cents. We were usually willing to agree to any scheme broached by any of the brothers if it was not too wild, so down the price went. The result was that people would not come, and so in that big Tabernacle, where we had been in the habit often of having nine-hundred-dollar houses, the attendance dwindled to thirty, and our dividend was one dollar each. That settled it. Judson was satisfied, the price was again put up, and the attendance at once revived. At the next concert there were twelve hundred present. At the concert following there were a good many hisses for our anti-slavery songs. Judson squelched them by remarking that he was done eating geese.

We met with more opposition in New York City that year than ever before. Much fault was found with our cheap prices, and certain elements were shocked by our calling our fellow-beings men and women, instead of "gentlemen and ladies." We well understood that the root of all the opposition was because of our steady blows at the system of slavery, and as the criticisms all came from pro-slavery publications, we kept our temper, and pushed our good work steadily on. As a sample of the kind of "blows" some papers gave us, and as indicating the ingenuity and ability displayed in the attempt to prejudice the public against us, the following is perhaps as typical as any that could be quoted:

THE HUTCHINSON FAMILY

"Last evening at the Tabernacle the Hutchinsons gave one of their most agreeable concerts. A new song, written for a California company, was introduced, in which was a very happy allusion to the strong Free-Soil influence which prevails among the emigrants to that country. This was received with great applause; but while they were singing the next one, which contained a contrast between freedom and slavery, it was utterly impossible for the audience to restrain their feelings, and before the song was concluded, the Tabernacle rung again with the plaudits of the company. These musicians will leave to-day for Albany, and will be here again the latter part of this month."— *Evening Post.*

Written by one of the *prodiges*, and paid for at the rate of ten cents a line. Now then, it so happens that the Hutchinsons advertised that they would sing twenty songs, and sung only ten, with two abolition lectures, which, by the way, were hissed tremendously. This we are told by a friend who was present, there being no one about the *Merchant's Day Book* who cares enough for that particular sort of entertainment to waste his time "sitting out" one of the Hutchinsons' concerts, or listening to an abolition lecture by any of William Lloyd Garrison's disciples.

P. S.— Since writing the above we have received the following notice of the Hutchinsons, written *not* by one of this "serious family."

"The Tabernacle was tolerably filled Wednesday evening to hear these pinks again. The audience was composed of people of color, white-cravated Abolitionists, moral reformers, Grahamites, temperance lecturers, with a large sprinkling of women of varied situations, whose faces, from exposure in the great cause of moral reform, bear a striking affinity to an old hide well exposed to the weather on a crooked fence. As near as 'a man of the world' could judge, seven-eighths of this family are now engaged in procuring flannel shirts and moral tracts for every new born nigger baby. (*Vide* Burton.) Seriously, 'tis the most shallow, not to say sickening affair that has yet succeeded in gulling Gotham. A sensible person having seen them once will wonder why other people are such dunces. The truth is, hundreds pay their half-dollar as thousands did their quarters to see Barnum's woolly horse — fooled into it by the first victims and gulled into it by others who, having received tickets for their own family, advise their brethren and sisters to help the cause along. It is the practice of the 'family' to send tickets to all the clergy, heads of schools, abolition, tract, temperance and moral-reform societies. Who can wonder that with all these deadheads and their influence that the 'family' can make three or four hundred dollars a night, although there is not a line of *poetry* nor a strain of *music* in their composition? Better rhyming can be got at Thompson's or Marshall & Clark's — confectionery included — for three shillings a pound. The singing is just what is found in every well-regulated school district where the master boards round and a singing school is kept twice a week at three dollars a quarter. Positively no better.

"Now here is a specimen or two of the songs that brought out the greatest demonstrations, as all will acknowledge who were present. The 'family,' it must be known, wear their own collars turned down and of the size and shape of an open spelling-book.

"'Song — "The Standing Collar"

"'When first we went to England
The boys all about the town
Kept hollerin' out, "See them Yankees
With their collars all turned down"'

This verse is the most witty in the song and was greatly admired.

"'Song — "Eight Dollars a Day."

"'In the great city of Washington
The Congress members will have their sway,
But what do you s'pose they are thinking about? —
Why, it is eight dollars a day.
The members from the Southern States,
Where black slavery has a say,
Talk ill of Seward, Douglass, Hale, —
Why? for eight dollars a day!'"

"The conclusion of this verse, so touchingly anti-slavery and withal so caustic and witty, caused a tremendous sensation. The largest part of the listeners fairly leaped and screamed, and the feminines clapped and stamped. It was a great time, and this is a great country."

About this time my diary remarks that old friends steer clear of us, a little afraid of their own popularity, but we kept right on about our business.

On April 17th we went down to the steamer *Baltic* to see Horace Greeley sail for Europe. The start was made in a storm which was the fiercest for a long time, and tidings came in thick and fast of disasters along the coast. We were particularly anxious for the safety of the man in "the old white coat," and were solicitous for fear he was suffering unusual inconvenience from seasickness, after his departure.

April 22d the six brothers then in New York sat for a group picture, which I still have and cherish highly. It shows Jesse, Caleb, Joshua, Judson, John and Asa as they appeared at that time.

At the close of this season's concerts, which were profitable, notwithstanding all our unusual experiences, some of the boys went home. Judson went to a hydropathic institution in Brattleboro, Vt., in search of health, and I made arrangements for a tour on my own account to the far West. I secured lithographic portraits, and other unusual advertising devices, and in these preparations took quite a little time. Meanwhile I spent much of my time with Sister Abby, at her home in New York City, and also visited my good friend Prof. O. S. Fowler.

My intention to go alone on this trip was changed by the discovery that Judson cherished a desire to go with me.

So I made a trip to Brattleboro with my material,

JESSE   JOSHUA   JUDSON   CALEB   ASA   JOHN
THE SIX BROTHERS — (p. 288)

found Judson convalescent and we united again and sent express word to Brother Jesse at Lynn to also go with us to the glorious West. He responded with alacrity.

Holding a successful concert at Bennington and one at Troy, N. Y., we reached Cleveland. Here we came in association with Judge Spaulding and Salmon P. Chase, who made known the project of holding a mass convention at Ravenna on June 25th, and desired us to unite with them in the enterprise. As they expressed it, "We desire to mass the democracy on the side of liberty and against the slavery of the country."

We arranged to return after a visit to St. Louis, and to our Brother Zephaniah, who resided fifty miles away in Greenville, Bond County, Ill., and join them in this attempt to turn the tide of popular prejudice into the channel of sympathy for the slave and free slave movement. We stopped on our visit to Akron to attend the first Woman's Rights Convention in Ohio. In fact it was the first in the country except one in Worcester a short time previous.

Leaving our friends after a few concerts in Cleveland, we took a steamboat at Cincinnati and floated down the Ohio River to Louisville, where a man was taken on board, a sort of colporteur, who had three thousand large volumes, a "Bible Defence of Slavery." These he was ordered to distribute all along shore, though most were designed for Missouri. Without regarding possible consequences, we entered into a discussion, criticizing him for his sacrilegious attempt to bolster up the nefarious traffic in human souls by compromising the Scriptures in its defence. Occasionally we would introduce a song on our side, this caused quite a sensation, but while the peddler was wrathy, some passengers expressed themselves warmly in favor of the principles we enunciated.

The sequel of this affair was somewhat against our financial success, for he gave information concerning us to the authorities on arriving at St. Louis. However, we arranged affairs in our usual manner — advertising in the papers and posting in the city. The proprietor of the hall, Mr. Wyman, was a Massachusetts man (a Yankee), and he boasted he was born under the shadow of Bunker Hill, so we supposed we should have success in our dealings with him.

Leaving the matter in his hands, we left for our visit to Brother Zephaniah, fifty miles away, with the expectation of returning in one week and filling the engagement.

Through Egypt (so-called in that part of Illinois) we travelled with carriage and span, and, like the Israelites, wandered about for days, depending upon the heathen to direct us to the land of Canaan

After being misdirected scores of times, we came to the farm cottage on a Sunday and saw one of our tribe, Zephy, leading his daughter up the lane through a grove from the school-house where they had attended a prayer and conference meeting. We embraced each other, and tears of joy flowed as we spoke to him of home and New England, and sad were we all again, as he tenderly inquired concerning the death of our beloved father, who had passed " over the river " since we last met.

We conversed on the welfare of our tribe, and spoke of farming on the prairie so far from market. We talked of the politics of Illinois and the condition of the anti-slavery sentiment ; and well I remember how his countenance brightened when he said, " We have the coming man in the person of Abraham Lincoln; He will shine and become a leading star to guide the bondman out of slavery and save the country." He had seen him and came *en rapport* with his kindly magnetic influence. And so we found Lincoln, for the country and the slave, a mighty power in the hands of the Mighty One, to bring joy to four million hearts and save the Union. We met this great patriot later in Springfield, Ill., and afterwards many times.

While we were at our brother's one day we walked out into a sparsely-grown grove on his farm. Suddenly we noticed a great commotion among some robins. They would fly toward the ground and then back again, apparently in great distress. We looked up in the top of a sixty-foot tree, and there saw a big black snake, which had climbed up and was devouring a nest of young robins. We threw stones and sticks at him, but failed to dislodge him. Then Zephaniah hurried back to his house and procured an axe, and soon we had the tree felled and despatched the serpent.

We spent several days in sweet conversation and song, and for the benefit of the neighbors gathered them in to hear us. Zephaniah had several young unshod horses; and when the time approached for us to start to fulfil our engagement, we mounted them and rode through the forest to Greenville Centre, six miles and a half from his house, where he was well known. It was the county-seat, and a large number came out to a concert which we gave in the evening.

From there we moved on to a place not far from Greenville, where we spent the night. During that time the wind blew, the thunder rattled as I never heard it before, and the rain fell in torrents. However, in the morning we mounted our ponies, and attempted to ride. They would slip so that it was impossible to stay on their backs. We found shelter in a little old shanty, and waited until a Missourian came along, with four mules drawing a picturesque vehicle known as a "prairie schooner." He agreed to carry us through to the river.

After a lunch in the shanty we bade a long farewell to Zephaniah, our brother, who had in the years before shared with us so many of our toils and triumphs. He had acted as our advance agent in some of our most successful engagements, and was always a sympathetic and whole-souled man. It was our last meeting with him. In 1853 he passed away.

As we rode along toward Alton, where Lovejoy met a martyr's death, we observed many people and teams hurrying away. Probably fifty teams passed us. They told us cholera was raging in the town. So a mile outside the place we took lodgings and stayed until morning, when holding our breath for fear, we hurried through the plague-spot to our boat.

We were quite solicitous, for Brother Judson had for several days been threatened with an attack of the same scourge, but we were relieved by his convalescence; so reaching our destination ten miles away (St. Louis), we hastened to inform our Bunker Hill Yankee boaster of our arrival. We found him at his home in quite a reticent mood. "Well, watchman, what of the night?" Then we learned he had committed a cowardly act, for the slave power would drive all manhood out of any Northern dough-faces. Some spy had betrayed us, and we were informed by this Mr. Wyman that he could not let us have the hall, for the papers had spoken against us, but if the mayor would give us a license or a permit he would open the hall.

We later found he had arranged previously with the mayor to prohibit our singing. On our way to the mayor's office we were advised of the circumstances. This lessee had been induced to make a public announcement at the hall a night previous — that this Hutchinson Family was not the real family he had read of; that he had been misinformed, and therefore no concert would be given by this company. Then we found scurrilous articles in the papers, calling upon the people to put us down and not permit the concert. But still we repaired to the office of the mayor. Addressing ourselves in a courteous manner to His Honor, we asked a permit to go on with the concert. Rushing out from behind his desk, and doubling up his fist in a pugilistic way, he dashed up to us like a furious cur, with a threat: "You are Abolitionists; you have no business here; we will give you no protection. Get out of the city as quick as you can."

No expostulations would appease his wrath, and we were obliged to withdraw from his presence. Noticing groups of strangers at the corners of the streets, with angry countenances and indulging in deriding remarks as we passed by, we were convinced we were in great peril. We hastened to arrange our affairs, settling bills that had been contracted on account of the concert to the amount of one hundred dollars, dispatched our baggage to the river, and went aboard the steamboat bound to Chicago. The song "America," "My country, 'tis of thee, sweet land of liberty," we were in a position to quote in ridicule, as a satire upon our "liberties."

Our loss was probably not less than two thousand dollars, but in the midst of our disappointment, some ray of hope would beam in upon our despondency, and we were consoled by the reflection that our consciences were clear. The time would soon arrive when our boasted patriotism would cease to be a mockery in the face of true liberty. We felt that freedom and slavery could not exist under the stars and stripes, and that the conflict was inevitable.

We felt we were favored in having so peaceful an exit, and soon were facing towards the North Star. We thought how many poor fugitive bondmen had left the Southern plantations, seeking for liberty; and by this incident were more than ever fired with zeal in our holy crusade against this slave traffic. We felt the time would surely come, and in some way the Lord would provide "a way of escape." And it did come afterwards, when near the close of the war, which was fourteen years later, we were welcomed back to this slave-ridden country and extended the freedom of the city, for by the proclamation of Abraham Lincoln, Missouri had become a free State. But I anticipate.

The news of this defeat reached the ear of William Lloyd Garrison, and on our return to Boston, meeting him on State Street, he referred to the affair and said, "Another feather in your cap, my friends."

It was June 12, 1851, when we shook the dust of St. Louis from our feet, and sailed away, up the Mississippi. A very intimate acquaintance and friend, Hon. Amos Tuck from New Hampshire, ex-member of Congress, with his lady came forward to greet us, and as we related our adventures they expressed their indignation at such treatment. They were going to Chicago, having just returned from Minnesota, and they spoke in praise of the glories of that upper land, while they importuned me to go and settle with them. No slavery there! freedom to worship God!

We had an ocular demonstration of steamboat racing. Another steamer followed us up for several hours, endeavoring to get ahead, but our craft was not willing that she should run us down, so our boat fired up — turpentine, tar, pitch, rosin, were thrown under the boiler to raise the steam. The danger of our boat and crew was imminent; all were on deck ready with life-preservers to meet a catastrophe, realizing the danger, yet hoping our antagonist would be humbled. After several attempts to run by, the boats came together; then there was a crash and our boat having the advantage, held her bows to the demolished guard, crowded her rival to the bank and held her for a while; then leaving the whipped craft we sailed away up the Illinois. Then we sang the victor's song, and after some pleasant conversation with our New Hampshire friend, thanked God for safety and returned to our stateroom.

The Illinois River runs slowly; we shouted to the people on the banks, and they came down to the boat to learn what such music meant. By request, in the evening we sang to quite an audience in the cabin. A great flood overflowed the banks, many villages were inundated, and thousands were rendered homeless by the spread of the waters. We took a canal boat from Naples. The sleeping arrangements were ugly, with three narrow apartments on a side. I could have slept, but a neighbor snored so loudly that I gave up the attempt. We saw numerous birds just right for game, and a dozen were soon on the ground. It was just my luck to have sold my gun a short time before the game came in sight.

Arrived in Chicago and meeting friends, we made known our experience in St. Louis. Immediately our case was taken up, the papers were full of indignation at this uncivil conduct, and plans were made for a public demonstration. Tremont Hall was engaged, and the citizens turned out *en masse*, crowding the largest room in the city. It was a benefit of two hundred and twenty-five dollars. This was a substantial aid, and we were happy.

After more concerts we took a boat for Racine, and meeting with success took a carriage to Milwaukee, where we sang to a full house; then bade adieu and took a boat again for Chicago. On board a robbery was committed: two hundred and fifty dollars were taken away from a poor fellow, but the robbers were discovered and induced to refund what they had taken and the matter was compromised.

At Chicago we met a true friend in the person of a Mr. S. T. Mann, who proved a lover of the Hutchinson Family and continued to be the same wherever we met him. Bidding adieu to the city of mud, we took a boat for New Buffalo, Mich. On the way we met a Mr. Maynard whose daughter, Caroline B. Maynard, had shown us great courtesy in Buffalo, N. Y. He gave us good notices in his paper in the latter city.

Arriving in Detroit, June 21st, we took a boat for Cleveland, and retired at once to our berths, all in one stateroom. The night was warm, and having to leave the door ajar, I took the precaution to put my money under my pillow, while Judson had his, fifty dollars in gold, loose in his pocket, and this left in an exposed position. About midnight I was in a half-conscious state, and thought I saw the shadow of a man leaving the stateroom. Judson awoke and said, "Who went out?" "Can't tell; look to your money." "'Tis gone," said he. He kept it in his watch-pocket. Surely, the gold was gone. Cautiously I dressed, and stepping out upon the deck I saw some person returning towards our door. I stepped up to him and said, "Sir, do you belong to this boat?" He was "mum," and I was sure that this was the thief. I kept close on the lookout and right by him, and soon my two brothers came to my aid. Judson being satisfied that this was the thief, accosted him thus: "Give me my money?" We followed him close, and Jesse notified the officers of the boat. I said to the culprit, "Give back the money, and we will let you go." He denied having taken it. "Give it up quick, the officers are coming." He pulled out a roll of bills, and offered it to Judson. "Don't want that, give me gold." Then with a long sigh, he slowly drew from his pocket the identical money he had but a few moments before stolen from my brother. The officers confined the culprit, and when we arrived in Cleveland, he was handed over to the authorities and jailed. We called on him in jail, and cheered him with songs. Next day he was tried, and we endeavored to get him good counsel, our friend Burr, whom I had met in Concord; and he was released on the ground of having committed the act in doubtful waters, between the States and Canada, so we were relieved from suspense and the poor fellow was at large.

Then came some more concerts at Cleveland, and visits to our dear friends the Severances, and on Mrs Burr, a very intelligent lady, who later divorced from Burr, married a Mr Burleigh and became a Unitarian preacher in Brookline, Conn.

About this time the Bloomer dress was coming into vogue and many of our female reformers vied with each other to indorse the peculiar costume, and would smile when the men would compliment the style. Mrs. Severance and Mrs. Burr were foremost in the city to wear the garment openly. I was pleased with the convenience of it, and wrote to my wife, sending her some patterns. I later found she at once donned the dress.

While at Mrs. Severance's we met with one of the best of women, Mrs. Francis D. Gage, the poet and philanthropist. She handed me a new production, "One Hundred Years Hence," and at the meeting next day at Ravenna it formed part of the programme. Before we left Cleveland, Salmon P. Chase came in, on his way to our promised convention. We took cars, and arriving at the hotel preparations were made and a procession formed; we three, Judson, Jesse and John taking the lead. We sang as we rode to the grove, where the meeting was called to order. Some Whig paper remarked later: "The procession consisted of three people led off by the Hutchinson Family." Among the speakers were Joshua R. Giddings, S. P. Chase, Judge Spaulding, Rev. Mr. Mahan, Professor at Oberlin College, and the Hutchinson Family. We sang songs appropriate to the occasion between the speeches; one song was written by Mr. Day, a colored man. Jesse spoke a few words, and read the song given me by Mrs. Gage, which was well received. The meeting continued without adjournment about four hours, until four o'clock, when the speakers vacated the platform and took seats among the audience and we had the field and the faces and hearts of the intelligent people. We sang our usual programme, about twelve or fifteen selections in number, retaining the audience about one hour and a half, and though they had sat so long, the expressed regret at the closing was that we could not sing more.

Our friends Messrs. Chase and Spaulding seemed very well satisfied, and pronounced the convention a success.

FREEDOM'S CHAMPIONS—(p. 298)

We received for compensation the income from the sale of our song-books, about eighty dollars; and as we retreated from the field to our hotel, all completely exhausted, we thought the switching of the Democratic political car on to the tracks of Free Soil was a success, and like the matchless senative would use up the Whigs and pro-slavery men and leave nothing but the hat and boots. So we went to rest believing in the good time coming.

June 26th we took the cars at Hudson, and sang another concert to the people. How gratifying to us this opportunity to utter in song the sentiments of our hearts, for we boldly declared our opinion of the reform of the day, whether they would hear or forbear.

Then we went again to Ravenna, for the people wished to hear more of our music. Judson preached some on the evils of tobacco and pork-eating. My diary says at this point: "O God, purify my mind! I will trust in Thee. Let me to-day promulgate some new truth, is the prayer of my heart."

Many young men came to say farewell, when we returned to Cleveland and held another popular concert in the Melodeon. Our concerts were disturbed by the ringing of the nine-o'clock bells, so dearly revered by the generation which commands a salary, and feels a glory in rolling o'er the human heart a stone. What a nuisance it is to the sensitive ear, just as one is pouring out his very soul in affectionate sympathy, to hear this banging of iron bells, dispelling every vista of harmony and sublimity, thus being compelled to close with disgust, mingled with shame at such lack of public appreciation.

June 29th we had a real welcome at the house of T. C. Severance, who always extended his hospitality to us poor pilgrims.

Brother Asa, who had, since we parted in New York in the spring, spent his time at the old homestead in New Hampshire, came to join us once more, and our trio was complete. Judson and I welcomed our bass singer, and rejoiced to mingle our voices once again. Good news came from home; mother was well and our wives prospering.

June 30th, another concert in Cleveland, Asa joining with us, and Brother Jesse attending to the business. Many bouquets were bestowed upon us, and the singing was all a success. Many young ladies admired our cause and showed us courtesy, and many a souvenir was pressed upon us.

We went to Elyria, where we were greeted with a fine audience, and the good people received us gladly and bade us God-speed. Away again in the weary stage to Oberlin. Many students came out to greet us, and congratulated us. We went upon the green in the afternoon with them and joined in our favorite sport, "Fox and Geese." This game served a double purpose, giving us athletic sport and lessening the monotony of our calling.

Here we found a true, radical spirit of reform, anti-slavery, temperance and woman's equality. I believe this the first college where a black man was recognized as a brother and both women and men could be educated and graduated together. Some eight hundred students and citizens gathered into the Tabernacle. Judson's remarks were well received, and the radical songs were loudly applauded. President Finney spoke in an approving manner of them.

These happy days we contrasted with the scourging we received at poor St. Louis, and so took courage. Here we met Miss Mary White, who was the soprano

THE TRIO OF BROTHERS — (p. 300)

of the choir — a lovely spirited lady whose voice seemed to blend with our's like that of our dear Sister Abby, who was still away from the circle at her home in New York. So we consulted with Miss White about joining with us, but the son of President Finney gave an encouraging word for love's sake, and we left them alone to their love-making and passed on, a disappointed trio, back to Cleveland and took a steamboat to Painesville, for no Lake Shore Railroad was yet built.

On July 4th we had a rather peculiar experience in Painesville. Arriving at the town on the preceding day, we found our old friends of the Baker Family also there. Soon after, we were waited upon by a committeeman named Steele, who desired to know if we would not sing for the celebration of Independence Day, in a beautiful grove near by. We declined. He wished us to set a price, but we refused to do that.

We were just then feeling, as did many other Abolitionists, that to join in the celebration of the natal day of the country was to, in a sense, approve its recognition of the system of slavery, and we could not do that. Nevertheless, we loved the land of our birth, and hated to refuse, so Jesse told him that if we had the spirits of singing on the following day, we would come and give the company gathered one song. On that day, therefore, after a ride into the country with the Bakers, Jesse composed an appropriate song, and we went to the grove to sing it, but the committee informed us they had made other arrangements. There were three thousand people in the gathering. Soon, to our astonishment, the announcement was made from the platform that the Hutchinsons had agreed to sing, and had then backed out, unless the people would pay them seventy-five dollars. This was untrue, and we felt deeply the attempt to injure us. We resolved to refute the imputation, and taking our stand by the platform, Jesse requested an opportunity to make a statement. The committee held a consultation, and refused to grant the privilege. We then determined to cry out, whether or no, and just as the assembly was dismissed, Judson stated in loud tones that the Hutchinsons had been belied. Jesse also denied the slander, as did Asa Steele made a lame attempt at an answer. We went to dinner with friends, and on our way back found the people still assembled, listening to toasts and speeches. Jesse mounted the platform, and made a short speech in favor of brown bread, and then said the Hutchinsons were present and would favor the company with a song "A song, a song!" rang through the trees, and we at once began to sing our "Cold Water Song," but were prevented from concluding it by some of the ugly partisans of the committee. We left the stage, and returned to the hotel. Then the committee waited on us in relation to the church we had engaged for our concert They told us we should have it, but said there had been some effort made to cheat us out of it. We concluded it was wise to stay indoors until six o'clock, and then we went to the church. The doors were locked. I hurried to one of the trustees, and asked the reason. He said it was because we had refused to sing during the day, and furthermore that the mob would disturb us if we went into the house. I calmly told him I did not fear a *mob*. Finally, we got his permission to sing on the steps of the church. Accordingly, we mounted them, and asked the people gathered, over a thousand, if we should sing. A united shout, " Yes," was enough to thrill us to action, and we commenced, and continued for two hours, procuring our instruments to aid us.

While we were in the middle of the song, "Behold, the Day of Promise comes," we saw a crowd of roughs coming near, making a good deal of noise. We expected difficulty, as they joined the group of listeners gathered near the steps of the church that each auditor might get every note of our songs. But as soon as they came within hearing of our music, they quieted down, mingled with the orderly ones, and we went on and finished our programme. Afterwards one fellow said he had intended to "break us up," and do us injury, but when he caught the sound of our harmony, he was entirely thwarted. He had a stone to throw, but dropped it suddenly. After the concert was over, many offered to pay us, and large numbers attempted to put a quarter into our hands, but we refused all such kindnesses. When we had finished singing, we visited a ladies' fair, and contributed our mite towards putting blinds on the church to which we had been refused admittance. Ever after that when we visited Painesville we were received with great *éclat*. The next night we were at Chardon, and some fifty people came down from Painesville to hear us. From thence we travelled through several Ohio towns until we came to Jefferson, the home of Joshua R. Giddings.

The following interesting statement in regard to the Painesville riot was written in 1874, by Col. J. F. Morse, the oldest member of that celebrated Fourth of July committee:

PAINESVILLE, September 28, 1874

DEAR SIR —Complying with your request coming from sources which I respect, I will proceed to write an imperfect narrative of some events which transpired nearly a quarter of a century ago, when the people of Lake County, Ohio, assembled at the village of Painesville on the Fourth of July to celebrate the seventy-fourth anniversary of the Declaration of Independence

On this day, consecrated to universal freedom, there was a violent outburst of pro-slavery passion and fury quite incredible when contemplated from the standpoint of the present time.

When some time previous to the fourth day of July, 1852, the citizens of Painesville began to make preparations for celebrating that day, it was suggested the songs and music of those unrivalled singers, the Hutchinsons, would form an attractive and appropriate feature of the commemorative exercises, if their consent could be obtained. It was known that they were to sing at an anti-slavery meeting to be held at Ravenna, Portage County, O., prior to the Fourth of July, and several persons from Painesville attended the meeting at Ravenna with the view of making such an arrangement with the Hutchinsons as would secure to the people who joined in the celebration the rare enjoyment afforded by the music, the wit and humor of these renowned artists. No definite engagement was made with the Hutchinsons at the interview had with them at Ravenna by these people, Messrs. Rockwell, Jennings, Steele and Morse. The Hutchinsons could do no more than say to those gentlemen that if subsequently they found it compatible with their other engagements they would sing at Painesville on the coming Fourth of July. The question was subsequently settled by a correspondence with the Hutchinsons, C. C. Jennings and J. F. Morse acting as a committee for that purpose, the former agreeing to give a concert in Painesville on the day of the celebration, and the latter agreeing to procure a church or hall to be used for the concert. With his usual promptitude Mr. Jennings obtained the written consent of five of the six trustees of the Methodist church, so that it could be used by the Hutchinsons. They arrived in Painesville in time to fulfil their engagement.

In the programme of exercises for the day the committee of arrangements advertised that the Hutchinsons would sing certain songs or pieces selected by themselves. To this the Hutchinsons objected. They would only consent to sing during the public exercises pieces of their own selection or composition.

A majority of the active members of the committee of arrangements were determined to exclude everything from the proceedings which could give offence to the sensitive pro-slavery people who might be present at the celebration, and would not yield. Neither would the Hutchinsons, as without the expression of the sentiment which they cherished, their singing would lack the inspiration which was its greatest charm. The committee of arrangements were enraged and excited in a most extravagant and unreasonable manner at this non-compliance of the Hutchinsons, and were determined to prevent their holding a concert, by which it was expected that they would receive some compensation for the time and money expended in meeting an engagement entered into for the gratification of their friends and the public in this section of the State.

The committee succeeded in communicating to a large crowd of people in an incredibly short space of time the fury of their own causeless indignation, so that the timid became alarmed for the safety of their property if not of their lives. The trustees of the Methodist church withdrew their consent to the occupancy of their building by the Hutchinsons, alleging that they were apprehensive of its destruction by an infuriated and incensed people. Mr. Jennings asserted his right to the occupancy of the church upon the faith of the written consent of the trustees and agreed to indemnify them for the loss of the church if it was destroyed.

When the time came for admission to the concert, a crowd of people were collected around the door of the Methodist church. Some were seeking admission, others were trying to repel them by noisy and threatening demonstrations. Mr. Jennings, disregarding all this opposition, took a position at the door of the church to receive the entrance fees. Very few had gone in when he was confronted by a stalwart and determined member of the committee of arrangements with threats of being ejected from the church by force. Mr. Jennings is a man of large statue, possessing moral and physical courage not likely to fail him in any emergency. He met those threatening demonstrations with such firmness of deportment that the assailant subsided without attempting any violence. In the meantime, the Hutchinsons arrived at the door of the church. Undismayed they surveyed the crowd in front of them, and after taking in the situation, they changed the programme from indoors to an outside free concert for the entertainment of both willing and unwilling hearers.

All attempts of the latter to drown the tuneful harmony of their voices by the rapid firing of cannon from an adjacent eminence or by shouting and throwing fire-crackers and other hissing and explosive missiles among the listening throng were ineffectual to silence or disconcert these courageous men. They said their say, and sung the songs of their own selection without discriminating between friends and enemies.

This paroxysm of pro-slavery madness speedily subsided and left those who were so violently affected by it to reflections not unmingled with shame and regret. Some of the gentlemen most conspicuous in exciting the disorders on this occasion subsequently made ample apologies to the Hutchinsons for their mistaken zeal.

Very cordially yours, etc., J. F. MORSE.

We made our headquarters with the great Abolitionist, Giddings, during our stay in Jefferson. He was very courteous toward us. We played ball for old acquaintance sake, and talked of the slavery question and the prospects of Daniel Webster. Giddings considered the great expounder of the constitution politically dead. The lapse of time showed that he was right. I thought of the reflections in my diary after my first meeting with the great statesman, when he was so attracted by the wine-glass, when Giddings told me that at one of Jenny Lind's concerts in Washington, Webster shocked the audience by three times rising and profoundly bowing to the Nightingale, at very inopportune moments, the explanation being that the noted man was irresponsible for his acts. At Ashtabula we found the story of our experience in Painesville had prejudiced the people against us, a very annoying circumstance. Stopping at the hotel I overheard some young men talking of us. They said the song, "Man the Life-Boat," was a good one, but so many "isms" would not go down. We went to Detroit, where we gave two concerts. We took tea at the house of the ex-mayor, Mr. Ladore, and met several old acquaintances, Messrs. Tucker, Palmer and others. After a concert at Ann Arbor, we returned to Detroit, and from there went to Buffalo. Here we settled with Jesse and he went home. I sent fifty dollars to him at the depot by a boy. Later I got a telegram that he had not received it. We looked up the boy, and he confessed that he had opened the letter, given forty dollars to another boy, and spent the rest. We hunted up the other sinner and recovered fifteen dollars of our money. Then we took the note of the first boy, Sammy, and took him along with us for security, hoping to do him good. He sold song-books at the door, and made himself generally useful. We had fine houses at Auburn, Rochester and Syracuse.

In Rochester, the year before, we had postponed two concerts, one to prevent interfering with Jenny Lind, and the other to accommodate a benefit by Madame Anna Bishop. For the latter act we were thanked by the Firemen's Benefit Association, and now it showed itself bread cast on the waters, for the fire laddies and others crowded out to our entertainment in such numbers that we were obliged to advertise a return concert a few days later. It took us forty-five minutes to get through the crowd of ten thousand seeking admission. Then came concerts at Oswego, Sacket Harbor; and with our last Rochester concert our season ended.

The summer was spent in Milford, in our usual manner. I made an attempt to establish a "union" store, I remember, and was rather chagrined at the slow way in which the townspeople took the matter up. In September the trio of brothers made another start, and gave concerts all through Southern New Hampshire and Vermont. It was successful, and the only unusual incident was the mortifying discovery that our youthful *protégé*, Samuel, who was with us, had repaid our attempt to save him from a life of viciousness, by rifling my trunk of the contents of a bag of silver (one hundred and twenty-five dollars), and left the bag stuffed with wads of paper. This was in Greenfield, and we soon got upon his track and found him nine miles away headed for Northampton. He was sent to the Reform School, to see what virtue there would be in that course of treatment.

We made some lasting friendships on this trip, as well as renewing others. At Keene we stayed some days with M. T. Tottingham, a prominent business man, president of the Cheshire County Musical Association, and were also handsomely entertained by William P.

Chamberlain, who for many years held a leading position in musical circles of the town. He took us to his father's farm, a few miles out, where my wife and I spent a very pleasant day. At Hanover, one of the students, Clinton Averill, showed us a good deal of attention. At Northfield, Vt., Governor Paine was particularly kind to us. At Burlington the poet humorist, John G. Saxe, was at our concert, and in fact accompanied us on the journey from Montpelier. He was a jolly companion, and we enjoyed his society very much. We also took tea with our friend Allen and his wife, whom we knew from the lady's former residence in Hancock. Mr. Conant, of Brandon, put us under obligations by his kindness. At Castleton we found our townsman John Fuller. My little daughter Viola was with me on this tour.

We got home October 30th, and by November 9th Judson had notified me he was ready to start out again. November 25th we were off. After a few days of preparation in Boston we sang to an immense audience in South Boston. We also gave concerts in the Melodeon and in Chelsea. Jenny Lind was giving concerts at this time, and we lent her the Melodeon three evenings, postponing our own concerts.

This was after her contract with Barnum had expired. Her agent came to Boston, and in looking for a suitable hall, could find none that pleased him so well as the Melodeon. We, however, had a contract for it. In those days, an evening in a Boston hall was worth many hundreds of dollars to us. But we released it to him, he paying us three hundred dollars, the rent of the hall, and giving us thirty-dollars-worth of tickets to the prima donna's concerts, so we heard Jenny to our hearts' content. She had a very bright, ringing, silvery-toned voice, accompanied with depth and strength. Singing in Charlestown, later, Judson and Asa took bad colds. The consequence was that when we reached Providence we were quite hampered in our work. At our first concert, where there were sixteen hundred people, Judson was so hoarse he broke down. The concert was postponed, and on the evening substituted seventeen hundred came. He was no better, and the people got their tickets back. Then we went to Boston in search of relief. We had a date for a concert there, and filled it, though Asa and I alone entertained the sixteen hundred auditors. Then Judson went home to Milford, while I went to Lowell to postpone another concert. From Milford we had to send a messenger to Providence to postpone the postponed concert. Finally, December 17th, we were able to start again, going to Boston, Newton and Providence, where our long-delayed entertainment came off. While here we heard unpleasant news from Jesse. He had lost his wife, Susan, a few months before. They had buried all of their five children previously. When we began our fall singing, we were unable to agree on the terms by which he should act as our advance agent; we now learned that he had started out as manager for our friendly rivals, the Alleghanians. The result of this arrangement was that as he knew all our routes we came into frequent conflict, often reaching the same city simultaneously. We still loved our brother and wished him success, but we were grieved. We went next to Pawtucket, Groton and Lowell. At the latter city both my children sang in the concert "The Yankee Boy." Viola was hardly five years old. This was her first public appearance.

From Lowell, bidding our families good-by, we proceeded, by way of Hartford and New Haven, where of course we sang, to New York. Here we found Jesse, Abby and Ludlow, and many friends. Jesse was making plans for a Californian trip with his company. After some weeks singing in the city and vicinity, we went to Albany, where great enthusiasm was manifested over our singing. On January 28, 1852, the State temperance convention occurred in Albany. On that evening we sang to at least three thousand people, in three different churches, it being impossible to get all our temperance friends into any one building. The Maine law was just becoming popular with these people, and great things were expected of it. I recorded my belief that the glorious day was surely coming, and that this law would drive King Alcohol from the country. Then we went to Troy, and coming back to Albany, introduced for the first time the song, "Do a Good Turn when You can." This song Jesse had found somewhere on his travels, and had put it in an envelope and mailed it to us; we receiving it at our hotel in New York a few days before this concert. We at once set it to music. The words were as follows:

"It needs not great wealth a kind heart to display,
If the hand be but willing, 'twill soon find a way,
And the poorest one yet, in the humblest abode,
May help a poor brother a step on the road
Then if we enjoy life, why, the next thing to do
Is to see that another enjoys his life too,
And though poor be our purse, and though narrow our span,
Let us all try to do a good turn when we can

"The fair bloom of pleasure may charm for a while,
But its beauty is pale, and inconstant its smile,
Whilst the beauty of kindness, immortal in bloom,
Sheds a sweetness o'er life, and a grace o'er the tomb
Then whatever of fortune a man may have won,
A kindness depends on the way it is done;
And though poor be our purse and though narrow our span,
Let us all try to do a good turn when we can"

This trip up the river for a week was very profitable for us. We went back to New York for another series of concerts, and then proceeded to Philadelphia. We found Joshua there, giving concerts, and attended one as soon as we arrived, singing one song by request of the people, and to show our good-will. Joshua's concerts, we found, were giving good satisfaction. We always looked for trouble in the city after the attempt of the mayor to shut out the colored people; but during this visit we had many of them in our hall without the slightest attempt to disturb them or us. We greatly enjoyed visits at the homes of the Mitchells and Samuel Brainard, a good-hearted Quaker. Our concerts were given in Sansom Street Hall, and there were eight or nine. We also sang in Rev. Mr. Moore's church, for the Philharmonic Society, and at a monster temperance meeting to three thousand people. Other places visited during this time were Norristown and Westchester.

Baltimore was visited next. A rather unpleasant reception awaited us. Some young men of pro-slavery tendencies had placarded the streets with appeals to the citizens not to allow us to sing. We went to the mayor, and he sent fifty police-officers to the hall on the evening of our concert. The attendance was small, and the blue-coats awed the roughs so much that there was no disorder. We felt these things hard to bear, as we went on to Washington, but consoled ourselves with the reflection that the bright spots would come by-and-by.

In Washington we took lodgings in the National Hotel, where Henry Clay was stopping. We repaired to the Capitol early, as usual, and heard an address by William H. Seward. Soon after our arrival we had a letter from President Fillmore, politely declining an invitation to attend one of our concerts. I met our friend Giddings as usual, and he introduced me to Horace Mann, with whom I had an hour's conversation on Spiritualism. Salmon P. Chase also took me under his wing, and introduced me to many of the senators, one of whom was Charles Sumner. At one of the president's levees, I met "Grace Greenwood," Ole Bull, Daniel Webster and others.

Next we went to Harrisburg, Pa., where my wife joined me. Proceeding to Pittsburgh, we spent several days. On Sunday we sang "Where shall the Soul find Rest" in one of the churches. The clergyman in charge responded "Yes, yes!" as we concluded, fell backward, and was so affected for some time that he could not go on with the service. His wife and children were so frightened that they rushed up the pulpit stairs to aid him. There was a good deal of excitement. We considered it a grand development and demonstration. Mr. Giddings was with us during our stay in Pittsburgh. We stayed in Pennsylvania for some time. My wife often sang with us, making a quartet, as in the days when Abby sang. She had given up the bloomer costume before this period, as she was more or less annoyed by the comments of rude boys as she passed through the streets. Later we went to Cleveland, where our good friends, the Severances, entertained us, and to Columbus, where we met Gough once more. At Columbus no church would allow us to sing, and the most available hall was under restrictions regarding the colored race, so we sang in the dissecting-room of the new medical college, the tables being removed. The Legislature then took the matter up, and tried to pass an order to allow us the use of the Representatives' chamber, but it failed by a small majority, and we returned to our dissecting-room. There was great good-will shown, and we had as happy a time as though we had been permitted to let our songs ring through the halls of legislation. Concerts in Sandusky, Springfield, Erie, Buffalo, Auburn and Utica followed, and then Judson went home, and the rest soon followed. I was rather discouraged, for Judson had announced that he would sing no more with us, and we felt that we had given our last concert together. We were mistaken. A short stay in New York for shopping, and then we were in Milford once more.

June 9th we all went to Concord, sang in a big temperance convention, with Gen. Neal Dow and Rev. E. H. Chapin, D.D., of New York, as speakers, and gave two concerts.

Then came an interval of farming. Viola came down with scarlet fever, and that made days and nights of anxiety and watching. In August we gave some concerts in Nashua, Manchester, and other places. One day I started from Concord for Meredith Bridge, where I was to give a concert in the evening. By mistake I got in a car bound for Claremont, and was forty miles out of my way before I discovered the fact. I had been busy talking with an acquaintance in the train, whom I assumed was also bound to my destination. Suddenly glancing out of the window, I saw a train, moving in an opposite direction. "Where's that train going?" I asked. "To Meredith Bridge," was the reply. "Then where does this go?" asked I. "To Claremont." "Well, I want that train," I exclaimed, as I grasped my bag and ran for the door. The train was then some distance off, but the engineer of the train I had left saw my dilemma, and sounded his whistle. "The train's gone; you can't get it," said a man whom I passed. "Well," said I, "I'm going to try." The engineer of the Meredith Bridge train, hearing the whistle, stopped it three-quarters of a mile away. It was against the rules of the road for the train to go back, but Conductor Wright left it, and coming to meet me, took my bag and my arm, and assisted me to it. This same Mr. Wright has been in Washington for thirty years, acting as superintendent of the street-cleaning department. I filled my engagement that night. Then followed a series of concerts among the mountain resorts. My wife's serious illness called me home. She recovered after many days of suffering.

October 15th we started out on a short trip through Vermont and New Hampshire. We visited Rutland, Brandon, Middleton, Poultney, Bennington, Brattleboro, Fitzwilliam, Winchendon (Mass.), and some other places. Then we spent some weeks trying to settle a mixed state of affairs at home, resulting from Brother Caleb's illness.

On December 9th, in company with my wife, I went to Andover and being joined by the brothers on the following day, gave a concert. We called on Harriet Beecher Stowe, the author of "Uncle Tom's Cabin," at the home of Professor Stowe, her husband, then connected with the theological seminary. She suggested the feasibility of public readings of her book, interspersed with some of our anti-slavery songs. On our way home in the cars a young girl who dressed in male attire was put off the train. I was very indignant, for I believed it the right of a woman to dress just as she chose. Next we sang in Dover, and then in Salmon Falls. Stopped with our friend John Sawtell. While here, Sunday, December 19th, we sang at a baptismal service. One convert was sprinkled, and three taken to the river, two being immersed and one baptized by pouring. The ice on the river was so thick that it bore the greater part of the two hundred who attended the service. It was a bitter cold day. Concerts in Haverhill and Georgetown followed, and then we once more turned our faces "down East." Biddeford, Portland, Bath, Hallowell, Augusta, and Gardner listened to our songs. At the latter town we came into competition with my much-admired friend, Prof. O. S Fowler. As his lecture was free, he got the largest audience. He called on us after the concert, and my diary forgivingly remarks that phrenology is a true science.

We went on to Waterville, Lewiston, Portland again, Saco, Bath again, Biddeford again, Kennebunk, where we sang in a hotel, fitting up a stage of an old gate from a fence in the yard. January 19, 1853, we sang once more in the old Camenerum Hall, where we had given one of our early concerts, ten years before. My diary contains a sad reference to the fact that my old friend Knowlton, who was very kind to us at our first visit to the city, was sleeping in the church-yard.

January 13th we sang at Amesbury. We went to the home of John G. Whittier. The poet was in ill health and unable to attend our concert, but his sister was there.

After this we spent a week in the vicinity of Boston. During this period we dined one day with Mrs. Richard Hildreth. She had just completed a crayon likeness of Judson. Her husband was at that time at work on his celebrated history of the United States

Then we started on another trip One of our first stops was at Newburyport. During the night there was a cry of fire, and our doorkeeper, Mr. Hastings, supposing it to be a summons to rise and proceed on his journey, hastily dressed himself, and seizing his valise, started for the door. Then he found to his chagrin that it was only midnight, and the rest of us were soundly sleeping.

Soon after we were in Fall River. The landlord of our hotel very politely started to show our rooms. He forgot himself, however, and instead, ushered us into the room where he kept his liquors. I told him we preferred a bedroom to a bar-room, and he appeared quite nonplussed. At New Bedford, at the request of our friend Colonel Hatch, we sang for the benefit of the Methodist church, Lucy Stone's name also being on the programme. The great advocate of universal suffrage dressed in bloomer costume in those days, and was at the zenith of her popularity. We sang several selections, then she talked, and we finished the meeting with songs.

Up to this time Lucy Stone had taken no money at her lectures. She sometimes took up a collection to assist in paying expenses, but seemed to have an impression that as she was advocating somewhat unpopular reforms, the people would not pay to hear them presented. I told her differently. "They'll pay," said I, "and be converted just as fast as if you crowded it down their throats for nothing." I realized that the matter of her lectures was of a most interesting character, and well worthy of pecuniary reward. She followed my advice, charged twenty-five cents thereafter, and, at a little later date. meeting her in New York State, I found that she was making money. We spent quite a period in concerting on Cape Cod. At Harwich we were the guests of our old friend Franklin Sears, and had the pleasure of meeting Charles C. Burleigh, reminding us forcibly of the joy of meeting a friendly face in a strange land. Our hall was very much crowded. Mr. Burleigh was compelled to sit on the stage, using my melodeon box for an opera chair.

March 14, 1853, this tour ended. We went home and at once began negotiations with Hayward Hutchinson, son of my oldest brother David, to go out on the road as our advance agent. He did not go, but soon after went to Baltimore and commenced a business career that made him both famous and wealthy. As it turned out, some time passed before we sang again. April 6th we received news that Jesse was at Cincinnati, sick. He had previously taken the Alleghanians to California, and, after a successful tour, severed his connection with them. Remaining in the gold country for a time, he finally took passage home, coming by way of Panama. When part way on his journey some one of the company discovered that a trunk, containing twenty thousand dollars in gold, had been left behind on the isthmus. He volunteered to return for it. Going back, he secured the trunk, but missed connection with the next returning boat by a half-hour. The consequence was that he had to wait three weeks for another. When he finally left, he had contracted the fever which carried off so many men who braved the unaccustomed climate of the isthmus, and was barely able to reach Cincinnati alive.

Here he found good friends in our Uncle Kendrick Leavitt and his family. As soon as possible after we learned of the circumstances, Judson went to Cincinnati, and as his reports were discouraging, Asa and I, with our wives, soon decided to go also. We stopped a few days at New York, and then went to Sister Abby's house in Orange, New Jersey, for further news. Just before that, while we were in New York, Brother Joshua came, on his way from Philadelphia to his home. We had some pleasant interviews. While talking with him on the grounds of the Croton Reservoir, where we had gone for a walk, I remember speaking of an impression that a little later he and I would be doing certain things together and some of the boys would be gone. While at Abby's one day — it was April 27th — I tipped back in my chair, and slept. I dreamed some one came in and handed me a letter. The only thing I could make out in it were the characters "Z. K." I awoke with the dream troubling me a little, and at once took the train for New York. Going to my hotel, the landlord gave me a letter. I was still thinking of my dream, and had meantime recalled the fact that in our boyhood days we had been in the habit of calling Brother Zephaniah "Z K." On opening the note, it proved to be from Joshua, and said "Z K is dead. Died the 19th of April." How glad was I to think that his brothers had made their visit to him before his death; and now another brother was waiting the summons. A few days later I went on to Cincinnati, with my wife. Then followed days and nights of watching and of alternate hope and despair. Our brother Jesse was cheerful, but dangerously sick. Some days he would rally and we would begin to hope. His three brothers would take turns in caring for him. He had been removed to a water-cure a little outside the city, in hope that he would recover. The days wore on until May 16th, when just as I was preparing to leave Uncle Kendrick's to relieve Asa, word came from him that Jesse was dead. He died easily, retaining his faculties to the last. The next day we left for home with the body. The funeral occurred at Lynn on the 20th.

In justice to Jesse and to his faith I ought to say here that his belief in Spiritualism was a comfort to him in the supreme hour. At intervals during his sickness he would look up with the greatest delight, and converse with his wife and children, who had passed on before, and whom he quite evidently thought he saw. "Here's Jimmie," "Here's Charlie," he would say. When a more normal condition from this of ecstatic joy came, he would say: "Oh, John, I've seen my wife and my children! They have appeared." He spent much time from day to day in making verses and rhyming.

It was the work of many weeks to settle the estates of our brothers. Meanwhile, I remained at Milford. One day I had a conversation with Oliver Lull, the village lawyer, on slavery. He spoke in pacific terms of the South. I said: "I suppose, in keeping with your Democratic proclivities, if war was inevitable, you, sir, would be inclined to favor your Southern allies, and draw your sword in defence of their rights as against the North." I can never forget his reply, as raising himself to his full height from his seat, he answered, "No, never! I would be a volunteer in the armies of the North, and fight for liberty and union." For thirty years his widow has been clad in the habiliments of mourning for a brave husband, soldier and patriot, who sacrificed his life in defence of his country. All who fought under Colonel Lull cherish his memory.

About this time my mother visited New York, to see Abby, in company with Sister Rhoda. When she returned to Milford, we met her at the depot with our horse handsomely trimmed with laurel, in honor of the event. Brother Caleb's health gave way during this period, and we could not help being impressed with our slender hold upon life.

July 1st and 2d we varied the monotony of a farmer's life with concerts in Pepperell and Townsend, and on the Fourth we joined in the local celebration, singing in the town hall. On the 21st we gave a concert at Manchester, Mass., and the following night sang in Gloucester. Remaining on Cape Ann a few days we spent a delightful Sunday at Annisquam, and on the following day tried to catch fish in Ipswich Bay. They did not bite, and we therefore sailed up the Essex River to the town of Essex, hailing the carpenters in the shipyards with songs, landed, and in the evening gave a concert.

After this we spent a good deal of time at High Rock, giving concerts at near-by places. Our singing was mostly as a quartet, the place so long filled by Sister Abby being taken by Abby Marvel. She was our cousin, niece of my mother, and took her musical ability from the Leavitts. The "Lynn Bard," Alonzo Lewis, was a frequent visitor on High Rock. He composed several songs for us, but they lacked the singable quality we desired, and none of them were ever given in public. He was a good wood-carver, and when we first started public singing made a cut of us in our concert gear — which was then a blouse with belt and flowing sleeves, and giving the effect of the costume of the pilgrims — which was used on our announcements for a long period.

In August, Brother Asa with his wife went to Nantucket, and Judson and I thought it a good opportunity to go to Martha's Vineyard camp-ground and give a concert at Edgartown.

We left New Bedford on Saturday, in the yacht of our friends Mr. and Mrs. Taber. We hailed a New Bedford whaler on the way, and found her returning from a thirty-months' voyage, with three hundred barrels of oil. After fishing around Gay Head a while, we bid the crew of our boat adieu, and started on our way to the camp-ground. When it was too late to go back, we discovered that we had been landed at the wrong point, and so lost our way to Holmes Holl. We asked the advice of some friendly Indians, and they told us to pursue a certain course until we came to a creek, which we must cross. It was late when we reached the creek. The ferryman had gone in for the night, and on seeking him out we found him deaf and dumb. We were unable to make him understand what we wanted, and began to despair, when we found some small boys with a boat, crab hunting. For eighteen cents they agreed to take us over the stream. Then we were directed to the house of a man who would row us down the creek to the camp-ground, fifteen miles.

We took supper with him and then tried to sleep. It was a hot night, and the mosquitos were so thick that we were driven out of doors by them. Finally we took our sheets and used them as curtains for our bed, and thus got some slight relief. It was impossible to sleep, however, and we counted the hours — one, two, three, four, — and at half past four we rose, prepared to resume our journey, and pushed off. It was a tedious route, and we were well brushed by overhanging bushes most of the way. At the camp-ground a friend to whom we were introduced invited us into his modest hut, or cottage, and we got some sleep. We were courteously received by the good Methodists, listened to the services, and at night went to Edgartown.

Here Asa joined us; and though I had been sick all day, on Monday evening we gave a concert, and then concerts in New Bedford, Newport, Bristol, Providence,

Pawtucket and Mystic Bridge. At the latter town, we found on arrival that no bills had been circulated. Asa at once borrowed a big bell, and while the rest of us put out bills he proclaimed the concert through the streets, thus getting out a good audience. Other Connecticut towns visited were New London, Stonington and Mystic.

September 2d. High Rock was sold at public auction and became the property of Asa and myself. We at once made arrangements to remove our belongings from Milford to the stone cottage that had been built on the rock by our brother. It was in a sightly location just under the face of the rock, and is still one of the prettiest of the many cottages that adorn the property. Before he built it, there was some speculation whether Brother Jesse would have any water, building on a rock some two hundred feet high. He called in the aid of a clairvoyant, who, walking out on the sward pointed to a certain spot and told him to dig down a stipulated number of feet. He would then find three rocks peculiarly placed, and on removing them would find beneath a living spring. He followed the directions minutely, found the three rocks and the spring, which has never failed all these years.

We made arrangements with a family to occupy the cottage and board us, with our wives and children. From that time High Rock became fully identified with us as the home of the Hutchinsons.

"In the State of Massachusetts, in the good old town of Lynn,
There's a famous range of ledges, as eye hath ever seen;
Two hundred feet the highest point looms up this rugged block,
And it's known throughout New England as 'Old High Rock.'

"Upon this noted eminence, far o'er the ocean blue —
And a hundred miles of landscape the eye can clearly view —

Rocks, mountains, seas and rivers the painter here could chalk,
And sketch a scene the world to vie, from 'Old High Rock'

"Just half a century ago we sought this sightly spot,
And underneath its lofty dome my brother built his cot,
And here the tribe of Jesse sang, and made the people talk
Of the friends of right and progress, at 'Old High Rock'

"This rock had noted visitors in stirring days of yore —
Garrison, Rogers, Douglass, Phillips and many more,
Upon its lofty summit for freedom they would talk —
Ah, those were proudest moments in the story of High Rock!"

Saturday, October 8th, we went to Lowell and opened her most famous audience-room, Huntington Hall. Soon after we started for Springfield and other western Massachusetts towns, Hartford, New Haven and New York. It was a repetition of other years' experiences — large audiences, many meetings with old friends. We stayed a while with a Dr Wellington. Suddenly his daughter came down with small-pox, and we sought the friendly shelter of the home of Mrs. Van Vleet, where we had often stayed before. While at Dr. Wellington's I had a talk one day with Frederick Douglass and Charles C. Burleigh, who were calling, in regard to dramatizing "Uncle Tom's Cabin." I believed a great deal of good would come from so doing. I wrote to Mrs Stowe in regard to the matter, after finding they agreed with me. She wrote in reply that she did not think public sentiment sufficiently advanced to warrant success in dramatizing the book. The immense success in the presentation of the play that came later fully vindicated my judgment. During this season in New York, I became very much attached to Frank B. Carpenter, the artist and author, whose famous painting of the signing of the emancipation proclamation now hangs in the Capitol, and whose other great painting of the signing of the treaty of Washington is now in the possession of Queen Victoria. In my diary for November 25th I speak of going to his house to tea, and viewing his portrait of Sister Abby. This portrait now hangs in the room where these words are written. In after years it was given by Sister Abby to my son Henry, he having given her another handsome portrait of herself, painted at a later date.

How shall I describe this picture? It is of Abby, the youngest child of the Tribe of Jesse — "the innocent, affable, genial, loving, charming Abby, the household pet." So one of her brothers described her, in a published tribute. But its writer was not one of the brothers who was her constant companion for so many years of artistic and moral triumph. Joshua knew Abby, and loved her well, but he could not know as I knew the inspiration of her presence in the hour when together we faced cheering thousands in the excitement of some of our greatest efforts; the courage she imparted when, a fearless, queenly soul, without the slightest suspicion of unwomanliness, she stood shoulder to shoulder with us while maddened men hissed our utterances for emancipation; the cheer of her presence when we all were wearied with the exacting demands of constant rehearsals — the bane of a musician's life; the solace of her presence when exhausted by days and nights of travel and the strain of renewed appearances in concert. Abby was strong in her convictions, earnest in her faith, cultured in her performances, gentle in her manner, full of hope, full of soul, full of love. However her brothers might be criticised, Abby disarmed criticism. With her full share of faults, for she was human, she had charms of manner and a heart full

ABBY HUTCHINSON — (p. 324)
(From Painting by Carpenter)

of virtues that totally eclipsed her failings and made every friend, man or woman, her lover in the purest sense. Looking back through the mists of those beautiful years, I realize that the words set to her own music, that have been sung by the children of America for nearly a half century, were more than a sentiment of her heart, — they were the expression of her life:

> "Bright things can never die,
> E'en though they fade,
> Beauty and minstrelsy
> Deathless were made
> What though the summer day
> Passes at eve away,
> Doth not the moon's soft ray
> Silver the night?
>
> "Kind words can never die;
> Cherished and blessed,
> God knows how deep they lie
> Stored in the breast,
> Like childhood's simple rhymes
> Said o'er a thousand times,
> Aye, in all years and climes,
> Distant and near."

Gifted, earnest, noble, true, with a magnificent voice, the light of our lives, the joy of our hearts, does any one wonder that it was a crushing blow to her brothers — a life-long sorrow — when one who did so much to make the family's work successful was compelled by her devotion to the man to whom she had given her heart to withdraw from it? From that time until she died, wherever she was — Hartford, New York, Orange, Italy, the Holy Land, Africa, Alaska — was the Mecca to which our hearts turned. As the years passed by the dark hair silvered, marks of age changed the youthful texture of the skin, but it only made her more lovely to us, and we might appropriately have repeated the words written in compliment to some other such gracious soul, who had grown beautiful in age:

> "Die when you will, you need not bear
> To Heaven's gate, a form more fair
> Than beauty here on earth has grown
> Keep but the lovely looks we see,
> The voice we hear, and you will be
> An angel, ready-made for Heaven."

But it is the Abby of long ago that looks at us with speaking eyes from this canvas. It is an accurate aid to memory in reproducing the face and form of our dearest sister. If Carpenter had never painted the works that have made his fame world-wide, this portrait, accidentally discovered perhaps, as many a noted Copley portrait has been found, would some day have given its painter posthumous glory. It is a half-length, life-size portrait. The subject sits in a natural posture, her guitar in her hand, the fingers in position, as though just preparing to sing. The head is erect, and she seems about to open the full, red lips, to express some noble sentiment either in song or speech. But it is not to the beholder she is addressing herself. The large, expressive eyes do not follow one as is the case of many a family portrait which has terrorized the small boy or girl left alone with it at dusk. She has paused, perhaps, and looked away from you an instant, as she considers whether it shall be " Jamie's on the Stormy Sea " or some other favorite ballad that shall be sung. Her abundant brown hair is parted simply in the middle, brushed back from the high, intellectual forehead, and in careless waves half covers the shapely ear on either side, being caught at the neck, and forming a fit setting for the well-rounded cheek and chin. Abby never changed the dressing of her hair, materially, as long as she lived. It is as it was when I dressed it for her before every concert in Great Britain. The artist has not neglected a detail of her features. The finely formed nose, the classically penciled eyebrows, the statuesque, yet perfectly natural pose of head and neck, the physically perfect outline of face and form, are all there to the life. The light is from above, slightly shadowing the right cheek. The dress is rich in its simplicity. The shoulders are clothed in white, of some gauzy material, half-concealing the flesh-tint beneath, gathered at the throat in a plain collar of the same fabric, and with flowing sleeves, turned back at the wrist. There is an overdress of blue brocaded silk, with open sleeves, and waist well calculated to bring into prominence the perfection of the figure. The finely-modelled hands are emphasized by the shadow of the finger-board of the guitar falling across the left. A wrap of reddish hue, shading on brown, falls over one arm and rests on the lap. All these details of color add to the general effect while detracting nothing from that face, which would arrest attention anywhere. There has been the closest attention to values, in bringing out the delicacies of texture in the garments and accenting the beauty of complexion and feature, but these are nothing beside the triumph of art in the reproduction of the soul of the sitter speaking from those eyes and that lovely countenance. All these details might have been painted and still it would not have been Abby. But far beyond the artistic worth of the portrait is the fact that it is my sister's preciously cherished self that seems to be there. I love to sit and contemplate it when the afternoon sun sheds a mellow radiance through my southwest window. Then the sun seems to bring into strong relief every detail of the figure, and it seems as if my sister must speak again. If photography can do it, my readers shall have its best reproduction of this portrait, but it needs a view of the original painting to obtain a correct idea of the real beauty of the work, for photography fails here, as it always does in portraiture, when compared with the brush in the hands of the master. I am blessed in its possession, for it is a continual reminder of that gentle, though strong presence that for sixty years made my life richer. Though I think of her with tears, often they are tears of gratitude and joy mingled with sorrow and loneliness, for it is no small comfort to feel that one has enjoyed communion with such a spirit for a lifetime:

> "Oh, though oft distressed and lonely,
> All our cares are laid aside,
> If we but remember, only,
> Such as these have lived and died."

January 16th, while we were still giving concerts in New York State, our brother Caleb died. It had been his lot to spend most of his life in Milford, but still he had frequently sung with the family in anti-slavery and temperance work, and was fully identified with them in his sympathies. It began to seem as though death was surely on our track; and full of care as we were, we felt keenly our loss.

Our concerts in New York, New Jersey and Pennsylvania continued for many weeks. A notable feature of them was my solo, the "Ship on Fire." I think I have already referred to the unusual effect it often had on our audiences. It may be well to give a short history and description of the song.

Almost every day, somewhere on the broad seas of our planet, may be witnessed the tragedy of a ship on fire. Every mariner has seen the conflagration which has destroyed valuable cargoes and endangered the lives of the men and women aboard. The song first represents the vessel at sea encountering a storm of thunder and lightning, the passengers and crew falling on their knees and pleading for mercy. It commences thus:

> "Storm o'er the ocean flew furious and fast,
> And the waves rose in foam at the voice of the blast,
> And heavily laden the gale-beaten ship
> Like a stout-hearted swimmer, the spray at his lip.
> And dark was the sky o'er the mariner's path,
> Except when the lightning illum'ed it in wrath
> A young mother knelt in the cabin below,
> And pressing her babe to her bosom of snow,
> She prayed to her God 'mid the hurricane wild—
> 'O Father, have mercy, look down on my child!'"

Five hundred times, at least, I sang that song, with my brothers Judson and Asa playing the accompaniment, and interested audiences listening. The story goes on:

> "It passed, the fierce whirlwind careered on its way,
> And the ship like an arrow divided the spray,
> Its sails glimmered white in the gleam of the moon,
> And the wind up aloft seemed to whistle a tune
> There was joy in the ship as she furrowed the foam
> And the fond hearts within her were dreaming of home,
> The young mother pressed her fond babe to her breast,
> And sang a sweet song as she rocked it to rest,
> And the husband sat cheerily down by her side
> And looked with delight on the face of his bride
> 'O happy,' said he, 'when our roaming is o'er
> We shall dwell in our cottage that stands by the shore,
> Already in fancy its roof I descry,
> The smoke from its hearth curling up to the sky—
> Its gardens so green and its vine-covered wall,
> And kind friends are waiting to welcome us all—
> And the children that sport by the old oaken tree'—
> O, gently the ship glided over the sea"

At this point in the song the scream of "Fire!" was heard Judson's voice sounded it ventriloquilly. Instantly I would turn my head in the direction from which it was supposed to proceed. Asa would follow with a rumble on his viol, in exact imitation of the roll and rattle of a fire-engine hurrying through the streets. The effect on the audience was always electrical. Often there would be a stampede. They would rise in groups from their seats until the whole audience was ready to start for the door. Meanwhile I would continue the song, and sometimes it would arrest their attention and they would quiet down, but usually it was with some difficulty they would be persuaded to remain long enough to find it was an illusion. At one place, Utica, we sang in a church, and the sexton was in the gallery. We observed that he started on a run for the bell-rope. He had grasped it, and was just giving it a vigorous pull when he was seized by two people who assured him that there was no fire. By the ordinances of Utica five dollars went to the person who first rang in an alarm of fire, and he was very unwilling to loosen his grasp, believing his tenacity would be rewarded. Another case was in Vermont. This was also in a church, and an influential citizen sat in the body of the house in the centre of a pew. When we had reached the point in the song I have indicated, he arose, and climbing over the people, rushed down the aisle and out of the edifice, shouting "Fire!" at the top of his voice. Soon he found his effort was a solo, and returning to the church, he stood in the vestibule until we had finished the song, and partial quiet had been restored. Then in came the six-footer, his head hanging, and filled with chagrin. As he re-entered his pew, he looked up and said: "Mr. Hutchinson if you'll sing that again, I'll agree not to disturb this audience!"

At Kingston, in New York, the audience made a simultaneous rush for the door, and it was with great difficulty we got it quieted. Then there was a hearty laugh to think how they had all gone out for an airing. Next day a New Englander had occasion to call on the local judge, who was present at the entertainment. He remarked, "I saw you were at the concert last evening." The judge's only reply was, "Yes; it was a —— Yankee trick." We always had to have this song on our programmes, for if we did not, it was called for. At Oswego, N. Y., during this tour, the people threw up the windows and looked for the fire. At Canton, Penn., they rushed out of the hall to the fire-engine house and had the machine out on the street before they were reassured. At Springfield a similar scene of disorder was enacted. The song closes as follows:

"'Fire! fire! fire!' it was raging above and below,
And the cheeks of the sailors grew pale at the sight,
And their eyes glistened wild in the glare of the light
'Twas vain o'er the ocean the waters to drip,
The pitiless flame was the lord of the ship,
And the smoke in thick wreaths mounted higher and higher—
O God, it is fearful to perish by fire!
Alone in destruction, alone on the sea,
'Great Father of Mercy, our hope is in Thee!'
Sad at heart and resigned, yet undaunted and brave,
They lowered the boat, a mere speck on the wave
First entered the mother, enfolding her child,
It knew she caressed, it looked upward and smiled
Cold, cold was the night, as they drifted away,
And mistily dawned o'er their pathway the day
And they prayed for the light, and at noontide, about,
The sun o'er the waters shone joyously out
'Ho, a sail! ho! a sail!' cried the man o'er the lea,
'Ho, a sail!' and they turned their glad eyes o'er the sea,
'They see us, O they see us, the signal is waved,
They bear down upon us, they bear down upon us,
Thank God, we are saved!'"

Our engagements took us to Washington, where we heard Seward and Sumner speak on the Nebraska bill. A little later, during the same year we brought out our famous anti-slavery song, "Nebrascality," which subjected us to a great deal of criticism and caused some disturbances in our concerts. At Salem, Ohio, during April, we were guests at the home of Mr. Barker, whom we had met in England, a man who seemed to me one of the greatest reformers I had seen. As we sat by the fire one day I fell asleep, for a half-hour. When I woke Mr. Barker told me I was not aware that I had been sleeping seven years, and playfully went on to enumerate the changes that had occurred: Woman had her rights, the slaves were free, the cause of temperance had advanced, there was a millennium on earth, and Christ had in reality begun to reign. His optimistic prophecy as yet is largely unfulfilled. Here we also met Henry C. Wright, an old soldier in the good cause of human rights, and the author of the famous story of the "Hutchinsons' Repentance." At Pittsburgh, we greatly appreciated the society of Abby Anna Wade, the poetess and scholar. Keeping on through Ohio, we in the course of time reached Cleveland, "our Western home," where we spent many days. At the house of the Severances there were many pleasant discussions, none of us agreeing entirely, but all being united in spirit. Here, also, we met Abby Kelley Foster and Dr. Snodgrass of Baltimore. Coming back through New York State, we met at Binghamton Senator Dickinson, and also visited S. F. B. Morse, the inventor of the telegraph. Our series of concerts closed May 29th, having lasted nearly eight months.

We had not been back on High Rock three days when every drop of blood in our veins was made to boil by the excitement in Boston over the rendition of Burns, the fugitive slave. Asa and I went to Boston, and going up Court Street at first secured a stand in the window of a dry-goods store opposite the court-house. It was a stirring though disgraceful scene we gazed upon. Several regiments of militia had been ordered out by the Governor, to prevent disorder, and the United States troops, with fife and drum, were also out. There were bands of music, and cannon, to awe the people who it was feared would make a strike for liberty and free that poor miserable black man. Every avenue leading into the street was crowded with people, and every window and roof was black with them. It was estimated that a hundred thousand were massed about the street, silent, quiet, but indignant that Boston was compelled to witness such an outrage, the logical result of the fugitive slave law. Meanwhile, the unfortunate colored man was cowering in the court-house, a few rods away, tremblingly waiting for the signal to escort him through State Street to the United States gunboat bound South. The excitement was at the highest pitch, and none were more excited than I. I felt I must do something. As I passed out of the building, looking towards Washington Street, I saw stretched across it, above the heads of the people, a huge coffin, suspended by ropes, bearing upon it the significant word, "Liberty." I was enthused. Here we were in sight of Bunker Hill, where my ancestors had fought for this very idea of Liberty! Pressing my way across the street, into the court-house, past the guards at every turn — I wore a tall white hat, and had bundles of papers under my arm, and presume they thought me on official business — I had nearly reached the room where the fugitive was confined, before a sentinel bade me "turn back." I had a notion I could exchange clothes with him and remain, while he escaped, but I was foiled. Then the procession moved, more like a funeral cortege than anything else, the musicians hanging their heads as they played, for, though in performance of their duty, they were men of free New England, and their hearts were with the prisoner

The soldiers passed, and soon we went home. That night from the piazza of the stone cottage on High Rock, we told the story of the day to a large gathering of Lynn people. We also sang many abolition songs. Finally some one suggested that Commissioner Loring, who gave the order that the man should be sent back, be hung in effigy. At once clothing was procured, and being taken to our stable, was stuffed with straw. Two stakes were placed in the ground on the summit of Prospect Rock, a sightly eminence fronting the cottage, and with a rope around the figure's neck, it was suspended from a cross-bar. Soon some one shouted, "Let's burn!" and a match was touched to it. Thus the judge was both hung and burned in effigy on old High Rock. In referring to this, my diary says:

"How we cheered when the body was hanging! We sang some songs to the crowd which had been gathered by the sight of the flames. I hate slavery and shall pray with all my might for the poor slave. God of Heaven Shall tyranny always usurp the sway? No! The good time will soon come and we shall have a free country"

Then followed many happy weeks at High Rock. I record the fact in my diary that we were "getting to be Know-Nothings," but most of the space is taken up with stories of fishing parties and social gatherings. Among those who came to stay with us was Frank B. Carpenter, and many a pleasant walk I had with him in "Rocks Pasture" now the beautiful and populous Lynn Highlands; then a barren, rocky tract, as its name implies. John Lewis Robinson, my life-long friend, was usually in our fishing-parties. Wendell Phillips came down to preach for the "Free church" which for so many years after had the ministrations of Rev. Samuel Johnson, that staunch friend of human and religious freedom, and we gave concerts in aid of the building-fund of the chapel of the society, which still stands on Oxford Street. Another loved friend who came and later established his home in Lynn, was Lloyd Glover. He was an engraver on steel, and was, unless I am mistaken, the designer of the "greenback." His home was afterward located on Ocean Street, where his wife died. He prospered in business, and after a time had flattering offers from Chicago, which he accepted, and went West. He met his death by the accidental discharge of a gun, as he was getting into his boat on a hunting expedition. While he was on the visit to High Rock to which I refer, we one evening sang a song expressing the sentiment, "I would not die in springtime," "summer," etc. He followed our song up with a verse of his own, concluding with the thought, "I would not die at all."

But changes were coming for us, of which another chapter shall treat.

CHAPTER VIII.

IN THE GREAT WEST.

"The brave in every nation are joining heart and hand,
And flocking to America, the real promised land;
And Uncle Sam stands ready with a child upon each arm,
To give them all a welcome, to a lot upon his farm.

"Then come along, come along, make no delay,
Come from every nation, come from every way,
Our lands they are broad enough, don't feel alarm,
For Uncle Sam is rich enough to give us all a farm."

THE early months of 1855 were devoted to singing on the New England circuit, and to duties at home. No particular incidents recur to my mind for record here. Then followed a tour in New York, and after that a summer rest on High Rock and at Milford.

The Kansas excitement was then at its height. It led to action on our part which resulted in the establishment of a new town, Hutchinson, in Minnesota, though it was many years after that I assisted in setting in motion the influences that resulted in founding Hutchinson, Kansas. The story of Kansas is a thrilling one, for the territory was during these years the theatre of much of the slavery agitation.

Franklin Pierce was inaugurated President of the United States on March 4, 1853. He congratulated the country on the peace it was enjoying, on the cessation of strife because the Clay compromise of 1850 had settled many mooted questions, and assured his countrymen this repose should suffer no shock if he had power to prevent it. Time, however, demonstrated that he did his full share to upset these reposeful conditions. A short time before, the Kansas agitation had begun, and it raged practically without abatement until war times.

On Tuesday, August 28th, there came to Lynn a gentleman named Thayer, of Worcester, who was acting as agent for the Emigration Society, endeavoring to secure recruits to swell the number of Free-Soil emigrants in Kansas. He lectured in Lyceum Hall, explaining the necessities of the case. The Missouri Compromise having been set aside, and the territory opened to settlement, there was a great demand that the New England spirit should arouse and answer the call of "Bleeding Kansas." Asa and I sung at this gathering, which was large and enthusiastic. As I listened to the appeal, I determined to go home and arrange my affairs, and emigrate to Kansas. On the way, I saw Asa. "Asa," said I, "what do you think of it?" "I think well of it," was his response. We at once hurried to our house, packed up a few things, got out our buggy, and at 10.30 started over the road to Milford, fifty miles, to find Judson, and enlist him in the enterprise. All night we took turns in driving, one sleeping meanwhile. When we got there and told our story, Judson at once said, "Boys, I am ready."

So in September we commenced a tour fraught with unusual incidents. We crossed Vermont and New York States, giving concerts all the way, and thence proceeded through Ohio, Michigan and Illinois to Wisconsin.

When we reached Rockford, Ill., we met an old acquaintance, William Butler. He had been on a tour up the Mississippi. We told him we were going to Kansas. He said, "I beg you will not go there until you have seen the upper Mississippi River." The result of this advice was a change of plans. We brothers often disagreed in our discussions, but it was always our custom to let the majority rule in the final decision. In this case, I was very loth to give up our plan of taking part in the Kansas crisis, but Judson and Asa were favorable to changing our route, and I finally acquiesced.

Our concerts consumed two months. On November 9th we reached St. Paul. We gave a concert, netting us good returns, and made the acquaintance of Colonel John H. Stevens, B. E. Messer, with others who joined enthusiastically in our scheme. Meanwhile, I was reluctant, still longing to do something practical in Kansas. After a few days spent in looking up land warrants, we started on Friday, November 16th, in search of a town site. In the party were Judson, Asa, John, E. E. Johnson (our agent), L. N. Parker, B. E. Messer, John H. Stevens, Lewis Harrington, Henry Chambers, I. H. Chubb, John F. Califf and Roswell Pendergast. We had two wagons and four horses. We started from Minneapolis, and our first halt was at Fort Snelling, for supplies, one hundred dollars' worth. There were four hundred soldiers in the place. Next we stopped at Shakopee. We stayed at Gibson's hotel, and gave a concert at an hour's notice. As soon as it was found we were willing to give an entertainment, Judson Blanchard, a brother of Hon. Stillman S. Blanchard, in 1894 a member of the Massachusetts Senate, mounted a horse and rode through Shakopee, announcing the fact. At this place Chambers was loading the traps for the morning start. Among them were a number of rifles and shotguns. In pulling the guns from a stack, the heaviest loaded rifle was accidentally discharged. The ball grazed his head, went through the floor above, through another room, and lodged in a rafter. As we proceeded, we saw an abundance of flowers and plenty of game. On November 17th, at night, we camped in the woods. It was cold, but we had a good fire in front of our camp, and were a company. We had game for food, and after supper jolly enjoyed songs and Indian dances for a while and then laid down together. The next night we reached Glencoe. Here we received two additions to our company, Andrew J. Bell and W. S. Chapman. Colonel Stevens was another of the settlers of this new town, as was Mr. McLeod, for whom the county was named. It had been settled the May before, and at this time had but a dozen houses, mostly log cabins. We had a room to sleep in, but the windows were not glazed, having cotton cloth only partially covering them. The weather continued very cold. Our objective point was only fourteen miles away, and the next day found us encamped upon our claim, on the bank of a murmuring stream, the middle fork of the Hassan River. We shot some game. Harrington shot an otter. The animal formed a part of our breakfast, and the skin, worth eight dollars, he gave to Judson, who afterwards wore it for a tippet. The next morning, while getting breakfast, Johnson shot a partridge. It dropped nearly into the frying-pan and was soon plucked and cooked for breakfast. A little later most of the party went on a scouting expedition. I did not feel well enough to go prospecting, and so stayed behind, and made preparations to build our pre-emption cabin, striking the first blow of an axe to any tree on the claim. While at work I lost a highly prized picture of my children, Henry and Viola. It remained there all winter, and was found next year in making a clearing. I have it now, the cover eaten off by some wild beast, but the picture as good as ever. While the party was out, they came upon a beautiful sheet of water which they named "Judson Lake." It still bears the name. In the evening we held a meeting and decided on the exact spot for the town site. We voted to establish two towns, on either bank of the stream, one to be called "Hutchinson" and the other "Harmony."

The next day we took a survey of the town. We were given our choice of farms, adjacent to the town sites. I was not able to select one above another, but finally took one, mostly all woodland. Judson made the first claim on the west; Asa's was on the east, mine on the north. The next day we started on our return journey to Minneapolis. After making contracts for the erection of cabins for our occupancy when we returned to Hutchinson, we went on with our singing tour.

Mr. Dix, the family historian, tells the story of the founding of Hutchinson as follows:

"In December, of the year 1855, Judson, John and Asa Hutchinson resolved, after due deliberation, to visit the great West, and accordingly proceeded to the new territory of Minnesota, where the fertility of the land and the beauty of the country — as well as the advantageous prospects held out to settlers — induced them to take up some prairie lands to the west of the Mississippi River, about sixty-five miles from the city of St. Paul. Here they founded a settlement, which they called after their own name, and the town of "Hutchinson" was added to the many others that were constantly springing up on the prairie and in the wilderness of the West. [It was the second town on the great Prairie.]

"At that time Minnesota was considered as not only the land of aspirations and dreams, but the land where aspirations and dreams were realized. Fact, poetry and romance all combined to lavish eulogy on the growing territory, whose healthful atmosphere seemed to resemble the fabled fountain, which restored the youth of man; and whose generous soil, to use Douglas Jerrold's pithy expression with reference to that of Australia, was so rich, that if you tickled the earth with a hoe, she would laugh with a harvest. The Falls of Minnehaha had been immortalized in flowing verse, while the beautiful Indian maiden, Winona, like the New England Madawiska, was honored by tradition as a heroine

"John W. Hutchinson cut the first tree that had ever fallen by the hand of the white man in those regions, and it was used in the construction of their log cabin. Around this nucleus of a settlement, other cabins arose, and the town of "Hutchinson" continued to gradually grow and extend until 1857,— in fact, at that time, it was becoming quite a large settlement. A hotel, that almost first want of a new place, early provided 'good entertainment' for travellers. Farms appeared one after another, and all in that productive section were soon in a thriving condition. The Hutchinsons worked with untiring energy, and corn and grain of all kinds were extensively cultivated by them, and also by the other settlers. Sheep and cattle dotted the pastures, and the vocalists became successful farmers. But, notwithstanding their agricultural avocations, they did not altogether abandon singing, having quite too much music in them for that So they started off occasionally to give concerts, and exchange the music of the flail for that of the platform And while they were thus singing, the crops were growing! They had taken with them to the West a superabundance of Yankee energy, and it found vent in vocalism."

The St. Anthony *Express* of that year, speaking of this enterprise, said:

"In addition to several well-known citizens of the territory (printed at the opening of the article) in the above list our readers will observe that the Hutchinson Family, with their agent, E. E. Johnson, are included in the enterprise, which is a sure guarantee of the success of this new and interesting embryo city — even without the help and influence of those names which have been so long known to never look back from the plough when once hold of the handle

"The company have now about twenty men in their employ, erecting houses and public buildings Messrs Harrington and Bell have completed the survey of the town site The several proprietors of the town have subscribed liberally for different objects. The site is situated in Town 116, Range 29, in Davis County, 14 miles west of Glencoe The Hutchinsons will be on early in the spring to occupy their claims. Judson expects to return in March, Asa, John and Joshua will be here on the first boat, at which time their houses will be completed Mr. Chambers has men at work on them now.

"The town is to be on the liberal order. No sectarianism will be tolerated. All churches are to have their rights. The schools are to be on the union plan. No lots will be disposed of for grog shops.

"From all we have been able to gather, we are satisfied they have a beautiful portion of the territory for their future home. Glencoe is the key of all future towns in that part, but we learn that Hutchinson is most pleasantly located in the valley of the *"Hassan"* (Indian name for Crow) a clear, rapid stream of water about four rods wide, surrounded with beautiful groves and fertile prairies. Game is represented to be very plenty. The workmen about the town often see deer, elk, bear, wolves and otter. A carpenter stamped one of the latter animals to death last week. As many as ten otter have been seen playing at once on the ice that divides the village site.

"With a clear sky above, the rich land below, we may expect to see in a short time a large town built up in Hutchinson."

The name "Harmony" for the north half of the town was soon given up, as the Legislature passed an act permitting larger town sites. I sent to Boston, and secured four hundred dollars in gold. With this I went to St. Croix, and after giving a concert, which Judge Flandreau — the United States official whose duty it was to enter town sites — attended, invited that dignitary to my room at the hotel. He was clearly much pleased with the concert, for when I told him I had a town for him to enter, and asked his charge, he said seventy-five dollars. There was no limit to the fees, and I was well aware he might have charged five hundred dollars if he chose. Judge Flandreau was an able and brave man, as his subsequent acts in leading the settlers in defending the territory against hostile Indians fully demonstrated.

When we returned to Minneapolis we learned to our consternation that the Mississippi was frozen over so that boats could not sail. We were therefore obliged to charter a team to go down the river bank. As we had an extra seat, we invited a passenger to accompany us.

This man was Charles G. Ames He is to-day known as one of Boston's leading clergymen of the Unitarian faith and had been preaching in the new country. He was my bed-fellow twelve nights, and we had some very interesting talks. On our way down the river we held a number of meetings and gave several concerts. Ames tended the door, and made interesting remarks. At one place our songs were hissed by a land agent in the audience. Ames promptly silenced him by a few sharp comments. One Sunday we spent in Rochester, now a large city, then containing only three cabins. We sang wherever we found inhabitants. By the time we reached modern means of conveyance, it was so late we had to return East to fill our engagements, and so we did not reach Kansas at all that year.

I am reminded that I have not yet mentioned "Blucher"; Blucher was a dog. Before leaving Minneapolis for the wilderness, as I expected to encounter bears, wolves and other wild animals, I determined to buy a dog. My inquiries were soon met with a large, noble bull dog, for which I paid fifteen dollars, and at once named him Blucher. I found him a very useful companion in Hutchinson. At one time I was driving cattle across the Crow River, but after they got into the water, they refused to come out, notwithstanding my pleading and yelling. In this emergency I called Blucher, and addressed him somewhat like this: "Blucher, you see the predicament I am in; you see those cattle in the stream; now, I want you to go into the water after them and bring them to this side; but I do not want you to bite at them or bark at them; simply drive them out of the river." Blucher seemed to comprehend this appeal to his intelligence, and he started. He obeyed instructions to the letter, except an occasional growl at an unruly animal; and he brought all of the cattle out of the river as requested. Blucher remained faithful to every duty required of him for the year and a half of his life at Hutchinson, at one time singling out a heifer he was directed to get and holding her from the herd, and at another time seizing a dangerous ox, in protection of his master, but he finally came to an untimely end in my absence, by being shot for having visited the original log-cabin home, which I have mentioned. I had turned it over to an emigrant family, and small-pox broke out among them. My noble Blucher, through the fear of spreading the disease, thus became a sacrifice for the good of mankind. It cost me sixty dollars for his keeping one winter. The man who boarded him for me had to bake Indian cakes, and break them up for his food.

We reached Lynn once more on April 1, 1856. A short trip to Milford and concerts in Boston and Providence, and our season ended. A few days were spent in attending to business matters and packing. The old ocean never looked so pleasant. On April 21st, we left Lynn, as my diary put it, "forever." Judson joined Fanny and me at Painesville, O., and we gave songs, on our way to St. Paul, at Adrian, Hillsdale, Coldwater, Mich., at each place having to apologize for the absence of Asa, who for some reason failed to connect with us anywhere on the road. Finally we reached St. Paul and Minneapolis, and here Asa joined us. It rained for fifteen successive days, and we had trouble in getting off to our home beyond the woods. Finally the brothers went on, and I stayed some little time in the vicinity of Minneapolis, and went 120 miles up the river to Little Falls, where I entered some land at St. Cloud. Giving concerts, May 29th I, too, reached Hutchinson.

The next few weeks were full of hard work, ploughing, and getting in crops. I was accustomed to it, however, and the soil yielded better than that of Milford. Had an unruly ox that got away from me occasionally, as I have said before. June 23d I was off again, to Chicago, where my wife — having occupied my claim with me, according to law — left for the East. The brothers were there too, and we gave several concerts in Chicago, thence travelling to leading places in Illinois, Iowa and Michigan. At St Paul we sold a share in our town to Ole Bull. We returned to Hutchinson in a big wagon. One night we spent with a Dutchman, Asa and I sleeping on his hay-mow, and Judson and Jerusha using the wagon for a boudoir. The next day we came across some Winnebago Indians, and sang them some songs. We went in swimming with one of them. We enjoyed witnessing his manner of diving and swimming. When we reached Hutchinson again, we proceeded to occupy our claims. We had comfortable log cabins, covered with bark. Asa and I occasionally made the situation a little less dreary by sleeping together, half the night on each claim. It was a satisfaction to see the town growing very fast. Within a fortnight of this time we were singing before overflowing audiences in Saratoga, and the big towns intervening, and less than a week later were again on High Rock.

Then followed a summer of combined work and play. It was mostly work, however. We vibrated between Lynn and Milford. On one evening I was singing in Milford the next forenoon talking to my wife in the Stone Cottage in Lynn, and by night singing in Fitchburg. We brothers, with Sister Abby, made a short singing tour of the White Mountain region, and without her, travelled across the New England States and New York as far as Buffalo. Then followed many weeks of hard work improving the property at High Rock. The only tour for singing that season was one as far as Bangor made late in December. This was followed up by concerts in the early months of 1857 in southern New England, New York City, Philadelphia, Rochester, Elmira, Buffalo, Cleveland, Toledo, Chicago, Racine, Madison, Rockford, Galena, Dubuque, Kansas City, La Crosse, and intervening points to St. Paul, from which place we set out once more for our town, Hutchinson, which we reached May 10th. Then came days of hard labor shingling and boarding the new house on my claim, setting on foot a movement for a new school-house, and caring for various other interests. While in the town the year before, a clergyman took up a claim, and on Sundays he would preach to the people, if it did not happen that a minister came in from Glencoe. This year, however, there was no minister, and so on Sundays I got in the habit of gathering meetings, where I was not only chorister but preacher. The subject usually turned on the thought of the good time coming. Meanwhile the saw-mill machinery we purchased the previous year in one of our many trips away from the town had been set up, and when I was not finishing my house or preaching I took my turn at running the saw. In June I took a trip to St. Paul, and invested in many acres more of Minnesota land in Scott County. Then I went back to Hutchinson, where in a few days we were able to house our Sunday meeting temporarily in a new store. The monotony of life at the saw-mill was sometimes varied by the appearance of a bear, when all hands would drop work and give chase, usually with no success. In July we

JOHN IN THE SAWMILL.—(p. 346)

sold shares in the mill to Lewis Harrington, Chubb and Chambers, and a company was formed. Soon after we all took a trip to Lynn, where we spent September, and by the middle of October had sung our way back to Hutchinson. In about a week I was off singing again, without Asa, and soon was joined by Judson, who came on from the East. We sang all winter, mostly in Minnesota and Wisconsin towns and as far east as Columbus.

Of course, we made many trips to Hutchinson from time to time, though it was long years before the place became the thriving town it now is. During war times it nearly became extinct because of its practically total destruction by hostile Sioux.

In 1862 there were not only reservations of Winnebagos in Minnesota, but of Sioux and Chippewas. In the spring and summer of that year, the United States Government at Washington received information from various sources that convinced it that the Indian tribes of Utah, Colorado, Dakota and western Nebraska were likely to ravage the territories and frontier States. It seemed that emissaries from the Southern Confederacy and adventurers from Canada,— the latter acting on the theory that war with England was inevitable,— had been at work among them endeavoring to get them to make trouble so as to create a diversion from the war that was engaging the Government's attention. In addition to this dastardly conspiracy, the Indians were themselves irritated because of the action of the agents in paying their annuities in legal tender notes instead of the gold provided by the Government, and because of delay in payments on the part of the Indian Bureau. As a result of its information, the Interior Department early in the summer issued an advertisement warning the public of danger in taking the overland route to the Pacific.

The settlers in Minnesota, notwithstanding these warnings, were as a rule unsuspicious. It happened that I was at Hutchinson a week during August, and having come from Washington, where there was an excellent chance to become acquainted with the rumors, I warned the people against trouble that might come.

I met a United States recruiting officer the day before I left Hutchinson, and told him he ought not to take any more of our young men away, for the Indians, still holding their ancient grudge against the settlers, would suddenly appear. I then felt that I should call a meeting and inform the three hundred inhabitants of my suspicions. The settlers gathered, and began to consider the wise course to adopt, and plans of escape in case of an attack were suggested. The people were thus put upon the alert, although no definite action was taken at the time. The gathering was mostly women. When the uprising was more imminent another meeting was held, and the settlers decided to leave for Glencoe, fourteen miles distant. But at this point one settler, named McCuen, came in from his cabin, and in agitated tones declared that his daughter, who was very sick in the cabin, could not be moved with safety across the country. "I must stay and perish with my daughter, if necessary," said he. At this the whole council declared that they would stay with him and defend themselves. At once a strong fort was begun in the public square, and it was soon completed. This timely precaution saved many lives, though it did not prevent the devastation of the town.

On August 14th four drunken Sioux Indians were roaming through the western part of the territory, being intoxicated on whiskey obtained from a white man. They had a violent altercation as to which was the bravest, and determined that the test should be the killing of a white man. In their condition, it did not take long for several murders to be committed. Then becoming sober, the savages fled to their village, Red Wood, and told their chief, Little Crow, what they had done. Little Crow was one of those in the conspiracy for the general uprising, he being the head of that portion of the Sioux on the Minnesota reservation. He at once saw that retaliation would come for the act of the drunken murderers, and planned to forestall it by taking the initiative in the attack that had been agreed upon. On August 18th he started out with a band of from two hundred and fifty to three hundred warriors, and went to the agency at Yellow Medicine, and commenced a slaughter of all the whites there. The agent, Mr. Galbraith, was absent, but his family fell victims to the tomahawk. Word reaching Fort Ridgely, a force of forty-five soldiers was dispatched to Yellow Medicine. They were ambushed, and half the number were slain. Then, flushed with victory, the savages began again their work of fire and slaughter, violating and killing women, beating out the brains of infants, or nailing them on doors, and in fact perpetrating every species of atrocity their fiendish natures prompted. On the 21st they attacked the village of New Ulm in Brown County, but were driven back. The Chippewas began to be uneasy also, but did not join Little Crow, and in fact in a few days offered to fight the Sioux, but the authorities declined the proffered aid.

While matters were in this condition Governor Alexander Ramsey sent four companies of the Sixth Regiment of Volunteers from Fort Snelling. Two days later seven more companies were sent. Colonel (later General) H. A. Sibley was detailed to command the forces, and mounted volunteers were called for. Many responded. It fortunately happened that the Third Minnesota Regiment was on parole at St. Louis, and on September 4th it arrived. On August 23d New Ulm was again attacked, and Judge Flandreau, whom I have before mentioned, headed a company of citizens who repulsed the savages. On the next day a detachment under Colonel Sibley came to their relief, and raised the siege, and two thousand women and children, who had sought refuge in the village were taken to a place of greater security. Colonel Sibley then went to the relief of the little garrison at Fort Ridgely, which had been resisting the siege nine days. The Indians then proceeded northward, burning and killing in the scattered farms as they went. There was a massacre in Breckenridge, and then a siege of Fort Abercrombie, in Dakota Territory.

On September 3d a force of one hundred and fifty Indians suddenly appeared at Cedar City, in McLeod County. They attacked a company of volunteers and drove them to Hutchinson. Simultaneously another band attacked Forest City, but were repulsed by the citizens. The band at Hutchinson burned the house of Dr. J. Benjamin on Section 18, four miles north of Hutchinson, first taking out what they wanted by way of bedding and clothing, then went over the hill to the house of W. W. Pendergast and treated it the same way. Two or three unoccupied houses near by were also burned. A few days later the savages returned to Hutchinson, burned the mill we brothers had built in 1857, the fine house of Mr. Chesley, the school-house, and all other buildings excepting two houses and also attacked the fort. Happily, they were repulsed, and the scenes of violence which had occurred elsewhere did not come in Hutchinson. The Indians retired in the direction of the Iowa border, and Colonel Flandreau was sent after them, at the head of five hundred men. An extra session of the legislature was called, and Major-General Pope was sent to take command in the war. The Indians retreated before him, and were engaged in a final battle, September 22d, at Wood Lake. Little Crow escaped across the border with his women, but five hundred warriors were captured. They were tried, and three hundred were condemned to death by hanging. Only thirty-eight were executed, however. One of the number was a negro named Godfrey, who had shown more cruelty than any redskin. It was ascertained that between one and two thousand Indians were engaged in the massacres. The killed numbered some five hundred, and from twenty to thirty thousand fled for their lives. The property loss was something like three million dollars, and seven thousand homeless people were dependent on charity for their subsistence the following winter.

During the months that followed, Little Crow was occasionally heard from in Canada, to which he made at least two trips, one to get a new reservation for his people, the other to purchase firearms. Both requests were refused. On July 3, 1863, a Mr. Lamson, of Hutchinson, was a short distance from his farm with his son, hunting deer. Mr. Lamson was in a thick growth of hazel brush. His son was a short distance away, both looking for deer. Mr. Lamson, while gazing a little distance ahead, to a ridge of land fringed with hazel brush, saw an Indian picking berries. He was taking no chances, in the excited condition of the country on the Indian question, and so crawled up to a small oak-tree, took deliberate aim, and fired. The Indian was wounded, and Mr. Lamson at once dropped on his hands and knees and fled back into the bushes, and out upon a "hay road," leading down into a hay meadow He crossed this road into a prickly-ash thicket, where he remained. His son stayed in the bushes on the opposite side. The Indian recovered from the shock, and came down the hay road in the direction of Mr. Lamson. His son rose in the brush, and fired, hitting the savage in the breast, and killing him. Before he died, the Indian's son came out and talked with him. As soon as he was dead, he took his father's pony, rifle and ammunition and fled toward the north. Lamson and his son, as soon as the darkness came on, returned to Hutchinson greatly frightened, and told their story. The next day a party went out, secured the Indian's body, which was soon identified by General Sibley as Little Crow, by his double wrists. The son, who succeeded to his father's dignity, was soon taken by the soldiers in a starving condition near Eagle Lake. Little Crow's scalp now hangs in the rooms of the State Historical Society at St. Paul.

On leaving Hutchinson, in 1862, I went down to Owatonna, south of St. Paul, some seventy-five miles. As we were entering the town we heard of the trouble at New Ulm In the next town as our stage passed the hotel, we saw two teams loaded with volunteers going to the defence of the threatened town, bearing firearms and flags. It was a tearful scene as the women gathered around their husbands and lovers, bidding them farewell. One mean fellow on the coach was unkind enough to harrow up the feelings of the anxious listeners by alleging that the Indians had attacked St. Paul, and made

Governor Ramsey a prisoner. The attack upon Hutchinson seriously retarded the growth of the town. Many went away, and when I chanced into the place some months later it seemed to me the property was practically worthless. Soon a word came that a quarter-section of it was to be jumped, it having been ascertained that Chambers, who pre-empted the town site, was not naturalized. Wm. E. Harrington, therefore, pre-empted the quarter-section again, and my son Henry furnished the land warrant, receiving as compensation twenty-five acres which are now in the centre of the town.

CHAPTER IX.

THE SWARMING.

"What need of all this fuss and strife,
  Each warring with his brother,
Why need we, in the crowd of life,
  Keep trampling down each other?
Is there no goal that can be won
  Without a squeeze to gain it,
No other way of getting on
  But scrambling to obtain it?

"Oh, fellow men! remember then,
  Whatever chance befall,
The world is wide in lands beside,
  There's room enough for all."

THE year 1858 marked a period of nearly two decades since the Hutchinsons, spurred on by the restless ambition and musical enthusiasm of the younger members of the family, and captained by Brother Joshua, gave their opening concert in the Milford church. The condition in life of each had greatly changed in that time. Father and four brothers had passed into the great Beyond; every one of the original quartet was married, and the marriage of Abby had resulted in her practical retirement from the concert platform, though her love of music and progress, as well as her affection for her brothers, led to occasional tours with them of short duration. Meanwhile, families were growing up about us. Our wives were musical. Jerusha, Judson's wife, had no ambition to appear in concert; but Lizzie, Asa's wife, and my wife, Fanny, were both singers of experience, and pleasing to the public. Judson had a daughter, Kate, who was gifted with a remarkably musical voice, and without exception the children of Asa and John were singers of high promise. Each brother saw in his little family the germ of a successful concert troupe.

I have before referred to the strong regard for the family institution and love of domesticity that characterized us. It was this that made a loadstone of home, and however attractive the successes of the concert platform, drew us thousands of miles back again, wherever we wandered. I had long before become as attached to High Rock as ever Jesse was, and the farther I got from it, the stronger seemed the influence that drew me back to it. Asa in time made a permanent home in Hutchinson, and lies buried on the banks of the Hassan, the river he loved, but though I at one time lived in Hutchinson long enough to gain a voting residence, my heart was in Lynn, and soon I was again permanently located on the beautiful highlands I so dearly loved. In this year, 1858, I began the erection of Daisy cottage, on High Rock, the house in which I lived until the building of Tower cottage, my present home, on the same property. At this time, and for many years after, Asa lived in the Bird's Nest cottage, built by Jesse some time previous to his death, just east of the Stone cottage. Daisy cottage is west of the original stone house. Judson never removed from Milford. At this time he had built a sightly house in that town.

It was natural that each of the brothers should enjoy having their families with them, in their concert triumphs. It is also self-evident that such a plan would be cumbersome and rather expensive. It was agreeable to all concerned that the wives should travel with the party, but the children were rather out of the question. And then another difficulty arose. Abby had demonstrated the feasibility of uniting one female voice with ours successfully. For a long time Lizzie had been taking vocal lessons, and was clearly a candidate for Abby's place. My wife, however, was a good alto singer, had often sung with us, and it became evident to Asa's mind that so long as he cherished objections to Fanny's singing in the quartet it was hardly wise for him to propose that Lizzie should do so. So he began to cogitate the subject of concerts by the "Tribe of Asa," his children Abby and Fred joining their father and mother in song. Judson had no desire to sing apart from us. His was an affectionate, clinging nature, and he could hardly bear the thought of leaving the brothers he depended upon so much. As for myself, I firmly believed the correct policy of the brothers would be to stick together. The conditions were more potent than my theories, however, and though I fought against them, the final result of the changes so soon to come to us was to give the country several bands, simultaneously singing in various localities. Of course these great changes were not brought about without some friction, but that is in the past, and only needs the merest mention in this record.

Towards the close of 1857 Judson and I started from Hutchinson with the intention of singing our way East. Asa was not through fixing up his farm, and so stayed behind, later coming on with his team to Chicago, where we had our pictures taken in a group. Asa was expecting his wife, and as soon as she came, instead of joining us as we had hoped, he started off on a concerting tour with her, giving most of his entertainments in Maine. Judson and I went to St. Paul, and from there I went to Stillwater, to give a concert and enter our claim for that portion of Hutchinson called in those days "Harmony," while Judson went down the river. It was getting late in the season, and I found I must go on or be frozen in. Taking the boat, I met a friend named Martha Loomis. She was a seer. She told me Judson was waiting to see me in Madison. He was in distress, she said, and desired to see me very much. As we approached Prairie du Chien the water was freezing so fast that it was with great difficulty the boat was brought to the wharf. Here she stuck fast and remained. However, we were able to land and took the cars at night for Madison. Here I found Judson and his wife. He was very glad to see me, and we at once made arrangements to sing a while together. The following day was Sunday. My diary simply says we spent the day singing together, and writing letters to family and friends, the weather being very cold. (The next day it was ten degrees below zero.) The "singing" referred to was the composition of the famous song "Mrs. Lofty and I," which was soon after brought out by Sister Abby, and for many years — in fact, has always — remained popular. Judson composed the melody. The words were placed on my melodeon, and while he stood at my side with his violin and made the tune, I accompanied him. The words of the song were written by Mrs. Gildersleeve Longstreet, of Buffalo:

> "Mrs. Lofty keeps a carriage,
>   So do I,
> She has dapple grays to draw it,
>   None have I,
> She's no prouder with her coachman
>   Than am I,
> With my blue-eyed, laughing baby,
>   Trundling by
> I hide his face, lest she should see
> The cherub boy, and envy me

"Mrs. Lofty has her jewels,
  So have I,
Her's she wears upon her bosom,
  Inside, I;
She will leave hers at death's portals
  By and by,
I shall bear the treasure with me,
  When I die,
For I have love, and she has gold;
She counts her wealth, mine can't be told.

"She has those that love her station,
  None have I,
But I've one true heart beside me,
  Glad am I,
I'd not change it for a kingdom,
  No, not I,
God will weigh it in his balance,
  By and by;
And then the difference 'twill define,
'Twixt Mrs. Lofty's wealth and mine."

From Madison we went on giving concerts. We made a proposition to Sister Abby after a while, to get Asa back and have her join us in a series of concerts by the original and ever-popular quartet. She consented, and Asa wrote us he would come. Abby joined us in Buffalo, but Asa changed his mind, and didn't appear. So we gave trio concerts in New York State and Vermont for a number of weeks. Mr. William V. Wallace attended to our business. Meanwhile Judson was exceedingly anxious and worried about Asa. Abby left us; and Judson, still excited and worried about Asa, conceived several impracticable schemes to fill our company. One was to hire a celebrated German pianist of Milwaukee, to tour with us, and another was to add an entire colored minstrel troupe to our combination. I told him we'd better not hire anybody. Finally he grew tired of waiting, and left me. Just after he had gone, Asa and his wife came. Meanwhile my family had come on from Lynn, and Asa taking his wife and I my children, we went to Philadelphia and gave some concerts. Then we separated and with my wife, Henry and Viola, I gave quite a series of concerts through New Jersey and Pennsylvania. It was a terribly broken year, as I remember it. The conditions that culminated in the John Brown raid at Harper's Ferry and his subsequent execution, were staring us in the face, and the long-expected war was imminent.

Judson, meanwhile, tried his hand at concerts. With his daughter Kate, and William Vincent Wallace, he started out. His announcement was a curious literary effort, but it brought him lots of business. I have before me as I write a hand-bill reading as follows:

CONCERT.

"Music hath charms to soothe the savage breast,
Rend a rock, or calm a hornet's nest"

The original
JUDSON J HUTCHINSON AND KATE L HUTCHINSON,
of the Hutchinson Family,
with the accomplished Pianist and Tuner,
WILLIAM V. WALLACE,

Would most respectfully say, that they are coming this way,
and on a certain day, or evening, intend to
sing and play

At ——— Hall, to rich and poor and all, who listen to this call
The time to commence is eight o'clock,
Before that time the people can talk, and those who come
must be in at eight — it is apt to disturb if
you come in late

The price of a ticket is fifteen cents, and none who listen will
grudge the expense The programme contains the
very best songs, each one introduced just
where it belongs

"The Good Time Coming," "The Good Time Come,"
When men will drink water and cease drinking rum;
"Zekle and Huldy" and "Old Uncle Ned,"
The song of the outcast in the street found dead;
"'Tis sweet to be remembered where'er we may be;"
"I live for those friends who live to love me,"
"The Shells of the Ocean," and "My Mary Ann,"
"The Little Maid" and the "Humbugged Man,"
"Millions Lie Bleeding," "The Italian Song,"
"We All Wear Cloaks," "Right over Wrong;"
"Hard Case of the Lone One," "Mrs. Lofty and I,"
"Forty Years Ago," "Carry Me Back to Die,"
"Come This Way, Father," "Sword of Bunker Hill,"
And quite enough more three half-hours to fill

Tickets obtained where they're left to be sold! And those who've
no paper, or silver, or gold, can leave with the
door-keeper as they pass in, the amount
in jewelry, jews-harps or gin-
ger, children's shoes, jack-
knives, dry-goods or
honey, or any-
thing else,
EXCEPT BOGUS MONEY!

Children who are pledged not to cry or to laugh, can come in with
their parents for seven cents and a half. The blind and
cripples pass free at the door; and the rich must
buy tickets and give to the poor

———

The Melodeon is splendid, and as will be seen,
Comes from the head of firms, Estey & Greene;
The prices are easy, and all those in want,
Can have them supplied, at Brattleboro, Vermont.
We can tune your pianos, and all early callers,
Can have them tuned good for from one to three dollars
All lovers of music take your families hither,
NO POSTPONEMENT ON ACCOUNT OF BAD WEATHER

But notwithstanding the hilarity of the announcement, Judson couldn't stand being alone. He longed to be with his brothers. I had been singing with my folks in Maine, and they wanted me to go on, when a despatch came from Hutchinson for me to go West to divide the town. Leaving my family I went, and stayed five or six weeks. All the shareholders in the town received their lots. Judson was worried about our affairs; and with his wife, and Asa and wife, we held a meeting. Asa wouldn't consent to go concerting unless his wife could sing too. Jerusha, Judson's wife, was opposed to Asa's wife and wouldn't allow him to have anything to do with the scheme. Judson was exceedingly excited about the matter. Meanwhile, I wanted to go on. Judson took Andrew Hutchinson, his wife's brother, and Jerusha, and went off singing. Asa had a team, and for a while I sang with him and his wife. I had to leave them at Rochester, Minn., and then went to meet Judson. Found him at Janesville, Wis. It was two o'clock in the morning when I arrived. About this time I received word to come home. I was building Daisy Cottage, as I have said, and was needed. I left Judson with the hope I would return. He was waiting, hoping Asa would come and meet him. Jerusha was still opposed to his singing with Asa, and so he told me to bring Kate. I told him to keep on with his single concerts until our return. When I reached Lynn I found a good deal to engage my attention in regard to my house. Fanny wanted me to sing for the benefit of the Free Church, and I agreed to give a concert there. I was nearly ready to start West again, when to my surprise, Judson came to me. We gave the concert at the Free Church together. Judson was thoroughly discouraged. He had brought home some songs, one of which was

"Hark, I hear an angel sing,
Angels now are on the wing."

Though my family were anxious to go to singing with me again, I decided to start out with Judson. Times were bad, and expenses going on, and I did not see any other way to do. I noticed in Judson a deep settled melancholy. The disappointments of the world had preyed upon his mind so that it was impossible to know what to do for him. Our concert for the church was given in Sagamore Hall, by the two brothers with the assistance of Kate and my children, on January 8, 1859. It was on Saturday. On Monday I observed Judson standing motionless in a moody state. I endeavored to wake him up, rubbed him, and did all possible to cheer him. The next day, Tuesday, I went over to Daisy Cottage with him. The masons had plastered it, and as the furnace had been put in, I tried to keep his mind employed by having him prepare the wood for a fire to dry the walls. There was a cold east wind, and the mercury was below zero. At dinner Judson ate heartily. I had a severe headache, and stayed in my home in the Stone Cottage all that afternoon. My reflections were not pleasant, for I was worried about my brother. He had become so despondent that he had distinctly said he would never go to Milford again. What to do I did not know. Tea-time came. Meanwhile, my headache had grown worse, and I was in a profound perspiration. Fanny called me to tea. I roused myself up, and seated myself at the table. "Has any one called Judson?" I inquired. He had not been seen for some time. I told Henry to go over to Daisy Cottage and try to find him. The thought came to me like a flash that he had made way with himself. Henry came back. He had not found him. "Did you go down in the basement?" I asked, for I remembered that Judson had been at work there. I hurried over to the house, and descended the ladder into the basement, for the stairs had not been built, and looking toward the furnace in the dusk, I could see his form, apparently standing as though he was in one of his moody fits of abstraction. As I got within a few feet of him I saw a line about his neck, and knew that my fears were realized. I grasped him and took him down. Spoke to him, but alas! there was no response. Just then somebody came in above. It was my hired man, there to watch the fires. I called him, and continued to rub Judson, hoping to bring back the life that had fled. With grief and agony of soul I assisted in carrying the body up the ladder and home. The funeral was held at Milford on the following Saturday. I sang Judson's new song, "Hark, I hear an angel sing."

Those were dark days, and I hasten to change the subject. My mother, brothers and sisters, and my immediate family never seemed more dear than then Judson, my dear Judson, had gone home. To my mind a star of brightest magnitude had been added to the immortal constellation. The shadow that had been over him ever since the days when his mind first became clouded, nearly a decade before, I believed was removed, and that noble soul, that had in it so much that could help and uplift humanity, was released from a bondage that had so hindered its fullest development. It is idle to discuss further the causes of our sorrow. Had reason been enthroned, my brother would have been the last man to hurry his own exit from a world where, however great might have been his own private trials, he was an instrument for brightening and blessing so many other hearts

Not long after this I made an arrangement with Brother Joshua to do some singing with me. With my children, we gave our first concert in Ipswich, following with others in Malden, Charlestown, Beverly, Danvers, Essex, Cambridgeport, Abington, Plymouth, East Abington, North Abington (where we met Mrs. Mary Wales, the lady the brothers had unsuccessfully tried to have join with them in Abby's place, at Oberlin, a few years previously. We stopped with her over a Sunday), Hanover, and so on through many southern Massachusetts towns, and thence into Connecticut. We spent a little while in June at New York and Orange, N. J., visiting Sister Abby and mother, who spent a long time with her daughter at this period.

The summer was spent at High Rock, making improvements. Asa came on from the West, and for a while I had a visit from Abby. In September, with my wife and children I started concerting again, first visiting southern New Hampshire and then central and western Massachusetts. This series of concerts consumed the rest of that year. Meanwhile, the slavery agitation was slowly but surely reaching a crisis. On the night of October 16th John Brown, with eighteen companions, seized the United States armory at Harper's Ferry, and a day later it was retaken by Colonel Robert E. Lee and a company of marines sent from Washington. When captured, Captain Brown's band had been reduced to six, and he was wounded and apparently dying. The honest old man, lying on his pallet, made no attempt to conceal his design, a wholesale liberation of slaves. In December of the previous year he had made a raid from Kansas into Missouri and carried off eleven slaves, conducting them to Canada. During the civil war in Kansas, he had been an active participant, defending Ossawatomie from the Missouri invaders. Two of his sons were among the killed when Harper's Ferry was retaken. Brown was tried for treason and murder. He showed his earnest, upright spirit in his remarks at the trial, where he denied any purpose to promote insurrection among the slaves, but did not hesitate to say that he had hoped to free them. He was convicted, and sentenced to be executed December 2d, at Charleston. The day was solemnly observed throughout the country by the friends of freedom, meetings being held, bells tolled, and other evidences of grief for the brave martyr for freedom being shown.

On the night before the execution, we were singing in Barre, Mass. There was a great deal of conservatism in the town. Before closing the entertainment, I mentioned that the fatal deed would take place on the morrow. The concert was given in the town hall, and I invited the people to gather at the steps of that edifice in convention at the hour when the execution would presumably occur. At the appointed time the audience assembled. We sang an appropriate song or two. We were fortunate enough to have with us a young man, John G. Crawford, whose native town was Lancaster, N. H., who had been in Kansas with John Brown, and who knew him well. He made some very appropriate remarks. For a quarter of a century since he has occasionally turned up in towns where I have given concerts and told the story of this Barre meeting to the audiences. The meeting closed at about half-past ten. The execution was to take place between certain hours. Finding it would be impossible to obtain the keys of any of the conservative churches, I had arranged with some eight likely boys, of whom my son Henry was one, to see to it that every church bell was rung at a specified hour. They went off in couples, and every one managed to get access to a bell-rope. As the gathering dispersed the bells tolled mournfully for about five minutes. The boys found their way from the churches as they had entered, and none were molested. The raid and execution of John Brown caused a variety of emotions. Garrison and the peace Abolitionists, did not countenance the act, but approved the motive which prompted it. Many of the more militant Free-Soilers, like Colonel Higginson and others who were in the plot, gloried in it, though deploring its fatal consequences. The leaders of the new Republican party, notably Henry Wilson, felt that it was a set-back for the cause they advocated. Some time after I recall meeting Wilson at Litchfield, Conn. We talked the situation over, and he expressed the opinion that John Brown had done great injury to the cause by his unwise action. I differed with him. It seemed to me, that however imprudent the act, it had been the prelude to a great work, soon to be accomplished. John Brown was in the skirmish line of the forces of freedom, that grand army of the republic that was finally to secure emancipation. I was well acquainted with Wilson. A year previous his friends had come to our hotel in Boston to ask us to go to the State-house and sing. The contest that culminated in his election as United States senator was on, and they evidently expected us to sing some abolition songs to cheer and unite the voters. We went up and sang "Where shall the Soul find Rest."

It was April, 1860, before we again saw Lynn, the intervening time being occupied with concerts in Connecticut and western Massachusetts. After a stop at home of a day or two only, we left for New York, and travelled through the northern part of that State for many weeks. Then we went into New Jersey, and after singing a while there, returned to New York, where we stayed until October. A hurried trip to Lynn and Milford and we were again in harness, singing with Sister Abby in New York State once more — singing for freedom, and urging lovers of freedom to unite in the election of Lincoln, whom we believed would emancipate the slaves, as he did.

Meanwhile, Asa had commenced in the West a career with his tribe. For many years he sang with Lizzie, his daughter Abby, his son Fred, and later, Dennett. Alas! the latter is now the only one left of the "Tribe of Asa," but only a day or two before writing this I received word that he had put his own Hutchinson Family into the field for concerts, under the name of the "Hutchinson Family Young Folks." So the name and the fame of the Tribe of Jesse will be, I trust, perpetuated through him.

The remainder of this history will largely deal with the experiences of the Tribe of John, because the materials are at hand, and I am more familiar with the details, but it will be seen from time to time that the various tribes united for a while, though never permanently. Joshua, with Kate, Judson's daughter, and Walter Kittredge, spent many seasons in concerts in northern New England. At one time he was concerting there, the Tribe of John was in central and western, and the Tribe of Asa in southern Massachusetts. It also sometimes happened that Asa would give concerts in the West, and that I would strike into the same circuit the following season. As time went on, however, we managed to avoid coming into collision.

Perhaps it may not be out of place for me to give at this point one or two quotations from the newspapers printed at the time of our starting out in tribes of our own, to indicate how we were received:

A correspondent of a New England journal wrote:

"Long years have passed since I heard them (the brothers and Abby), sing together their brave songs of human freedom, of temperance advocacy and universal brotherhood, and I had for many years lost sight of the matchless "elder brother" who was the guide and counsellor of the rest. Judge then of my surprise, when traversing the streets of your quiet village, I was attracted by a placard, announcing that the 'Hutchinsons' with John at their head, would give a concert at Phœnix Hall on Wednesday evening. He had, at last, 'turned up.' The hand of the man whose heart throbbed so much in sympathy with my own, would again meet mine in friendship's grasp — his voice again awaken memories 'of the old time entombed.' I lost no time in calling on him at his hotel, and found him as hearty, genial, and whole-souled as ever, with a 'family' of his own, to do the singing *à la* Hutchinson. I need not say I attended the concert — money would not have hired me to stay away — and I hope I am not supposed to be able to transmit to paper all the pleasure I felt in listening to their harmonious vocalization. I really could not do justice to the subject. The 'brothers and sister' it seemed to me, never in their palmiest days, excelled these 'parents and children.' The father's voice has grown rich and mellow with time, while his love of fun, and his ability to 'raise it,' has in nowise decreased. The children are chips of the old block, chock full of music, and never so happy as when *enjoying it out*, for the edification of those who have the taste to appreciate it."

The *Boston Journal* said:

"THE HUTCHINSONS. — A new feature was introduced in the concert of this well-known family (or rather that portion of them still left in New England) at the Mercantile Hall, last night, by the performance of two young members of the 'family' from a later generation, children, we believe, of John Hutchinson, the funny man, and chips of the old block; imperturbable and easy while singing the most laughable comic songs any one could wish. They are pretty, keen-eyed youths, possessing voices rarely attained, and evincing great discipline in the cultivation."

A Connecticut paper said:

"The sweet voices of John and his children, Henry and Viola, not omitting the alto of Mrs H., seemed to carry us back in remembrance to the days when the old family — three brothers and Abby, too — made light so many sad hearts with their songs. We have always thought the Hutchinsons of the days gone by were superior to any other band of singers. When we say, then, that the present troupe possess almost the same wonderful harmony and blending of voice, with full as much originality of style, we need not further express our admiration for their singing. They do not need the praise — they would certainly scorn the flattery of any critics. Their music speaks for itself."

Another paper said:

"The memory of the sweet and pathetic tones, together with the noble and benignant countenance of the senior, John Hutchinson, will never be effaced from the mind of any person present. His countenance in singing is love and benignity itself, and his voice sweetness and majesty. At times the tones are charming beyond description. The son and daughter are superb singers, and their manner exceedingly pleasing."

CHAPTER X.

IN WAR TIME.

"We wait beneath the furnace-blast
  The pangs of transformation ·
Not painlessly doth God recast
  And mould anew the nation.
    Hot burns the fire
    Where wrongs expire;
    Nor spares the hand
    That from the land
  Uproots the ancient evil.

"Then let the selfish lip be dumb,
  And hushed the breath of sighing,
Before the joy of peace, must come
  The pains of purifying.
    God give us grace
    Each in his place
    To bear his lot,
    And, murmuring not,
  Endure and wait and labor!"

THE election of Lincoln, and the strong sentiment for freedom and union that made it possible, were firebrands to the spirit of secession that had been so long smouldering in the South. For many months the disloyal cabinet of Buchanan had been plotting to give the Slave States the advantage in the impending conflict, by storing munitions of war and supplies in the South, while the pusillanimous president looked helplessly on. I remember singing in Springfield during this period, and visiting the armory. The people there were all quiet, not a word was spoken, but many of them were packing guns to send away. I asked the reason, and all the answer I got was that it was done at

ABRAHAM LINCOLN — (p. 370)

the command of the Secretary of War, John B. Floyd, and probably they were to be used to fight Indians. I was suspicious of their reticence, and thought the public should know of the circumstance, and so acquainted the *Springfield Republican* with what I had seen.

To the minds of all but the over-sanguine, the election of Lincoln meant secession, and secession meant war. It was a peculiar fact, however, that even after many States had held conventions and formally passed resolutions withdrawing from the Union, a desire to avoid a conflict seemed to blind the eyes of the people to the real situation. I, however, was convinced that war was inevitable when Fremont was defeated by Buchanan.

During the campaign that had resulted in the election of Lincoln, I had been very industrious in his behalf. Wherever I was, in railroad trains, at hotels, at the door of concert halls, on the street — in fact, at any place where I could get a group of hearers, I had been urging the election of "Honest Abe." We had been singing in New York State, and along the line of the Harlem railroad. Abby had been temporarily singing with us, and we were now preparing for city concerts. I found myself to be overworked. The care of the concert tour and of my two children had worn upon me. It had been my habit nightly to stand at the door and take tickets and money, following this labor up by stationing a substitute there, and going on the stage to sing and manage the concert.

For our series of concerts in New York and Brooklyn we secured the largest halls to be had. After a few concerts the labor had been so great that I was obliged to take a rest, and during the month of December, 1860, and a part of January, 1861, I was very much affected by pulmonary troubles. I took a severe cold, and was threatened with pneumonia and quick consumption; but by dint of perseverance in exercise and a proper diet, I soon began to recuperate. My sister Abby invited me to Orange, N. J., and there, with good care, I completely recovered. Then I resolved to go to Washington. My brothers David and Andrew had attended the inaugurals of Pierce and Buchanan, they being Democrats. I now desired to view the inauguration of the man of my choice.

I remember going over to the depot in Jersey City on the day Lincoln left New York for Washington. The train not being made up on his arrival at the station, he sat in an open barouche a short time, surrounded by his friends. Meanwhile, we were in a balcony of the building. During the interval of waiting we struck up a song:

"Behold the day of promise comes — full of inspiration —
The blessed day by prophets sung,— for the healing of the nation.
Old midnight errors flee away; they soon will all be gone;
While heavenly angels seem to say, 'The good time's coming on.'
   Coming right along,
   Coming right along,
The blessed day of promise is coming right along.

"Already in the golden east the glorious light is dawning,
And watchmen from the mountain tops can see the blessed morning
O'er all the land their voices ring, the harvest now we're reaping,
Awake, sad heart, now comes the morn, arouse, there's no more weeping
   Coming right along,—
Oh! I hear the angel voices — 'We're coming right along.'

"The captive now begins to rise and burst his chains asunder,
While politicians stand aghast, in anxious fear and wonder
No longer shall the bondman sigh beneath the galling fetters,—
He sees the dawn of freedom nigh, and reads the golden letters,—
   Coming right along,
Behold the day of freedom is coming right along!"

When Lincoln heard our song, the good soul looked up and recognized us. He seemed to be very much pleased. He had attended our concerts in Springfield, his home, and of course was aware of our sentiments on the great questions agitating the land, which had led to his election. The presidential party seemed to linger until our song was sung, and then passed to the train. Then Lincoln went on to his great work in Washington, the journey being accomplished with safety, though there was great anxiety on the part of his friends. He was established in Seward's home and watched over with the most tender and vigilant solicitude.

On my way to Washington, I passed through Baltimore, and stayed at the house of a friend, Nehemiah Hayward. His family were still in sympathy with the system of slavery, and had one or two slaves at their command. I said to Mrs. Hayward, "I am going to Washington to help inaugurate an anti-slavery president. We are going to liberate the slaves." "Why, Mr. Hutchinson," said she, "do you mean it?" I answered that I did, and a further discussion ensued on the way this was to be accomplished. My idea was that the means might be a war measure, or some peaceful method that might be devised, but I was sure the good time of emancipation was very near at hand.

While in Baltimore, I had an opportunity of learning the origin of the term "Secesh." Two drunken men were on the street, staggering along, when one said to the other, "If they wa-nt to secesh, let u-u-m se-se-cesh!" and the other thick-voiced gentleman, addressing his companion, declared "if you are secesh-h, I am secesh-h-h-es-h too!——if I ain't!"

In company with a friend I arrived in Washington

on the morning of March 4th, Inauguration Day. The word was soon passed around that General Scott had placed his forces on many of the roofs of the buildings along Pennsylvania Avenue, with guns loaded, ready to discharge upon the mob if it should show itself disposed to interfere with the progress of the procession. The soldiers could be seen peering over the edges of the roofs. Soon the procession started, proceeding through the avenue between lines of soldiers, acting as a guard, its entire length. Arriving at the Capitol, after the president-elect and suite had succeeded in coming down the steps upon the platform, they found themselves in the midst of a gathering of twenty thousand people, with scarcely standing room for themselves. Looking from the crowd we could observe on the platform the familiar form of Stephen A. Douglas, who had disputed the great national questions with Lincoln on the stump in Illinois in a famous senatorial contest a few years before. As Mr. Lincoln removed his hat, Douglas stepped forward, politely took it, and held it during the delivery of the inaugural. As the oath was administered, a colored man, who stood at one corner of the platform by a flagstaff, seemingly inspired by the momentous act, seized the halyards and raised the stripes and stars to the peak. As it floated proudly in the breeze over their heads, the incident seemed prophetic to me. The negro seemed to be helping in the ceremonies that were to pave the way to his own emancipation. After a few sentences uttered by Lincoln, I was pained to hear his deliberate statement that he would prove true to the Constitution, and would carry out the law of the land in regard to the return of fugitive slaves. The remark filled me with consternation, but I did not then consider, as afterward, certain facts. He was surrounded by the bitterest traitors, who had dogged his steps from his home in Illinois to the capital, putting him all the time in danger of assassination. I was later convinced that his announcement of the obligation resting upon him rendered him comparatively safe, and enabled him to take the oath of office.

The same day, after the inauguration I returned to Baltimore

When I reached the depot in Washington I found it full of men who seemed completely possessed with a spirit of evil. They had had no chance to kill a "nigger" all day. They were "plug uglies" and as they swarmed about the station they kept up in a grim, growling, nasal tone, the refrain of "Dixie":

> "In Dixie's land I'll take my stand,
> And live and die in Dixie,
>   Away, away,
> Away down South in Dixie."

From Baltimore I went to Philadelphia, where after some successful concerts in that city and adjoining places, I determined on one more season in New York City. The excitement over the rebellion had reached a fever heat. I conceived the idea of showing my patriotism by having a big star-spangled banner printed as a part of the poster announcing my concerts. It was quite a task to engrave it on wood and print it in colors, much more than it would be to-day, with our improved chromatic printing devices. It was done, however, and a few weeks later, when the flag of Sumpter was fired upon, I had the satisfaction of seeing my device become popular. In the three weeks after that event, my printer realized eight hundred dollars by printing impressions from that same flag-block, the calls for them being numerous from all over the loyal States. I also had a very handsome shield, with stars, designed, and printed in colors. This cost me sixty dollars. On this the announcements of concerts were printed.

There was the most intense excitement in New York, and earnest solicitude for the weal of the Union. The storm was fast gathering, and finally we read on the bulletin boards, "Our flag is dishonored! Fort Sumpter in Charleston has been fired upon this very day!" It was true. The rebels under Beauregard had begun their work. Then followed scenes on Nassau Street such as had never been seen before A rushing to and fro, showing great intensity of feeling, deep sympathy and high resolve. In my own heart, however, I rejoiced, for I felt the end was near, and to find a sympathizing friend to talk to, went into the *Independent* office. One of the editors, Mr. Joshua Leavitt, sprang from his chair and embraced me. He said, "I am no more an Abolitionist. The war spirit will take care of abolition. 'Whom the gods would destroy they first make mad.'"

There was great enthusiasm. A hall was soon secured, and recruits were solicited. Some one saw me and said, "Come in and sing 'The Star-Spangled Banner'" As I raised the tune their voices took it up, and it was glorious to hear them sing

"And the star-spangled banner in triumph shall wave
O'er the land of the free and the home of the brave."

It was folly to attempt to give popular concerts amid such excitement in the city. Though I had engaged the noted basso, Carl Formes, to sing with me, and secured a hall that would seat two thousand, I gave it up, and rested easy for a while. Meanwhile I sent my children to school at Eagleswood, Perth Amboy, N. J., an institution kept by Theodore D. Weld.

When the Eighth Massachusetts Regiment reached New York, on its way to Annapolis and Washington, I stood on Broadway as it passed. One of the officers, a Marblehead man, whom I recognized, inquired the way to the Park, and I at once responded by taking a position by his side and marching along with the brave Essex County soldiery. I had one of the flags, of which I have spoken, furled on a stick. Suddenly a soldier stepped forward from the ranks, seized the flag, and swinging it round, unfurled it. He then passed it back and returned to his place. I heard some of the talk of the volunteers, such as: "We'll whip them out" in so many days, etc. I wept to hear it. When I thought of my own experiences in the South and my observation of the spirit of secession, I said, "O boys, you don't know what you have got to meet!"

"Brave boys are they,
Gone at their country's call,
And yet, and yet, we cannot forget
That many brave boys must fall."

After a while we started out to sing in Connecticut. I published an announcement that for the present the profits of our concerts would be devoted to the soldiers' aid societies, and issued editions of our songs for sale to aid the same object. We were comparatively successful, and sang along up to the Fourth of July. On that morning I passed from the town where I had just sung at a very early hour. I heard a unusual noise, like the rumble of battle. It did not sound like thunder, but like the discharge of musketry and artillery, floating over my head. It seemed like the echo of a terrible conflict. We spent the day at West Colchester. It was being celebrated by a big drum corps, which had taken possession of the town hall. We went in and joined in the observance, singing "The Star-Spangled Banner" several times. In the middle of July we settled down once more at High Rock, and endeavored to rest our voices. I devoted myself to building a retaining wall along the Essex Street front of my premises. I was at work for some weeks on this wall, and during this time the first battle of Bull Run occurred. "Mr. Hutchinson," said a man, "are you building a fortification?" I thought High Rock was quite a fortification in itself. This wall was superseded by the "Centennial wall," built in 1876. August 11th we all drove over to Lynnfield, where the Twenty-second Regiment, recruited by Hon. Henry Wilson, was encamped and here had our first experience in singing in camp. We tried to sing such songs as would give new courage to the daunted, stimulate the hesitating, and comfort those who were leaving home and all that was dear to endure the unknown issues of battle. Many words of thanks and praise were spoken by officers and men. I was entertained by Wilson's attempts to drill the regiment. It seemed much more like the work of a raw recruit than that of an ex-general in the State militia. A drill-master stood at his side and prompted him in giving the orders. He had quite a time trying to tell the recruits to "right shoulder, shift." Of course, however, it had never been intended that Wilson should take the field. He did good service in raising and getting two regiments ready for the army, but his best work was as chairman of the Senate Military Committee.

On August 23d I sang at the memorial of Theodore Parker in Boston, spending the night at the home of Samuel Gould on Worcester Square. The next day I

DAISY COTTAGE   HIGH ROCK IN 1864 — (p. 58)   TRIBE OF JOHN   OBSERVATORY   STONE COTTAGE

took my first ride from Boston to Lynn in the horse-car "over the marshes." It was a tiresome journey then to what it is to-day in the swift moving electrics of the Lynn and Boston road. During the following autumn I visited the Lynnfield camp many times, with Asa and our families, singing songs of patriotism and courage. In November the Tribe of John went singing through New Hampshire and Maine, and in December while singing in Haverhill and Lawrence, I "had a call" to go to Washington. I left the team in which we travelled, for my wife and children to drive home, and started at once. I found the field was open for us to sing at the capital, for many meetings were being held, and the war spirit was high in every quarter. So I sent for my children to come to me, and also secured the services of Frank Martin, son of a ministerial friend, to sing with us as bass. A friend, by the name of George W. Atwood, whom I had met in England many years before, recommended that we take the Smithsonian Institution for our entertainments, and he assisted me in getting up a concert at that place, which was very successful. Soon after my arrival in Washington, I sought out Salmon P. Chase, Secretary of the Treasury. He expressed himself as very much pleased that I had come to the city. I had often met him at Columbus, Cincinnati and other places, and was at the conference when he was first nominated for Congress. He had been a true Abolitionist, and with my uncle, Kendrick Leavitt, was on a committee to form the first anti-slavery society in that region.

Soon after my arrival I met Chaplain R. B. Yard, of the First New Jersey Regiment. He was then located amid thirty thousand troops near the Fairfax Seminary in Virginia, and though he was aware there was some risk in the venture, invited me to come there and give a concert to his "boys in blue." I told him I would come as soon as I could get the requisite pass within the lines, and at once set to work to get it.

Meanwhile we gave concerts in Washington, and kept our eyes open to the notable events transpiring. On one evening after giving a concert at Georgetown we were driven to the White House. The occasion was a levee. President Lincoln at once recognized me. Both he and Mrs. Lincoln treated us with great kindness, and in the course of the evening asked us to sing. We sang "The War-drums are Beating — Up, Soldiers, and Fight!" We suffered under a slight inconvenience in singing. The key of the piano could not be found. As a contemporary writer put it, "The instrument belonged to the mansion, and possibly, in the latter part of Mr. Buchanan's occupancy, more discord than harmony prevailed in the presidential dwelling." When the key was discovered, it was found that the piano was in shocking bad tune. No music stool could be found, and altogether it was evident that Mr. Lincoln and his family were thinking of something else than music in those days. The same writer says: "'There's nae luck aboot the house,' might perhaps have been played upon the rattling old keys, but it would have been little less than treason to have attempted 'Yankee Doodle' on such a rickety box of wires." At President Lincoln's request, I sent for my melodeon, and sang the "Ship on Fire," he having heard me sing it before at Springfield, Ill. I can seem to see our martyred President now, as he stood, only a few feet from me, holding his sweet boy, "Tad," by the hand. We were warmly applauded as our songs concluded. The room was as full as it could be

SINGING TO LINCOLN — (p. 386)

It was natural that in my dilemma over obtaining permission to visit the camps, I should again seek out my old friend Salmon P. Chase. He was more than willing to do all in his power to smooth our pathway for us, and at once sent me to Simon Cameron, Secretary of War, with just the right sort of introduction to secure the coveted pass. Cameron courteously furnished us the following document, jocosely remarking: "But mind you don't sing secesh!"

WAR DEPARTMENT, January 14, 1862

Permit the "Hutchinson Family" to pass over bridges and ferries, and within the main lines of the Army of the Potomac. They will be allowed to sing to the soldiers, and this permit will continue good until 1st February, 1862. SIMON CAMERON, *Secretary of War*

While I was getting the pass, I turned, and there by the window stood General B. F. Butler. He seemed to be in deep thought. I think now that he was hoping to be appointed Secretary of War, for so far as I can learn, the issuance of this permit was Cameron's last official act. The next day he was superseded by Edwin M. Stanton.

Then followed our visit to the camps. Crossing the long, carefully guarded bridge over the Potomac from Washington, we soon passed the guard to General Franklin's division, under convoy and patronage of Chaplain Yard. We had intended to give a concert on the same afternoon, but unforeseen obstacles prevented. One was given in a magnificent church, that evening, on the elegant grounds connected with the Fairfax Seminary, meanwhile taking quarters and messing with Chaplain Yard and Surgeon Welling, where we were most hospitably entertained.

We had fixed the price of admission to the entertainment at one dime. The church would comfortably seat one regiment, so we arranged that one regiment at a time should come. The First New Jersey Regiment was to hear us on this first evening. Another New Jersey regiment had expected to hear us in the afternoon, and many of its members therefore came to the evening concert. The result was a very large crowd, soldiers sitting on the floor in the aisles, and standing in the rear of the pews and around the walls. It was an enthusiastic and largely sympathetic audience, and the programme went off splendidly, until we sung the famous hymn by John G. Whittier, which I had adapted to music, two verses of which head this chapter. Of course, we were aware that the army of the Union did not entirely consist of Abolitionists. Many of the brave men who composed our audience had enlisted to save the Union, but had yet to learn the lesson that time only taught Lincoln, that the backbone of secession must be broken by the abolition of the system it was inaugurated to sustain. The song was this:

EIN FESTE BURG IST UNSER GOTT (*Luther's Hymn*)

> We wait beneath the furnace-blast
> The pangs of transformation
> Not painlessly doth God recast
> And mould anew the nation
>   Hot burns the fire
>   Where wrongs expire,
>   Nor spares the hand
>   That from the land
> Uproots the ancient evil

> The hand-breadth cloud the sages feared
> Its bloody rain is dropping,
> The poison plant the fathers spared
> All else is overtopping
>   East, West, South, North,
>   It curses earth,
>   All justice dies,
>   And fraud and lies
> Live only in its shadow.

What gives the wheat-fields blades of steel?
　　What points the rebel cannon?
What sets the roaring rabble's heel
　　On the old star-spangled pennon?
　　　　What breaks the oath
　　　　Of the men of the South?
　　　　What whets the knife
　　　　For the Union's life? —
　　Hark to the answer: *Slavery!*

Then waste no blows on lesser foes
　　In strife unworthy freemen,
God lifts to-day the vail and shows
　　The features of the demon!
　　　　O North and South,
　　　　Its victims both,
　　　　Can ye not cry,
　　　　" Let slavery die!"
　　And union find in Freedom?

What though the cast-out spirit tear
　　The nation in his going,
We who have shared the guilt must share
　　The pang of his overthrowing!
　　　　What'er the loss,
　　　　Whate'er the cross,
　　　　Shall they complain
　　　　Of present pain
　　Who trust in God hereafter?

For who that leans on His right arm
　　Was ever yet forsaken?
What righteous cause can suffer harm
　　If He its part hath taken?
　　　　Though wild and loud,
　　　　And dark the cloud,
　　　　Behind its folds
　　　　His hand upholds
　　The calm sky of to-morrow!

Above the maddening cry for blood,
　　Above the wild war-drumming,
Let Freedom's voice be heard, with good
　　The evil overcoming

Give prayer and purse
To stay the curse
Whose wrong we share,
Whose shame we bear,
Whose end shall gladden Heaven!

In vain the bells of war shall ring
Of triumphs and revenges,
While still is spared the evil thing
That severs and estranges
But, blest the ear
That yet shall hear
The jubilant bell
That rings the knell
Of slavery forever!

Then let the selfish lip be dumb,
And hushed the breath of sighing,
Before the joy of peace, must come
The pains of purifying
God give us grace
Each in his place
To bear his lot,
And murmuring not,
Endure and wait and labor!

What a prophet Whittier was, and how clearly he saw what so many of his countrymen were slow in seeing! His prophecy was addressed to just such patriots as those to whom we were singing, but it needed just such opposition as it met to draw the attention of the army and the country to its truth. It might have saved us trouble to omit it, but it was not a characteristic of the Hutchinsons to forbear when a message was put in their lips. It seemed a testing-time for us, but it also served to open the eyes of the country to the devotion to the "peculiar institution," the opposition to emancipation, and consequent lukewarmness, not to say treason, of men in high places in the army, who were then the hope of the nation in the hour of its extremity, and a forlorn hope at that. No sooner had we finished the verse:

"What gives the wheat-fields blades of steel?" etc.,

than a solitary hiss was heard, from a corner of the room. Major Hatfield, commanding the regiment, was seated in a front pew of the church, and immediately rose, and turning to the part of the room from whence the sign of disapprobation had proceeded, indignantly said that if the interruption was repeated the offender would be put out of the house. "If there is to be any putting out, you had better begin with me," retorted Surgeon Oakley of his own command, evidently the culprit. The major, to whom the surgeon had made threats of disturbance before the concert commenced, then said, "I can put you out — and if I cannot, I have a regiment that will!" At this the soldiers rose to a man, amid much confusion and cries of "Put him out!" But no force was resorted to, and order was finally restored. The surgeon was heard sending a messenger for his pistols to defend himself. We at once bethought ourselves of our old expedient, and soon the soldier boys were melted to tears by the beautiful song, "No Tear in Heaven."

"No tear shall be in heaven; no gathering gloom
Shall o'er that glorious landscape ever come,
No tear shall fall in sadness o'er those flowers
That breathe their fragrance thro' celestial bowers."

Chaplain Merwin, a chaplain at large, had used his good offices to help restore quiet, and there was no further disturbance, but after the concert certain persons refused to mess with the conciliatory chaplain. Major Hatfield, who interfered so decidedly in our favor, was afterwards killed, during McClellan's retreat from before Richmond.

After the concert we retired to our quarters. We could hear loud talking in those adjoining, and could see nothing but trouble ahead. Soon General Birney, brother of James G. Birney, the noted Abolitionist, came into the place, with others, in full sympathy with us. We freely sang our radical pieces to them. Subsequently Birney told me he just escaped a challenge to fight a duel because of the matter. We felt that we had done nothing wrong, and our consciences were clear. The hour was late, but we understood a chaplain to have full control of his quarters, and so sang as long as our callers desired.

The next morning Chaplain Yard received a message to appear before General Kearney (afterwards killed in battle). When he returned it was with a sad countenance. Very great excitement had been caused by the proceedings of the night before, he said. Surgeon Oakley had complained of our singing; and the authorities had gone so far as to take the keys of the church from him. It was doubtful if the concerts would be permitted to proceed. Soon there came a second message, calling for both chaplain and singers at General Kearney's headquarters. We at once tramped through rain and mud to that place. General Kearney rebuked the chaplain and vocalists for singing without first submitting a programme of their songs to the authorities, and added that he "could not allow the concerts to go on."

"General," I said, "I have a permit from the Secretary of War to sing. We are no strangers to the soldiers, many thousands of whom know and have heard us — whatever the officers may think and feel on the subject."

"I rule supreme here," remarked the general quickly.

"You are Abolitionists; I think as much of a Rebel as I do of an Abolitionist."

After saying this, however, the general seemed to hesitate, and the matter still appeared to be open when we left him. Soon after we reached our quarters, nevertheless, a fresh message came from him that we must forego all singing in the camp. This did not settle the matter, for subordinates must report to their superiors. When the news was sent to General Franklin, the following order came.

HEADQUARTERS, ALEXANDRIA DIVISION.,
CAMP WILLIAM, January, 1862

MAJOR HATFIELD — You will please send to these headquarters, as soon as practicable, a copy of the songs sung by the Hutchinson Family last night in the Seminary Chapel

By order of Brigadier-General Franklin,
JOSEPH C. JACKSON, A. D. C.

It was the work of several hours to make copies of all the songs, but they were finally taken to the general by Chaplain Yard. He took them and wished to have the objectionable song pointed out. He read Whittier's song, and said, "I pronounce that incendiary; if these people are allowed to go on, they will demoralize the army." The chaplain again returned to us, depressed and sad.

Another concert had been advertised. Many members of the regiment came and expressed their regret when it was announced that it was forbidden.

It was then Saturday night. Late in the evening General Franklin issued another order, evidently by instructions from General McClellan, who paused in his hot pursuit of means to carry out the country's mandate "On to Richmond!" to consider our innocent exhibition of treasonable propensities.

HEADQUARTERS, ALEXANDRIA, VA.,
January 18, 1862.

GENERAL ORDERS, NO. 3.

By command of the Major-General Commanding U. S. A. the permit given to the Hutchinson Family to sing in the camps, and their permit to cross the Potomac, are hereby revoked, and they will not be allowed to sing to the troops.

By order of Brigadier-General Franklin.

J. C. JACKSON, A. D. C.

Official—JAMES M. WILSON, A. A. G.

Headquarters, 1st N. J. V.

This seemed to settle the question of further proceedings, especially as I at the same time received a verbal message to leave our quarters. It was late and the weather was bad. I at once wrote a note to General Franklin, asking permission to stay with our friends until Monday morning.

I still retain the original copies of all the correspondence I have quoted, as also this letter. In it I said:

FAIRFAX, January 18, 1862.

GENERAL FRANKLIN:

DEAR SIR. Having had my pass, granted by the Secretary of War and General McClellan, revoked, and not being able to remove to the other side the Potomac at this late hour, I ask of you the privilege of remaining with my friends the Rev. Mr. Yard, and Dr. Welling, till Monday, or if not, till Sunday morning, when at your command *we leave.*

Wishing the best success to our glorious army, as when we came into its lines,—"God save the Commonwealth."

Yours, with the greatest desire for law and order,

JOHN W. HUTCHINSON.

This was sent to Capt. E. S. Purdy, Assistant Adjutant-General, turned over to General Kearney, who forwarded it to General Franklin, with this endorsement:

JANUARY 19th.

Respectfully forwarded. Yesterday morning I had given the directions to the Hutchinsons to forego any further concerts.

P. H. KEARNY, *Brigadier-General.*

Soon the letter came back, with this further endorsement:

HEADQUARTERS, January 19, 1862

BRIGADIER-GENERAL KEARNEY — There is no objection to these people staying until Monday morning, if they behave themselves properly. W. B. FRANKLIN,
Brigadier-General Commanding Division

Of course we determined to be good, and stayed over. On Sunday Chaplain Yard went to General Kearney and obtained permission to use the chapel. He also asked if there would be any objection to his having a choir to sing. The general said no. The request was the result of an effort to give soldiers who had been disappointed a chance to hear us sing. When his service began the Hutchinson's were there and those soldiers who were desiring to do so, heard Chaplain Yard's choir, though they were forbidden to hear the Hutchinson Family. In the evening Chaplain Merwin gave a temperance lecture, and Chaplain Yard kindly lent his choir to sing temperance songs. The next day my daughter Viola received a twenty-dollar gold-piece sent her by the soldiers.

The next morning Henry and Frank Martin went on to Washington. I intended to follow with Viola on the boat from Alexandria, but the fog prevented its departure. Chaplain Yard said he would take me across the bridge in his carriage the next day, so I concluded to remain. I accepted an invitation to accompany the two chaplains on a visit to Colonel Farnsworth's regiment of cavalry, quartered a mile or so away. We started in a buggy, Chaplain Yard driving, with Merwin on one side and I on the other. The horse was high-spirited, and had not been harnessed to a buggy for months, being used only with the saddle. We had not gone far when the horse, being nervous from his harness, took fright going down a hill. We were in the utmost danger. I reached my arm around the chaplain and got hold of the right rein, pulling so hard that it broke. This was fortunate, for the strong pull on the other rein caused him to swerve from the road and knocked the vehicle against some trees, demolishing it, but leaving us unhurt. The frightened animal cleared himself, and with only the thills ran back to camp. Thousands of soldiers looked on at this catastrophe, and many shouted, "Forward movement!" Poor fellows! they had been waiting in the mud many weary months for a forward movement.

When we returned to our quarters, we learned that an officer had been asking for the Hutchinson Family, and finding that some of us had remained, had remarked that we "might as well have gone off." On hearing this, being anxious to give the authorities no ground for charging us with disobedience of orders, I determined to go at once and not risk disturbing the peace. So we went to Alexandria, where we called on General Montgomery. He took us to his own quarters, where we sang him psalms and hymns, and conjointly with the provost-marshal, he invited us to give a concert in the place. We declined for the time being.

When I returned to Washington from Alexandria, I went immediately to Chase. I found him at his home, and told him my experience. Said he: "I want you to write out me that song, and I'll submit it to the cabinet. I'm Secretary of the Treasury; Stanton is Secretary of War, and he thinks just as I do."

As soon as I conveniently could, I passed to Chase a copy of the Whittier song. I had by this time discovered that the episode was one of far more importance than its merely personal bearing would indicate. There had been a good deal of complaint of McClellan, but thus far he had not before taken it upon himself to so directly countermand the action of the war secretary, who would naturally be his superior in a matter of this character. However, I did not wish to see a matter so closely identified with myself in any way embarrassing the administration, and therefore on the next day, the cabinet being in session, I sent in a note to Secretary Chase, requesting him, unless his judgment dictated otherwise, not to give to the papers the fact that the subject was under consideration. The next morning all the papers were silent on it, but I went to the treasury department, and met Mr. Chase on the stairs going to his office. He grasped me by the hand, and smilingly said: "I want to tell you that the poem was read at the cabinet meeting and they were all in your favor. Mr. Lincoln remarked that it was one of just the kind of songs he wanted the soldiers to hear. He also said you should have the right to go among any of the soldiers where you were invited to sing."

A few days later Representative Lovejoy, of Illinois, brother of the martyr Lovejoy, offered an order of inquiry concerning McClellan's arrogant attitude to Congress. It was the beginning of the end for that officer. Soon after he was allowed to report at Trenton, while another man took charge of the destinies of the Army of the Potomac and the campaign against Richmond, in which he had so signally failed. Two years later, when he was a candidate for the presidency, practically every man who took the stump for Lincoln found occasion to say that though "Little Mac" was not able to drive out the rebels, he did drive out the Hutchinsons.

After our pronounced vindication of course we no

longer hesitated about giving concerts in Alexandria, as we had been invited to do. In the meantime, owing to the inclemency of the weather and the tendency of his soldiers to sickness and disease, Colonel (afterwards General) Farnsworth had found quarters for them in the vestry of a large Southern Methodist church, that had been forsaken by nearly all its worshippers, who had joined the Rebels. When we arrived we were ushered into this room, and introduced to the soldiers by Farnsworth, who invited me to mess with him at his headquarters, in another building. He said he wanted me to have the auditorium of the church for the concerts, and desired me to go to General Montgomery and get a permit. I waited on Montgomery, found him exceedingly cordial, and as he was in charge of that department, he at once gave the permit.

Returning to Colonel Farnsworth, we had been but a short time together, and were eating our dinner, when he received a note from General Montgomery, stating that the sexton of the church, and he one of its trustees, had waited upon him and protested against opening it for any purpose. He said: "I leave the matter with you and Mr. Hutchinson and the sexton." The colonel at once said: "He leaves it to us three. We are in the majority. The church will be opened." He sent an orderly for the key. It was a hard task to get it, and it was only obtained when the obdurate janitor was informed that if the key was not forthcoming, the troops would break in the door. On that he succumbed. As the time for the concert drew near, I discovered that there was no gas. I at once went in pursuit of some one to order it turned on, and was sent to a man named Stewart, who was a Union man, married to a Northern woman, and was very courteous. He told me to find a man named Bell. I hastened to a book-store, stepped up to the man, and said: "We are to have a concert to-night in the church, and desire the gas turned on." He brusquely retorted; "You'll not be allowed to sing in that church. I have been a Union man so far, but have suffered enough. I'll go down to the mayor and have it stopped." "I'll go with you," I quickly replied. He took me to a large warehouse, and up a flight of dark stairs, across the floor above to an office in the corner. He opened the door, and there I saw some twenty men, evidently of the "Secesh" order, discussing the success of the "cause." "Mr. Mayor," said Bell, addressing one of the men, "here's one of the Hutchinsons, who wants to sing in the Methodist church. If I was mayor, I wouldn't allow it." "Mr Bell," said he, "I'm mayor of the city, to be sure, but I've no control in this military department." Then turning to me, and shaking my hand heartily: "Why, Mr. Hutchinson! I am glad to meet you. I remember hearing you sing in Beecher's church." It appeared that the mayor had been educated in the North. It was pleasant, indeed, under conditions so strained, to hear such a friendly greeting. Mr. Bell was baffled, and leaving the building, mutely walked up the street towards the church. Finally he pointed to a gas-house down a side street "There," said he, "you go and tell them to put on the gas, and mention my name." Night had come on, and I hurried down to the gas-house, and then to my quarters to make ready for the concert. When I arrived at the church, I found a glorious audience to greet me. We sang our "prohibited" song, it being loudly called for, and also many other radical songs, among them "John Brown's Body." General Montgomery sat on the platform, and at the close of the concert resolutions in our favor were adopted. The next night we gave another concert.

This closed our singing before the army. We had done what we intended to do and were satisfied. The incident of expulsion caused a great commotion among the people of the North. All the Washington correspondents referred to it, at more or less length, and as in the case of our expulsion from Philadelphia, a great deal of good resulted from the discussions which it provoked. We had been before the public too many years to care seriously when unfriendly papers seemed to find virtue in the action of General McClellan, and their attempt to prove us "traitors" because he seemed to dislike our songs, only made us smile.

Horace Greeley, in his "American Conflict," thus refers to this incident:

"A portion of the melodious Hutchinson Family having been attracted to Washington by the novelty of finding the public halls of the city no longer barricaded against the utterance of humane and generous sentiments, had there solicited the Secretary of War's permission to visit the camps along the Potomac in order to break the monotony and cheer the ruggedness of winter with the spontaneous, unbought carol of some of their cheerful, heartfelt songs. General Cameron gave their project not merely his cordial assent, but his emphatic commendation, and thus endorsed, they received General McClellan's gracious permission. So they passed on to the camps, and were singing to delighted crowds of soldiers, when an officer's quick ear caught the drift of what sounded like *Abolition*. Forthwith, there were commotion, and effervescence, and indignation, rising from circle to circle of the military aristocracy until it reached the very highest, bringing thence the following order." (The order of General McClellan and the poem of Whittier are then quoted.)

"Arlington," a noted Washington correspondent of the time, writing to a New England journal, gave the following description of the affair, which I quote as a sample of the comments made, as well as to show the necessity there was of our putting before the public an accurate story of it, which we did soon after:

"WASHINGTON, January 23, 1862

"The Hutchinson Family have been here for the last five weeks, giving concerts. On Friday they passed over into Virginia, intending to spend a month among the camps, cheering the hearts of the soldiers and enlivening the monotony of camp life with their sweet melody. They gave their first concert on Saturday evening at Alexandria Seminary, three miles from Alexandria, in the division of General Franklin. The audience was composed entirely of soldiers of the First New Jersey Regiment. The hall was crowded, the brave boys were delighted, and everything passed off pleasantly, until the singing of Whittier's beautiful lines commencing

'We wait beneath the furnace blast,'

when amid the general and hearty applause which followed, a loud and spiteful hissing was heard from some one in the audience. The soldiers became indignant, and a major of one of the regiments remonstrated against the hissing, saying he would be obliged to eject any persons thus insulting the vocalists. On this announcement, up rose Dr. Oakley, Surgeon of the New Jersey First, and said, 'If there is to be any putting out, you may as well begin with me.' Some excitement ensued, and a determination was manifested among the soldiers, who have all along suspected the Dr. of secesh sympathies, to kick that gentleman out of the hall. Through the exertions of one of the chaplains, order was finally restored. The matter was immediately reported to General Franklin, who at once ordered the surgeon and major under arrest, and soon after an order came through General Franklin from General McClellan, revoking the 'pass' of the Hutchinsons. General Franklin directed their immediate return to Washington, but as it was now half-past nine o'clock, and the roads in the most wretched condition, Mr. Hutchinson wrote a polite note to General Franklin asking permission to remain over Sunday. The latter returned the note with the following insulting endorsement. 'There is no objection to these folks remaining until Monday, if they behave themselves.'

"Now all this occurred within sight of the residence of a family named Godwin, in which there are some five or six young ladies, who, it is alleged, have been promised passes to go South whenever they are disposed to do so, — carrying, of course, all the information they can to the enemy. The bands of the regiments are also sent to serenade them, and on these occasions orders are given to suppress the national airs, as being offensive to these traitors in crinoline. Many of the higher officers in the army are declared to be in secret sympathy with the rebellion. They are regular graduates of West Point, and generally look upon and treat the volunteer officers with contempt. It was of the military school at West Point that Senator Chandler declared in a recent debate, that 'since the days of Judas Iscariot, there had never existed an institution that had produced so many traitors.'

"The foregoing statements are made on the authority of an officer in General Franklin's division, whose post is in the vicinity of the Godwin's residence, and who is cognizant of the facts relating to the disturbance on the evening of the concert. I have since seen Mr. Hutchinson, who corroborates all that the officer has stated, and has shown me the correspondence which has passed between himself and the military authorities on the subject. Your readers may rely, therefore, on the correctness of the foregoing narrative."

The writer here reproduces the song, on the ground that many readers may like to see the beautiful lines, the singing of which had given such offence to those secret sympathizers with secession, and judging from the ridiculous action of General Franklin, well-nigh produced a general disruption of our army. He then goes on:

"For giving expression to these sentiments, the Hutchinsons have been driven from the camps of our army. It is due, however, to the soldiers to say, that almost to a man they condemn the outrage, but, with the fate of the major before them, they dare not manifest openly their sense of the wrong. They are subjects of a petty tyranny from officials who, it is feared, have too little sympathy with the cause in which they are enlisted. It is idle to talk of rebels at Ball's Bluff, in the Potomac batteries, or behind the entrenchments at Centreville or Manassas. The traitors are *here* — in our own camps — at the head of our armies — in the Capitol itself. They stalk unblushingly into the Senate Chamber, and mingle in the most secret councils of senators. Their eager eye is watchful, and their ready tongue may whisper the tidings in the listening ear of treason."

Colonel Edward Livingston Welling, Secretary of the Third Army Corps Union, and a successful physician of Pennington, N. J., to whom I have referred, was present at the concert, being then a member of the First Regiment. He was then a pro-slavery man. Our singing, however, converted him and he was ever after a warm friend of emancipation. He has maintained a firm feeling of friendship for the family ever since those eventful days. Writing to my daughter Viola a few years since, he said:

"How time flies! It seems but yesterday that we had such thrilling and grand old times in the seminary, when we were so much in advance of the glorious 'Proclamation of Emancipation' which had to come, and which, when it did come, made the name and the memory of Abraham Lincoln immortal. I can almost hear, ringing in my ears, those thrilling, majestically truthful words

"'What gives the wheat fields blades of steel?
What points the rebel cannon?' etc.,

and as in days of yore, I can e'en now feel the hair rising on my head, as the answer peals forth — '*Slavery!*'"

Pleasantest of all the comment and correspondence called out by this incident was this, from Whittier:

AMESBURY, 6th, 3d month, 1862.

MY DEAR H. — I am glad to know that there is any *sing* in my verses.
Of course I can have no objection to thy use of them. If thee can get any music out of them, I shall be pleased and gratified.
Whatever General McClellan may do with my rhymes, I am thankful that Congress is putting it out of his power to "send back" fugitive slaves as well as singers.
After all, I do not think it strange that a Quaker's song should be thought out of place in the army.
Wishing thee and thine health and happiness, and hoping that you may live to sing of the deliverance of our land from slavery and war, I am very truly thy friend,

JOHN G. WHITTIER.

The remark in Whittier's first paragraph evidently refers to a conversation I had with him in Amesbury, before the war. Whittier was calling on me and said, "Do you want to know the one desire I have above all others?" I told him I would be pleased to hear from his own lips a statement of this supreme desire. "It is this," said he, "that I may so write my verses that they may be sung."

In all the years since, wherever we have been singing, we have been greeted by thousands of soldiers who remembered the thrilling incidents of those days in the camps and seemed to have an attachment for us because of our songs to the brave boys of the Army of the Potomac.

After singing in Alexandria, we once more returned to Washington. Some of the members of General McClellan's body-guard gave us an invitation to sing before them in private. To compensate us, they purchased large numbers of tickets for a concert, and attended at a church where it was held. The provost-marshal of the city was present at this concert. We sung about all of our radical songs, amid great applause. They so frightened the pastor of the church, however, for fear some of his congregation should be disturbed by their anti-slavery sentiments, that he refused to let us have the edifice for another. Then we made an arrangement with the Young Men's Christian Association to give concerts in its hall, dividing the profits. Our experience here affords an additional illustration of the peculiar conditions existing in Washington, where were gathered all sorts of men, some friendly to the administration and some not — Union men, copperheads and doughfaces. The departments swarmed with men who did not know their own minds. Their experience made them useful, but though they might have been theoretically in favor of the success of Northern arms and the establishment of universal freedom, they were not only afraid to say so, but were disposed to object to any one else saying so either.

The president of the Y. M. C. A. had been for a long time a clerk in the Treasury Department. He seemed pleased to see the money come in from our concerts, but evidently something troubled him. Finally he came to me after one of the concerts and with a good deal of hemming and hawing managed to evolve a suggestion, that considering the exciting conditions prevailing it would be wiser to drop references to the slavery question in our programmes. I thanked him for the hint, but gave no indication of what I would do. He correctly inferred that I would do nothing of the sort and so wrote me a long letter of four pages, in which, after beating all about the bush, he succeeded in again delivering himself of the same idea. A few days later I called at the Treasury Department and went to his office. Desiring to introduce the subject of my call pleasantly, I referred in tones of satisfaction to the news just received of the success of one of our armies in battle. Then I told him I had just been calling on my friend of many years' standing, Secretary Chase. He looked startled, and seemed even more surprised and ill at ease, when I said that I had been invited as a special guest to a reception at the secretary's house. Suddenly I said: "Oh, I received a letter from you!" "Yes," he responded, "have you got it with you?" Unthinkingly, I drew it from my pocket. He snatched it and put it into the fire burning in the room. Then I told him I would relieve his mind of further anxiety regarding our anti-slavery utterances, by giving up the concerts. The man evidently thought I was in a position to show his letter and perhaps secure his dismissal, but I said nothing further of the matter.

On the following Sunday we sang at the Capitol. N. P. Willis was in the city at the time and in writing to his paper, the *Home Journal*, made a reference to the incident

"WASHINGTON, January 12, 1862.

"With the charm of novelty, as to time and place—the additional relish, that is to say, of 'game out of season'—I have had, to-day, two *warm* experiences, for mid-winter, at Washington—a summer stroll through the grounds of the Capitol, and the hearing of Cheever's abolition sermon in the House of Representatives. June never had a softer or summer day than this January twelfth, and a more volcanic outburst of human utterance was probably never listened to, than Cheever's astonishing of those legislative chairs, this Sabbath afternoon! Whether the hearer did, or did not believe in the parallel drawn from the text—that Lincoln was 'Pharaoh' and Fremont 'Moses,' rebellion the 'Red Sea' and 'river of blood,' and that abolition would be the 'letting God's people go,' at the now last command of an angry Jehovah—the persuading thereto was oratorically tremendous!

"At the close of the service, the portable melodeon of 'the Hutchinsons' was brought into the centre of the Representative hall, and the four famous vocalists broke forth with a quartette of Wendell Phillipsism (an anti-slavery *hymn*), by way of doxology. It was exceedingly well sung—only, a little perplexing to remember, that this musical family had done the same thing for the just-denounced 'Pharaoh' a few nights before—bringing in their melodeon (as I had innocently been delighted to see them do), and doxologizing, in the very same way, the departing guests of a *levee* at the White House. That the 'Egyptian Ruler's' heart is not yet altogether hardened, however (and therefore still worthy of being sung to), I am happy to bear witness, for, chancing to look around at the conclusion of this latter song, I saw the eyes of our tall 'Pharaoh' brimful of tears!"

Among the selections sung at the meeting in the Capitol referred to, was "The Slave's Appeal," which created a great sensation. After it was over, a slaveholder invited us to his house to have "a talk," but we were pressed for time and could not go.

Acting on the principle that misery likes company, and knowing that General John C. Fremont had been cashiered, or at least ordered to report at Washington from his Missouri command, for issuing an emancipation proclamation, while I had been obliged to return from the army for singing emancipation songs, I seized the first opportunity that offered to call upon him. He was just in the state of mind for communion, and we related our mutual greivances. Then our talk wandered to our hopes for the success of the war, and our regret at the apparent lukewarmness and delinquency of President Lincoln and the government, failing because of the dilemma of discord on the part of the leaders of the army to declare emancipation. We discussed the contrast furnished by Jeff Davis, who fully controlled every man in the South, united to fight to maintain slavery. I said that it seemed to me dangerous to delay the great movement. As I looked at it, not only the friends of the slave in the North, but in Canada and over the sea stood ready to assist in a contest for his emancipation. Looking him fully in the face, I said: "John C. Fremont, a million of men can be marshalled under the slogan of 'Fremont and Victory!'" "The time is not yet," was his reply. I felt that my visit to him was timely and delightful. We afterward enjoyed many pleasant hours with him and his beloved and popular wife, Jessie Benton Fremont.

Our experiences with Secretary Chase were of the pleasantest character, though some of them were rather unusual. We had hardly reached the city before his daughter, afterwards so well known as Mrs. Kate Chase Sprague, invited us to come to the house for an evening. These calls were often repeated. On one occasion he invited me for a social evening and at the appointed time I repaired to the house in company with Henry and Viola. The bell was answered by a servant I inquired if Mr. Chase was at home and told him I had an appointment to come that night He said Mr. Chase was in his library. He took the verbal message and returned, saying that Mr. Chase was very much engaged and could not see company. I said there must be a mistake, and he went once more to the great secretary, returning with the message, "Mr Chase wants you to send him your card." I discovered that I had no card with me, and as I had as usual, plenty of concert tickets handy, sent one of them. The servant returned a third time, and said: "Mr. Chase says there is no concert here to-night." We left the house in surprise and wonder The rude treatment we had met was inexplicable. I recalled statements I had heard, however, that when busy, Mr. Chase had no recognition of engagements, and felt somewhat relieved. We happened to know that there was to be a grand war meeting at the Smithsonian Institution and consequently went there. We were met at the entrance by one of those in charge, my arm was taken and we were at once marched to the stage. We sung to the immense audience and in the enthusiasm of the hour forgot the Chase incident. This was during the period of the concerts at the Y. M. C. A. Building. On the following evening I had gone to the hall and was standing at the door as the people came in, when a letter was given me. I was just about to go on the stage. The letter had no envelope, in the ancient style, and as I glanced at it in my haste, the writing being far from handsome and difficult to decipher, concluded it to be from some indifferent person and thrust it into my pocket unread. Then I forgot all about it. That night I woke at midnight and thought of it I lit the gas, found it, and discovered it to be from Chase. It was as follows:

Friday eve.

My Dear Friend —Allow me to explain a mistake When the card marked "Hutchinson Family Concert, 50 cents," was brought with the remark of the servant that the gentleman said "there was to be a concert here to-night," I naturally supposed that you had given the tickets to some friends to be present this evening, and, as Nettie is ill, though I trust not seriously, at Philadelphia, and Katie went off suddenly last night to be with her, I thought it not best to have anything like a concert in the house to-night and sent word to the supposed concert comers that there would be none. It never occurred to me that the comers were you and your children. Why did you not send your name instead of a ticket? After the door had closed some minutes it flashed through my mind that I had sent away the very friends I most desired to see. Won't you all come and take dinner with me at six tomorrow? Yours cordially, S. P. CHASE.

JOHN HUTCHINSON, ESQ.

Soon after he invited me to come to his house for a more pretentious reception. He said: "I want you to come, and I will have whoever I can invite of the members of the government, leading generals, and others who understand the gist of this war. You may sing and talk to them as much as you please." A day or two later I wrote to him that if he would pardon the suggestion, and if it would be consistent with etiquette, I should be happy to have him invite General Fremont and "Jessie" to the reception. His reply was this:

Monday, 3 Feb.

DEAR FRIEND — My engagements for Wednesday evening will prevent me from being able to receive you then, but Thursday evening is free. Can you come then? If possible for you, you will be very welcome.

As neither General Fremont has called on me, nor Mrs. F. on my daughter, it will be impossible, consistently with the rules of society here, which one is obliged to observe, to gratify your wish in respect to them; which otherwise I should gratify with as much pleasure to myself as to you. Yours truly, S. P. CHASE.

On the evening of the reception Mr. Chase was near the door to welcome the guests when I came in. The room was already well filled. Mr. Chase beckoned me into his library before introducing me. Sitting down on one side of the library table, I on the other, he said: "My excuse for denying you the privilege of meeting Fremont and Jessie was explained somewhat in my letter. But there are other reasons. The attitude of Fremont is not approved by the administration. When this great question is finally adjusted, the proclamation of emancipation must come from the government — from Lincoln, not from a general."

I was presented to a notable gathering indeed. Among them were Hon. Carl Shurz, ex-Governor Boutwell, of Massachusetts, Senator Howe and lady, Mrs. Governor Andrew, of Massachusetts, General Shields, Mrs. General McDowell and many others of equal distinction. We had a very good opportunity both to sing and speak our opinions. During the programme we rendered "John Brown's Body." When we came to the words "Hang Jeff Davis to a sour apple tree," I noticed a downcast look of disapproval on the secretary's face. Soon after he sought a quiet opportunity and said to me: "If I were you I would not sing that verse again. The point is this: when emancipation comes, we shall have no further quarrel with the South. That will mean an end of war. We shall then be a united and reconstructed people, in harmony again."

One day Chase wrote me a note, inviting me to call and remarking that he would that day be under the necessity of seeing the brokers — "who sing very different notes from yours." That evening, when I reached his house he said: "Oh, how glad I am to see you! I have been thronged with the bankers and brokers of Wall Street, Philadelphia and Boston, some two hundred of them in my office all day." He seemed to be in great distress because of their proceedings. They had given him to understand that the issue of greenbacks, which was to represent the credit of the government, must come under the banking system, or they would refuse to loan the government money. Those were days of trial for the great financier, and it was not strange that he was sometimes depressed.

The fact that it became difficult for us to get a place in which to sing won for us great sympathy from the colored people, who gave every possible evidence of their appreciation of our labors for twenty years in behalf of the enfranchisement of their race. When the doors of the white churches were closed against us, they offered us the use of their own houses of worship.

On leaving Washington, we went once more to Philadelphia, and besides opening a new hall, many concerts were given. "The Furnace Blast" at once became the most popular of our selections, because of the publicity given the fact of its prohibition. George Burleigh, the poet and friend of anti-slavery, published at this time in the *New York Independent* a poem, "Free Song on the Potomac," dedicated to the Hutchinsons, which was as follows:

"Ha, *Tape* and *Tinsel*, will ye stop
   The swelling tide of freedom's song,
E'en while the Judgment Hour lets drop
   God's lightning on the towers of wrong? —
Forbid the fearless free who fling
   Their lives on battle's combing wave
To hear their Mountain Warblers sing
   Our ransom with the ransomed slave?
But truth divine can pass your line
Without your word and countersign
      The winds will wing it,
      The birds will sing it,
      The seas will ring it,
The shouting brooks from the hills will bring it,
And your shattering cannon-peal shall fling it,
      Wherever a slave may pine.

"Sweet songsters of the Granite Hills,
  Birds of the rock and forest oak,
Wild-bubbling as their own free rills
  Their music, through the cannon-smoke,
Rained like the sky-larks from her cloud;
  And might have laid the fiend of Saul,
But makes your haunting fiend more loud,
  Whose javelin seeks the life of all
Unjustly strong, from out your throng
You drive the Flock, but not the Song!
    The winds will wing it,
    The birds will sing it,
    The seas will ring it,
The shouting brooks from the hills will bring it,
And the scream of your roaring shells will fling it,
    Wherever the weak bears wrong

"Not clanging horns nor rumbling drums
  The tones that deepest thrill the land,
The Resurrection angel comes
  With Freedom's trumpet in her hand!
Its blast will call the living dead,
  Redeemed, from Slavery's Hadean tomb
To find our welcome, or instead
  Peal the last charge of flying Doom!
The hour of fate will never wait,
Ye hear its judgment knell too late
    The winds will wing it,
    The birds will sing it,
    The seas will ring it,
The shouting brooks from the hills will bring it,
And a nation's dying groan shall fling it
    Through the shattered prison-gate!

"Once old chivalric honor reigned,
  And bards were sacred, e'en to foes,
They kept the glory heroes gained,
  And sang high deeds that shamed repose
But cheer, my Warblers! fly away
  To sing more clear in smokeless air,
The herald Angels sing to-day,
  Nor ask a tinselled tyrant where,
From heaven's blue cope the song of hope
Thrills down the bondman's dungeon slope,

>   The winds will wing it,
>   The birds will sing it,
>   The seas will ring it,
> The shouting brooks from the hills will bring it,
> And a rescued nation's voice shall fling it,
>   Where the last lone slave may grope "

Soon after we went to Boston for concerts. We were under contract to sing for some lecture committee, but they found the hall we desired, Tremont Temple, had been engaged by Wendell Phillips, who was to lecture. He not only granted us the use of the hall, but postponed a lecture and came to hear us himself. The Melodeon, in which for so many seasons we gave our Boston concerts, had disappeared. Years after, I was in Boston one day at a store on Washington Street, buying some gas fixtures for the house in which I now live. Sitting in the back of the store, waiting for the clerk, a scene suddenly flashed across my mind. It was of our family, singing before an audience in the Melodeon, and it came before me with such vividness that when the clerk came back I said: "My dear fellow, I have been thinking of our singing in the old Melodeon. Tell me if I am in the vicinity of its site?" "Why," said he, "You are right where its stage would be if it were still in existence."

After this came numerous concerts in New York, Trenton and contiguous places and a series of concerts on Long Island for the benefit of the soldier's home in New York. Then we winged our way across the country, by way of Pittsburgh, Ohio, Indiana, Wisconsin, and Minnesota, concerting, of course, to Hutchinson. Here everything appeared prosperous, but I took occasion to warn the inhabitants against the hostile tribes of Indians. They did not share my apprehensions, but in a few weeks had a chance to judge whether I was right. But this subject is treated more fully in another chapter.

I have given some inkling of the way our Potomac experience was received by our friends. It would take a large volume to reproduce all the controversy that raged about the subject. A few further quotations of the newspaper talk must suffice.

One pro-slavery paper, the *Warren Journal*, said:

"The Hutchinsons, the notorious abolition family, who were drummed out of the New Jersey camps as traitors, and who sang in the court-house some weeks since a number of abolition songs and one very abusive of that brave and gallant Jerseyman, General Kearney, will visit this place again, on Monday next. Of course all the enemies of General Kearney, who wished that on the bloody fields of Mexico, where he lost an arm, "he would be welcomed with bloody hands to a hospitable grave," and who now sympathize with those who would blacken his fair name and reputation, while he is absent from home, giving his best efforts to crush out and put down this unrighteous and unholy rebellion, will give their countenance and support to his traducers. We know we have a certain class, who will joyfully embrace this opportunity and we expect great efforts will be made to fill the court-house."

Another sample shot:

"A CONTEMPTIBLE SPIRIT.—The *Pioneer* of yesterday indulged in one of its characteristic obscene attacks on the Hutchinson family, because they did not favor it with any patronage. It is true the Hutchinsons labored under many embarrassments. Their musical instruments were broken while in transit to this city, and they could not obtain others. The night was extremely cold, which prevented a large audience, and added to their other difficulties. But the animus of the *Pioneer's* attack is manifested in the following paragraph:

"'Although they sang some ballads quite well, their "liberty, humanity and fraternity" *buffoonery* spoiled it all.'

"It seems, according to this, that to advocate 'liberty and humanity' is *buffoonery*. Of course that Copperhead concern was never guilty of such 'buffoonery.' It never 'spoils it all' with 'liberty and humanity buffoonery.' That isn't the style of rebel papers.

"The Hutchinsons are noted for their patriotism and love of freedom. For years they have sung their songs of freedom, and that, too, when they were ostracized by a portion of the community for doing so. Now, the sentiment of the community agrees with their songs, and it is only occasionally that a nasty cur flings his obscene filth upon them. The Hutchinsons can ask no higher compliment than abuse from this ribald sheet, for their 'liberty, humanity and fraternity *buffoonery.*'"

The above was in the *St. Paul Press*, afterwards consolidated with the *Pioneer*, which it so severely criticizes. It might seem that the words it quotes hardly deserved so harsh treatment, but the portions of the notice it does not quote were fully as bad as it says.

About this time the *Troy Times* printed a letter from a correspondent, who said in part:

"Sirs: On one page of the *Whig* this morning I waded through a column of muddle, designed to refute the almost self-evident fact of the paper's disloyalty, and on another page, I find the following:

"'The Republican organ which brought a negro minstrel to task a few days since, for singing a harmless verse about the times, will, no doubt, feel much aggrieved at the Hutchinsons, for giving utterance to the abolition hymns of last evening.'

"The editor and his associates can see no difference between the meanness and pusillanimity of a public performer, in deriding and abusing a poor, despised, oppressed race — too humble to retort upon their persecutors with either wit or violence — and the utterance by the Hutchinsons of sentiments expressive of future universal freedom, future happiness, and future deliverance from oppression. We should not be surprised to read in the columns of the *Whig* any day some such article as this: 'Dr. Beman, who took a chap to task a few days since for singing publicly a harmless verse about the desirableness of following lying and cheating as a profession, will no doubt feel much aggrieved to learn that the choir of an uptown Methodist Church sang publicly, and with utter shamefacedness, last Sunday, the following abolition hymn, written by one Montgomery:

"'He comes to break oppression,
To set the captive free,
To take away transgression,
And rule in equity.

"'He comes, with succor speedy,
To those who suffer wrong,
To help the poor and needy,
And bid the weak be strong.'"

"'We shall only add, that if the elders of the above referred to church allow the singing of such inflammatory hymns in future, the *Whig* will not hesitate to fearlessly denounce them.'"

Here is a specimen of the fine art of "blowing" from a paper in Springfield, Mass. It will be observed that the effort to conceal the real reason for the dislike of our critics always miscarries. At some point in the article the objection to our advocacy of abolition is unwittingly or otherwise inserted:

"THE HUTCHINSON FAMILY.—The 'Tribe of John' concerted Friday night at Union Hall. John wears a shirt collar of the Byronical style, the size of a horse collar, as a badge of Spiritualism, and has a patriarchical look; that is, John has, not the collar. The collar has a look of affectation, or a bid for notoriety; it looks too much like a quack medicine sign, and it looks as if he had made a mistake in putting his shirt on, and put it on wrong end up. It is fair to presume that John's kind of spirits wear shirts, from his wearing a collar as a badge. John's horse shirt collar is prodigious; it would be just about right for a shirt collar for an elephant, or would make a good shroud for Tom Thumb, or a stay-sail for a '74' ship, or a Fourth of July flag, after the stars are all wiped out, or a cover for an emigrant wagon, or an army tent. It would be all the bedclothes we should suppose John would want. Another gentleman and two ladies accompany John; their singing sounds like ventriloquism, or as if it came up from their toes, and sounds like young thunder. The gentleman who accompanies John looks as if he might be a lady in male attire. The greatest difficulty they seemed to have in singing was they could not bite off the tunes. When they commence unravelling a tune they can't stop its unravelling. The songs they sung were mostly old ones, such as we have heard them sing before. They are charming singers. The young lady stands most too stiff; she looks as if she was froze stiff. We are not much of a judge of music, but we know that if it was not good singing, it was good hollering. The young lady, we think, bids fair to make as fine a singer as there is. We very much doubt if she has her equal of her age in any country. Of John it is not necessary to speak. His reputation is at least United States wide. The other two are star singers. John does not talk distinct enough in making announcements, and their singing is like all singing, the sentiment is Greek to the audience, because the pronunciation, we think, is unnecessarily smothered — an affectation.

We look forward and expect to see a reform in this, when singing words will be as distinct as speaking them, and more melodious, and therefore more captivating. The singers, complained, justly, we presume, of the echo spoiling the effect of their singing. [It was a fact, that this was as miserable a hall, acoustically, as we ever were compelled to sing in.] The young ladies in the audience pronounced the young gentleman singer handsome. Were we a young man, we should pronounce the young lady handsome. John spoiled the programme by making his foolish stereotyped abolition speech that he always makes. The *whole* audience was disgusted by this miserable nonsensical stuff. John proves the old saw true, 'that good singers are never smart.' Democrats that do not wish to be insulted will stay away from these concerts until John mends his political manners. John is a born Yankee, and has never been born again, and we don't think he ever will be. He will always say 'keow' and 'heow,' and sing abolition songs after all the white men are dead, and if all the white women should die, we don't think John would be at a loss what to do, and would be all the time in congenial company and much happier than he is now at times. The young man acted the drunkard a great deal better than a raw hand, and John's face is pretty red for a Yankee, unless eating too many sour apples is the cause of it."

A Western paper said:

"The Hutchinsons gave one of their exhilarating concerts at Brewster Hall, last Thursday evening, and notwithstanding a rainy night, had a full house. It was decidedly the best entertainment that it has been our privilege to enjoy since our advent to Waterford. Patriotism, mirth, sentiment and religion all took their appropriate places in the performance, and called forth rapturous applause from the delighted audience. They sang without stint their 'Songs of Freedom,' for which they were exiled from McClellan's camp a few months ago. We admire the Hutchinsons for the manly advocacy of what they believe, no less than the power and sweetness of their singing, which has won them a world-wide reputation. Let them sing on — sing for truth, liberty, religion and humanity. We wish there were more Hutchinson families, to aid in the world's amelioration."

A paper in Mt. Clemens, Mich., made this comment:

"This is a land of liberty, and a country where freedom of speech and a free expression of opinion are the bulwarks that guard our civil liberties. Such at least has been the proud boast of the American people during the last half-century. But there are some dark spots where a certain class of men yet endeavor to choke down such doctrines and place a gag upon such thoughts as conflict with their own south of Mason and Dixon's line, down in Egypt, Illinois, and here in Mt Clemens, do we occasionally hear of an attempt of this kind. The Hutchinson family of singers (a family whose reputation has gone before them), advertised a concert in this place for last Tuesday evening and secured the Court House for that purpose. But some of the unterrified Democracy having been told by one of their street oracles that they were the Hutchinson family that General McClellan ordered out of the Army of the Potomac because the songs of freedom that they sung to the soldiers had a tendency to 'demoralize the army,' — an effort was at once made on the part of the 'constabulary force' to shut off the exhibition, and on Tuesday night the house was closed against the concert.

"'Some men clothed with a little brief authority,
Play such fantastic tricks as make the devil blush.'

"The operation was repeated on Wednesday night — or attempted to be — but the house was finally opened and lighted. Then another difficulty there was no corporation officer to be found to give the license, hence the concert was a free one, a collection being taken up to defray expenses, etc.

"Now, what is the effect of all this, what impression is naturally created by such a display of backwoods verdancy and lack of cultivation? What do our officials think of accomplishing by descending to such petty political poltroonery as this last exhibition? Sensible people cannot but feel greatly disgusted, and wish for a change."

In Rockford, Ill., there was a Democratic mayor. We gave a concert. At its conclusion, as I stood at the door, a bill of ten dollars for the privilege of singing was presented to me. The concert had not been very remunerative, and this license would eat up all the profits. However, I paid the exorbitant charge, under protest, and writing a letter to the mayor, stating my grievances, left the place. Subsequently I got a letter from the mayor, saying he was sorry the incident had occurred, and also that if I came there again, I could be sure of the freedom of the city. In a few weeks I appeared again in Rockford, and as I passed through the place to fulfil another engagement, left cards of admission for the mayor and city council to another concert I proposed giving. When I returned, I was at the hall to meet my audience, when, just before the time for commencement, while I was standing at the door, I was approached by an officer, who presented me another bill of ten dollars for a license. I was astounded at the act, as I had depended on the assurance of the mayor, and was sure I would not be again molested. To get out of the dilemma for the time being, I said, " I must go and give my concert; I cannot pay the tax." " You will pay or you will not sing," was his tart response. " I will sing and I will not pay," said I, and quick as thought there came into my mind a plan to avoid the payment. So I went on the stage, and told the audience that owing to the inclemency of the weather and for other reasons I had decided to postpone the concert. I inquired how many would consent and the vote was unanimous. I could see the officer in the rear of the hall ready to arrest me. Then I said: " Dear friends, I cannot turn you out in this inclement weather after you have so kindly come here, without giving you a specimen of our singing. It is to be understood, however, that you may all receive your tickets at the door to the postponed concert, and that those who desire may have their money refunded." The audience cheered me, and we then sang the first number on the programme, and continued for an hour and a half, until it was concluded, to the great delight of the auditors. Before we had finished the programme, the cause of the " postponement " was whispered about. When the company dispersed, it was observable that no person asked either for tickets or money. The face of the baffled officer was pitiful to look upon. I was smiling.

"Well," said he, "I'll see that you are waited upon." "Go ahead," I replied, "the concert was postponed. The vote was unanimous, as you saw."

The next morning I waited on the mayor. I told him how I had been treated, and that depending on his letter, I made no effort to secure a license. "Well," said he, "you didn't send us any tickets." I told him, that he was mistaken; I had left tickets with the clerk of the hotel. This surprised him, and he said he would go and see about it. I went with him. The clerk said he put the tickets in the post-office, directed to the mayor. We went to the post-office, and there the postal clerk found the package. After this convincing proof that I had not ignored the city government, and had told the truth about the matter, the mayor was ready to do anything. He went with me to the office of the city attorney. He opened the door and introduced me. The attorney shook hands and laughed. "Well" said he, "I'll defend you with no expense, whatever comes." He had heard of the affair, and was immensely pleased at the way I had escaped from the difficulty. He went to the clerk and told him to stay all process. He had already been instructed to do something to bring me to terms, if anything could be done, which he doubted.

Before taking final leave of the subject of the expulsion from the Potomac, I desire to say in justice to the memory of the heroic General Kearney, that I subsequently heard that long before his death while facing the enemy in battle, he expressed his regret at his action; as he had become fully convinced of the worth of emancipation, and entirely in sympathy with the government in its conduct of the war.

The story of our experience, with the Whittier song,

was published in practically every Union paper in the North, and, I was told, in nearly every paper in England.

During this year, 1862, on February 17th, my youngest son was born at Lynn. I named him "Judson Whittier," for my lamented brother and the poet whose song had led to such momentous experiences. Though Judson's health has always been frail, he still lives to be my daily companion. During his childhood he was often with the family on its travels and participated in its entertainments. His gentle, loving soul, and spirit of devotion and helpfulness have bound him with most tender cords to my heart, and these sentiments have of course been strengthened by the necessary attention and care required by his infirmities.

The year 1863 was the year of Jubilee, for with January came emancipation, for which we had so long labored and prayed. I was singing in northern New York at the time the proclamation was promulgated, and recall that I was taking a tramp between Sandy Hill and Glens Falls with my agent, Cyrus Brett, when I heard the news. At last the sky was clear, and we were full of grand expectation of noble results.

After a pleasant experience during the spring in the region named, Brett left us and went to Long Island, where he held summer singing-schools and conventions for a while. At Eagle Bridge, N. Y., I had met a man by the name of Jack Whitcomb, who was a fine harpist. He believed we could work together well, and desired an engagement. Sending my wife and children to Mont Vernon, N. H., for a while, I agreed to go to Morristown, N. J., for one trial. The concert pleased me so much that I made an engagement with him for a number of concerts. We went to Boston and from thence to Portland. Then I took a large number of bills and got on board the Maine Central road. At each town along the line, I dropped off a bunch of bills with a card to the postmaster requesting him to engage the largest church for me. We went up the road as far as Farmington, giving concerts with good success. The young man would play the harp, and I played my violin, the programme of songs being thus pleasantly varied. On our arrival in each town we would go to the hall and he would rehearse, the music of his harp being very soothing to me.

Then I went back to Lynn, Whitcomb going with me. Asa had just returned from a concert trip to Cape Cod. His wife had been with him, and also Fred. His daughter Abby had been unable to sing, owing to a bad throat. I found Asa anxious to join me in some concerts on High Rock. So I sent to Mont Vernon for my children, and they joined Asa, Whitcomb and myself, in some as unique concerts as we had ever given. They were given on the crest of old High Rock, and the tickets were five cents. The people turned out *en masse*. We had a half-dozen or more ticket sellers and takers, stationed at the various approaches to the rock. During the day we would wind balls of old cloths, and soak them in oil. These would be placed in pans on the top of posts, at intervals, and lighted after dark. They burned quite steadily for an hour or more, and boys stood ready to replace them when they burned out. There was a *café* for refreshments in the observatory. The audience gathered mainly on the eastern side of the observatory. Although thousands came to the rock every night, no accident befell any person who clambered up the hill. During this series of concerts we brought out "Rally round the Flag,

ON HIGH ROCK IN WAR TIME—(p. 416)

Boys," and "We're Tenting To-night on the Old Campground."

"Rally round the Flag" was the composition of George F. Root, and its history has been given in his own words. A very handsomely illustrated gift edition of "Tenting To-night" was published a few years since, but no history of it was attempted. It may be appreciated here.

"Tenting To-night" was first heard in public from our lips, on the summit of grand old High Rock. Its author was Walter Kittredge. He was a native of Reed's Ferry, N. H. His sisters came to Milford to school when he was a young man, and later worked in the cotton mill in that town. During one of his visits to them Kittredge became acquainted with Joshua. He took lessons of Joshua, and finally went on the road with him giving concerts. The two, with Kate Hutchinson, Brother Judson's daughter, gave concerts through New Hampshire and Vermont for six years.

In 1863 Kittredge was drafted into the army. That night he went to bed the prey of many conflicting emotions. His heart was fired with patriotism, but full of grief at leaving his home, and full of dread of war. In the middle of the night he awoke with the burden still on his mind. He thought of the many dear boys already gone over to the unseen shore, killed in battle or dead from disease in the camps, of the unknown graves, of the sorrowful homes; of the weary waiting for the end of the cruel strife, and the sorrow in the camps, of the brave boys waiting for the coming battle, which might be their last. Suddenly the thoughts began to take form in his mind. He arose and began to write:

> " We're tenting to-night on the old camp-ground;
>   Give us a song to cheer
> Our weary hearts, — a song of home,
>   And friends we loved so dear.
>
> " We are tired of war on the old camp-ground.
>   Many are dead and gone
> Of the brave and true who've left their homes;
>   Others have been wounded long
>
> "Many are the hearts that are weary to-night,
>   Wishing for the war to cease;
> Many are the hearts looking for the right,
>   To see the dawn of peace.
>   Tenting to-night,
>   Tenting to-night,
>   Tenting on the old camp-ground."

Being a musician, a tune for the song easily came to Mr. Kittredge's mind, and after copying both words and music, he at once came to Lynn, and went to Brother Asa, at Bird's Nest Cottage, High Rock. After they had looked it over together they called me in to sing the solo. Asa sang the bass and the children joined us on the chorus. Kittredge at once made a contract with Asa to properly arrange and publish the song, for one-half the profits. That night we sung it for the first time on High Rock. As everybody knows, when Ditson brought out the composition, it was an instant success. In less than two years its author and my brother had a thousand dollars each from the profits of the song.

Our next venture was a series of concerts in Boston. We chartered the Meionaon, and had good success. Finally, the tribes separated again, and I went West, taking in the small towns at first, in order to get the company properly united in their work. Just before I started, Bernard Covert, the composer of the immortal "Sword of Bunker Hill," and "Jamie's on the Stormy

Sea," came to me and desired to act as our advance agent. This work he did to my satisfaction. Meanwhile, Asa's tribe took a more southern route. My harpist left me to join the Peak Family.

Our first concert in 1864 was given at Saxonville, Mass., on January 4th. Then in succession came concerts at Concord, Groton, Feltonville, Gardner, Fitchburg (where on the following evening, Sunday, we gave a sacred concert for the benefit of the Sanitary Commission, Covert singing with us), Shirley, South Royalston, Orange, Athol, Montague, Greenfield, Shelbourne Falls, Deerfield, South Deerfield, Conway, Amherst, Belchertown, Florence, Easthampton, Holyoke, Hadley Falls, Holyoke again (this was a Sunday evening concert, and a minister present pronounced it better than a prayer meeting), Old Hadley, Hatfield, Ashfield, Cummington (when I sang at the centennial anniversary of Bryant's birth, at Cummington in 1894, I was told that I sang in town many years before, but was unable to recall it, until my diary refreshed my memory, then I recalled singing there with Frederick Douglass and Remond as speakers in a Sunday antislavery meeting at the invitation of the Brown Brothers, E. R. and D. L.), Williamsburg, Thompsonville (Conn.), Suffield, Windsor Locks, Windsor, Chicopee Falls, Hartford (where we gave a benefit to Covert in addition to our regular concert. He was a dear good fellow, unselfish and kind-hearted and very suggestive. His selections of songs were always of the very best, but physical disability led me to let him go a little later), Meriden, Plainville, Winstead, Waterbury, Naugatuck, New Haven, Bridgeport (where we went to the campground and sung to a regiment of colored soldiers), Norwalk, Danbury, Ridgefield, Wilton, and thence to

New York City; and in Brooklyn, on Sunday, March 27th, we heard our loved Beecher preach once more. On the following day we went again to Plymouth Church, to attend the funeral of Owen Lovejoy, brother of the Illinois martyr, and the member of Congress who introduced the McClellan resolutions, mentioned. That night we sang in Tarrytown, and followed with concerts in Haverstraw, Nyack (where we had first met Chaplain Yard, of Potomac renown, then pastor of a Methodist church), Piermont, Brunswick (N. J.), Princeton, Trenton, Lambertville, Newton, Doylestown, Bristol, Mt. Holly and Philadelphia. I lost my instruments on my arrival at Philadelphia, and we gave one concert with no accompaniments. Here we met Anna Dickinson, and had many interesting conversations regarding the future of the nation.

After a few days in Philadelphia and Baltimore we went to Washington. Here I was for the time the guest of Hon. John B. Alley, joining him in holding numerous receptions and also visited the White House. Frank B. Carpenter was at this time at work on his great painting, "The Signing of the Emancipation Proclamation." One day Chase was with me. Stanton was at that time away from the city, and as Chase was that day to pose for his portrait in the picture, Carpenter asked me to take Stanton's place. So on that day I posed in the place of the War Secretary. Any person who examines the picture will see that when Chase posed it was necessary for Stanton, or some one in his place, to be with him.

Several concerts followed in Philadelphia and vicinity. While singing here word came to me that a man had been operating in New York State, in the vicinity of the Hudson River, in a way to exasperate the people and do us injury. He secured some of our programmes and announcements and had duplicates printed. With these he would visit a town, announce the coming of the family, sell all the tickets possible, and just before the date set, abscond with the money. Next word came that the swindler had got into Pennsylvania, not far from us — that is, some sixty miles away. He had come to a town, and some people happening to know we were not in the vicinity, telegraphed me to come up. He had meanwhile got some money, but aroused so much suspicion that he was anxious to get away. He said he would go to a certain boarding-house and see if the Hutchinsons had arrived. Others went too and learned that the Hutchinsons were not expected. On that he was faced down, taken back to the hall, placed on the platform, pelted with questions he could not answer, and finally succumbed to the demands for the money taken and sadly drew out his last dollar from his pocket and restored it. He was arrested and brought to trial, but as I had not arrived, the judge let him go before I came, and he at once put himself out of sight. Twenty minutes after his release I came into town. Some of the people were anxious to re-arrest him, but as the money had been returned, and he had been already taught a lesson by his experience, I did not care to press the matter.

In the course of the next two months we had worked our way back through New Jersey, New York, Connecticut and Rhode Island to Lynn. Then we went down to Cape Cod for some concerts, after which we allowed ourselves about two weeks of rest at High Rock and Milford. That was all the vacation we got that year. On September 23d we opened at Wrentham a series of concerts that were to extend across the States to Minneapolis and beyond, down the Mississippi to St. Louis and back over another route. It was July 7th of the following year before I saw Lynn again, and there was practically no rest from concerts in all that time.

I engaged "Cousin Maud" as soprano for this trip. Her name was Morgiana M. Porter, and she was a niece of my wife, daughter of her sister Caroline. My daughter Viola sang the contralto parts, and Henry sang the bass. Morgiana was rather too long a word to suit my ideas, so I changed its wearer's name to Maud. She became one of the pleasantest and most appreciated members of our company, and its survivors recall with satisfaction the months she travelled with them. Our first task was to have our pictures taken, singly and in groups, and have them printed by hundreds. Bowers, a Lynn photographer, did most of this work. I was pretty well acquainted with Mr. Bowers. He is now in the Lynn city government, and is a veteran. Once when I was in Saratoga Springs, I was shown the picture of an old woman who was quite a character in the place. She lived some two miles out, and came into town every day, begging for supplies. She was a harmless and picturesque person in her ancient sun-bonnet and shawl, with her basket and cane. I went out to see her, and found her face old and seamed and her whole appearance antiquated and quite out of date. I secured one of her pictures, and when I got home took it to Bowers. "Here" said I, "do you want to see a picture of Moll Pitcher?" The woman seemed the embodiment of what Lynn's famous fortune-teller must have been. Bowers borrowed the picture and making some copies of it, put one in his show-case, marked "Moll Pitcher." It created great excitement. The decrepit and toothless old settlers were called in, and all unanimously declared that the likeness was perfect, as they recalled her. They well remembered that old sun-bonnet and that old shawl. There could be no doubt of the genuineness of the portrait, which had from some source unknown so fortunately come to light. Life-size copies of the photograph were made, and the next history of Lynn that appeared contained the picture. It was a long time before any one had the temerity to question the authenticity of the portrait, the real history of which is here given for the first time. One day a waggish sort of chap examined the picture critically and then said to the satisfied photographer, "How in time did Moll Pitcher ever get a modern Bay State shawl?" Bowers at once saw the point, and cornered the market for Moll Pitcher photographs.

Our route led us first through some Rhode Island towns, then into Connecticut and New York. We gave one concert in Brooklyn, and while there we met Rev. J. B. Merwin, who with Chaplain Yard was so closely connected with our Potomac experience. Merwin was during the war a chaplain-at-large. He gave temperance lectures, and did other moral and religious work, wherever duty or inclination called him. We made a quick trip across the State, stopping only at Elmira, and were soon singing in Ohio, at Ashtabula, Painesville, Oberlin, Toledo, and elsewhere, then at one or two Michigan towns and to Chicago. Then at Battle Creek, Kalamazoo, Detroit and many other Michigan towns, and into Minnesota and Wisconsin. At Rochester I observed that the pastry was poor, and thought it would be a kindness to confide the fact to the landlord of the hotel. So I told him the crust was so hard one couldn't get a knife through it. He politely replied that it was made so on purpose; people came up there hungry, and it had to be made hard so they couldn't eat it.

We sung in Faribault. Years before, the brothers sung in this place when there were only a few houses, and one clapboarded house used for a hotel. But we had from three to five hundred people at our concert, and at its close resolutions were adopted to build a public assembly-room and name it "Hutchinson Hall." General Shields was present at the time, I remember. On this occasion we chartered a team at Faribault agreeing to pay so much a day to the driver to take us to Hutchinson and so on up the Mississippi River. We sang in St. Peters Friday night and in Mankato Saturday. Then we set out over the prairie fifty or sixty miles to Hutchinson, running the risk of perishing in a blizzard, for it was the 3d of December and a storm was raging. We lost our way, but really didn't realize our danger. Finally we came to a house and rapped on our carriage, to arouse the inhabitants. Somebody opened the window. We inquired the way to Hutchinson. Meanwhile the girls, who were back in the carriage, were giggling and making so much noise that in the storm the man could not hear us. Finally he banged the window down and left us to our fate, with no reply. However, we reached Hutchinson at two o'clock the next day, with no damage.

In our wanderings through the storm we came on a stack of hay. From this we groped our way into a barn-yard, which we soon discovered to be that of Mr. McCuen, the man who was kept in Hutchinson by the illness of his daughter at the time of the Indian raid. He gave us a warm welcome, and we found refreshments and sleep in his home.

We gave a concert on Monday and then proceeded to Glencoe, Shakopee, St. Paul, Fort Snelling, Minneapolis, St. Cloud, Monticello, Stillwater, Hudson, Hastings and Red Wing. Here Henry left us and went back to Hutchinson, where he stayed many months, being temporarily weary of concerting. I grieved over his decision, but made the best of it. He bought an axe at St. Paul, and in a short time, though having no previous experience, had cut one hundred cords of wood.

At Austin I met a man who had been canvassing for Greeley's "American Conflict," in Iowa. He told me he could give me the names of at least ten places where we could have a great crowd of people at our concerts. I made up ten or twelve bundles of bills, and sent them adrift. Each was directed to the postmaster of the place to which it was sent, requesting him to act as agent, and giving instructions in as simple terms as possible, to engage the largest church or hall in the place and post the bills conspicuously; to have notice of the concerts given in any previous entertainments that might be given, and also put notices in the papers, extending complimentary tickets whereever services were rendered. The result was ten concerts, netting me about fifteen hundred dollars. My method of proceeding at the church or hall was to have the people when they arrived at the place walk in and take seats. Then a short time before commencement I would take a box of tickets and station myself near the pulpit platform and ask those who had not already purchased tickets to come and get them. Often one person would be delegated to purchase fifteen or twenty tickets. Then with my box I would go around and take the tickets up, taking the money of any person who had failed to get one. In this way I could get quite acquainted with the people before the concert commenced.

Our concerts were given in Mitchell, Osage, Charles City, Waverly, Zanesville, Ill., Cedar Falls, Waterloo, Independence, Manchester, Dyersville, Dubuque, Anamosa, Marion, Cedar Rapids, Mt. Vernon, Toledo, Marshalltown, Nevada, Des Moines (here I stood at the door and took between three hundred and four hundred dollars directly into my hands; it was mostly in postal scrip, and my pockets were stuffed with it before I was through), Newton, Grinnell, Marengo, Iowa City, Tipton, DeWitt, Maquoketa, Clinton, Lyons, Fulton, Dixon, Mendota, Sterling, Morrison, La Salle, Davenport, Brockport and Springfield. The proceeds of these concerts were invested in United States interest-bearing notes, as often as I found a broker.

Then we went to St. Louis, where, as I have said in my reference to the far from handsome treatment received by the three brothers in the city a few years before, our reception was of the kindest nature, the mayor proffering courtesies and the people turning out to the entertainments in good numbers. We stayed several days, and were given the "freedom of the city," so to speak. John B. Gough was lecturing there at the time, and we had one more opportunity to enjoy the intimate society of the great reformer. He would spend the whole day with us, until the time arrived for him to take his nap, to refresh himself before the lecture. He was the jolliest companion imaginable. Some eight years later he gave me his autograph. I told him I was in the habit, when giving an autograph, of stating my age, weight, and prevailing disease, so he did likewise: "John B. Gough — age, 56; weight, 173; disease, salt-rheum."

Then we went into Illinois and Indiana and thence into Ohio, singing on our way. I had reached Hudson, O., when the news came, April 15th, of the assassination of President Lincoln by J. Wilkes Booth. There, as everywhere else, there was the greatest consternation and indignation. I knew so few in the place who could understand the case, that I jumped on the train and went to Cleveland. Here groups of men were everywhere gathered, discussing the nation's sorrow. Meetings were held and speeches made, full of patriotism and vengeance. We gave no concert that night. We could not sing, for we had no heart to do it. The next day, Sunday, I sang in church. On the following day W. Milton Clark joined our company as bass singer, as there seemed no probability of Henry's giving up the freedom of life in Hutchinson for the stage that year. It was over a month before we left Ohio, and then we went into the oil region of Pennsylvania, where we had unusual success, and from thence proceeded by way of New York State. J. Al. Sawtell, a family connection of my wife, was our agent at this time. We were at Fulton on July 4th. There was a celebration, at which Clark and I sung four songs. I played games with some five hundred children. In one I got the whole of them in one game, holding each other's hands and travelling in a circle. It took a big field to accommodate them.

Three days later I was in Lynn. Notwithstanding the depressing fact that I lost eight hundred dollars in one lump from my pocket while in St. Louis, and had suffered slightly from changes in the company, after settling with my singers I had five thousand dollars to show as the profits of the trip.

The fine observatory which had crowned the summit

of High Rock for so many years was gone. It was fired on the night of the receipt of the news that Lee had surrendered, and made a fine bonfire for the benefit of the surrounding country, albeit a little expensive for its owners, Brother Asa and myself. To make the situation a little more interesting, if not amusing, I was told after my return by a lad who ingenuously confessed himself to be one of the incendiaries, that the conflagration took place by my consent, if not at my request. The papers told the same story, and it is so recorded in the history of Lynn. While on my way to the depot, when starting on my Western tour, I met Charles Luscomb, a painter and neighbor, near his home on Pearl Street. There were others with him. He said: "John, we men think it would be a capital thing, when the news of the surrender of the Rebel army comes, to touch fire to the old observatory. Will you consent?" "That would be a fine thing," said I, sarcastically, and passed on. My remark was evidently taken to mean an assent to the project.

The summer was spent in Lynn, with the exception of a trip to Milford, and another to the mountains with my wife, Viola and Clark. Late in August the same singers started towards the West once more. The 31st we spent with the Oneida Community and the 3d and 4th of September with Gerrit Smith, at Peterboro, N. Y. We always cherished a high regard for him, and I have letters from the great reformer among my choicest possessions.

We found our old friend George W. Putnam, who was once private secretary to Charles Dickens, acting as agent for Mr. Smith in handling his estate. Mr. Smith attended a concert we gave in the church founded principally through his gifts. I recall that I sang "Will the New Year come To-night, Mother?" The people were greatly affected by the song. Mr. Smith told me afterwards that as he listened he felt a sudden inclination to weep. He sought to suppress it, and, as he looked around, saw all those near him using their handkerchiefs. Then he found the tears running down his own cheeks and he said to himself, "cry on" He said he never tried so hard to keep from crying, and failed. In 1875 I wrote the following tribute to his memory:

"We honor and we emulate the honest, true and brave
Whose heart of love and tenderness the warmest friendship gave
With sympathetic action, and impulse all for good,
He labored long and truly, and firm for right he stood.

"Faithful as a father, husband, brother, friend,
Generous, philanthropic, looking to the end;
The noble man of fortune, a prince of loyal deed
With heart of broadest charity, a boon for human need

"We loved his manly bearing, his voice so rich and sweet,
Breathing out Freedom's sentiments when friends of truth would meet
That voice we'll hear no longer, but the great truths that he said
Shall be remembered evermore, though the reformer's dead"

After a few weeks in Ohio we returned to Lynn again, and in October made a tour through Rhode Island and Connecticut and thence into New Jersey, where we finished the year 1865.

CHAPTER XI.

MORAL REFORM WORK.

"Who votes for woman suffrage now
Will add new laurels to his brow,
His children's children with holy fire
Will chant and praise their patriot sire.
No warrior's wreath of glory shed
A brighter lustre o'er the head,
Than he who battles selfish pride,
And votes with woman, side by side
　　Oh! we'll do nothing wrong
　　But sing you this song,
　　The good time for woman
　　Is coming right along
　　We'll sing you this song,
　　The chorus we'll prolong,
　　The good time, good time,
　　Vote it right along."

THE day of emancipation had come. The war was over, and the necessity for singing the songs of freedom, except as a reminiscence, had passed. But ours was a moral mission, nevertheless, and we still felt there were many reforms demanding our attention and support. One of these was temperance. Another, peace. Still another, the legitimate offspring of abolition, was universal suffrage. The ballot was in the hand of the negro, as a citizen of the Union. We believed it should be in the hand of woman, not only as her absolute right, but as a temperance and reform measure. The years following the war, therefore, found us allied with the temperance workers as ever, and also singing for uni-

CLOSING EXERCISES, CHRISTIAN COMMISSION.   (p. 41)

versal suffrage as we had formerly sung for universal freedom and brotherhood.

We commenced 1866 with my son Henry still in Minnesota, and the concert company consisting of my wife and Viola, Milton Clark, bass singer, and myself.

In January we went to Washington. We gave several concerts here, in Rev. Mr. Garrett's church and elsewhere. The colored people gave us great ovations. We boarded at the same house with Schuyler Colfax, soon to be Vice-President, and ate with him at table. He took a great liking to Viola, and was very kind in his attentions to her. I had many pleasant conversations with him in regard to the condition of the country. I found him a true American, and loved and honored him.

On February 11th we attended the closing exercises of the United States Christian Commission, at the Capitol. Rev. Prof. Lemuel Moss, in his "Annals of the Christian Commission," has given a detailed story of the exercises, which were listened to with the closest attention by an audience completely filling the Hall of Representatives. The crowd was so great that many were turned away. The hall was draped in memory of Lincoln, who took a prominent part in the third anniversary, a year before. Speaker Colfax presided. The meeting opened with the singing of "Jesus shall reign where'er the sun," by the vast congregation, led by Philip Phillips. Rev. Dr. Boynton, chaplain of the House, lead in prayer, and the Scripture was read by Rev. Dr. Taylor, secretary of the American Bible Society. After a speech by Colfax, George H. Stuart, chairman of the Commission, read letters from Secretary Stanton, Secretary Seward, Chief Justice Chase, Generals Grant, Sherman, Meade, Howard, Thomas, Butler,

Ord, Meigs, Surgeon-General Barnes, and Admiral Farragut. After speaking by Charles Demond, of Boston, Phillips sung "Your Mission," and then followed speaking by Rear-Admiral Davis, Rev. Herrick Johnson, Hon. J. R. Doolittle of Wisconsin, Major-General Augur, Rev B. W. Chidlaw, of Ohio, Bishop Simpson, and the home secretary of the Commission, Mr. Moss. We sung "I live for those who love me," and "The Good Time Coming." Although he sent a letter, General Grant was there. I remember he sat directly behind us as we sung, and congratulated Viola on the success of our efforts.

While in Washington we had the privilege of listening to Bancroft's eulogy on Abraham Lincoln in the Capitol; a fine deliverance. After a few concerts in Baltimore we went into Pennsylvania. Our tour through this State was followed by a long-to-be-remembered singing trip to Lake Superior.

For many years the greater part of my financial investments had been made through Ludlow Patton, husband of my Sister Abby. He had been quite successful as a Wall Street banker and broker, and had a reputation for conservatism. But a short time before the war, I had a dream. I awoke in the morning with the suggestion in my mind, "Buy gold; it will be at a premium as a result of the war." Thinking the matter over, I was convinced that there was some merit in the impression, and immediately went to Ludlow, and urged him to take whatever money of mine he had on deposit, together with all he could spare and whatever he could borrow, and buy gold. I told him I fully believed the coming conflict would place the metal at a premium. He did not agree with me. "You'll lose your interest," said he. He was then paying me six per cent. He said he was opposed to buying gold under the peculiar circumstances. Rather abashed at the reception of my scheme, I subsided and went home. Before the war was over, gold was selling for $2.60. The next morning at the same hour I awoke with another impression, "Buy cotton; it will greatly advance in price." I made haste to Ludlow with this — reaching the office half an hour before his arrival — and asked him if it would not be a good scheme to buy all the cotton we could get hold of and store it until the demand for it came. This suggestion was also received with indifference. Undoubtedly, he argued, cotton would advance in price, but the charges for storage would eat up all the profit, and he said that dealing in cotton, or speculation, was out of his line. Cotton was then selling at 11 cents a pound. It went up to $1.65. When my dream prophecies were realized, Ludlow told his friends on the street of it, and thereafter they used to come to me often and ask my opinion of the money market.

My son Henry left singing and agriculture, for a while, and connected himself with the engineering corps of John C. Campbell in surveying the route of the St. Croix and Lake Superior Railroad Company through the white-pine forests of northern Wisconsin, from the St. Croix River to Lake Superior. He rose rapidly in position, and when the survey was completed he retired with honors, and with the compliments of the chief engineer.

When we started for Lake Superior the survey was in progress. When we reached Superior City it had been completed, and at our hotel we found my son Henry, together with Lewis A. Campbell, nephew of John C. Campbell, the chief engineer of the survey. L. A. Campbell was a promising young man, son of

Judge Campbell of the New York supreme bench, and a veteran of the war, having been confined many months in Libby and other prisons. It was a fateful meeting so far as he and another member of my party was concerned. Within a year there was an engagement and not many months after, my daughter became Viola Hutchinson Campbell. Inviting both these young men to join us, we soon reached the steamboat with all our impedimenta, and put off on the lake, toward Milwaukee. All the towns along the lake gave us very remunerative concerts. We visited many of the copper mines and sung to the miners, on one occasion seven hundred feet below the surface. We obtained some valuable mineralogical specimens. We saw one nugget of copper which had caused more than two years' work in removal. It had been conveyed to the surface by powerful steam appliances. It weighed several tons. We learned that the more copper there was in a body the more unprofitable it was to mine, as it could not be blasted and it was difficult to excavate about it. The work must be done with chisels five or six feet long. Powder has no effect on the metal. We were told that the squatters and miners had an understanding that if any one found a piece of silver the fact was not to be known to the employers, but the ore became the joint property of those present when it was found.

Mr. Campbell left us at Milwaukee and we continued our concerts, keeping in the direction of Hutchinson. We arrived there August 31st. On the previous day we were stuck in a slough. This deep, bog-like hole, impassable during heavy rains, was crossed by a bridge. Our horses failed us, and backed us off the bridge into the slough. We finally got the horses out, and by using oxen on the solid ground, attached by a long chain to the carriage, saved that also. We stayed in Hutchinson or the vicinity for quite a while. I had gained a residence there, so that on November 6th I was able to vote in favor of that town as the county seat. We were disappointed, however. The honor went elsewhere. Going back in the direction of Milwaukee on the 29th of November we were privileged to sing at the close of a lecture by our dear old friend John B. Gough. The closing days of that year were spent in Chicago.

The early weeks of 1867 were devoted to concerting in Illinois and Iowa. At Iowa City we found the landlord of the hotel to be Robert Hutchinson, who used to sing in the choir of the Baptist church in Milford with me in boyhood days. At Des Moines we spent an hour with the governor of the State, talking brotherhood. In February we were in Nebraska, and had at least one notable as well as unpleasant experience. We had been several days in Nebraska City, and determined to cross the Missouri River on the ice to Bartlett, where we intended to take the cars to another place. In going over we found we were near to floating ice. In the midst of our dilemma, little Judson, then five years old, pleased to be at liberty, ran toward an opening. Viola ran after him, and caught him just before he would have fallen in. Some one on the shore, seeing our danger, tied a rope to a canoe, and got us ashore, two at a time. Our bills were out for concerts for ten days ahead, but news came that the track was destroyed by a recent great storm, so that we could not proceed. There seemed to be nothing to do but make ourselves as comfortable as possible. There was no hotel, but fortunately there were plenty of bags of grain and corn in the depot, and making a fire to keep us warm, all the waiting passengers spent the night on the bags. The next day I was able to secure a room for my wife near by, but the rest of the party stayed in the depot three days.

Then we went to Council Bluffs. Here we met Mrs. Bloomer, the promoter of the costume, who told how she came to adopt it. The dress had been worn in the Oneida Community before she appeared in public with it. Singing our way back through Illinois and Ohio, we gave our last concert for the season at Toledo, April 22d, and then went to Lynn, where we arrived on the 24th, after an absence of nearly two years.

Less than a month was spent at home, and then we began to make plans to go into the field of reform in dead earnest. The Legislature of Kansas that year voted to submit to the people three propositions for amendments to the Constitution, one to strike from it the word "white," thus enfranchising all male citizens of the age of twenty-one years, without respect to color; another striking out the word "male," thus enfranchising all women of the age of twenty-one years, without regard to color; third, restricting the elective franchise to loyal persons. The result of the action was to inaugurate one of the historic political battles of our time, the first contest for woman suffrage in this country.

During the spring, Lucy Stone had gone into Kansas lecturing in behalf of the emancipation of woman. With the exception of her advocacy of masculine dress and the fact that though a married woman she continued to use the name of "Mrs. Lucy Stone," the impression she created was of the most favorable character. When she returned, she communicated to me her conviction that the Hutchinsons could do a work for suffrage as singing evangelists second only to that they

REPRESENTATIVE WOMEN—(p. 457)

did for abolition, by going into Kansas in this crisis. I remembered how years before I had been disappointed in my plans to go to "Bleeding Kansas," and saw in this opening an opportunity to do for the State in another direction what I had been unable to do then. I also was thinking seriously of buying a new township, and establishing the "Hutchinson" in Kansas that failed of being founded when Hutchinson, Minnesota, was settled. Brother Asa was living in the other Hutchinson, and I felt like leaving it to him, as he had become so fully identified with it. Mrs. Stone later put me in communication with Colonel S. N. Wood, of Cottonwood Falls, Kan., chairman of the committee of prominent friends of universal suffrage, who had taken up the cudgels in favor of all three of the proposed amendments. I was not long in making an agreement with him to go campaigning in the State. Susan B. Anthony, Elizabeth Cady Stanton and other prominent speakers were engaged, and it was agreed that the campaign should commence in earnest on the second day of September, and close November 4th, the election occurring on the following day. Recalling my advice to Lucy Stone several years before, that she should charge an admission fee for her lectures, on the ground that the people absorbed reform ideas fully as well if they had paid for them. I made no stipulation for salary from my Kansas friends, but I arranged to give paid concerts in as many of the large communities as possible, agreeing to speak in the neighborhood of a half-hour in addition to singing. The arrangement of places and dates was left to the committee, and it also took care that hotel accommodations, stabling for our horses, and halls were provided. This plan proved satisfactory to us, and apparently so to the committee, for immediately on the completion of the campaign, one of its prominent members started out with us on a tour of temperance concerts under the auspices of the State Temperance Society.

But before we started for Kansas a great many preliminaries must be arranged. On May 19th I commenced to pack my carryall for transportation West. This was not the famous carryall which our old "John horse" and his mate drew through New England and New York, but one of three similar vehicles built in Milford for the three brothers some years before. I packed two large trunks with bedding and household utensils, and stowed them away in the carryall before boxing it for its long journey. The trunks were to be left in Hutchinson. Then I billed the carriage for Milwaukee, and sent it on its way. On May 25th I left home and went to New York. The following day I spent at Orange, N. J., with Sister Abby, and at the home of Lucy Stone and her husband, Henry B Blackwell. We discussed Kansas matters mostly. I had been requested to sing as many suffrage songs as possible in the coming campaign, but found on examination that the national hymnology was surprisingly deficient in that class of poetry. I therefore wrote to a large number of our American song-writers, asking contributions to the cause. The responses were not numerous, and so I decided that I must depend largely on my own resources

Before I left New York I completed the details of the Kansas engagement After spending a happy half-day with my valued friend Frank B. Carpenter, I took the train for the West. I stopped over in Buffalo long enough to gently dun a man who bought a horse of me several years before. Perhaps the delay of my debtor was caused by a lack of enthusiasm over the fine points of the animal. He was a high-spirited horse. I bought him in Milford some years before for three hundred and fifty dollars. He was handsome, but his beauty did not make up for his drawbacks. Kicking was his particular pastime, but in addition to that he displayed a refinement of genius in plotting unpleasant situations for those who attempted to be kind to him, that would have given him a warm welcome to some anarchistic body. He amused himself by knocking me over as opportunity occurred. My nephew and namesake, John W. Hutchinson, a son of David, went into his stall one day, and he calmly crowded him to the wall until he begged for mercy. Asa's father-in-law carried the marks of a kick from him as a memento of a visit to Lynn. I was playing with him in the field one day when he arose and tried to dash me with his hoofs. I abstained from further amusement of that character. Another pleasurable pastime, for him, was trying to fall upon me, as a manifestation of playfulness. I sold him, and the purchaser made me wait ten years before he settled partially for him and he is not all paid for yet.

When I returned from the West, I had left Viola with Henry in Toledo, and before making this trip I had received word of her engagement to Lewis Campbell. I reached Toledo on May 29th, and found all well and happy. I spent the next two days persuading Viola to postpone her wedding, and go with Henry and myself on the Kansas campaign. When she finally consented, she decided to go home first, and to return and meet me in Kansas September 1st.

Then Henry and I started for Milwaukee, arriving June 4th. We made our home with Mrs. Severance, a physician and notable lecturer, and there I met Louise L. Whittier, a young lady who so interested me that I composed a song, "Louisa," which I dedicated to her. We also met a Mr. Watson, who afterwards married Mrs. Severance, and we agreed to give a concert with him on the following Monday evening. At Darien, our carriage came, forwarded from Milwaukee, and then we had a good time looking up a team. Finally we bought two gray mares, for which we paid four hundred dollars, a high price for the West. After getting harness and other necessary things, we started off. A short distance out of Darien we discovered that the gauge of our eastern carriage was too wide for western ruts, so turning back, we found a blacksmith shop. Henry took off his coat, and in two and one-half hours' time they had cut off the axle some five inches. On this road I was reminded of an experience of some previous years. Driving in from Milwaukee I came to a village where I wanted to get some blacksmithing done for my horse. I observed a big bull chained to a post. He was moaning as if in trouble. I stepped up to his head. He was making a musical though guttural sound, very like the basal tone of a bagpipe. At once I struck up the air of "The Campbells are Coming" in the same key. The villagers paused in astonishment at this unusual duet, the windows came up and somebody appropriately shouted out, amid the cheering, "Bully for you!" It was the oddest concert I ever gave. I had to take breath frequently. But the animal seemed to be able to sing a full minute without a breath.

In company with our friend Watson, we gave several concerts at Beloit, Janesville, Evansville and other places. At Elkhart we met our old friend J. P. Webster, author of the favorite ballad, "Lorena," but to be better known to fame as the composer of "The Sweet By-and-By." Our first meeting with him was in 1843. He came to the ante-room of our concert hall in New York, and was introduced to us by Bernard Covert, composer of "The Sword of Bunker Hill." We sang to him, and Covert sang to us. I do not remember that Webster sang, though I believe he had a promising voice. During their half-hour's stay, Covert said to me, "Mr. Webster has come to the city sanguine of success, but he hasn't a dollar." I took out five dollars and gave it to him. Webster never forgot this. After that we met him frequently. At this time he was a saloon-keeper. The drink habit grew upon him, and blighted his life. He had a nature that could suffer as much without breaking down as anybody, and he did suffer. He was kind-hearted, and despite his faults, one could not help loving him. In company with Dr. S. F. Bennett, he composed many songs beside those I have mentioned. "Who shall be my angel bride?" was one, which he gave me, and which I sang often.

A few years ago Dr. Bennett told the story of the composition of "The Sweet By-and-By." "At that time," said he, "I resided in Elkhart, Wis., where I kept an apothecary store, and was associated with Joseph P. Webster, a music teacher, in the production of musical works, I composing the words and he the music. It was in the fall of 1874, when we were at work on the 'Signet Ring' that we composed 'The Sweet By-and-By.' It was composed for that work, and first published in it. Webster was an extremely sensitive and melancholy man, and very prone to think others had slighted him. He was always imagining that some old friend had treated him coolly, and then dropping into a bottomless despondency about it until some casual meeting afterwards dispelled the illusion. One day in the fall of 1874 — I could give you the day if I had the copyright here — I was standing at my desk in my drug store, writing up my books, when in came Webster, looking uncommonly blue. I knew at a glance what ailed him, and said to him pleasantly, 'Webster, what is the matter with you?' 'Ah,' said he, 'nothing much. It will be all right by-and-by.' 'That is so,' I said; 'and what is the reason that wouldn't be a good subject for a song — By-and-By?' With that I snatched up a bit of paper and went to writing. Within fifteen minutes I handed him the piece of paper with the words of the hymn written upon it. 'There,' I said, 'write a tune for that.' Webster looked it over, and then turned to a man named Bright in the store and said, 'Hand me my fiddle over the counter, please.' The fiddle was passed to him, and he went to work at once to make a tune. I hardly think it was more than thirty minutes from the time he came into the store that he and I were singing together the words and music just as you see them here, on the nineteenth page of the 'Signet Ring.'" Dr. Bennett said neither he nor Webster were Methodists, as generally supposed, but liberals, rather Unitarian in sentiment. The story that Webster was drunk when he composed the tune, the doctor denied. He was in the habit of drinking, but not drunk that day. For many years the sale of the song, in sheet music, was from six thousand to ten thousand copies annually. It has been in nearly all the hymn books, the fee for its use never being less than fifty dollars. It was a source of great profit to the publishers, but brought the authors only three cents a copy.

I well remember the close of one of the great camp meetings at Martha's Vineyard a few years later. The Hutchinsons, just before the benediction, sang "The Sweet By-and-By," then a new song. The clergymen present then descended from the platform forming a line to give a final grasp of the hand to the audience. We also started to retire, but the people, who were supposed to keep moving past the speakers, crowded up to us so that there was a clog. I realized we were getting more than our share of attention, and requested my company to vacate immediately.

From Elkhart we went on to Evansville, the town where Judson advertised and then postponed his concert — going home to die. It was a sadly suggestive visit. Saturday, July 6th, we were at Richland Centre, where we stayed two days. While here I composed a verse which later became a part of a famous song of mine. It was as follows:

> "Now peace on earth, the hosts above proclaim the nations free,
> And all of every kin enjoy this boon of liberty
> We claim no creed for class or clan, but cherish all the good,
> So round the world there soon will be a glorious brotherhood"

At De Soto, on July 11th, I first met Linn B. Porter, the author and poet, whose acquaintance I have often had the pleasure of renewing in the years that have since passed. Sunday, the 15th, I spent in Decorah, Iowa, and there composed a song which was of so much value in the woman-suffrage campaign that followed, "Vote it Right Along."

We had sung our way up to this place, and had given a concert on Saturday night. As has before been stated, I had sent abroad for songs appropriate to the coming woman-suffrage campaign, but at this time had received no response. This dilemma suggested the thought, "Why not go to your room, and see if the muse will not come to you?" Acting on the suggestion, as soon as the door of the room was closed, an inspiration seemed to take possession of me. Placing my instrument in the centre of the room, and striking a chord upon it, words and melody embodying a new thought seemed to spring into life.

"Who votes for woman suffrage now,
Will add new laurels to his brow."

Every line and every verse carried a hope that we might be able to sing a spirit of liberty and justice into the hearts of the people of Kansas. When the war was concluded it seemed clear that here was one song that would do for the campaign. In due course of time Henry came in and sang the song, expressing his satisfaction with it, and we then went on with new hopes and aspirations toward our western home. The song was this:

"Who votes for woman suffrage now
Will add new laurels to his brow,
His children's children, with holy fire,
Will chant in praise their patriot sire.
No warrior's wreath of glory shed
A brighter lustre o'er the head
Than he who battles selfish pride,
And votes with woman side by side.

"This shall unfold his better part,
Delight the spirit and warm his heart.
No jealous thought shall haunt his brain,
And Eden's peace he shall regain;
For an equal partner shall be his bride,
No holy joy shall be denied,
As Equal Rights their motto'll be,
Together journeying o'er life's sea

"Their first great vote to close shall be
Those gilded haunts of infamy

The poor, besotted wretch shall know
That woman has shut the gate of woe
The light of truth shall shine again,
And temperance on earth shall reign;
The night of darkness shall disappear,
The millennial sun shine bright and clear.

"Then let us all unite in love,
To emulate the hosts above
Be just, and kind, and brave, and true,
Doing to others as they'd to you
Build high humanity's sacred cause,
Obeying conscience and its laws
We reach at last the ethereal sphere,
Know God, and all His works revere,
Behold the heavenly angels near.

CHORUS

"We'll do nothing wrong, but sing you this song,
The good time for woman is coming right along,
We'll sing you this song — the chorus loud prolong —
The good time is coming, boys, vote it right along!"

Going from Decorah our carriage became stuck in a slough. We broke the two whiffletrees, and the situation looked desperate. By means of a rope, our best horse drew the carriage out. It had been a wet season, and we encountered bogs and sloughs and mud everywhere. Crossing one deep, wide stream the water came into the carriage. The off horse lost his courage and laid down in the stream, being almost drowned.

Finally, after various experiences, we arrived in Hutchinson on July 27th, and put up at Pendergast's Hotel. At this point Henry became dissatisfied with the situation, and quit my company for the time being. A new bridge was being built, and his services in laying the foundation were besought by the contractor. He worked with them two weeks. I found the hotel altogether too open. There was no plastering on the laths, and the opportunity I desired to compose and practise music for the Kansas campaign in quiet could not be afforded there. In that pioneer prairie settlement hotels were few and boarding-houses unknown, and therefore a serious problem presented itself. However, on the following day I set out on a voyage of discovery. My efforts were fruitless, but suddenly I descried my old log cabin on Main Street. It was the first house built in Hutchinson. At once it occurred to me that it might be feasible to utilize it. Going in, I found it occupied by an old man named Strickland. He had been a colporteur evangelist, but was now using my property as a blacksmith-shop. Although he was on the premises without invitation, and the ceremony of rent-paying had never presented itself to his mind, I had not the least idea of disturbing him. "Anybody occupying the story above?" I asked. "Nobody; nothing but cinders," was his response. "Where's the stairway?" "Gone, long ago." Seeing it was impossible to get up by an inside route, I went and got a ladder and climbed through the unglazed window from the outside. The floor was covered with about two and one-half inches of cinders which were cleared away for quite a space by a shovel borrowed for the purpose. Some nice new hay was procured and covered the floor. Over this I spread an old carpet. Then a bedstead was improvised by mortising into the logs of the house to support the frame, and filling up my straw-tick, a bed was prepared. Before retiring that night, my heart overflowed with gratitude for these rude accommodations, which afforded me, nevertheless, a much-coveted opportunity of being alone, in peace and quiet. Setting up my instrument, as I touched the keys, there came to me these words, "The fatherhood of God, and the brotherhood of man."

Before seeking my primitive bed, I had composed a couple of verses. I never slept so serenely and happily. I had hung up a canvas curtain at the window. Waking in the morning, and putting it aside, the sun streamed in and I felt glorified. I arose and resumed work at the instrument. In a day or two the words were completed and the tune composed. As before stated, I inserted the verse composed in Wisconsin. The remaining verses were:

"We'll raise the song of triumph when we see the hosts advance,
Our banners streaming high, and its mottoes shall entrance
As the golden words they read, they will quickly join our van,
And vote for the cause of freedom and the brotherhood of man

CHORUS

"The fatherhood of God, and the brotherhood of man,
The cause of true religion is spreading through the land
Oh, the fatherhood of God, and the brotherhood of man!
We'll talk and sing, while on the wing, and ring it through the land

"Columbia's sons must lead the way, raise high the lofty standard
Of equal rights they now maintain, though once to slavery pandered
Our country shall this banner bear; 'Free Suffrage' is our motto,
For liberty they'll work, you see, and vote the way they ought to

CHORUS

"For the fatherhood of God, and the brotherhood of man,
The cause of arbitration is spreading through the land
The fatherhood of God, and the brotherhood of man,
This message that the angels bring, we'll sing it through the land

"Let discord and contention cease, that fill our hearts with sorrow,
A ray of hope dispels the gloom, there's sunshine on the morrow
The truth for man proclaimed by Christ far centuries ago,
Its resurrection cheers us now, and, oh, our hearts o'erflow

CHORUS

"With gratitude to God for the brotherhood of man,
We all revere the higher law, do a good turn when you can.
The fatherhood of God, we obey His high command,
This message that the angels bring, we'll sing it through the land

"List ye sorrow-stricken people to the voice of truth to-day,
On the world the sun is rising, error's clouds shall flee away
True hearts watching for the dawning, earnest seers their joys foretold,
Look, ah, look, the field of promise, white with harvest, rich as gold
Ever hopeful, never doubting, always working for the right,
Loving, waiting, watching, longing for the millennial day of light

CHORUS

"The fatherhood of God, and the brotherhood of man,
Proclaim it through the nations, this glorious Christian plan
The fatherhood of God, and the brotherhood of man,
Come join with us this chorus now and waft it through the land"

As I worked away, singing on the choruses, entirely oblivious of possible listeners, Strickland in the room below, hammered applause on his anvil. It seemed prophetic That sentiment was to be forged with peace and good-will toward men.

That cabin, of which I have spoken, finally was sacrificed, *pro bono publico* It was situated in North Hutchinson, the portion we originally designed calling "Harmony," and was a pre-emption cabin for the town site For a long time it was the only hotel, thirty often sleeping in the upper room mentioned. One day some of the citizens were discussing the probability of its being so decrepit that it should be torn down, to prevent injury in case it should fall They thought they'd have a little fun, and so proceeded to demolish it. They found that far from being unsafe, they had undertaken a big job. The whole company had to chop to get the roof down It seemed a pity that the most historic, because the first, building in town should have been so needlessly destroyed.

On August 8th I sent to the *Post* newspaper office in Detroit, in which Carl Shurz was interested, for ten thousand copies of my songs and the address to the people of Kansas, which we afterwards used very effectively. The whole was bound in a small pamphlet. Perhaps the address should go in here, as a matter of history:

> "Hail to the land whereon we tread! our fondest boast,
> The sepulchre of mighty dead,
> The truest hearts that ever bled,
> Who sleep on glory's brightest bed,—a fearless host."

"MEN AND WOMEN OF KANSAS.— With the love of God and man in our hearts, we come to cheer the desponding and elevate the hopes of the most sanguine. Awake then, brothers and sisters of the West! Let your light shine forth. Lay hold on the great weapon of the true Republic, *the ballot*, to ameliorate the condition of common humanity. Let not the glory won by your sons in the early struggles to establish constitutional freedom, be dimmed by any weariness in well-doing. May the history of the past, fraught with strenuous efforts, and so successfully triumphant in the glorious cause of human freedom, serve as a beacon light to encourage you onward and upward, in the radical work of equal rights, equal suffrage, woman's suffrage and the brotherhood of man, until the light of truth shall burst forth with radiant splendor and the millennial day begin to dawn. Turn not back upon your worthy stand taken as leader in this glorious conflict. As the eyes of the world were upon you in the days of the past, when John Brown led forth his little band, conquering and to conquer — so to-day they watch with earnest solicitude your public acts and efforts; trusting, as in the conflict of arms you outrode the storms of secession, treason, war and slavery, so in the peaceful revolution of your political future you will stand foremost in the galaxy of States — the *first* to adopt equal suffrage. Let the voice of woman plead its own cause; let the sympathizing heart, true to the instincts of her own nature, beat for the right, that the *vote* on this all-absorbing question may roll up such majorities for woman suffrage as to shame the few opponents. Come, then, ye young and fair maidens, whisper a kind word of advice in the ear of your betrothed. With the conditions of plighted vows mingle a promise to vote for woman's redemption, and Kansas, *the Queen of the West, shall truly guide and guard our Ship of State to the haven of peace and progress.*"

On the evening of August 8th, the whim seized me to give the public the benefit of my new songs. It was easy to secure the co-operation of the boys of Hutchinson, who drew my carriage along the main street. In the carriage I put up my melodeon, and lighted it up. Boys were less skittish than horses under such conditions. So I went singing through the street and did not lack for an audience. When I reached the hotel I saw Henry, who had not yet resumed negotiations, sitting with his feet on the window-sill. When I had finished what I ever after called my "F O G. B. O M." song, he approvingly clapped his feet together. This I deemed an omen of approaching capitulation. I was right. The next night he joined me in a concert at the public hall. Meanwhile, I had varnished my carriage, and two days later we started for Kansas.

We took a bee-line, as closely as we could reckon it, from Minnesota to Kansas, passing over the prairies of Iowa and crossing Missouri, singing in every town and village we could reach at night. We would bait our horses on the road often, having grain in our carriage, and pluck ears of corn and roast them for a lunch. Our custom on entering a village was to shout out as we passed along that there would be a concert that evening in the largest hall or church. The response was always gratifying and often we would have as much money to show at the close as if we had advertised the entertainment several days ahead. We were two weeks in getting from Hutchinson, Minn., to Atchison, Kan., and during that period had many interesting experiences. During one of our concerts in Iowa I recognized in the audience a lady whom I had met in England twenty years before. It was Mrs. Constance Russell, sister of Mrs. Rebecca Moore, for a lifetime a contributor to woman-suffrage papers and ever since our visit one of my most valued English correspondents. Finally, after fording rivers, wading sloughs, climbing innumerable guide-posts in the dark and encountering other obstacles to progress, we reached Atchison on August 31st. We were under agreement to begin our work September 2d. In Kansas we met Miss Olympia Brown, one of the advocates of suffrage. She rode in our carriage with us several days and as a prelude to our campaign, sang at her lecture the night following our arrival in Atchison.

On the next day there was a great woman-suffrage convention in Atchison, at which we sang. In the notable company there assembled were ex-Governor Charles Robinson, one of the heroes of the early days of Kansas; Senator S. C. Pomeroy; Susan B. Anthony, the directing genius of the campaign; Elizabeth Cady Stanton, Miss Nichols and many other lesser lights. I had expected to meet Viola on my arrival, but she was delayed at St. Louis, and did not come until the evening session of this convention. Just before she started she met our old friend Chief Justice Chase on Washington Street in Boston. He bade her God-speed, saying that the cause of suffrage was near his heart, and remarking that he hoped we would have great success in Kansas.

Our understanding was that we should sing in all the big conventions all over Kansas. Miss Anthony made the arrangements for these conventions at my suggestion. She had many consultations with me and my advice to "Susan," as she was affectionately known wherever suffragists congregated, was that she let Dr. Robinson go out speaking with Mrs. Stanton, and that she establish headquarters in Lawrence. She did so. Judge S. N. Wood, as I have before said, made the original plans, but ill health compelled him to desist from anything but a general oversight of the work as chairman of the committee, and the active manœuvering devolved on Susan. Mrs. Stanton would lecture in a town, and give a notice of a coming concert by the

Hutchinsons. A week later we would come, find all arrangements for our entertainment provided, and give our concert. I suggested to Susan that it would be good policy to have as many temperance meetings as possible, thus enlisting the active aid of the temperance people in our cause. She agreed with me, and we held them in Lawrence, Atchison and other places.

October 3d I wrote to Wendell Phillips, at Susan's request, stating the promising condition of the work and hoping to enlist his sympathy and co-operation. The fields seemed white for harvest, there were many good speakers ready to go out, but very little money to pay expenses. Phillips was unresponsive. Susan and he had not been in sympathy for some reason and he seemed disposed to let her fight her own battles.

On October 5th Miss Anthony and I held a temperance meeting in Ottawa. My diary records: " Mr. Whetstone lives here. I think him a handy man for dull times.' Our concerts were given in Lawrence, Topeka, Marengo, Junction City, Seneca, Albany, White Cloud, Atchison, Oscaloosa, Paola, Ossawatomee, Ottawa, Mound City, Fort Scott, Plato, Oswego, Humboldt, Burlington, Emporia, Medina, Wyandotte, Leavenworth and other places.

On November 4th we sang at the polls, and Mrs. Stanton talked. This was in the city of Leavenworth. At my suggestion coffee was served to the voters. As is well known, the suffragists were defeated. Immediately after this, the Hutchinsons started out and went over the ground again, in company with Mr. A. Hunting, agent of the State Temperance Society, singing for temperance where they had previously sung for suffrage.

Amid the mass of notices, sets of resolutions, and

other souvenirs I retain of this interesting suffrage campaign, I can only reproduce a few, to give the reader some slight idea of the way the varying elements received us. Here is one resolution:

"*Whereas*, the Hutchinson Family have spent ten weeks in this State, singing for 'impartial suffrage,' and having made many converts to the glorious cause through the influence of their sweet and characteristic songs, giving three or four concerts in the large towns and cities to crowded houses,

"*Resolved*, That the Impartial Suffrage Association of Atchison County, Kansas, tender to them our sincere thanks for the services rendered to our cause, and the perfect satisfaction given to our citizens, by their sweet songs, and the chaste and elevating influence and high moral character of their concerts."

This was signed by the executive committee

The *Leavenworth Conservative*, Colonel Hoyle, editor, said:

"The Hutchinsons sang at the Baptist church last Saturday evening to a crowded and intensely delighted audience. The principal musical connoisseurs of the town pronounced themselves delighted beyond any former experience. The memory of the sweet and pathetic tones, together with the noble and benignant countenance of the senior John Hutchinson, will never be effaced from the mind of any person present. His countenance in singing is love and benignity itself, and his voice sweetness and majesty. At times the tones are charming beyond description. The son and daughter are superb singers, and their manner exceedingly pleasing. As they sing for 'equal rights for all,' it is certain their influence will be powerful for good. As in the conflict against slavery and treason, loyalty had all the true poetry and music, so now the party which is loyal to humanity and progress is possessed of these allies. God confers these royal gifts of poesy and song only on those who are loyal to Him."

Contrast the foregoing with this, from the *Ottawa Home Journal*:

"THE HUTCHINSON FAMILY.—This celebrated family of singers gave an entertainment at Pickrell Hall on Monday evening, which was largely attended, although the tickets of admission were fifty cents each. They are travelling under an engagement with the advocates of female suffrage, and are striving to sing the people of Kansas into an acceptance of the 'pernicious proposition.' Futile as their efforts will evidently be in this direction, they furnish a delightful evening's entertainment. They must be sacrificing many profitable engagements in large eastern towns in their zeal for this heresy, and much as we regret to see such talent so misdirected, we are thankful that such sweet singers can be heard upon these prairies.

"They were apparently hard driven to find poetry the sentiment of which could be made to sustain a proposition so hostile to poetic feeling as is female suffrage, and so their songs upon this subject were original. But an agreeable variety of sentimental, patriotic, temperance and comic songs, all rendered with that delightful harmony and soul-inspiring fervor which has made them famous all around the world, gave to the occasion an agreeable variety. The party consisted of John Hutchinson, and a son and daughter."

Before starting on our temperance campaign, we found time to cross the border into Missouri, and sung at Kansas City. The *Journal of Commerce*, Colonel Van Horn, editor, of that place, said next day:

"THE HUTCHINSONS.—The concert of this troupe last night was not so well attended as we could have wished, though there was a good house, and one that appreciated their excellent music. Their old songs have the ring of true merit, and were finely sung. The concert passed off well, with the exception of the sudden leaving of some parties who took exception to some of Mr. Hutchinson's remarks on emancipation and universal suffrage. Of course a person has a right to shut his ears against anything that offends him, but it is unquestionably bad taste to make a public exhibition of one's dislike, thereby disturbing the harmony of any assembly. The day is passed in Missouri when free speech can be frowned down by opposition. Universal suffrage is foremost among the great aims of the day, and will override all opposition. Fossil Democracy cannot stem the tide of the new order of things."

A few days later, following a concert at Manhattan, Kan., Josiah H. Pillsbury, editor of the *Independent*, wrote me as follows:

DEAR FRIEND.—I regret that I did not know that you were to leave here this morning. I wanted to have seen you before you left. I am glad you have visited our State and town. You have done good. Your work will hasten the triumph of equal rights and the reign of temperance "The Fatherhood of God, and the Brotherhood of Man" will be sooner realized by your efforts. God bless *you* and your dear children. Among the brightest of my recollections of the past are the few evenings I spent in listening to the concerts, more than twenty years ago, when Judson, John, Asa and Abby formed the quartette. Those memories have been refreshed, and others, equally pleasant, added, by the sweet songs of John, Henry and Viola. My experience is only that of tens and perhaps hundreds of thousands. Again I thank you for coming to our State. Good-bye. Yours, for the elevation of humanity,

JOSIAH H. PILLSBURY.

Simultaneously with the above I received the following from Rev. Lewis Bodwell, pastor of a Congregational church in Topeka:

DEAR SIR AND BROTHER.—I cannot leave you without an excuse for my seeming neglect on Friday. Though Friday and Saturday are a preacher's busiest days, I counted on the privilege of once more listening to your music, though I could not give a Friday night to any singers *but* the Hutchinsons. The over-weariness of my wife, on returning from an afternoon at "Society" and the coming of an old friend, kept us much against our wills.

We trust that you will long continue in the work of furthering the love of the beautiful in music, as wedded to the pure in morals. As a people still

"We wait beneath the furnace blast
The pains of transformation,"

but

"God give us grace,
Each in his place,
To bear his lot,
And murmuring not,
Endure and wait and labor."

Simply as "good old Yankee singers" your place and lot and work are well defined, and I trust you are rejoicing in the belief that the seed which you and yours have been sowing, has not all fallen by the wayside, or on the stony ground, or among the thorns.

"For right is right, if God *be* God,
And right the day must win;
To doubt would be disloyalty,
To falter would be sin."

The harvest shall come, "first the blade, then the ear, after that the full corn in the ear." As your fellow-believer in "The Fatherhood of God, and the Brotherhood of Man," dear friends, God-speed and farewell,

LEWIS BODWELL.

While singing in Kansas I met C. C. Hutchinson. He was a pioneer of experience and ability, having assisted in the settlement of several towns. I told him the story of our settlement at Hutchinson, Minn., and the ambition I then felt and still retained, to found a town of the same name in Kansas. Asa was settled in Hutchinson, Minn., and my disposition was to go elsewhere. I asked him if he would not like to take hold with me in the enterprise of establishing such a town in Kansas. He responded at once that he would be pleased to do so. After our second meeting arrangements were entered into. I agreed that if he would make the preliminary arrangements, I would put the name and a description of the town on my bills and programmes, as I went from place to place, and so advertise it and secure settlers. He readily agreed to this plan. Of course my idea was to invest largely in the enterprise as I had done in Minnesota. Mr. Hutchinson said he knew of a very desirable town site on the line of the Atchison and Topeka Railroad, which had not yet been taken up, and this location was of course satisfactory to me. Just as our negotiations had reached this stage, Mr. Hutchinson received a telegram from Hastings, Minn., that his wife was sick. He left abruptly. I was very much engaged in my concert work, and had to press on, having full confidence that in due season I should have word from him to fulfil my part of the engagement. A year and a half later I heard that Mr. Hutchinson had taken up the site we had discussed, was building his town, and was very sanguine of success. He built a dam across the stream miles above the place, and brought water to the town by a canal. In later years, while concerting in that vicinity, I visited the town, and told the story. Mr.

Hutchinson is now in San Francisco, engaged in the land and irrigation business. In 1893 I wrote him and asked him if he recalled the circumstances I have narrated. He seemed to suffer from a loss of memory, for his reply was as follows:

MY DEAR RELATIVE AND FRIEND:—I am very sorry to have confirmation from you, that all of the good old original family of singers are gone but yourself. May you yet enjoy many happy, useful years.

I do not understand the design or object of your inquiries. I well remember our many pleasant hours together in 1868 [?], and I have, now that you recall it to mind, a dim recollection of some talk as to our establishing a town. But after that I received such severe blows in business, etc., that I supposed, as you never brought up the matter again, that you had forgotten or dropped it.

When I established Ottawa, it was proposed by my associates to name it Hutchinson, but I was comparatively unknown at that time, 1863, and I thought Ottawa a better name, from local associations. The site I had in mind in those days, and probably mentioned to you, was in Osage county, nearly two hundred miles away from Hutchinson, Kan., founded by me in 1871. You say I have an important city bearing *our* name, to which I can only say that you also have, in Minnesota, an important city "bearing *our* name." But honors are easy, and really unimportant, in these matters. I as really selected, arranged for, and located Ottawa, but two others claimed the glory.

At Hutchinson, Kan., is a man bearing our name, and many people think *he* founded the place. I took him into my employ the first year of my settlement there; he has remained there constantly, has prospered, and bears his honors (accorded by *new* settlers), without blushing.

Very truly yours,   C. C. HUTCHINSON.

While on our temperance campaign in Kansas during December, we entered a town where the leading saloon-keeper had, as he supposed, got the community fully in sympathy with the spirit of license. He offered us the free use of his hall, a spacious room adjoining his saloon, saying, "You can sing all you want to now; I have got license. My father was a Congregational minister, and I was born in Vermont. I don't drink this liquor, but I sell it. I came to Kansas to make money, and I'm bound to make it." His remarks indicated an utter lack of principle which shocked us.

The months spent in Kansas were among the most pleasurable of our long concert experiences. Added to the other emotions which made the work pleasant, was the saddening reflection that this was probably the last season with my daughter, for the loss of Abby had convinced me that I could not hope for much assistance from her after her household altars were set up. So I cherished the fleeting moments and valued them accordingly. Our last concert in Kansas was given on December 16th. Then we started on our homeward journey, our plans including a trip through Illinois to Chicago, and then concerts in the principal cities until we reached Washington. We issued an advance circular, with a list of dates for some weeks ahead, and for a time all went merrily. At Jacksonville, Ill., I met Col. G. P. Smith, editor of the *Journal*, and made provisional plans with him to come and sing in the presidential campaign the following autumn, in case General Grant should be nominated, as seemed probable. Concerts in Bloomington, Springfield, Decatur, Peoria, Galesburg and Monmouth closed the year.

The month of January, 1868, was spent in Iowa and Illinois, and we reached Chicago on the 31st. By this time we were reminded of the advice given by Tony Weller to the genial character in "Pickwick": "Samivel, beware of Vidders." Ole Bull had a sagacious advance agent named Widdows. He had possessed himself of one of my lists of advance dates, and was politely putting the great virtuoso in about two days ahead of us as fast as we went along. His prices were a dollar a ticket, and ours only fifty cents, to be sure, but it was too much to ask the average concert goer to pay one dollar and a half so nearly at one time. So we concluded to change our plans, and give a few concerts near Chicago, until Ole Bull's tour had carried him a little farther away.

At Bloomington, on the 5th of February, I got my life insured. Stillman Churchill was chairman of a committee of Good Templars, for whom we sung. He was also a life insurance agent. On the morning after our concert, he came in to pay us thirty-five dollars. At once he began to talk business. He asked me if I had my life insured, and I told him it had been my effort to lay up a competence for my family, in case of my demise and I had none. He urged the matter upon me, and was so importunate, that I saw no way of escaping from him. So I said: "You insure for any length of time?" "Yes." "And for any amount?" "Yes." "Well," said I, "you may give me five dollars' worth." He took five dollars out, paid me the thirty, and I left him. When I got home I found the policy had been mailed with a polite request that I pay the balance necessary to give me a reasonable amount of insurance, but I made no response. I still have the policy, all the life insurance I ever secured.

On the 8th of March we closed our concerts and started for home. On the 10th I was in New York, and besides seeing Sister Abby and her husband, saw Louisa T. Conger, the "Louisa" of my song composed the year before, she having since married. Of course Lynn friends were glad to see us when we returned. On April 8th, with Edmund Quincy, I called and renewed my acquaintance with Charles Dickens, then making his last tour of America. We saw him at the Parker House, in Boston. Many friends were there.

On April 15th came the wedding of my daughter, to Lewis A. Campbell, of Toledo. The ceremony was in the Free Church, on Oxford Street, and the officiating clergyman was Rev. Samuel Johnson, my life-long friend. Although he had been in the ministry many years, I understood that by some strange happening this was his first solemnization of the marriage service, and his embarrassment was far more palpable than that of either the bride or groom. A merry party partook of the wedding breakfast at Daisy Cottage, although plans we had made for a photograph of the gathering were spoiled by rain. Then my daughter left me for the West. I was doubly bereaved, for I had not only lost her mild and happy presence from my home, but was deprived of a very important member of my concert company. It was only the next day that I was introduced to a Mr. Ridgway, in Boston, and invited by him to call and listen to the singing of his sixteen-year-old daughter, Graziella. I went soon after, and found her not only to be a fine vocalist, but an excellent pianist as well. The result of my hearing was her engagement to sing with us. She appeared with us in many concerts, to the satisfaction of our audiences. Afterwards she sang in the Camilla Urso Concert Company, and in Italian Opera in the Academy of Music, New York, and later with Ole Bull. She was very fond of singing my "Fatherhood of God, and Brotherhood of Man," and it was not long ago that I called at her pleasant home in New Haven, Conn. — she married long since — and we sang it together.

On Tuesday, May 14th, there was a great convention in Cooper Institute, New York, the second anniversary of the Equal Suffrage Society. Lucretia Mott, who had served as president of the society, resigned, and

Mrs. Elizabeth Cady Stanton was chosen in her place. The speakers were Mrs. Stanton, Miss Anthony, Miss Olympia Brown, Frederick Douglass, C. C. Burleigh, Lucy Stone, Mr. Blackwell, and others. I went on with Henry, and sister Abby joined us in the singing.

Returning home, on the 20th, I made a trip to Milford. On the 27th Henry and I attended the anniversary of the Anti-Slavery Society at the Meionaon, in Boston. After Phillips's speech, we sung "One Hundred Years Hence," it being followed by great applause:

> "One hundred years hence what a change will be made
> In politics, morals, religion and trade;
> In statesmen, who wrangle or ride on the fence,
> These things will be altered a hundred years hence.
>
> "Then woman, man's partner, man's equal will stand,
> While beauty and harmony govern the land;
> To think for one's self will be no offence,
> The world will be thinking, a hundred years hence
>
> "Oppression and war will be heard of no more,
> Nor the blood of the slave leave its print on our shore;
> Conventions will then be a useless expense,
> For we'll all go free suffrage, a hundred years hence"

On May 29th the Free Religious Association held its anniversary at Tremont Temple. Men of every denomination took part. Sister Abby, who came on to attend, joined Henry and I in singing "The Fatherhood of God, and the Brotherhood of Man." When we had closed, the presiding officer remarked, "The man who made that song stands higher than any man in this world." Abby turned to me and said, "John, you are the most honored man on earth." I had already published the song, in Chicago, Ill., and it was having a good sale. On May 31st, I had a visit from an old acquaintance, Richard D. Webb, of Dublin, Ireland. The day previous we had gone to the beautiful Pine Grove Cemetery, in Lynn, to witness the first Memorial Day decoration of soldiers' graves, the custom being inaugurated that year by order of General Logan, Commander-in-Chief of the Grand Army.

The following week we filled a number of concert engagements in southern Massachusetts, Miss Ridgway singing with us. These were followed by other concerts until the cold weather interfered. Then duties about High Rock engaged my attention for a while. During this summer religious mass-meetings were held nearly every Sunday evening on the rock. In August my daughter came on to visit us. On the 19th I started back to Toledo with her. Leaving her there, I pushed on to Jacksonville, Ill., and saw Colonel Smith. Grant and Colfax had been nominated, and I arranged with him to take the stump in Illinois and help sing the great soldier into the presidential chair, as I had helped Lincoln eight years before. Then I went to St. Louis and thence toward Kansas.

One of the saddest experiences of our long years of service in the concert field, was going from place to place where we had been before and made friends, inquiring for this and that one, and finding him gone from earth forever. Every important town in America, almost, has a connection in our minds with friends whom we never shall meet again in this world. To compensate for this was the counter experience of meeting here and there, unexpectedly, friends whose memories were kept green because of scenes we had witnessed or good times we had enjoyed together. At St. Louis on this trip I met Rev. J. B. Merwin, who was with us in the Potomac camps. We had a good time relating our experiences since then.

I wonder if my reader has ever given a thought to the fate of the team which I drove from Minnesota to Kansas the year before. The horses had faithfully done their duty in bringing us there, and after we travelled with them in the Kansas campaign, I sought on arriving at Lawrence to leave them in good hands for the winter. So I made a bargain with a livery-man, to take horses and carriage, be responsible for them, and use them judiciously to pay for their keeping. I hadn't been away from Lawrence five weeks before I received a bill of sixty dollars from this man. I at once wrote to a Lawrence friend to take the team away. He wrote me in return that he had done so, and placed it in the hands of a responsible man, on the terms I had originally made with the livery-man. He failed to mention this person's name.

On August 24th I arrived at Lawrence, rather curious to see what condition my team was in, and also wondering who had it. I had been in town but a short time, and had but just begun to make inquiries, when I saw my horses being driven down the street. Their driver was ex-Governor Robinson. On seeing me, he at once invited me to get in and ride with him to his place, six miles out. He soon began to talk about the team. His wife, he said, was very fond of the horses, and drove them to town every day. Finally I ventured an inquiry, "Mr. Robinson, where is my carriage?" "Oh," said he, "that's all used up." I found the carriage on my arrival at the farm, in an old shed, completely played out. It had evidently been exposed to the action of the weather all the season. It seemed that the governor and Rev. I. S. Kalloch, who had been prominently identified with the opposition to woman suffrage the year before, had during the winter taken it and rode several hundred miles into Indian Territory, to look up some railroad scheme. It was in pretty bad condition. I went to the governor and told him that I had engaged to sing in Illinois for Grant and Colfax, and that my carriage must be fixed up. He demurred, but finally told me to take the carriage down town, and tell the repairer to expend from three to five dollars on it, at his expense. I went, grieved to think of this unfortunate winding up of the woman-suffrage campaign.

Arriving at the carriage factory, I told what was wanted, and at once took off my coat and went to work to help. I hadn't been at work more than three-quarters of an hour, when Dr. Robinson came riding down in haste, took the carriage-builder aside, and had a private talk with him. Finally the repairs were made, and taking it back, on the following morning I prepared to tackle up my team for a long journey. I said, "Doctor, I had a water-pail, hammer, wrench and a buffalo robe; also a whip that cost me three dollars." The doctor gave me a fifty-cent whip, a superannuated pail, and an old horse-blanket, remarking that he guessed they would do. Considering the fact that he was the possessor of a magnificent farm and large landed interests beside, I was not quite satisfied. Then he wanted to trade horses. I told him I did not see how I could. He said he would give two house-lots in the suburbs of Lawrence for them. Finally I left him and drove toward Missouri.

I drove as fast as the team would go, but I found I could not reach Atchison that night, so I finally untackled my horses, hitched them to the wheels of my carriage, took a club as a protection from danger and curled up in the carriage for the night, with no company but the dear old moon looking down in pity. At four o'clock in the morning I was awakened by a noise, "rip, rip!" and found my straw hat gone. It had dropped from my head during the night. This filled me with apprehension, for I had no other. Looking out of the carriage, I saw it in possession of an old sow and a litter of ten pigs. It was badly torn. I jumped out and saved the remains, and putting the sorry headgear on drove into Atchison. There I found my niece Estella, Mrs. Dr. Sawyer, and she not only gave me a good breakfast, but repaired the hat. As soon as possible I resumed my journey into poor, afflicted Missouri, but soon found I would be unable to reach Illinois in time, by this method of locomotion. Plodding along I kept meeting the most woe-begone-looking people, riding horseback and talking "secesh." They were beaten but not whipped. They viewed me with suspicion "Where'd ye come from?" "Where ye goin'?" they would ask. I kept my club handy and did not dare go into the houses, for I had been told that this was the worst part of Missouri, the home of the border-ruffians who invaded Kansas and sacked Lawrence. In that place, by the way, one man, a Methodist clergyman, whom I later found preaching in Omaha and Salt Lake City, told me that when the raiders came he was hidden in the cellar of his house. The raiders ransacked the premises and then declared their intention of firing the house. His quick-witted wife asked permission to save a carpet, which was granted and the ruffians temporarily went elsewhere. Taking up the carpet, she called the fugitive from the cellar and rolled him in it. Then by main strength she carried her strange bundle out and stood it up against a tree. He remained in momentary expectation of being shot during the destruction of the premises, but the raiders, assuming that nothing but a carpet was standing there, left him unmolested.

On September 1st, I reached New Cambria. It was settled by Scandinavians. I thought it might be a good place to leave my team, for I saw it was impossible to reach my destination with it. Finally I saw some neat looking children playing in front of a house. "Children," I said, "run in and tell your father and mother I've got a team for them." They did so and the parents came out with countenances bright with surprise. I explained to the man that I should have been in Jacksonville two days before, and that I desired to leave the team with him for its keeping until I was able to come and get it. He consented, drove me to the depot, where I took the train for Quincy, Ill. I learned that the man's name was Moses Williams.

I might here say, that a few weeks after I received a bill from the carriage maker at Lawrence of thirty dollars, for repairs on my vehicle. He did not do more than seven or eight dollars' worth to it and I helped him do that.

On the next day, September 2d, I reached Jacksonville, and sung at a political gathering of Republicans where Richard Yates, the great war governor of the State, spoke. I learned that it was the design of the State committee that Henry and I should travel and sing with Yates. Henry had not arrived, so I sang alone. Yates made a beautiful address. Henry came the next day. We made a similar arrangement with the committee to that in Kansas, which was that they should pay us nothing, but provide entertainment and halls free we singing at the political meetings in the daytime, and giving a paid concert in the evening. Of course they freely advertised our coming. Among the towns that we visited was Greenville, the home of my brother Zephaniah, of lamented memory. Oh, how tender were my thoughts of that dear brother, with his wise head, genial wit and fascinatingly whimsical nature. I recalled the time, years before, when he was our business agent. He stepped up to us, at the hotel in New York, and patronizingly remarked, " Boys, I'm going to pay you off." We had taken fifteen hundred dollars at our concert the night before. We held out our hands expectantly, and he munificently vouchsafed us one cent apiece. As I stated in relating the visit of Jesse, Judson and myself there many years before, Zephaniah's farm was over six miles from Greenville. Henry and I took a carriage and drove out there. I determined that I wouldn't ask anybody the way, but see if I could recognize the place. At last we came to a grove. " This must be the place," said I, " and yet I thought that barn stood another way." I opened the gate. " Good morning, my good friend," I said to the man in the yard, " will you tell me if this is the farm Zephaniah K. Hutchinson settled?" " Certainly, this is the place," was his response. He invited me into the house. I was startled. The man much resembled my brother, and his wife was the image of my brother's wife. His name was Jonathan Keppler. He told me I was right about the barn. It had been turned around. Zephaniah had planted some three hundred selected trees, and when we made our visit they were loaded with fruit. We visited my brother's grave and dropped tears of genuine grief to his memory.

Wherever the name of Richard Yates is known, there, alas! is known also the story of his great weakness. If we had needed additional examples of the ravages of the drink habit for our temperance meetings, he would have furnished them. He was a fine speaker, a very gentlemanly man, and a man of good heart. At Champaign, after our concert, he came and shook our hands, remarking, "We are going to have one of the grandest campaigns ever inaugurated in the West, together." His words did not prove true, to our sorrow and disappointment. At Danville he was not in condition to appear, and the next morning he rushed out of his hotel and started for the East. We next heard from him at Toledo, still going, and therefore the newspapers inferred and stated, rightly or wrongly, that important business had taken him to Washington. He was to speak in Decatur that day, and at the specified time we took the train for that town. A committee, with a band of music and carriage, was at the depot to meet Yates. I had to tell them he had gone, no one knew whither. We were escorted to the wigwam. Twenty thousand people were in waiting to hear the speaker. We sang, to their great satisfaction, and I talked. General Francis P. Blair, the Democratic candidate for Vice-President, had been recently delivering himself of sentiments that had aroused a good deal of comment, and I took him off as a "Curiosity," to the delight of the multitude. The wigwam was a long, low-studded building, with all the windows taken out. The committee, in its emergency, bethought itself of another man who had come home under the influence of liquor a few days before, but who could speak if in his senses. His house was sought out, and he was found asleep. A little brandy put to his nose revived him, and he was taken to the wigwam. He took off his coat, and commenced beating the air, his wild gesticulations entertaining the crowd, if his words did not.

The next day Yates's son came to us and anxiously inquired for his father. We broke the sad news of his escapade as gently as we could. All he could do was to wait until some newspaper paragraph gave him an inkling of the senator's whereabouts.

"Oh, rum, what hast thou done?
Ruined mother, daughter, father and son."

How sad the reflection! As my mind reverts through the vista of years to the numerous examples of our poor, weak brothers and sisters, who have fallen victims to this fell destroyer, I feel that the dark curtain of forgetfulness should be drawn over these causes of woe — the mantle of charity should hide from the rude inspection of idle curiosity these revolting spectacles. Let not the strong ones boastfully and exultingly glory in their fortune, or tauntingly refer to the unfortunate, but while

"Admitting their weakness and evil behavior,
Leave with meekness their sins to their Saviour."

"Dick" Oglesby spoke with us the next day, at Bloomington. At Kankakee, two days later, the committee met us at the depot with a carriage drawn by four white horses. The speakers were in a barouche drawn by four cream-colored steeds. The procession was the finest in the State. We sang all day. At Lockport we were entertained over Sunday at the house of a deceased friend, Rev. Mr. Codding, a liberal-minded preacher, who had been an earnest anti-slavery man, and had done a great deal for the cause of emancipation. Fifteen years had elapsed since last I saw him, and it was two years or more since he had died. With a sorrowful heart I accompanied the widow to the churchyard, and had pointed out to me the spot where his body lay. He had been a noted spiritualist.

While stopping at this place I had a vision. I awoke at three o'clock in the morning, Sunday, September 20th. I felt rested, but soon quieted down, and fell into a half-slumber. I seemed to have a view of, as I thought, the other sphere. I thought I saw a curtain, partially drawn apart, and in the space behind it who should appear but my father, brothers, and one or two sisters, all long since dead. While looking at them, they arose and together moved forward and formed a semicircle. Just then my dear mother entered, and they surrounded her. Instantly I awoke. I was filled with hope. As soon as morning came I told my dream. At once I wrote to Asa. I said, "Asa, don't doubt again; I have seen a vision. Saw my mother in another world." I went about my vocation. As soon as the mail could reach me in reply, from Minnesota, word came from Asa: "Mother died that very night, in Milford." Now Milford was fourteen hundred miles away.

I have already told much of my mother's history. She was a woman of great natural affection for her family, and though her descendants numbered many score before her death, there was room in her heart for them all. She had a great musical gift, loved poetry, was an earnest Christian, and one who faithfully tried to do her duty to all mankind. A prominent publication thus editorially referred to her death:

"A MOTHER IN ISRAEL — The granite hills of New England produce character. The men and women who climb their heights, or labor under their shadow, think as well as work. They do not always grow rich, but they bring up in contentment and virtue families that go forth and subdue the earth. The more quaint and old-fashioned style of people is indeed passing away — the patriarchs and matriarchs of simple habits and marked qualities. The death of one of these, Mrs. Mary L. Hutchinson, the mother of the celebrated Hutchinson family of singers, is briefly noted on our seventh page. She was a woman of cheerful temperament, of strong feeling, and of decided character. Early in life she embraced

Baptist views, and was a zealous defender of them to the last, though in other respects her doctrinal belief varied from the tenets of that denomination. She had the psalms and hymns of Watts by heart, so that she never needed the printed page, and was so fond of them that lines, couplets and verses would find their way into her ordinary conversation, often with amusing appropriateness. It was from her the children inherited their remarkable musical talent, and her voice retained much of its power to the end. A hymn-book was buried with her in the coffin, and the funeral services were conducted at the rural school-house, where all the children received their education, and several of them who were able to be present added touching interest to the occasion by singing appropriate songs of faith and hope. She was married but once, surviving her husband ten or twelve years, was the mother of sixteen children, thirteen of whom lived to adult years, the grandmother of fifty-two, and the great-grandmother of twenty-eight; being thus the ancestor during her life of ninety-six persons."

Continuing our campaign work, on the 22d of September we were in Chicago. At least fifty thousand people filled the great court square on either side of the Court House. In each place was a platform. We would sing on one side, and then the speakers would take our places, and we would go to the other. Among the orators that day were Governor Oglesby, General Logan, Emery A. Storrs, and our war-time friend, Gen. John P. Farnsworth. I remember that among the pieces sung by Henry and myself were, "'Tis coming up the steep of time," and our "Curiosity Song." Of course the latter was so amended as to be a take-off on the opposition. Oh, it was something to be a Republican in those days! Then it was a comfort to be in opposition to the Democracy. Then it was a delight to see the letters "U. S. A" on the mail-bags, and other government material. For twenty-five years a stigma had been attached to them in our minds, for it meant a government that upheld slavery. We could not sing "America" honestly then, but now all this was changed, and we entered with enthusiasm into the work we had on hand.

On the next day we went to St. Charles, and General Farnsworth took us immediately to his home. In fact, this campaign brought only a repetition of our experiences all through our career. We received courtesies that put us under life-long obligation from friends wherever we went. As I look back over my professional life, I feel that to merely enumerate these kind friends would leave room for nothing else in this book. So I trust all such who read this will rest assured that they are gratefully remembered and loved, though not specially mentioned.

For a few days we had with us as speakers General Logan, General Farnsworth, and that prince of orators, Emery A. Storrs. Congressman Bates also spoke with us. We went with Logan to various places, and also visited his home, where we met Mrs. Logan, a woman whose acquaintance I was glad to renew in later years. General Logan was a grand, true specimen of the best in Americanism. On October 10th we sang in Peoria to twenty-five thousand people. On the following day we called on another oratorical giant, Col. R. G. Ingersoll, declined the wine he politely offered us, and laid out a plan of campaign for a number of meetings with him. The "Carpet-Baggers" turned out in full force at Peoria. Those who recall that campaign will remember that the "Tanners" and "Carpet-Baggers" played an important part in the parades. On this occasion, with a big carpet-bag on my back, I led the procession, with the motto, "My countrymen, all mankind."

Partly from principle and partly because of the warning furnished by Governor Yates, I made it in my way, besides having many talks on the Bible with Ingersoll during our tour, to give him numerous earnest temperance lectures. After I went with Yates, Governor

Oglesby blamed me for not taking care of him. I said, "I was not in charge of Yates; I did my duty and satisfied the people. I had not been told of Mr. Yates's weakness. If you blame me, I shall publish the whole story."

At Springfield, where Ingersoll and Governor Oglesby were the speakers, Yates again appeared. He expressed his desire to be with us once more, and speak while we sang. We were each grieved that our anticipations for a great campaign together had been disappointed. To please both Yates and us a meeting was appointed, and we appeared together. On the 26th we rode from Bath thirty miles in a hand-car, and then in a carriage fifteen miles to Pekin. From there we went once more to Peoria, stopping with Mrs. Curtenius, an old friend we had made in New York, years before.

On October 27th we were at Chicago again. There was a big rally at which Lyman Trumbull made a great speech. It was our last singing in the Illinois campaign. The next day we took the train to La Crosse, and at midnight took the boat *Key City* to Winona. We reached Rochester, Minn., on the 29th, where we had many old friends. There was a Democratic rally that night, addressed by D. S Norton, once a Republican. At the close there were calls for the Hutchinsons, and seeing an opportunity to help the cause along, we at once responded, singing our "Curiosity" song, and not sparing our friends, the enemy. The result was three rousing cheers for Grant and Colfax. Mr. Norton was quite welcome to all the satisfaction he got from the meeting. The next day we took the train for St. Paul; General Ramsey and other speakers were on board. We sang them "Grant, Our Great Commander."

"Fling wide the banner, boys, fling wide the banner;
For noble Grant, the people's choice, shout a loud hosanna.

"All doubt will ever pass away,
With Grant, the brave, we'll win the day:
In him the nation put its trust,
It heeded not each slander
Thrown out against the good and just,
Grant, our great commander

"Come soldiers, sailors, freemen all,
Can you resist your country's call?
Don't for a moment hesitate,
Come forth with truth and candor,
Vote for the man who saved the State —
For Grant, our great commander

On the 31st we sang in the Opera House at Minneapolis, at a Republican rally, Ignatius Donnelly, the great Baconian critic of Shakespeare, being the speaker. He gave a fine address. On Monday, November 2d, we started toward Hutchinson. Had a rough journey towards the Crow River, the track being under the mud for the last two miles of the way. A stage ride of seven miles after leaving the railroad took us to Watertown, where we gave a concert in the hotel hall. At four o'clock the next morning we started on a drive of thirty miles, reaching Hutchinson at noon. There was great excitement over the election, then in progress. Henry cast his first presidential ballot. We sung several songs in the street. Another effort was made to remove the county seat from Glencoe to Hutchinson, but it failed by one hundred and fifty votes. Lizzie, Asa's wife, and another lady, Mrs. Alexander, went to the polls and asked the privilege of voting, but were refused. The meeting unanimously voted, however, to help give them the right of suffrage, a significant fact, as indicating the character of the voting population of the town. We spent a day on Asa's farm, one mile from the village. Nearly one hundred acres of it were under the plow that year.

We gave several concerts in Minnesota during the weeks that followed. On Thanksgiving Day we had a big concert in Minneapolis. My brother Joshua, who had come on from the East, was in the audience, but did not make himself known until the close. He spent three days with me, appearing in concert with us one evening, and singing several songs. It was his first visit to Minnesota, and his keen eyes took in about everything of interest in the new country. His comments on it, printed in the *Cabinet*, are worth quoting:

HUTCHINSON, December 10

FRIEND BOYLSTON.—Although I make no pretention to journalism, I thought to give you a little of my travels in the great Northwest I left our own granite hills on the 16th of November, but lingering by the way in New York, to fill professional engagements, did not reach the great "Father of Waters," the majestic Mississippi, till the 26th Navigation having closed, I was obliged to take the rails from Prairie du Chien to Minneapolis. Hearing that Brother John and son were in the city, I hurried to the concert, at Pence Opera House, where they were greeted by the *élite* of the city. John, with his usual enthusiasm and some *new* songs, won their approval "The Fatherhood of God, and the Brotherhood of Man," a new production, was received with applause

While in the city I enjoyed the hospitalities of an old townsman, Mr George Holt, and with him I met your amiable merchant, Mr George F Stevens, who appears to have regained his health by coming to this cold but exhilarating climate. In fact, it is proverbial as the resort of invalids I met several in the cars, on their way from the East and South, emigrating expressly for their health. I suppose the people will die here sometime, but it seems almost an exception to the general rule A gentleman told me, who resided here (at Hutchinson) four years, that there have been but two deaths in that time; one an aged person, and the other a child—by drowning

Leaving Minneapolis I took cars to Crow River, thence by stage seven miles, thence by ox-sleds and on foot two days through the "big woods" (forty by thirty miles, with a growth of timber that puts our New England forests in the shade), with logs lying on the ground and standing, that I had the curiosity to measure — three and one-half feet in diameter and thirty or forty feet to the limbs. Oh, the immense wealth of this forest, inviting the enterprise of the world to make it available to man!

As I left the "woods" I came on to the prairie, and a five-mile walk brought me to the beautiful town of Hutchinson, situated on the western borders of the plain, skirted with a lovely forest of smaller growth, made so by the annual fires that have swept through them from time immemorial. This town was laid out in November, 1855, and although it has once been burned by the Indians, it still lives, and is being rapidly filled up by a most hardy and virtuous people. Men who came here were nearly all of very small means, not averaging over five hundred dollars, and have risen to permanent wealth. I learned that there were but two paupers in the county, and that one of them owns two hundred acres of land, fifty sheep, two yoke of oxen, five cows, etc.

A gentleman in this neighborhood, whose acquaintance I formed last evening, has a small farm of 2,500 acres. He is in the cheese business, and is intending to *enlarge*. But he is ready to sell his lands at a small advance, to encourage emigration. Why will men congregate so in cities, when such wealth is undeveloped? The soil in the main is unequalled for the culture of wheat and potatoes, and our New England corn is being introduced with great success. The farmers are holding on to their wheat, which ranges at seventy-five or eighty cents a bushel. The speculators are trying to get it into their hands, and they probably will. I should like to send a million bushels to New England at present prices, so we could afford to live there. If you will forward the funds I will charter a railroad, and we will get some wheat at our own price. I will give my services for a month to consummate such a plan — but enough of this.

Suffice it to say that this is a big country, and with General Grant at the helm, and the people at the wheel, we shall glide along successfully to a high and triumphant civilization. The thermometer ranges at 22° below zero, and is going down, as they say here, into the "roaring forties." Yours for human improvement and happiness. JOSHUA.

After leaving Minneapolis we sang at several Iowa and Wisconsin towns. At Boscobel, Wis., on December 20th, I found myself very homesick. Christmas was coming and I longed for Lynn. So I bought a box of poultry and started, leaving Henry at Chicago on my way. Viola was at home, and I thought it would be a good plan for me to surprise the folks as Santa Claus. Stopped to see Sister Abby in New York and reached

Lynn at midnight, December 24th. The surprise was complete.

A number of friends had been invited to Daisy Cottage on Christmas Day, and as no one knew of my arrival, it was suggested that I be "palmed off," so to speak, as a contribution from the West. So when evening came, I was securely done up in brown paper, tied with string, and placed in a corner, behind the piano. I confess I was rather anxious as to my appearance when the wrappings were taken off. When the hour arrived, the friends gathered round, all alert to see what could be the contents of the big bundle. My wife informed them that it arrived at midnight. At last the paper was removed by my son-in-law so that my face was revealed. For a few moments there was perfect surprise. They looked as though they were either deceived or looking at a splendid likeness of John W. Hutchinson. They finally realized that the spectre was no ghost, but quite alive. It was then remarked that as another guest, Colonel Allen G. Shepherd, then city marshal of Lynn, had not arrived, he should be subjected to the surprise for the benefit of the company, and I was tied up again. Soon Colonel Shepherd and another neighbor came in. We went through the form again. Shepherd went at me as he would at a rebel. He expressed much surprise that the rest of the company failed to join him in shaking hands and greeting me when the truth was discovered.

A good deal took place in a short time during my stay at home. That Christmas night, at midnight, a cry aroused me: "Father, come quick! Lyceum Hall is burning." I arose and looked out of the window at the ancient structure. Sure enough; it was doomed, though the roof timbers were still standing. "Here is glory enough," said I, "the filthy old hall is gone, and now Lynn will have a new assembly-room." So I went back to bed. Suddenly something said to me, "Why, you've got ten thousand dollars in government bonds in that vault!" It was true. My bank was located under the hall. I hurried up, dressed, and went down. By this time the Frazier and Bubier blocks, handsome brick buildings, were also in flames. It was a three-hundred-thousand-dollar fire. The brick vault was still standing. James N. Buffum, one of the directors of the bank, stood by, in a hopeful frame of mind, though smoke could be plainly seen issuing from the door of the vault. The next day the vault was cooled off and opened, the contents being found intact.

New Year's came next, and then my birthday, January 4th. On the 8th, my first grandchild, Cleveland J. Campbell, was born. As soon as possible after that I gathered my belongings together and started back to Chicago, where I had left Henry. I arrived there January 22d. Henry was well and happy, having spent the time with friends, and we at once went to work rehearsing for a series of concerts.

We spent many weeks in Chicago. We had hosts of friends there, engaged in the different phases of religious and reform work. During the fall campaign we had found time to attend Rev. Robert Collyer's church one Sunday, and as a consequence of that visit, were a little later invited to return and be at the dedication of his new church. This winter's experiences made us well acquainted with a large number of the churches and missions in the city.

But before taking up active concert work, we had quite an experience with the woman-suffrage reform. While I was in Kansas in 1867, Miss Anthony had called my attention to the fact that Mrs. Mary A. Livermore, who had become known to the public through her antislavery labors, and her work in the hospitals, lived in Chicago, and was showing an increased interest in the suffrage problem. Miss Anthony saw in Mrs. Livermore a great power to help the cause along, and desired me to be sure and see her when I was in Chicago, and secure her sympathy in a more definite way.

From the first I had doubts of the advisability of enlisting George Francis Train in the woman-suffrage cause. I saw in him an impediment to gaining the sympathy of just such people as Mrs. Livermore. For a year or two after the Kansas campaign, the question of the extent to which suffragists should endorse Train almost eclipsed the main issue.

Susan B. Anthony gave her full endorsement to Train from the first. No other leader was so fully committed in his behalf. She had planned to take Mrs. Stanton, Train and me on a woman-suffrage tour from Kansas to Boston. I declined to go with him after one experience of his peculiar manner of conducting a meeting. At the last convention in Kansas Mrs. Stanton and Train were to speak, and we were to sing. Before it opened I got word that Mr. Train was not quite ready to go on, and desired me to go ahead and sing. I returned a message that when the meeting was organized I would sing. I did not consider my family either a brass band or an orchestra.

To return to Chicago once more. The radical woman suffragists held frequent meetings after my arrival in 1869. I said to those who gathered that they ought to take measures to secure the good-will of the people in town. I realized that there was a prejudice to be overcome anyway, and that it was important to enlist the sympathizers together. I suggested that Mrs. Livermore be seen. They decided to make me a committee to wait upon her and invite her to come to the hall and be recognized as affiliating with pioneer woman suffragists of Chicago. Accordingly I called upon her. We had a conversation on the Kansas campaign. "Now," said I, "here is a chance. Won't you go down in response to the invitation of these people?" She responded that she would not be prejudiced. "We have suffered," said she, "as Universalists; we know what it is to be oppressed and despised. It behooves me to now treat with respect those engaged in this cause." I told her I was delegated to see if she would go down and speak to them and be endorsed as one of their leaders. She consented to go. On the way to the hall, however, she stepped into her husband's office, and there met "Mrs. Grundy." "Who were these people who had invited her? Were not many of them spiritualists; possibly some of them even free-lovers?" When she got to the hall in the Farwell Building she stood outside, and refused to enter and address them. My room was not far away from the place of meeting. I could easily hear the discussion. I saw there was something in the wind, but felt I had done my duty.

Then a great public meeting was proposed. Anxious to assist, I engaged Library Hall for a whole day and night. The convention was well advertised. Before the meeting day came, however, the same people who had drawn Mrs. Livermore away from the conference I had suggested, had crowded us out of our hall by paying for it in advance, the librarian supposing them to represent the same "suffragists" as myself. I was not with either party, but merely in sympathy with the woman-suffrage idea. There was no disposition to fight the matter on the part of the disappointed suffragists. Under the lead of Mrs. Waterman they hired Music Hall, and held their convention on the day advertised, February 11th. Meanwhile, I said, "It's our hall; let us go there. If the other element come, let them meet with us." They outvoted me, and so there were two conventions. I said to them, "My dear friends, I engaged that hall. I will sing for you two sessions." In the afternoon of the day I said to Henry, "We will go to Library Hall. My friends are there, and I don't propose to be reckoned out. I am a straight-out reformer, and I propose to go and show my colors." I went in before the session opened, and took a seat about one-half the way down the aisle. I previously told my son to take the melodeon to the ante-room of the hall.

I have before me the "call" for this convention, as it appeared in the *Chicago Tribune* of February 6th. It was headed by Judge Charles B. Waite, and an appeal signed by Mrs. Livermore follows it. She says: "It will be seen by the above call that the forthcoming Woman Suffrage Convention, to be held in Library Hall next Thursday and Friday, February 11th and 12th, is in the hands of the best people of Chicago Among the signers to the call will be recognized the names of judges, doctors of divinity, clergymen of almost every denomination, editors of leading papers, legislators, professors of theology, physicians, lawyers, merchants, eminent men of business, substantial and reliable men and women of society." She closed by saying, "Although our preparations have been made quietly, with no flourish of trumpets, they have been made wisely and well." It grieved me to have quite so much stress laid upon the respectable character of this gathering, simply because it seemed to be a reflection on the other.

The meeting was organized. Mrs. Livermore presided. Soon a man from Wisconsin was recognized. "Mrs. President," said he, "I perceive in the audience our veteran anti-slavery friend, Mr. Hutchinson. I trust he will be invited to the platform and to sing." Mrs. Livermore said "Will Mr. Hutchinson please come to the stage?" I looked, but could see no sign of Henry. Then I went to the stage. Susan and Mrs. Stanton were there, and I took a seat beside them. Then I rose and addressed the audience, telling them I would respond to their call to sing later.

The meeting went on. After a while Henry came in with the melodeon. Then we were announced. I said, "Dear friends, will you pardon me a prelude, by way of explanation? In the first place, with union we will have success. We cannot afford to throw out any individual on account of any difference of opinion on other points. I have this day sung to another convention of earnest woman-suffrage people who should have been here. I engaged this room." "Oh," broke in Judge Waite, looking uncomfortable, "we asked you to sing, not to talk." "I shall have the privilege of singing directly," I replied. "To bring this matter as it should be, I have engaged another hall, twice as large as this, where we shall have a union meeting to-morrow night."

"I'll come and speak," said Miss Anthony at this point. "I'll come too," said Mrs. Stanton. "And so will I," said Mrs Livermore. *Then* I sang the "Fatherhood of God." There was great enthusiasm. On the next night Farwell Hall was opened at my expense.

It was a thrilling meeting. Speakers were there to represent the different factions. Mrs. Stanton and Miss Anthony spoke. Mrs. Livermore came, but nothing would induce her to speak, and other speakers had to lengthen their remarks, and we increased the number of our songs to fill in the time.

One day, as Henry and I were passing along the sidewalk in front of Farwell Hall, where the Young Men's Christian Association was located, a highly spiritual appearing man accosted me, without giving his own name, saying, "Mr. Hutchinson, we should like to have you go into our meeting." We had given many concerts there. We went in. After the preliminary exercises, the gentleman invited us to sing. We sung our old favorite, "Mary at the Cross." The effect was electric. The man who had invited us in was Dwight L. Moody. At the close of the meeting he asked me if I would not sing for him on Sundays, at his great mass meetings in Farwell Hall. The result of our conversation was an agreement to sing for several weeks. We consented to sing on Sunday evenings. He agreed to make engagements for week-night concerts for us, in and around Chicago. The result was quite satisfactory. Often two thousand people were gathered in the Sunday evening meetings. We would spend a part of each Saturday in the Y. M. C. A. headquarters, arranging for the concerts of the following week. We took quarters in the building, and had our rent free. We loved to hear Mr. Moody talk, though for obvious reasons we could not agree with all his conclusions. On each occasion Mr. Moody was sure to say : "I have invited Mr. Hutchinson and son to sing for us that beautiful hymn: 'Mary at the Cross.'" This was perhaps the finest chant the Hutchinsons ever sang:

"Jews were wrought to cruel madness,
　Christians fled with fear and sadness,
　　Mary stood the cross beside

"Not she with traitorous lips her Saviour stung;
　At its foot her foot she planted,
　Midst the dreadful scene undaunted,
　　Till the gentle sufferer died,
　　Mary stood the cross beside

"She, while apostles shrunk, could danger brave,
　But no worship, song or glory
　Touches like the simple story —
　　Mary stood the cross beside

"Last at the cross and earliest at the grave
　And when under fierce oppression,
　Goodness suffers like transgression, —
　　Christ again is crucified,
　　Mary stands the cross beside"

It was some time after this, that Ira D. Sankey commenced with Moody the work that meant so much to the cause of Christian song. During the time of which I have been speaking Mr. Moody would often drop in at our week-night concerts, and offer an encouraging word. Many of the concerts were given in the various missions established by Mr Moody. This engagement continued into spring. On one occasion having some verses to sing in Farwell Hall, I had written them off, but had great difficulty in reading them. At the close of the meeting, I said to Mr. Moody, "We shall have to have more light. You give a great deal of light yourself, but my eyes need artificial light." "You shall have it," responded the great evangelist. On the next Sabbath there were three additional gas-burners on either side of the hall but I was just as unable to read, and at the close of the meeting said so. Mr. Moody opened his Bible and read from it easily. Just then Henry stepped up, and remarked, "Father, you're getting blind." He was right. It was the first time I realized I needed glasses.

During our stay at Chicago, we made occasional trips outside for a night or two. On one of these occasions, at Janesville, we met Dexter Smith, the song writer, with a combination company, consisting of the Halls, D. C. and Rudolph, cornetists, Camilla Urso, violinist, Graziella Ridgway, and others. Smith was anxious to have his company appear in Farwell Hall, in Chicago, but found that I had a contract under which I could secure it much cheaper than he. He had run the gantlet from Boston to Chicago, and was *en route* to the Pacific coast. Smith had come out to Janesville with his company to hear us. We had a good concert, gave satisfaction to the audience, and pleased Smith's company very much. The result of our meeting was an agreement to give a series of concerts together in Chicago. We agreed to pay all the expenses of the company except personal, and divide the proceeds. We went ahead and attended to our part of the arrangements. The announcements read, "Hutchinson's Grand Concerts, Dexter Smith, Manager." The first concert of the series was given on April 15th. It proved a mystery to the public and the papers. One said:

"HUTCHINSON'S CONCERT — We must call it by the name which headed the programme, though the only evidences of Hutchinson to be seen in the actual concert were the bright bunting adorning the stage, the scarlet screen at the rear, behind which evidently slumbered the time-honored melodeon, and the flowing locks and beard of the Hutchinson, called John, in the outskirts of the audience."

The fact was that just before the concert Camilla Urso rebelled. She had never agreed, she said, to play with any artists but the Halls and Miss Ridgway. The latter was very much chagrined at Camilla's attitude. We had brought her out, and she was very anxious to sing with us, but Camilla was firm. For our own part, it was no cross for us not to sing, and it involved no financial loss. The report I have partly quoted speaks of me in the outskirts of the audience. I went to see how the people were enjoying the entertainment. General Sheridan was in one of the balconies, and seeing me, he came down and met me. "Why, Mr. Hutchinson," said he, "I came here to hear you sing. I have heard all the bands I care to before, and I don't care for fiddles." I explained that we thought it not advisable to sing. He was the only person who said anything to me about our failure to appear. The next day there was a change. The Halls had been waiting for just such an episode to vindicate them in altering the status of things. Camilla was informed that on the 19th the company would sing with the Hutchinsons and without her. This programme was carried out and brought her to terms, so that the rest of the series she made no objection to appearing with us. That she cherished no ill feeling because of the occurrence was evidenced a few years later, when Henry succeeded Gaston Gottschalk as basso of her company, and travelled with her several months. At the close of this engagement, however, Smith changed his plans and took his company back to Boston.

When my engagement with Moody expired, I determined to go to Missouri, hunt up my horses and drive them East. I made an arrangement with a young law student to go ahead as agent and arrange some concerts, and, as was our custom, Henry and I sung our way until we reached New Cambria. Mr. Williams was surprised to see me. I had been gone so long that he had concluded I was never coming back to claim my team and thought he had got a good thing at no expense. He was loth to give them up and wanted one hundred and thirty dollars for keeping them. They were lean and lank, and the carriage was pretty well used up. By calling in three referees, I was able to compromise and paid him sixty dollars. Meanwhile a man in the village was laboring with my agent, he having his eye on the horses. I drove twenty miles away, somewhat in a quandary as to whether I should drive the horses to Massachusetts or sell them and proceed to New York, accepting invitations to sing for the suffrage and other May anniversaries there. I had written part of a song, " Unite, unite, to battle for right," and it was still forming itself in my mind. I was undergoing considerable mental excitement, and was in a brown study as to what was best for me to do, when in came the shyster lawyer who was acting as my business agent. " Here's the money," said he, handing me two hundred dollars. " What money ? " I inquired. " For your horses," said he. " Where are they ? " was my next question. He went with me, and sure enough, the New Cambria man had followed us up and bought them. He was just leading them out to be tackled to the carriage. I said to the hostler, " Take these horses back to the stable; this is no sale." I had simply told my agent to find me a customer. Probably he got something out of the bargain he had made. I went back to the house and began to reflect. I had had those horses two years. They had been a continual expense to me. I did not desire to own them and leave them longer in Missouri. I called the agent and told him he might let the man have the team for the two hundred dollars. Then I registered a vow within my mind. Those were my last horses. They cost me four hundred dollars and the carriage three hundred dollars. I concluded that if I did not know how to trade horses better than that, I would keep out of the business.

It was a three days' journey to New York on the cars. On the way I completed my song:

> "Unite, unite, to battle for right
>   The war has just begun,
> Through all the land let the cry go out —
>   'We've need of more earnest ones'
> Brave hearts and stout,
> A consummate enemy we have to rout,
> Come, join the suffrage van"

This I set to music before we reached New York. The Equal Rights Convention was in progress at Steinway Hall when we arrived. It was just the song needed. Mrs. Livermore was there, having decided to go on from Chicago and sift the subject. Among the speakers were the Burleighs, Mrs. Stone and Mrs. Livermore. They had been working all day. The resolution under discussion was one to exclude from consideration such extraneous subjects as spiritualism, free-love, etc. We came from the train just as the debate was at its hottest point, went on the stage and sung the song. Lucy Stone assumed a pacific attitude toward the people who were attacked and deprecated the broaching of the subject. The Burleighs agreed with her. Mrs. Livermore was firm, however, and our song was needed to assist in bringing the warring elements together. On the two following days the meetings were held in Cooper Institute and the Academy of Music, the speakers being Henry Ward Beecher, Frederick Douglass, Lucy Stone, Olive Logan, Miss Cousens and many others. On May 15th, at the Woman's Bureau the National

Woman's Rights Association was formed, Henry and I joining

At the close of this convention, we returned to Lynn. The rest of May was largely given up to attending and singing at anniversary meetings in Boston and New York. At the latter city we gave some concerts for the benefit of the Morning Star Sunday-school, at one of which Sister Abby sang with us. She was greeted with hearty cheers, it being her first appearance on the concert platform in many years. After our return to Lynn we gave a number of concerts in Lynn, Salem, Lowell, Lawrence and other places, for the benefit of this same Sunday-school.

In June of this year, the first of the great peace jubilees — projected by Patrick S. Gilmore, and given by him, with the assistance of Carl Zerrahn, and Dr. Eben Tourjee — occurred in Boston. There were 1,100 players in the great orchestra, over 10,000 singers, and 100 anvils in the great anvil chorus from "Il Trovatore" with cannon, electrically discharged, for sub-bass. Henry sung in the chorus, and we attended many of the concerts in the great Coliseum near the Public Garden. The only concert company that had the courage to compete with this aggregation was the Hutchinsons. We hired the Bromfield Street Church, and gave concerts each night. We put out any amount of dodgers, and hired boys, with banners eighteen feet high, to parade in the vicinity of the Coliseum. These banners bore the words, "One shall chase a thousand, and two shall put ten thousand to flight." It was a hit. Asa arrived on the second day, and Sister Abby came later. Mr. Pratt, the pianist of the Camilla Urso troupe, and Graziella Ridgway assisted us. We had numerous offers from talent from all over the country to join with us, but accepted no others, except that of Jules Perkins, who afterwards sang for many years with Parepa.

On Saturday, June 19th, in St. Paul's Methodist-Episcopal Church in Lynn, Abby, Asa, Joshua and I, with the assistance of Henry, gave a concert. It was the old quartet, with Joshua in place of Judson. It was the first appearance of an original Hutchinson quartet for many a year.

On June 25th, Abby and Henry with Lucy Stone Blackwell and Henry B. Blackwell, her husband, went to Rutland, Vt., and held a two days' convention, organizing the Vermont Woman Suffrage Association, the first in the State.

On July 3d, the living members of the Hutchinson Family held a reunion at Milford. David, Noah, Joshua, John, Asa, Rhoda and Abby, with many of their descendants assisted in laying the corner-stone of the town hall, with appropriate ceremonies. We gave a concert in the evening. While at Milford I sold my interest in the community block in the village.

Then followed a few weeks of quiet. Asa gave a few concerts in the vicinity of Cape Cod, and then, with his wife and daughter Abby went to Nantucket to visit his father-in-law. Henry, by a coincidence, went to Nantucket with another party, where he camped a while. The combined Hutchinsons gave a concert in the Methodist-Episcopal church while there. The attraction was clearly in that vicinity and so I started off too, and went to Martha's Vineyard.

I arrived at Cottage City in the midst of the camp-meeting season. It had some distinguished attendants that year. Among them were Governor Claflin of Massachusetts, Governor Sprague — then senator — of

Rhode Island, General Butler, Senator Henry Wilson, Senator Benjamin F. Wade of Ohio, Judge Thomas Russell and many others. I sent to Nantucket for the rest of the folks, and they all came. On the night they arrived we gave an impromptu concert from the steps of Mrs. Parkins's cottage, and when we sung "John Brown" all the distinguished men I have named joined in the chorus. We sang at the camp-meeting several times. On the last day of the meeting, August 23d, we gave a free concert at the preachers' stand, and raised three hundred dollars towards building a Methodist church in Hutchinson, Minn. When built, this church was named the "Vineyard Church," in honor of this camp-meeting, a name it still bears.

While at this meeting I met Samuel B. Spinning of Bridgeport, Conn., a bass singer of a good deal of ability, in company with a friend, Frank Benjamin, who was gifted with a very high tenor voice. I at once saw that they would be an aquisition, as members of my company. Asa thought the same. I had a talk with him, and he suggested that we might give some combination concerts together. I agreed, and we gave several, at Edgartown, Newport — where we also attended a great suffrage convention — Pawtucket, Warren, Fall River and Providence. I saw that Asa was planning to take both Spinning and Benjamin. So I said, "Boys, one of you should go with each. I need a bass singer and Asa needs a tenor voice in his company." This did not seem to suit them; they hugged round me until finally I agreed to give them four dollars per concert each, and pay all their expenses, and took them both. Asa and his family left us at Providence. I at once formed a male quartet. Our family never had a successful high tenor voice for such work. I used to sing the parts in a falsetto voice, but disliked to. Benjamin took this part, I the second tenor, Henry the baritone and Spinning the bass. We took up the Arion glees, and had good times singing them.

On September 10th we went to Lawrence and sang at a woman-suffrage convention with William Lloyd Garrison, Phebe A. Hanaford, and others as speakers. Earlier in the summer I had attended a similar convention in Newburyport, where Garrison spoke. The next night we gave a concert in Lawrence, and followed it up with others in Lowell, Methuen, Haverhill, Concord, N. H., Manchester, N. H., Derry, N. H., and other large towns in that vicinity. Under the head of Derry, Henry's diary says: "Father failed to arrive. Sam, Frank and I gave the concert alone very acceptably. How are you, 'Hutchinson Family?'" After this we made a short trip into Connecticut, my wife going with us, and then gave some concerts in the vicinity of Boston.

On October 20th we attended the Woman Suffrage Convention in Providence. Mrs. Paulina M. Davis presided. There was a good deal of discussion in regard to the recognition to be given the free-love factions, and the debate was particularly lively between Theodore Tilton, speaking for these people, and Colonel Thomas Wentworth Higginson, who thought the woman suffragists had no use for them. The Colonel rather got the best of the argument. It hardly seems possible that it is only a quarter of a century since these questions, which do not now enter to the slightest extent into the question of equal suffrage, were considered of so much importance. The next night we sung in Pawtucket for the benefit of the poor in that place, and on the following Sunday sang at a big temperance meeting at River Point. On the following Tuesday night we gave a monster concert in Providence, always our biggest concert town, with the exception of New York City.

The next day we were under engagement to Rev. H. W. Conant, of Providence, for seventy-five dollars to sing in the Temperance Alliance Convention. This turned out to be the forerunner of several seasons' work for him. At the close of the evening's session, Henry took a freight-car and rode all night on a tool box, *en route* for Hartford, where he arrived at six o'clock in the morning. The rest of us took a night's rest and then followed him. The Woman Suffrage Convention commenced before we arrived, and Henry sang the opening invocation with Sister Abby. He was an enthusiast. Isabella Beecher Hooker presided, and one of the most effective speeches was that of Henry Ward Beecher.

We concluded to stay in Hartford over Sunday and had a temperance mass meeting announced in the churches, to be held in Roberts's Opera House in the evening. On Saturday evening we called on Dr. Comstock and stayed to tea. A young minister dropped in, and to him I suggested the subject of a temperance meeting. He pushed back his chair and said, "Anything I can do to help you I will." I told him I had already engaged the opera house. He at once wrote out a pulpit notice and by ten o'clock that night started out. By morning he had seen every minister in town. There were three thousand present. The clergymen of the city spoke, and we sung. It was simply impossible to get in all the people who came. The proprietor of the opera house was unsympathetic. I had agreed to give him the receipts of the collection for the use of the hall. At the close of the meeting I remarked that I was weary. "You weary?" said he, "you have done nothing but sing a song or two." This seemed unkind, after all my care and anxiety in getting up a meeting which brought him thirty or forty dollars, the amount collected. The next Tuesday evening we gave a concert in the same hall, taking two hundred and fifty dollars.

A mass temperance meeting, at which there was a great audience, was held in Willimantic the next Sunday evening, at which C. C. Burleigh was one of the speakers. On the Sunday following we had a mass temperance meeting at River Point, R. I., at which I made the address. Between these meetings we gave concerts, as usual.

November 18th we reached New York City, with high hopes for a very successful winter season. On my way home from the West, the previous spring, I was walking up Nassau Street, in New York, when I saw a sign, "Literary Bureau." "What does that mean?" I said to myself. I went in and found the proprietor made engagements for lecturers. "Ever made engagements for music?" I inquired. He never had, but I told him I saw no reason why he should not, and he quite agreed with me. Soon after I reached Lynn, he came to see me at Daisy Cottage. I gave him some material and he advertised us. During that very year James Redpath, the author, came to see me in Boston, and after hearing some of our concerts jubilee week, gave me his card and asked me to call upon him. I thought I would make him my business agent, but on visiting him, found that he, too, had opened a bureau. He wanted me to go into it, but I told him I could not consistently do so, as I was already under an arrangement with the New York concern. Finally, to pacify him, I told him he might simply put my name into his announcements as open to engagements. Instead of doing this, however, he used my name very freely. The first I knew, he had made three engagements for us. I told him I could not take them. I was engaged to the New York bureau and I could not possibly let him make engagements without a conflict of dates. His course made trouble all that winter. The New York man found he was advertising me, and blamed me for it. However, Redpath persisted, and whenever I found I could meet his engagements without sacrificing the American Literary Bureau's interests, after getting their permit, I did so. Between the two, I was kept pretty busy, and we had to do a good deal more travelling than formerly to meet dates in different sections. The engagements I had come to fill at the present time were made by the American Literary Bureau.

On the threshold of these concerts, I encountered a snag in the indisposition of Benjamin to continue unless important concessions were made to him in the matter of salary. I let him go and he joined the Alleghanians, and their agent put them through to California. The real fact was that he was of no especial advantage to us except in quartet work. Spinning continued with me several seasons. Our engagement with the Literary Bureau gave us a hundred dollars a night. We gave a number of concerts in the city and then continued along the Hudson River, singing at all the large towns. While in New York, we were the guests of the Press Club, Oliver Johnson, president, at their annual banquet at Delmonico's, singing several times.